The Hollywood Horror Film, 1931–1941

Madness in a Social Landscape

Reynold Humphries

THE SCARECROW PRESS, INC.
Lanham, Maryland • Toronto • Oxford
2006

SCARECROW PRESS, INC.

Published in the United States of America
by Scarecrow Press, Inc.
A wholly owned subsidiary of
The Rowman & Littlefield Publishing Group, Inc.
4501 Forbes Boulevard, Suite 200, Lanham, Maryland 20706
www.scarecrowpress.com

PO Box 317
Oxford
OX2 9RU, UK

British Library Cataloguing in Publication Information Available

Library of Congress Cataloging-in-Publication Data

Humphries, Reynold.
  The Hollywood horror film, 1931–1941 : madness in a social landscape /
Reynold Humphries.
    p. cm.
  Filmography: p.
  Includes bibliographical references and index.
  ISBN-13: 978-0-8108-5726-1 (alk. paper)
  ISBN-10: 0-8108-5726-X (alk. paper)
  1. Horror films—United States—History and criticism. I. Title.

PN1995.9.H6H78 2006
791.43'6164—dc22
                                                    2006002576

Contents

~

Acknowledgments

Various institutions welcomed me during the summer of 1997 and provided not only the material requested but the sort of help and advice that makes research even more enjoyable. The George Eastman House at Rochester, New York; the University of Southern California (USC); and the Film and Television Archive of the University of California–Los Angeles (UCLA) put at my disposal prints of films (16mm, 35mm, and video) that I had not been able to view previously, not to mention the necessary technical expertise. The fact that I have since been able to obtain tapes of many of these films in no way alters the deep gratitude I wish to express to all those involved.

A special word of thanks for Ned Comstock of USC who helped me with the Special Collections held in the Doheny Memorial Library.

The Production Code Administration (PCA) files held at the Margaret Herrick Library, Academy of Motion Picture Arts and Sciences, Beverly Hills, are a veritable mine of information and are made available for research in surroundings that can only be termed ideal. My heartfelt thanks to the staff of the library.

I am most grateful to William Rothman, Anthony Slide, and Slavoj Zizek for their support and encouragement.

Thanks to Michael Grant, Gary D. Rhodes, D. N. Rodowick, Elias Savada, and Tom Weaver for their help and, especially, to Gregory Mank for providing an appropriate still.

My copy editor Laura Larson is to be thanked for making my life easier.

Nicole McCullough steered me through the production process by replying promptly to various queries. Last but not least, Stephen Ryan of Scarecrow Press has proven over the months to be a courteous correspondent with a keen eye for detail, always welcome qualities in the person with whom an author collaborates when preparing a manuscript for publication.

As usual when it comes to the use of the more complex aspects of computing, I have had recourse to the help of my wife, Martine Lannaud, who can carry out in a matter of minutes what it would take me countless laborious hours to accomplish. In such cases, gratitude knows no bounds.

From CIVILIZATION AND ITS DISCONTENTS by Sigmund Freud, translated by James Strachey. Copyright 1961 by James Strachey, renewed 1989 by Alix Strachey. Used by permission of W.W.Norton & Company, Inc.

Sigmund Freud Copyrights, The Institute of Psycho-Analysis and The Hogarth Press for permission to quote from *Civilization And Its Discontents* taken from THE STANDARD EDITION OF THE COMPLETE PSYCHOLOGICAL WORKS OF SIGMUND FREUD translated and edited by James Strachey. *Reprinted by permission of the Random House Group Ltd.*

~

Introduction

This book started as a research project, launched at the end of 1996, on the horror films produced by Hollywood in the 1930s. By the end of the following summer, both the content of the book and its very conception had undergone radical changes. As a result of more reading, the viewing of nearly a score of films at the George Eastman House, the University of Southern California (USC), and the University of California–Los Angeles (UCLA) that I had not previously seen, and several weeks spent studying the Production Code Administration (PCA) files at the Library of the Academy of Motion Picture Arts and Sciences in Beverly Hills, it became apparent that the original project was not satisfactory, for a number of reasons, all intimately connected.

To begin with, I felt it necessary to extend the period under discussion beyond that originally chosen: 1931–1936. At the same time I realized that an indefinite extension of that period into the 1940s ran the risk of both redundancy and a lack of coherency. Three aspects of the horror film of the 1940s therefore imposed certain limits. The films produced by Val Lewton for RKO Studios introduced new elements, on the level of both themes and representation, that call for a separate and quite different study. Universal Studios' decision to start remaking the successes of the 1930s in ways that too often amounted to opportunistic and self-indulgent parody rendered most of the resulting films far less interesting than their predecessors. And the numerous films produced by what are familiarly known as "Poverty Row" studios seemed to me to fall outside the concerns of this study or else resemble the remakes and parodies of the 1940s.[1] For a brief period, however, there was, I would argue, both a renewal and a widening of the concerns manifest in the films produced up until 1936. This period runs from 1939 to 1941, starting with the decision by Universal late in 1938 to make *Son of Franken-stein*, which, despite its title, is by no means either a remake or a form of parody. Indeed, it is arguably more successful on its own terms than either *Frankenstein* or *Bride of Frankenstein*. The period also saw the production of *Dr. Cyclops*, the first and only film of the period to be shot in Technicolor, and *The Wolf Man*. This latter film is of importance historically inasmuch as, far more than *Werewolf of London* in 1935, it "codified" the werewolf movie, therefore looking ahead to later developments. As such, it is as important, culturally and historically, as the film that launched the horror cycle of the 1930s, *Dracula*, which is notable for its presentation of the paraphernalia of the vampire movie that we now take for granted.

Other important films of this second period, such as *The Monster and the Girl* and *The Devil Commands*, prolong the tradition of the mad doctor or scientist, central in one form or another to the films of the period since 1931, the year of *Frankenstein*, *Dr. Jekyll and Mr. Hyde*, and *Murders in the Rue Morgue*. They also prolong a variety of themes that will be the subject of the four chapters of this study. It is the nature of these themes, in both how they are represented and how critical writing on the horror film has come to grips with them, which led to a feeling of dissatisfaction on my part with the methods employed, the conclusions drawn, and the presuppositions at work. At the risk of grossly simplifying a complex situation—and it is not my purpose here to offer an "instant history" of horror film criticism—I would argue that cultural approaches to the genre have tended to have recourse either to history as an explanation or to psychoanalysis as a method as if both went without saying, and that gender studies are too often guilty of excluding class and economics as essential social and historical factors. Thus, however informative and stimulating the work of David Skal, Andrew Tudor, and James Twitchell, on the one hand, and Rhona J. Berenstein, on the other, may be, an entire dimension of the horror film has been neglected, even repressed.[2] A few words of explanation are in order at this juncture.

In his book, in the chapter appropriately entitled "The Psychological Attraction of Horror," Twitchell asks the sixty-four thousand dollar question: "What is the sexual act that must be feared (and is especially feared in cultures where initiation horror myths are the most vibrant), lest real horror result?" He then promptly gives us his answer: "I think it is incest. I think that along with all the other phobic explanations for the attraction of horror (fear of insanity, death, madness, homosexuality, castration), the fear of incest underlies all horror myths in our culture that are repeatedly told for more than one generation."[3] Berenstein disagrees, drawing attention to "[h]orrors ability to trade simultaneously in more than one forbidden or culturally marginalized theme" and to "its celebration of multiple and shifting forbidden themes."[4] Twitchell is absolutely correct in highlighting the theme of incest but mistaken in seemingly putting it in a sort of watertight compartment separate from the intimately related themes to which he himself refers: death, homosexuality, castration. He goes on to make the following points: "*The 'grisly horror' of incest is socially learned. It has to be taught, and shivers are a most efficient teacher. Guilt occurs after an act; horror, however, can occur before—and may prevent the action.*"[5]

Twitchell is guilty here of a serious misreading of Freud. To state that "guilt occurs after an act" makes of guilt a purely ethical and individual matter that, if not necessarily conscious and assumed at every moment, evacuates the unconscious. Nothing could be further from the truth from a psychoanalytic standpoint. If Freud is to be taken seriously, then attention must be paid to one of his major discoveries, that the unconscious cannot represent negation, doubt, or hypotheses. Thus, when the little boy wishes his father would go away so that he can be with his mother, this desire, when repressed, becomes a *reality* in which "go away" means "die." The child will end up by resolving the Oedipus complex, but its traces will never leave him and can be reactivated at any moment, thus possibly producing traumatic feelings of *guilt*. But that guilt is not the result of an *act* but of a radically unconscious *desire*. The child who successfully resolves his Oedipus complex enters what Lacan calls the Symbolic Order, that of language and everyday life, which means overcoming the castration complex (in the form of the feared but imaginary punishment visited on the child by the stern, unforgiving father) and recognizing mortality as the inevitable outcome of existence.

Of the authors mentioned, only Berenstein has devoted a book-length study to the 1930s, limiting her attention to the key period 1931–1936. Apart from the hefty volume by Bryan Senn, this period has not received all the attention it deserves; those who have seen fit to write about the 1940s have neglected the films of the years 1939–1941 that complete this corpus. Critics have tended to focus on actors such as Boris Karloff and Bela Lugosi or, especially, on certain directors, such as Tod Browning and James Whale at the expense of others. This is due partly to a commitment to auteur theory, but it is also necessary to point out that these actors and directors share the distinction of having appeared in or directed the first sound films based on the two most celebrated horror novels of all time: *Dracula* and *Frankenstein*. And it is precisely to the novel that particularly stimulating works, inspired by Marxism or Freudian psychoanalysis (or both), have been devoted.[6]

Similarly, much theoretical attention has been paid to certain celebrated films, such as *King Kong*, at the expense of many more which are just as deserving but far less well known. It is, in fact, the modern horror film that has been the privileged object of theoretical study. Ironically, given that the role of gender studies—of which Berenstein's book is a remarkable example—has more or less coincided historically with a willingness to take the horror film seriously, it is therefore horror, since George A. Romero's *Night of the Living Dead* (1968) has benefited from analyses applying a psychoanalytic, ideological, or historical approach.

One of the constant elements of the "mad doctor" or "mad scientist" horror film is the way the character hides away from his fellow beings to carry out his research, either because it is monstrous or because he is convinced that nobody will be willing to take him seriously or give him the benefit of the doubt. I shall refer to this social and psychological tendency on his part as "isolation," a notion to which I shall have occasion to return and to which I shall lend a precise political and historical significance in the final chapter. For now, I shall simply suggest that the isolation of the mad scientist from his fellows is at once an unconscious representation of the idealist belief that classes function in physical separation from one another and the equally unconscious critique of this notion, couched in moral and individualistic terms that deny all question of class whatsoever. If the doctor/scientist is indeed mad, then this madness needs to be grasped in a precise social and historical sense that this study will define and that its subtitle, *Madness in a Social Landscape*, tries to circumscribe and describe.

The mad doctor is driven by an insatiable desire for truth and knowledge, noble sentiments that all too often lead to a rejection of society's most precious values (i.e., presuppositions) and to a striving for mastery and control over people and the environment. However horror films may portray the mad doctor as an extremist in his individualism, the fact remains that he must either accept certain constraints or else overrule them totally. Freud has much to teach us here. He drew a crucial distinction between what the subject demands and what he or she can achieve in a given situation, the difference between the two constituting a drive that will stop at nothing to attain its goal.[7] This refusal to conform, to submit to social constraints, to want to go ever farther to obtain some "ultimate" satisfaction, to refuse to restrain oneself, defines the behavior of the mad doctor. On occasion I shall have recourse to the Lacanian notion of *jouissance*, that refusal of prohibition that entails an unending but doomed drive to go "beyond." Lacan, like Freud before him, casts this drive in a particular light: the "death drive," the pertinence of which for the mad scientist is patent. Nothing and, in particular, no one must be allowed to stand in his way, and we shall have cause to describe and analyze the manifestations of cruelty, sadism, paranoia, and a total abandoning of the reality principle in the pages that follow.

Once again, it is Freud who has nicely summed up the mad doctor for us in a fascinating observation on mania. Here the ego and the ego ideal become one, with the result that the subject can simultaneously cast off those inhibitions imposed by the reality principle and consider himself free to indulge his desires without concern for anyone likely to be affected by such behavior.[8] I would argue that we can and must give a precise political resonance to these prophetic words of Freud. The drive of the mad scientist bears a striking resemblance to that of global capitalism and the ideology of neoliberalism, concerned as they are with mastery and control of people and nature, to be achieved in a climate of overweaning self-interest and indifference to the desire of the other who is transformed into an object to be exploited. The search for knowledge has now become the search for profit and the discourse of the mad doctor, who usually claims to speak "in the name of science," is in reality the economic discourse of the neoliberal big Other displaced onto the individual. The mad doctor's obsession with probing, dissecting, and reconstructing the body produces a state akin to that of the transformation of workers under capitalism into a sort of "fragment" of the whole production process. This in turn leads to alienation and a desire for wholeness to combat its negative effects, which brings us to the interrelated notions of fetishism, disavowal, and ideology.

By one of those delightful historical coincidences that theorists should rejoice in, *fetishism* is a term common to both Karl Marx and Freud. For Marx, fetishism functions to hide the very nature of manual labor in favor of the products of that labor that thus seem to exist "naturally" in the everyday world. For Freud, the fetishist is someone who, while knowing full well that the maternal phallus does not exist, nevertheless continues to believe in it. In the former case, a presence is transformed into an absence by way of ideology, whereas in the latter case, an absence is transformed into a presence by the discursive tactic of disavowal. Thus, the manufactured object becomes an object in its own right that homogenizes reality and represses all notions of class, economics, and, indeed, history itself; and the maternal phallus enables the neurotic to believe in a full presence that hides the lack that is at the basis of desire, itself the foundation of the unconscious and hence of the split subject positions taken up by the ego.

As Tony Williams has neatly put it, fetishism "is designed to suspend enquiry into what is really behind imaginary representations."[9] When this is a case of disavowal of one's senses, the better to deny a fact that threatens the imaginary stability of an equally imaginary nonproblematic reality, then we are dealing with fetishism in both the Marxist and Freudian senses of the term. This insistence on an imaginary presence or totality is the means open to human subjects to bracket off an unpleasant absence, an absence that questions their self-assured place in the world, their position as a self-centered subject who is master of all he says and surveys. Thus, a belief in the maternal phallus masks that lack at the heart of being, as does an ability to reify objects so that the relations between them supersede—indeed, replace—those fundamental relations between human beings that determine our real social conditions. There is always, therefore, an "absent cause" structuring both reality and the subject's apprehension of it.

It is here that Fredric Jameson's adoption of Louis Althusser's notion of history as an absent cause will prove most fruitful for our own undertaking, most notably Jameson's articulation of Marxism and Freudian psychoanalysis in the formula "the political unconscious."[10] No more than the characters themselves, whatever their status, can the films accede to the Real, Lacan's concept of what is radically other and to which the subject cannot give symbolic form by language. Yet, just as we make history without knowing we are doing so, the Real leaves its traces in the subject's unconscious. In both cases, the effects are experienced only after the founding event. Let us take anxiety, for example. For no apparent reason the subject is overwhelmed by a feeling of unease, of dread.[11] It is our aim here to try to bring to the surface the possible significance of the Real in both the properly Lacanian sense and the way it can be exploited from a Marxist standpoint (= the Real of history) to traverse the unconscious of the text to pinpoint the political forms it takes. As I shall show, cultural and sociological approaches that seek to explain both the content and the reception of the horror film of the 1930s as products of the aftermath of World War I, the Depression, and the rise of fascism are examples of critical blindness and insight.

If we return to the notion of anxiety, it must be apparent that this is hardly a concept that goes without saying, especially when the term is taken in a more common and less psychoanalytic sense. Could it not be argued, for instance, that a film that produces anxiety in the spectator is having a debilitating effect on him or her, blocking off any notion of reflection and instilling in its place a sense of intellectual and psychological paralysis that is profoundly conservative, even reactionary, in nature? Undoubtedly. Yet it could also be argued—and this is an argument that I find more satisfying and productive politically—that the average film, produced as it is for instant and unthinking consumption, produces a feeling of pleasure, satisfaction, and imaginary gratification that is debilitating in the extreme. In that case, it is once again Jameson who has put the issue succinctly for us when he states that "the profound vocation of a work of art in a commodity society" is "*not* to be a commodity, *not* to be consumed, to be *unpleasurable* in the commodity sense."[12]

Freud argued that the further the representation of the repressed (in a patient's discourse, in a work of art) is from the desire being repressed, the less likely we are to recognize it. Conversely, the closer the unconscious representation comes to giving that desire access to symbolization, the more likely it is that the original unpleasure associated with the repressed desire will become manifest again, provoking incomprehensible feelings of anxiety. Horror creates effects of a special kind on audiences, and critics are part of those audiences. This last point should be a question of stating the obvious, but it is not. As from the moment we ask ourselves the question "How?" and consider that it deserves an answer, the whole matter of subject positions and, by extension, of the very form of the discourse we enunciate comes to the fore. My concern is to show that certain discourses on the classic horror film demonstrate, in diverse ways determined by the films themselves, that something fundamental is being repressed, that the subject matter contained within these films influences unconsciously the way critics wrote and are still writing about the films in question. We shall see that certain situations produce reactions that cannot be explained away by ignoring them or adopting the attitude that they are mere incongruities or signs of incompetence or incoherence, a favorite tactic of defense in critical disavowal. When the films depict certain characters and situations in ways that elicit responses of puzzlement, rejection, laughter, incomprehension and so forth, then there is something *wrong*. When the critics draw attention to element X without stating why it is worth a mention, or when element Y is repeated many times within a large number of films without drawing critical attention, then I would maintain that the films are staging the repressed in ways that are making its presence felt in the discourse of the critics. The fascination produced by fetishism in the Freudian sense can easily be transformed into its opposite, anxiety, by the return of the repressed.

If we consider the horror film to be a collective fantasy, then the inability to tell the difference between reality and fantasy is productive and not necessarily the path to a refusal of reality. By being freed ideologically from the need to be "realistic"—which all too often means portraying the everyday referent as a nonproblematic given and thereby indulging in fetishism—the horror film can investigate themes and forms of behavior usually considered as "out of bounds" or even "mad." Any simple "cause/effect" approach can only, therefore, turn the film into a metaphor for something else, ultimately hiding textual activity and the logic of the signifier and enabling the spectator to misrecognize his or her position as an effect of the latter, just as he misrecognizes the point to which he is "ontologically involved" in the precise socioeconomic position obtaining both in the act of watching the film and within the diegetic world unfurling on the screen.[13]

This study is an attempt to turn the clock back to the days—not that long ago—before the notions of "the end of history" and "posttheory" had been concocted by those anxious to ensure that certain questions would never be asked again. Robin Wood has put his finger unerringly on the ideological stakes when he writes that the attempts to discredit Freud are "strongly influenced by the social-political climate."[14] The questions referred to are those Marxism asks concerning class, economics, and history, while certain answers not to everyone's liking can be found in the methods deployed by Freudo-Lacanian psychoanalysis. Thus, just as the ideologues of "the end of history" seek to present global capitalism as natural or inevitable since the collapse of the Soviet Union, henceforth passed off as a sort of "mistake" or hiatus in the smooth chronology of an unproblematic history, so "posttheory" can become a refuge for those anxious to transform the subject into a self-centered entity in keeping with immediate experience and access to the self. Thus chapter 1, "Curse of the Superstitious Script," has recourse to the PCA files to set the scene for the diverse ways questions were raised concerning the horror films of the 1930s by Hollywood, only for their implications to be repressed or disavowed. Already we can see at work a refusal to face up to the conclusions to be drawn, from both the films themselves and the reactions to them on the part of the press, both trade and national. The Real of incest, castration and death is central to our argument here, which also turns on the "blurring of boundaries" between the masculine and the feminine so prevalent to horror, then as now. This will remain a major theme under constant consideration.

Chapter 2, "Mad Doctors in Love," focuses in particular on the representations of sexuality, particularly that of the mad doctor/scientist. We describe and analyze the ways films can both reinforce and call into question socially and ideologically acceptable forms of desire. Through the character of Dr. Frankenstein we show the inadequate nature of arguments based on the binary opposition between heterosexuality and homosexuality, preferring to couch the discussion in other terms, where the character's actions lie outside the rigid boundaries drawn up by patriarchy. The films directed by Ernest B. Schoedsack are scrutinized as manifestations of hysteria, in particular the symbolic function of the character called King Kong. Just as Frankenstein refuses to bend the knee to recognized forms of behavior, both sexual and scientific, so Murder Legendre (*White Zombie*) strives to submit everyone, male and female, to his desire, thus becoming a form of primal father, or "obscene father of Enjoyment."[15] This leads on to discussions of such pathologies as sadism and paranoia and how mastery and control are exercised. Publicity material is most instructive here, particularly when it came to rewriting certain films to make them correspond to Hollywood's ideology of the commercial and the acceptable. Such rewriting, as we shall see, has much to tell us about the context in which the films were conceived and (meant to be) received, not to mention the unconscious values at work in the finished product projected on cinema screens.

Chapter 3, "The Road to (Dis)enchantment," takes up the increasingly important role played by the social dimension of the behavior of the mad doctor/scientist and the meaning of this behavior and of his experiments. The chapter opens with a discussion of Freud's *Civilization and Its Discontents* and his contribution to a theory of how society is based on repression and constraint. We then consider Herbert Marcuse's political reading of Freud in *Eros and Civilization*, in which we encounter the notion of "surplus repression": how the dominant social and economic class reinforces its control and succeeds in rendering it natural and acceptable. A detailed analysis of the brilliant 1931 version of *Dr. Jekyll and Mr. Hyde* and a brief discussion of the mediocre 1941 version show at work the theories put forward by Freud and Marcuse, and the remaining sections of the chapter build on this to introduce the "specter" of Marxist theory concerning class, economics and exploitation and how they haunt the horror films of the period under discussion.

The conclusions we draw from these analyses lead on to the fourth chapter, "History Is Made at Night," where we return to the question of history as "absent cause" in an attempt to show how critical writing on horror has evaded the pertinent implications of the role of history, in the ways it both determines the films in question and is represented (or distorted) in the diegetic world. We expand the question to embrace politics, such as the nature and function of colonialism in *The Mask of Fu Manchu*. This latter notion brings us to the related matter of the historical implications underpinning the theme of mastery and control: the attempt to dominate and exploit nature itself and how this is linked to and determined by capitalism's insatiable drive for profit and conquest, a drive as much psychic as economic and hegemonic. "Repression" is taken in all its senses, and Teresa Brennan's pathbreaking *History after Lacan* proves to be an indispensable guide.

Finally, via a discussion of Fredric Jameson's Marxist analysis of Utopia, I propose a reading of the theme of isolation. Hidden laboratories, forbidding dwellings, and remote islands can be seen to represent both a rejection of society and a desire to refuse that society's anti-intellectual thrust, its downgrading of intelligence. *The Black Cat* gives a more historical slant to the question of isolation by introducing World War I, but finally "isolates" the theme and its own conclusions in favor of a "happy end" in which the couple are reunited in a literal fiction that renders history irrelevant in the best Hollywood tradition.

Notes

1. If I have included *The Devil Bat* (1940), it is not simply because it stars Bela Lugosi but because the film's thematic approach to the character of the mad scientist is interesting, even innovative. The collective volumes devoted to Lugosi and Boris Karloff often do a fine job of rescuing forgotten movies from undeserved oblivion.

2. For publication details, see the bibliography.

3. James Twitchell, *Dreadful Pleasures: An Anatomy of Modern Horror* (New York: Oxford University Press, 1985), 93.

4. Rhona J. Berenstein, *Attack of the Leading Ladies: Gender, Sexuality, and Spectatorship in Classic Horror Cinema* (New York: Columbia University Press, 1996), 18.

5. Twitchell, *Dreadful Pleasures*, 96, emphasis in the original.

6. This is hardly surprising, given the way the Gothic novel brings together themes to which Marxism and psychoanalysis have long been drawn. And the implications of the vampire—his feudal past, his penchant for sucking victims' blood, his indifference to their sex, for instance—have led to a vast literature on his multifarious manifestations and their polysemy.

7. Sigmund Freud, "Beyond the Pleasure Principle," in *The Standard Edition of the Complete Psychological Works of Sigmund Freud*, trans. and ed. James Strachey (London: Hogarth and the Institute of Psycho-Analysis, 1955), XVIII: 42. Hereinafter this main work is referred to as *SE* plus the volume number.

8. Freud, *Group Psychology and the Analysis of the Ego*, in *SE* XVIII: 132.

9. Tony Williams, *Hearths of Darkness: The Family in the American Horror Film* (Madison, Wisc., and London: Fairleigh Dickinson University Press and Associated University Presses, 1996), 19.

10. Fredric Jameson, *The Political Unconscious: Narrative as a Socially Symbolic Act* (London: Methuen, 1981), 35.

11. We shall find the formula "for no apparent reason" occurring in the writing of a critic expressing puzzlement at a supposedly inexplicable element of a particular film. See "Specters of the World, Unite!" in chapter 3.

12. Fredric Jameson, *Marxism and Form* (Princeton, N.J.: Princeton University Press, 1971), 395, emphasis in the original.

13. The formula "ontologically involved" is Jameson's. See *Marxism and Form*, 322.

14. Robin Wood, "Foreword," in *Horror Film and Psychoanalysis: Freud's Worst Nightmare*, ed. Steven Jay Schneider (Cambridge: Cambridge University Press, 2004), xiv–xv.

15. I am thinking in particular of the use made of this formula by Slavoj Zizek and return to it on more than one occasion in the following chapters.

~

CHAPTER ONE

Curse of the Superstitious Script

The Text and the Critic

I shall open with *Bride of Frankenstein* and two letters written by Joseph Breen of the Motion Picture Producers and Distributors of America (MPPDA) concerning the evolution of the film's script. Universal had already written to James Wingate of the MPPDA on 25 July 1933 about the script—then entitled *The Return of Frankenstein*—and had been warned about the use of the word *God*.[1] This was the only problem raised at the time—religion was always a bone of contention between Breen and Hollywood—but Breen saw another difficulty in the script submitted to him the following year. In a letter dated 24 July 1934, he wrote to Harry Zehner of Universal stating that the word *mate* must be replaced by the word *companion* to avoid any sexual connotation.[2] This decision obviously raises a multitude of fascinating questions concerning how the monster created by Frankenstein related to sexuality. It is worth noting here that, whereas the scriptwriters conceived of a clear difference between Frankenstein and his wife/bride and the monster and his "mate"—the monster is instantly condemned to being less than human—Breen decided that the important question was one of "decency" and, by so doing, assimilated the monster to a human being, a blurring of boundaries that he cannot have wished consciously but that I ask the reader to keep in mind for later discussion, in this and subsequent chapters.

On the very same day he wrote to Zehner, Breen sent off a letter to Will Hays in which he enclosed a list of films reviewed by the censors of his

1

office. In it he mentioned the new version of the *Frankenstein* saga in these terms: "This is a sequel to the former picture and tells of Frankenstein's search for a mate." We have in this sentence a condensation of the problems posed by the film and frequently mentioned by critics—just whose "bride" is the film talking about?—and an eloquent return of the repressed: the word to be banned from the public sphere. One can easily put this down to Breen's double standards—if he and Hays are capable of discussing such base matters without getting carried away by lust, the audiences are another matter—but the question is surely more complex. I have raised it in part earlier: the uncertainty as to whether it is the scientist or the monster who is "in search of a mate" at once poses the question of hesitation concerning what a given film represents and how we describe and interpret the very ways by which it represents. The dimension of "sexual (im)propriety" becomes one of a sexuality that does not admit of a clear definition and hence of an unambiguous representation. This in turn goes far beyond the matter of the blurring of genders in this and other films, however important that may be, by raising the question of sexuality as a drive that cannot be reduced to an "either/or" opposition.

As I have suggested, double standards are at work in Breen's reaction to this version of the script of the film destined to become *Bride of Frankenstein*.[3] These, however, were not limited to Breen (or to the MPPDA and the censors), nor were they simply a case of hypocrisy. Rather, language here is representing a split subject position, a question of admitting what one wants to deny, or of denying what one knows very well to be the case. This can be ascertained by taking instances of the contempt of trade papers for certain films and their audiences and by seeing in what precise contexts such contempt could take form. Reviewing *Dr. Jekyll and Mr. Hyde*, *Variety* wrote (5 January 1932) that "labored adornment . . . weakens the production for mob appeal" and in its presentation of *Zoo in Budapest* (2 May 1933) evoked "things in it that will prove profoundly moving to film followers of fastidious tastes, but that probably will be lost on the gum chewers." In other words, artistry is wasted on the lower orders, who must not be asked to think. This point could perhaps be defended more easily as a thesis on the part of critics able and willing to think for themselves, but the thought processes of many of those writing about the horror film at that time suffered from strange linguistic and semantic deformations. Discussing *The Old Dark House* (1 November 1932), *Variety* bemoans what it sees as a flaw in the typical audience of horror films: it "seemingly doesn't expect coherence." The writer's notion of "coherence" is to ask whether anyone would spend a night in such company as that depicted.[4] This cheap jibe does not quite cover up the fact that its author either had not bothered to view the film or else was writing with the benefit of hindsight in order to laugh at what patently disturbed him. The occupants of the car who take refuge with the Femm family have the choice between spending the night with unfriendly eccentrics and possibly being buried by landslides caused by torrential rain. Their decision in favor of the former is therefore quite coherent, and it is not until morning that they realize they have risked their lives in the presence of a dangerous madman. The critic is disavowing his knowledge of the film in favor of a stance that enables him to feel superior and to misrecognize the fact that he would have done the same thing. To put it another way: with the benefit of hindsight, the critic will now look askance at old dark houses, thus repressing the difference between the time of viewing and the time of writing, the different status of his relation to knowledge at these two separate but unconsciously linked moments. Drawing on a variety of examples, I wish to argue that such disavowal and mis(re)cognition, the ability for contradictory ideas to coexist, was the very stuff of writing on horror and that this situation can tell us much about the films concerned and their effects on audiences.

The opposition set up between refined taste and the tastes of the "mob" surely partakes of the same psychic structure. On the one hand, you have people who come from a respectable social background and have been educated to think; on the other, you have those who always give in to what the former call "the baser instincts." The problem here is that a film such as *Dr. Jekyll and Mr. Hyde* concerns the dual personality of just one of these respectable people, which did not prevent *Variety*, in the review quoted earlier, from evoking the "baser self" having "its temporary way." The reason I insist on this is to be found in precisely the subject matter of so many horror films of the period: science. Perhaps I should say "discourses on science," as the representation of the theme, in whatever way, is always already determined elsewhere. Certain mad doctors and scientists are presented as sincere researchers and intellectuals anxious to help their fellow human beings and advance the cause of science. Others, of course, are mad sadists, but the fact remains that one of the most extreme cases, Dr. Moreau (*Island of Lost Souls*), succeeds beyond the wildest dreams of any scientist. This helps account for the critical discourses on science, a realm reserved for the educated, among whom the critic is eager to count him- or herself.

Let us consider the following remarks on *The Invisible Ray*. For *Motion Picture Daily* (11 January 1936), the film shows the "mysteries of advanced science," whereas *Daily Variety* (same date) evokes its "quasi-scientific tone." The first quote suggests a story adhering to scientific facts that are beyond the layman, the latter constitutes a perfect example of disavowal through the presence of "quasi": knowing full well that the film's vision of science is fictional and supernatural but nevertheless wanting to believe there is some scientific basis to it. On occasions this delicate balance is upset. The *New York Post* (22 April 1940) refers to the "pseudoscientific thrills" of *Dr. Cyclops*. *The Hollywood Reporter* (21 August 1939) writes of "some phony apparatus" in *The Man They Could Not Hang*. *Variety* (23 December 1932) dismisses the "manufactured chills" of *Mystery of the Wax Museum*. Sometimes the dismissal of a film can be quite violent: *The Walking Dead* leads *Variety* (4 March 1936) to denounce the "trite and pseudoscientific vaporings of the writers." On still other occasions, the balance is restored and justified. It is interesting here to consider the attitude of *The Hollywood Reporter* that had put a certain distance between itself and the first Boris Karloff/Nick Grindé film, *The Man They Could Not Hang*. Evoking the second in the series, *The Man with Nine Lives*, the paper claims "the premise is weirdly fantastic" but finds the film "immensely interesting" because the screenplay is "so soundly constructed."[5]

In this last example, we can see disavowal functioning on the level of the statement, inasmuch as a film's "premise" is a matter of the story, the reference to the screenplay suggesting that the film relies far more on characters and themes than on recourse to special effects, such as that staple, electricity. This in turn suggests that identification with characters and situations on the part of the critics must not be interfered with (too much) by the film's makers having recourse to obviously unrealistic devices to keep the story going. When these special effects call too much attention to themselves, when they become intrusive to the point of incredulity, then the balance between belief and knowledge cannot be maintained. The film ceases to give pleasure, which enables the critic to blame this on the film's incompetence, another way of admitting that the critic would have preferred to go along with the film to the end—and beyond—in his or her review. The terms employed by two journals when reviewing *The Monster and the Girl* are eloquent; the first quote is taken from *The Hollywood Reporter* (6 February 1941), the second from the *Los Angeles Examiner* (7 February 1941): "In spite of the horrible strain on audience credulity . . . one finds himself [sic] waiting eagerly for the next plot twist." "It's unbelievable, we admit, but director Stewart [sic] Heisler has told his story so well, we eagerly followed the tale to its amazing finish."[6]

We can note here the parallel between this desire for a particular—and particularly satisfying—ending and Freud's insight in "The Three Caskets": a work of art can provide knowledge about that which is denied to us in real life—namely, death.[7] Thus, the psychic function of disavowal, in order to keep at a safe distance (the knowledge of) castration and the inevitable implications of the Symbolic Order, implies a certain form of perfection corresponding to the denial of castration: the film takes some swallowing, but, nevertheless, how harmonious it is! This brings us back to special effects as so many fetishes, not only in the Freudian but also in the Marxist sense: no longer bearing any visible trace of the work involved, thus circulating—and enabling the critic's desire to circulate—as if free from all constraints. We can perhaps sum this up in the formula "seeing is believing," where Marxism and psychoanalysis meet in a revealing manner. From the Marxist perspective, it is a matter of not seeing something that is there: the labor of the worker. From the psychoanalytic perspective, it is a matter of seeing something that is not there: the maternal phallus. As the pressbook concocted for a reissue of *King Kong* in the 1940s put it: "Adventure to make you wonder if it's true . . . while your eyes convince you that it *is*."[8]

It is therefore hardly surprising to find sex being foregrounded the better to disavow it; nor that the word *uncanny* should float around, attaching itself "freely" to any and every available signifier. An eloquent example of the former tendency is the memo sent by one of Breen's censors/reviewers after viewing a print of *Bride of Frankenstein*. Referring to the sequence where the young shepherdess falls into the pool on catching sight of the monster and the attempts of the latter to help her, Islin Auster informs Breen that the sequence "will be lengthened to protract the suspense. It is understood that this scene will, in no sense, have a sexual connotation."[9] This is priceless stuff and shows the complicity between the studios and the MPPDA. On the one hand, you can excite audiences by suggesting that something horrible will happen to the young woman, despite the fact that it is clear the monster is trying to help her. On the other hand, you must film it so that no such titillation will be present. And this is precisely what happens. Whale's direction carefully avoids suggesting that the monster has designs on the shepherdess, whereas it is the censor's desire that reads in sexual connotations, the latter the product of collective desire, a desire to find in the film a representation of the forbidden that goes beyond the mating of the human and the "inhuman."

Given the constant evocation of death in horror films, particularly in those where a monster is created from corpses, anxiety can return at any moment. And Hollywood understood that it could sell films by evoking that which was at once feared and desired. The fear of death is offset by obtaining an imaginary knowledge of it where the spectator lives through a situation whose resolution enables disavowal to function. Thus, the Metro Goldwyn Mayer Studios (MGM) publicity campaign for *The Mask of Fu Manchu* refers to "uncanny mystery," an "uncanny laboratory," and "uncanny torture chambers."[10] This could be taken for a typical piece of linguistic exaggeration were other factors not at work. Later the same year posters used to advertise *The Mummy* coined the phrase "Karloff the Uncanny."[11] The word floats from statement to enunciation, from plot and situations to actor and production values. We know from Freud that the Uncanny occurs when something long familiar to us is alienated by repression.[12] When the representation of the idea repressed takes on a form that is not sufficiently removed from that idea, then the subject experiences unpleasurable effects, such as anxiety.

Numerous comments on horror films reflect this, starting with a letter from Breen to Harry Zehner of Universal (30 March 1935) concerning *The Raven*. Breen, who disapproved personally of such movies, felt more self-control was necessary on the part of the studios to tone down representations of characters or situations where too much detail was shared—in other words, where "stark realism" induced "excessive horror."[13] As can be seen from film reviews of the time, this amounts to admitting that certain films have come too close to something that must be kept hidden, that repression is not working.

The following examples will suffice to get an inkling of what is at stake. In its review of *The Old Dark House* referred to earlier, *Variety* makes its unease plain: "There's a bit too much reality involved, hence the disparities are the more flagrant and obvious." The *New York Times* (3 April 1933) found that Lionel Atwill's performance in *Murders in the Zoo* was "almost too convincing for comfort" and detected in *The Devil-Doll* (8 August 1936) "a menacing, chilling quality which makes it impossible for you to consider them [the dolls] too lightly."[14] I would suggest that the same can be said of a remark that is the simple psychic negation of the above. Writing to Carl Laemmle Jr. concerning *Murders in the Rue Morgue*, Jason Joy opined, "Because it is laid in a period so far away, we doubt if anything in the picture will offend French sensibilities."[15] We can rewrite these remarks as follows: The films cited refer to matters that are "too close for comfort," but this quality can be disavowed when far removed from the present.[16]

In which case, the reader might ask, why should the writings of Bryan Senn and Randy Loren Rasmussen reproduce, sixty years later, the unconscious discursive strategies that we have just analyzed? There are three main reasons. First, I was referring to films whose setting is distant from the time of shooting, placing the matter on the level of the statement, as did Jason Joy. All this does, surely, is to disavow yet again the function of the enunciation and hence of the subject positions created for the critic/spectator through the films' narrative and representational devices. Second, there is the question of the approaches adopted by Senn and Rasmussen. By going into such a wealth of detail in a laudable desire to inform his readers, Senn steers the films closer to that "stark realism" feared so profoundly by Breen. If all the details can never add up to a harmonious whole, they can nevertheless evoke what we have chosen to call the "absent cause" in a way that represents it and brings it "too close for comfort." Similarly, by a juxtaposition of heterogeneous thematic elements that he attempts to analyze both as such and through their narrative functions, Rasmussen constantly runs the risk of bringing out the repressed signified, maintained in this state of repression by the metonymy of desire, the constant slippage from signifier to signifier. The themes and characters thus fulfill the role of signifiers of *something else*. Or, as Slavoj Zizek Lacanically puts it, such books exemplify the "surplus produced by the signifying operation,"[17] that of the films, that of language itself. Third, we must not forget that time and history are not linear and chronological in the unconscious: the signifier will produce certain effects in the subject whether he or she is at a press show in the 1930s or writing generations later. But I am anticipating our later discussion somewhat.[18]

Certain analyses by Senn show that one can be alert and self-conscious (in a nonpejorative sense) and still manifest a desire to believe what one rejects. On *Mad Love*:

> First of all, the concept of the hands of a murderer being grafted onto the arms of a normal man, only to have the limbs retain their murderous skill, is patently absurd. But it is treated here with such serious care, and we are so drawn in by the fascinating characters, that it ceases to be a problem as the film builds its own reality with a superb sense of gothic style.[19]

We can note the structure of disavowal in the use of "But" to introduce the disclaimer whereby Senn writes as if the first sentence had not been written, for what he is saying in the second sentence contains a profound truth that should in no way be laughed at as a truism. Any and every work of art worth our attention "builds its own reality," just as language places and reconstructs the subject anew with every statement he or she makes or is interpellated by. And why should Dr. Gogol's experiments be considered any more "absurd" than those of Dr. Frankenstein, Dr. Moreau, or Dr. Pretorius? What is it in *Mad Love* that jars? Suffice it to point out here that the notion of a subject losing control of his words and actions as the character of Orlac the pianist does in *Mad Love* comes perilously close to a deconstruction of the autonomous ego that tends to elicit immediate condemnation in so many quarters. Senn's discussion of *The Walking Dead* would seem to indicate that this notion is acceptable if God is involved:

> The confirmation of an afterlife, the revelation that the guilty WILL by punished, and the assurance that there is indeed a God watching over us, ready to

take a hand, touch some very real and basic human needs. . . . They [the screenwriters] deliver the goods in the end, for the film's message is one of reassurance, and as such is rather appealing and, ultimately, satisfying.[20]

The Walking Dead tells the story of an innocent man returning from death in the electric chair and pursuing the gangsters who had him condemned. But he dies a second time before he can reveal what life after death is like. Science may be thus frustrated, but the unpleasantness of death—and, as we shall see in the next chapter, of something far more unpleasant as it concerns us in the here and now—is defused by the notion of God. As Senn does not give the impression in his book of being particularly religious, we must conclude that the desire to believe enables the subject to repress what he prefers to ignore.

The Ghoul tells of a British Egyptologist (played by Boris Karloff, who made the film in England after The Mummy) who believes in the ancient Egyptian concept of the afterlife and has himself buried with an object called "the Eternal Flame" that he will offer to the statue of Anubis installed in his tomb in order to enjoy eternal life. Describing one sequence toward the end of the film, Senn writes that "the unseeing idol of Anubis looks on" as Karloff, apparently brought back to life by the rays of the full moon falling on the door of the tomb, performs an act of homage to his god. The copresence of "unseeing" and "looks on" both confers life on the object and suggests a belief in some supernatural power: the fetishistic dimension of this kind of discourse is patent. Senn had already evoked the curse from The Mummy as not seeming "so very terrible," only to refer in the very next breath to "the feeling of dread one gets from the general scene." He also evokes the "deaths or curse surrounding those who made the discovery" of the tomb of Tutankhamen.[21] This latter remark is surely a case of displacement. If one can convince oneself that only certain people—those involved in the famous discovery—can be directly concerned by forces from the distant past, then one can deny the patent feelings of anxiety triggered by a film whose representation of death, as we shall show, brings us uncomfortably close to something much nearer to home than ancient—or modern—Egypt.

The excavation of the Egyptian tombs has for a long time produced theories of a superstitious nature concerning the powers of the gods, their beliefs and, especially, curses. It must be remembered that these theories appeared in real life prior to being incorporated into the discourse of film. Paul M. Jensen has this to say on the matter: "Ever since the discovery of Tutankhamen's tomb, news reports had fueled popular interest with speculation about a curse being attached to the tomb, and whenever someone even remotely connected with it died, the story was revived."[22] Jensen goes on to quote a French Egyptologist, Dr. Mardrus, who deemed it necessary "to take certain precautions, both against the visible and the invisible" and "to guard against the dangerous surroundings of the tomb." This was in 1924, and a couple of years later, following the death of the sixth person involved, Dr. Mardrus was reported in *The Times* as saying about the ancient Egyptians that he was "absolutely convinced that they knew how to concentrate upon and around a mummy certain dynamic powers of which we possess very incomplete notions."[23] One such victim, according to Jensen's research, even left a suicide letter in which he wrote, "I knew there was a curse on me."

Rather than dismiss this as the superstitious twaddle of yet another mad scientist (a real-life one this time), I would suggest we take it as seriously as Freud would have done. It is not a case of Mardrus's belief being the effect of a cause, but just the reverse: he believed in these forces *because* he had already submitted unconsciously to the need to believe. The whole question of curses therefore reinforces something always already there, and the "forces" he mentions were, by 1924, well known and analyzed: the Freudian theory of the unconscious.[24] Despite appearances—for it would seem that Mardrus conceived of a system outside of which a force exists that would now be called "alien" (such as attributing Stonehenge and the Pyramids to extraterrestrials)[25]— Mardrus really conceived unconsciously of a self-contained system of a profoundly homogeneous nature: literally everything can be explained by that system. This is summed up perfectly in an element of the script of *The Mummy* itself. Imhotep/Ardath Bey recounts how, after he was buried alive, the slaves were killed by soldiers so that they would not reveal the place; then the soldiers were killed. And what then? Who killed the soldiers? And so on, ad infinitum. That we do not see who kills the soldiers, whereas we do see the soldiers kill the slaves, and that the script should have recourse to the passive —"the soldiers were killed"—without an agent indicates the unconscious need to stop the cycle in an attempt to deny, precisely, that there is an element or "absent cause" over which the subject has no control. This can perhaps best be illustrated by an old joke from the 1960s that, by a delightful coincidence, concerns mad scientists.

Having come to the end of their financial resources owing to the lunacy of their experiments, two scientists decide to convince the United States to finance their future research. They fly to Washington to propose a scheme that will definitively put the United States ahead in the space race. Received by the president's scientific adviser, they reveal their daring plan: to put a man on the sun. The adviser looks at them aghast: "You're crazy—he'll be burnt to a crisp when still millions of miles away!" The scientists exchange knowing smiles; then one of them replies: "Don't you worry about that, sir, we've thought it all out. We're going to land him during the night."

Thus the sun is seen not as an element over which we have no control—Lacan's Real—but as an integral part of a homogeneous (solar) system having the same status and function as a planet on which the sun sets. This is also, of course, the structure of paranoia: a system in which everything fits, where nothing is external and where all elements can be explained (and thus controlled in the subject's delirium). What is external is what is needed to give consistency to the system: the unconscious.[26]

We are clearly in the realm of the "absent cause," as can be ascertained from the plot of The Black Room. A curse lies on the family: the younger brother will murder the elder one, and the deed will take place, in the future as in the past, in the Black Room. One member of the family hits on what he considers to be a solution: "seal it up—there won't be any Black Room." This response, of course, goes on two false assumptions. First, there is a simple and constant cause/effect syndrome at work, which reproduces itself without change. Second—and the two are linked—hostility between siblings can be eliminated in the way indicated, as if the room were responsible instead of being part of the fantasy scenario designated as a "curse." By banning the room in question from the Symbolic, the family's patriarch merely ensures that it will make its effects felt in other ways, and the entire film thus turns on the presence of the "absent cause."

I mentioned earlier the suicide of a member of the Egyptian expedition of 1924, and this item relates to another matter rooted in reality: the suicide of James Whale. It is still possible to come across comments referring to his death in "mysterious circumstances," despite the fact that it is now known that he killed himself by walking out to his swimming pool and falling in. The only "mysterious" element is why. We can only speculate. Whale was more or less excluded from the studios after 1940: his open gayness was not appreciated.[27] In this context one can reflect on another suicide, that of a leading French specialist on the horror film, Jean Boullet.[28] He, too, evokes a sense of mystery surrounding Whale's death, due to the kind of film that Whale made. It is here that we can see "uncanny" forces at work. For Boullet was also gay. His insistence on an unknown cause behind Whale's death was at one and the same time an understanding that Whale's homosexuality was a contributing factor and a sort of "knowledge of the Real," a drive that would eventually bring about Boullet's death from the same (absent) cause.

At one point in his book, Rasmussen is discussing The Black Cat and mentions the animal that gives the film its name: "Poelzig embraces and strokes his pet black cat as a token of the evil power that soothes away his doubts and fears. Werdegast recoils in horror at the sight of it. To him it signifies the potential evil of his own unrestrained hatred."[29] This surely partakes of superstition as it is the author's interpretation of the characters, not the film's representation of them: Werdegast is explicitly identified as suffering from an acute case of phobia. Having set up a whole series of binary oppositions to explain the behavior of the various characters and the intellectual thrust of the film, Rasmussen is forced back on superstition in order to explain the struggle that opposes Poelzig and Werdegast by overdetermining it with a series of parallels that calls for balance and a one-to-one symbolism. Such symbolism, unfortunately, must function according to the argument that each element of a text immediately means something else, and when that "something else" turns on an obsessional attachment to and horror of death, then discursive barriers must be raised to prevent discussion coming into contact with the unconscious desire at the heart of the film of which each spectator is the effect.

It is in Senn's discussion of the special effects in *The Invisible Man* that we find one of the most striking cases of disavowal, so it is not surprising that it concerns special effects in the context of a scientific experiment, thus bringing together both statement and enunciation. Evoking the famous sequence in which the invisible hero plays pranks on the "spectators" (I quote Senn) by running about his room so that he seems it is his shirt that has taken on a life of its own,[30] Senn writes:

> We have no doubts that invisible hands really are manipulating these objects. Even the more mundane gags involving simple props . . . , such as a chair pulled forward on its own and turning to face the fire before the cushion indents under the weight of an invisible backside, are so flawless and natural that suspension of disbelief never becomes an issue. From what we *do* see, we have no doubt that what we do not see is truly there.[31]

The "invisible hands" of the hero (level of the statement) are, of course, those of the technicians of the film (level of the enunciation), just as the "spectators" mentioned elsewhere are both the characters *in* the film and those *of* the film. Discourse creates an imaginary harmony that enables the writer/spectator to misrecognize his real subject position as an effect of narrative and, particularly, of the signifier. For what is being referred to in the last sentence quoted above, something that we are not duped into believing is there even as we believe unswervingly in its existence, if not the maternal phallus itself?

That the Invisible Man becomes visible only after death is a reminder of the impossibility of the Real as a part of reality. Just as the vampire crumbles away to dust when staked, so the Invisible Man becomes visible after death. What we first see as he becomes visible is something that resembles a cross between a mummy and a skull: freezing the image makes this eloquent. Obviously there is something amiss: either the man is visible, in which case he looks like any other human being; or he is invisible, but that changes nothing else concerning his physical state. That the film should represent him as if long dead indicates just to what extent such a scientific experiment is considered unconsciously as always already determined by the death drive. That a werewolf becomes human again when killed shows a return to order (natural, social, and ideological): better death in reality than an assimilation to the Uncanny.

One film that raises this issue in the form of a fantasy is *Death Takes a Holiday*. As the title indicates, Death decides to spend several days in the company of ordinary mortals in the shape of a certain Prince Sirki who has just died. During his stay in the home of an aristocrat, he meets a young woman and they fall in love. At the end of the film, she gives up the young man she is in love with to follow Death for eternity. If this is a fantasy, then it reveals the structure of fantasy according to Lacan: a veil or screen that the subject creates to keep the Real (of mortality) at bay. At the opening of the film the young woman who will fall in love with Sirki is driving through the country in the company of a group of aristocrats. Suddenly she feels "the strangest shadow" is following them, adding, "Sometimes it is close by and sometimes we almost lose it. Let's lose it, let's go fast enough to reach the illimitable." Shortly after, in the mansion where the rest of the action takes place, she suddenly screams and faints; as she does so the film cuts to a blackened part of the salon. On recovering she says, "There was something cold and terrible. I saw a shadow, an enormous darkness. And yet it wasn't a shadow as the moon shone through it. I felt something behind me, running." This imagery is repeated at the end of the film when Death appears as he is: a sort of black shape. He addresses the heroine: "Now you see me as I am, but I've always seen you like that: you haven't changed." Since there is no doubt that the opening encounter was with Death, the ending of the film can be seen as a sort of "appointment in Samarra," with the character finding at the end what she had sought all along. Thus, the car drive is a sort of literal "death drive." If Death chose that particular weekend and that particular house, it was because the young woman wanted something impossible beyond what reality could offer, while needing to cloak this in the fantasy of the perfect love. Which, of course, is what the film too must do; otherwise, it would be as completely unsettling as a "real" horror film rather than a whimsical fantasy. There are, however, sufficient elements in it to show that the manifest content, the discourse of love, is constantly threatened by the unconscious repercussions of the delicate subject matter of death.

Aging and dying are at the center of *Before I Hang* in which scientist John Garth (Boris Karloff) invents a serum that, mixed with a person's blood, can rejuvenate them by twenty to thirty years. He offers to use it on three old friends whose life span has about reached its term. They are all horrified. Garth cannot understand why, but the answer is not difficult to find. The men have already come to terms with death and have settled their symbolic debts: they can await the inevitable with serenity. What Garth proposes is tantamount to asking them to face for a second time not only death itself but also symbolic death, to go through different painful stages of their existence that, once overcome, they wish to forget. What Garth envisages as the answer to a dream is for them akin to a nightmare, and it is precisely this element of the Uncanny that insists in *Death Takes a Holiday*.

How do the films under discussion represent the characters and actions that, in however convoluted a way, have inspired what has been written about them? To what extent do they fit into the logic lucidly expressed by one critic reviewing *King Kong* (in the *New York Times*, 3 March 1933): "Needless to say that this picture was received by many a giggle to cover up fright"?

I shall begin with *The Mummy*, since the film turns on the function of a document that is the object of much superstition within the film: the Scroll of Thoth. This was the papyrus found in 1921 by a British expedition to Egypt where they uncover the tomb of High Priest Imhotep, buried alive 3,700 years previously for using the scroll in an attempt to bring his beloved princess back to life. On the lid of the casket containing the scroll is a warning to the effect that death awaits the person opening the casket. "What a terrible curse!" says Sir Joseph Whemple, leader of the expedition, and his colleague Dr. Muller (played by Edward van Sloan, the Van Helsing of *Dracula*) prevents Whemple's young assistant from opening the casket, for Muller is an expert in the occult and believes in the power of the word. Left alone, the young man cannot resist the temptation, removes the scroll, transcribes its hieroglyphics, and starts to read. The Mummy comes to life, takes the scroll and disappears, leaving the young man laughing hysterically. Years later he dies in a straitjacket, still laughing.

It is necessary to note at the outset the approach adopted by horror films of the period: the need to convince spectators to accept the supernatural premise, to suspend their disbelief quickly. This, I would suggest, indicates on the part of the films an unconscious understanding that something quite different from the supernatural is at stake, something far more difficult to come to terms with because it is firmly anchored in the innermost being of each of us and therefore something we can come up against at any moment. This is hardly the case with vampires, zombies and mummies. And yet we (want to) believe in them.

Belief in the power of the word is, of course, a trait in children and primitive peoples. That the rites, rituals, and incantations of the latter are used in horror films only goes to show how right Freud was to insist on the perseverance of those beliefs and stages of psychic development supposedly left behind by adults who look upon themselves as civilized. This, of course, is yet another dimension of the Uncanny. Thus, Sir Joseph is clearly unnerved by the curse, without accepting its validity. Once he finds the scroll, however—the main action of the film takes place in 1932, with Sir Joseph back on another expedition—he "knows" what has happened and now believes, like Muller. We are clearly faced here with a case of interpellation, where the subject unconsciously recognizes itself in a discourse and acts accordingly. As with the real-life Egyptologists, Sir Joseph already believes unconsciously. This is overdetermined by the film presenting Muller as filling the place of the Subject Supposed to Know. Retroactively, therefore, Sir Joseph "interprets" what happened in 1921: life after death does exist. Either he believes something that he knows to be false, or he accepts that, for no apparent reason, a subject can be annihilated in his being and become irrevocably insane. Such uncertainty about one's own possible future is too difficult to bear. Hence the old adage "It's just as well we don't know what the future holds in store for us." We would dearly have this knowledge, yet we fear it as something far worse than not knowing. For the future, inevitably, means death, but no person can possibly face experiencing certain forms it can take, such as that which befell the assistant.

If *The Mummy* wants us to believe, it nevertheless needs to cushion the blow of desire. One device is to portray the representatives of otherness as more superstitious than ourselves. Thus, the Nubian servant of Sir Joseph comes under the sway of Ardath Bey, the reincarnation of Imhotep, as can be seen from the way he is so easily frightened and kneels to kiss his ring. Such a gesture, it should be added, is common in Western religions such as Anglicanism and Catholicism. On another level, the Nubian is being denounced as betraying Sir Joseph's trust by "going over" to the enemy, but the point I want to make is that the relation of the Nubian to the Mummy parallels that of Muller and Sir Joseph to the occult.

That the film partakes of this structure of belief can be seen in a most revealing sequence that takes place in Ardath Bey's home. By the power of suggestion—telepathy—he has enticed there Helen Grosvenor, the young daughter of the British high commissioner in the Sudan whom he takes for the reincarnation of the princess for whom he suffered the horror of being buried alive. He reveals the past to her through hypnosis, the film presenting it as a sort of flashback. As his tale ends, she wakes up, remembering nothing. Suddenly we hear the horrible yelping of the dog she brought with her. She rushes out to see what is wrong, and Ardath Bey follows her. Yet we see nothing. There is, of course, nothing to see, or, rather, the film cannot show us anything as the incident brings into play the structure of disavowal in ways that show up the fashion in which the film is manipulating the spectators. Earlier in the sequence, Ardath Bey has evoked the young woman's spirit, which has taken many forms over the ages. The camera cuts to his cat running away and apparently hiding. This can only be interpreted by audiences as an indication that something hideous is to happen (such a use of animals is made in *Werewolf of London* in which a cat suddenly goes berserk just before the main character's transformation). In the next sequence, however, we learn that the dog was killed and that a white cat was on its back, which encourages us to believe the cat to be the reincarnation of an Egyptian god or else is under the spell of the reincarnation of Imhotep, much like the Nubian, thus assimilating the racial other to an animal. The dog—completely superfluous to the story—is thus yanked yelping into the diegesis in order to make us believe. Retroactively, we reinterpret the cat's running away so as to lend credence to what we learn later. Here, as elsewhere, notably in vampire films, the concept "seeing is believing" is transformed into "not seeing is knowing," which, readers will remember, is simply a rewriting of the formula referred to earlier as designating a belief in the maternal phallus.

It is patent from this sequence that the film offers, the better to deny it, a perfectly rational explanation for Ardath Bey's control over the young woman: hypnosis. That the unconscious explains her belief in and response to what he tells her is hardly conducive to exploitation by Hollywood, which preferred to pour scorn on a genuine theory of the concept at the same time as it inscribed it into the very body of its texts. *Dracula's Daughter*, as we shall see presently, is eloquent on this strategy. A revealing occurrence of the matter is the first meeting between Helen Grosvenor and the son of Sir Joseph. Needless to say (but I shall say it anyway), he falls in love with her, but on the mode of displacement by saying "there's something about you." She, however, is made of sterner stuff: "Do you have to open graves to find girls to fall in love with?" This vigorous frontal attack reminds him that she looks like the Mummy the new expedition has just discovered: the object of Imhotep's sacrilegious love. In other words, he displaces onto a purely coincidental resemblance a subjective relation to death that is neurotic. And a similar relation to women, we could add: that "something about you" surely corresponds to the "in you more than you" analyzed by Slavoj Zizek, the "something" in the subject, notably the female subject, that resists symbolization.[32] By the same token, the hero is no more able to choose than Sir Joseph is able not to believe, which underpins the neurotic relation to death and castration. This sequence is also crucial for grasping the unconscious project of the film. Despite its wish to show that love Hollywood style will triumph, the film falls unwittingly into the discursive trap it laid for the spectator early on. When the young assistant removes the scroll from its casket, we have a point-of-view (POV) shot: his hands are our hands. Familiar stuff, but like any such device encouraging identification, it leaves its trace on the spectators' unconscious. The young assistant is now replaced by Sir Joseph's son, the film's hero inasmuch as he is our representative in the fiction as the one able to save the heroine through his love (the fact that actor David Manners is an uninspiring substitute for such a stand-in does not change the narrative function of the character). As such, the spectator identifies with the son on the level of traditional heterosexual desire just as he or she identified with the assistant on the level of the desire to know.

The Return of the Repressed

When Renfield insists on taking the stagecoach on to Borgo Pass, where he will be met at midnight by someone from Dracula's castle, the villagers inform him in horror of the vampires. Renfield dismisses this as "superstition." He is, of course, the first person to be vampirized, thus showing the fate of those who do not believe. As Van Helsing states pointedly later in the film, "the strength of the vampire is that people will *not* believe in him." The parallel with *The Mummy*, down to the use of the same actor Edward van Sloan, is striking. What I wish to stress in the following sequences—the drive in Dracula's coach from Borgo Pass to the castle, Renfield entering the castle, and his meeting with Dracula—is the way Renfield systematically refuses to pay heed to what his senses tell him. Behind Renfield's scornful rejection of peasant superstition lie both class prejudice on the part of the Westerner and a desire to maintain a belief in an object the human eye can only represent via a hallucination: the maternal phallus. This is essential to an understanding of the film.

On no fewer than four occasions, Renfield sees something he refuses to accept. The first occurs when he leans out of Dracula's stage to tell the driver (whom he and we have seen earlier) not to drive so fast: there is no driver, only a bat hovering over the horses' backs. With a look that shows both amazement and horror, Renfield draws back into the coach *so as not to see.* The second is a continuation of this. When the coach finally stops, Renfield alights and addresses the driver again; he stops in midsentence when he sees there is nobody driving. The third instance occurs when the castle door opens, as if by magic (as the saying goes). Renfield mounts the steps, his hesitation indicating an awareness that something is wrong. The fourth is Dracula descending the huge interior staircase to greet him: the count passes through spiders' webs as if they were not there, whereas Renfield is forced to brush them aside with his cane when he follows the count upstairs.

Ushered into a large but cozy room with a fire, Renfield makes this strange remark: "It's different from outside, more cheerful." I wish to draw attention to a discrepancy between the apparent meaning of this statement and the actual words used. It would seem obvious that Renfield is comparing the room in which he now finds himself with the hall of the castle, which seems abandoned, but the use of the word *outside* suggests the absent term *inside.* Strictly speaking, there is only one "outside," in front of the castle, but just as Renfield had to walk up steps to enter the castle, so he had to walk up a staircase to gain access to the space that he now calls "cheerful." Certainly there is nothing cheerful about the castle hall and staircase, nor about the exterior. It becomes clear, therefore, that "inside" is divided into a sort of antechamber—the hall and the staircase—and the room where Dracula and Renfield talk and do business and where the latter has a meal. It is in this room that Renfield signs, as it were, his death warrant by simply acting as if nothing untoward had happened. We shall see presently that Van Helsing acts in the same way, but in a reversed form: just as Renfield continues to refuse to believe while unconsciously knowing, Van Helsing continues to believe while unconsciously refusing to know.

At one point in the film Mina is "visited" by Lucy; although Mina has already received the "visit" of Dracula, she is not yet under his control, whereas Lucy, the first victim, has died and is now therefore a vampire. Mina's way of describing this encounter should not be passed over, She tells Harker and Van Helsing about it, adding, "Then I remembered Lucy was dead." It is surely a most remarkable thing to forget one's best friend has died! If Mina were under the count's spell, then she would not have mentioned Lucy so as not to arouse Van Helsing's suspicions, so we must interpret her remark as indicating a desire to repress Lucy's death because she knows what it means. By that, I emphatically do *not* mean that Mina knows she is heading for the same fate, although that could be the first step in an interpretation. Rather, it would suggest that she knows unconsciously not who Dracula *is* but what he *means.*

Let us return to Van Helsing and his remark about what constitutes the vampire's strength: people not believing in him. Later in the film he evokes "the little-known facts which the world is perhaps better off for not knowing." This surely contradicts the earlier claim by encouraging ignorance, whereas Van Helsing is a firm believer: by believing in vampires, one can take the necessary precautions—which he does systematically—and destroy them. This apparent contradiction on the level of the script has, of course, nothing to do with incompetence or studio tampering. If it remains in the film, it is because its meaning interpellates the text and the spectator and provides an understanding of what is being signified. For Van Helsing is just as careless as Renfield when it comes to using the information one's senses provide—indeed, far more so.

Vampirized and considered insane—he has been found on the boat that has unwittingly brought Dracula to England—Renfield has been locked up in Dr. Seward's sanitarium where Seward and Van Helsing can keep an eye on him. However, Renfield keeps on escaping from his cell, wandering about the hospital and participating in the conversations between the two doctors. This is completely illogical on a conscious, cause-effect level, but its meaning has nothing to do with such logic. A nurse called Martin is in charge of Renfield, and he is played as being a bit of an idiot, doubtless because of his proletarian background. How can a competent nurse allow his patient to escape all the time? What is striking is that Van Helsing takes no notice of Martin and what he has to say, as if the man were irrelevant; this is a prejudice due to class difference. Yet there are no traces of Renfield having broken out of his cell (and he escapes with a bewildering regularity and facility), except once: the bars have been broken. This should surely alert Van Helsing: either Renfield has passed through the walls of his cell, which means he is a vampire, or Martin is incompetent. The breaking of the bars is a sign of superhuman strength, another pertinent trait of vampirism (exploited for blatant special-effects purposes in John Carpenter's *Vampires*). This, however, is the only time an explanation is given and still Van Helsing does not react.

The fact is that Van Helsing does not listen to Martin at the outset when he says he heard wolves. This is all the more surprising as Van Helsing knows that vampires can turn into wolves and, to Harker's remark that he has seen a dog running across the lawn after Dracula has left the sanitarium, replies, "Or a wolf?" So Van Helsing takes the situation seriously yet refuses to pay heed to the crucial information supplied by Martin. We can put it down to his scientific hubris as well as to class prejudice, but something else is at stake.[33] Van Helsing knows vampires cast no reflection in mirrors, and we have already seen a shot reflected in a mirror where Dracula, although present in the room, is absent from the mirror. Zizek has drawn the necessary conclusion: the vampire is an *objet a* and as such cannot be seen in a mirror.[34] I shall reformulate this in more explicit terms, as I have already done elsewhere.[35] The lack of reflection in a mirror is an uncanny return to the mirror stage from the vantage point of the Symbolic. If there is no other person alongside the subject, then this absence represents the lack that constitutes the subject. In other words, the shock of this absence is due to it reactivating an unpleasant fact that the subject has had to accept but that he has repressed, while carrying the unconscious traces of this knowledge with him or her for all time. *The vampire is thus the locus of castration.*[36]

This hardly settles things, but it does bring us a little closer to the heart of the matter. When Dracula evokes "things far worse than death," it is this dimension of (his) being that is making its presence felt. *Dracula's Daughter* will enable us to approach the question from a somewhat different angle, via the character of Dr. Garth, a psychiatrist who chooses to believe for reasons having nothing whatsoever to do with being forced to change one's mind because of the testimony of one's senses. We have already seen how Van Helsing in *Dracula* prefers not to listen because he needs to maintain a certain form of belief in vampires. This can only be seen as a mode of defense against what he cannot face up to in the person of the vampire: his own castration. The structures of disavowal in *Dracula's Daughter* are even more insistent, for reasons that will soon be apparent.

The film begins where the earlier one had left off: Renfield killed by Dracula in Carfax Abbey and Dracula duly staked by Van Helsing. The latter gives himself up to the police, and the ensuing comic aspects of the opening sequences are there in an attempt to displace the issues. The police sergeant and constable responsible for arresting Van Helsing keep an eye on the two bodies while the vampire hunter is escorted to London.[37] The constable looks in on the coffins and suddenly sees something burrowing under the floor. He runs back to the sergeant and claims there are rats in there. "No rats in Whitby jail," replies the sergeant (all this is played for comic effect). He in turn goes to inspect his charges and discovers that the burrowing has continued to the point where the ground is starting to open up. He retires hastily and says to his colleague, "Rats!" On the purely superficial level, encouraged by the film's feeble attempts at humor, this is a case of honest-to-goodness cowardice. I shall venture to interpret the sequence along the lines defined in this chapter: the sergeant disavows the testimony of his senses so as not to recognize that something outside his comprehension is taking place. Inasmuch as the two uniformed policemen are stupid and cowardly (after all, we are in Britain as Hollywood conceived it), this would hardly rate a mention, were it not for the fact that Garth functions in a like fashion and that this places the film on a most interesting terrain that, like the floor in the prison, threatens to open up and engulf Garth and the spectators.

Garth may be a psychiatrist, but he clearly has no truck with such nonsense as psychoanalysis. When questioned by Countess Zeleska—only the audience and her servant Sandor know she is Dracula's daughter—as to whether he believes the dead can influence the living, he retorts curtly that he does not. One could cite the Oedipus complex to counter this interesting manifestation of denial, but let us continue with the interview where Garth adds, "Your strength lies within yourself." She has only to fight her problem. Garth sees himself as a scientist and thus as a man of reason; he respects Von Helsing because he studied under him in Vienna, but there are limits. Clearly the film is taking a swipe at Freud, but as so often when Hollywood denounces things about which it knows nothing, the knowledge repressed—the existence of the unconscious—returns to haunt the text in no uncertain fashion.

One of the countess's victims, a young woman called Lily, finally emerges from the coma into which being vampirized has plunged her. Garth, the man of science, immediately decides to hypnotize her: "You must remember," he commands. What he does not know, unlike the audience, is that the countess used her large signet ring to hypnotize Lily before taking advantage of her.[38] The light from the machine used to hypnotize her resembles the lighting used to symbolize the power emanating from the ring, so Garth succeeds beyond his hopes in reminding the victim of what befell her: she goes hysterical and then dies. What must be noted here is how she replies to Garth's questions: first she talks as if in conversation with the vampire, then with Garth, and then with the vampire again. As a result, she suffers a complete loss of identity: her very being is threatened, and it is Garth who is at the origin of her suffering. By forcing Lily to repeat what she has experienced, he forces her to remember what she has forgotten, in the reflexive sense used by Lacan when discussing little Hans.[39] She has in fact successfully resolved her Oedipal complex, but Garth has not. She has therefore to endure not only the shock of the return of the repressed of castration but also the shock of returning, on emerging from her coma (a defense mechanism) as from a form of death. This places Lily before the annihilation of her being, and she dies so as to escape the horror of the situation, an impossible knowledge of death Garth sadistically submits her to (again) in the name of his own thirst for knowledge as imaginary certainty. This "thirst" is as vampiric as that of the countess and is insisted on by a detail designating the text's unconscious: Lily addressing now the vampire, now Garth, *as if they were the same person*. *Dracula's Daughter* displaces onto Lily the woman the castration anxiety of Garth the man and has her die in his place. If the male ego has doubts about knowledge and women, the source of these doubts must stem, not from a feminine position, but from the clear-cut one of patriarchy.

Garth blames it all on the vampire, but Lily would still be alive if he had not forced her, by repeating what she experienced, to bring sufficiently close to consciousness what she had repressed originally and that which she must forget, like little Hans, in order to continue living. This denial of responsibility on Garth's part is promptly followed by his changing his mind: vampires do exist; Von Helsing was right. He gets the chance to put this to the test when Countess Zeleska entices him to her castle in Transylvania so that she can vampirize him and live for eternity with him. Garth now finds himself in a most uncomfortable position: the countess's powers of hypnosis are stronger than his will (in *Dracula* Van Helsing successfully resisted the Count). Thus the male is weaker than the female. Neither Garth nor Hollywood can accept this, even if their reasons are the wrong ones. When the countess mocks him, accusing him of killing Lily, Garth replies, "I don't believe in your spells or your magic." And this despite the fact that, momentarily, she has got the upper hand. It is only because Garth is anxious to defend his secretary, abducted by the countess, that he manages to focus his mind on the young woman and thus resist the "spell." This disavowal of what he has just experienced—a most unscientific attitude, let it be said, and akin to Van Helsing's disavowal of his senses in *Dracula*—is overdetermined by a displacement: he focuses his attention from the countess to the secretary. By so doing, he can at one and the same time assert his phallic rights and deny both castration and his belief in the maternal phallus, symbolized by the masculine bearing and behavior of the countess. The female vampire is just a bit more uncanny than the male.[40]

Mark of the Vampire has aroused controversy by suddenly revealing, some ten minutes from the end, that all we have seen is nothing but an elaborate plot to confound a murderer, first by inducing in him by word and deed the belief that vampires are at work in the neighborhood, then getting him to repeat under hypnosis the way he killed his victim a year previously. My argument will be not only that the film falls into the trap laid for the character—and the spectator until we become privy to the plot—but that the various manifestations of disavowal it musters hide something of a radically different kind. We shall attempt to identify what this is before extending our analyses in order to grasp the form of the unconscious discourse structuring all the films under discussion here.

As Bryan Senn has pertinently asked, what are we to make of the film's numerous inconsistencies? If the film is really saying, as it is, that there are no such things as vampires, only actors playing their role to trap Baron Otto into a confession, then what is the purpose of the extended opening sequence of peasants with garlic everywhere, including in a baby's cradle? Why the discussion between the doctor and travelers to the effect that there are vampires in the area and that they should spend the night at the inn? Why are we shown Luna, daughter of supposed vampire Count Mora (Bela Lugosi), flying like a bat in human form? None of these incidents takes place within the baron's sight or hearing, so they can only be aimed at the audience. They cannot therefore be explained as part of the charade. One such inconsistency, however, can be explained. Two servants recount how they saw a bat enter the house and turn into Count Mora; we see it happen. Here there is no problem, providing one adopts the formula of the point of view and the inherent ability of the image to lie, not necessarily in itself, but according to who (re)presents it. What we see therefore is not a bat changing into a human vampire but *a visualization of how the servants told the tale*. And as we learn at the end that they are part of the plot, this can be interpreted as a discursive device to hoodwink the baron—and us with him. The baron and the spectators *want* to believe, and the servants' discourse promptly interpellates this unconscious desire and represents it visually.

The other occurrences, however, can pretend to no such purely narrative explanation. They can nevertheless be explained. What is being repressed in *Mark of the Vampire* is, as we shall see, something that cannot be admitted. Just as the film shows a group of characters convincing the baron to believe in something that does not exist and whose presence is a decoy, a lure, so what the film is repressing leads to the text introducing elements that exist to prove—nevertheless—that vampires do exist. Once again, a belief in our blood-sucking friends is preferable to knowledge of a kind that is too disturbing for words—except that it is precisely through words, and a precise image, that this knowledge insists despite all the ballyhoo to keep it at bay. No garlic or crosses can do that.

At one point, Professor Zelin, who leads the plot to unmask the baron and is the person who hypnotizes him at the end, makes the following remark: "We can't undo what's been done." He is referring, with apparent rationality, to the fact that carelessness has led to the daughter of Sir Karell, the murder victim, being "visited" by a vampire. I propose to see in this remark a striking manifestation and confirmation of a thesis of Freud's. In *Inhibitions, Symptoms and Anxiety*, he points out how the ego's tenacious attachment to reality leads it to have recourse to a variety of means in order to maintain in a state of repression a desire that interferes with that reality. The ego can even go so far as to adopt quite unrealistic tactics. These can consist of attempting to undo, by simple denial, not only what has already been carried out in reality but even the *consequences* of the act in question.[41] We shall now see that the mise en scène of the plot creates a situation where the repressed is manifest in a disguised and displaced form; that the "trick" ending is an attempt to undo by denial what has been done, said and shown; and that the inconsistent elements are remnants that exist to call attention to the vampire, not as something that exists but as something that *signifies*.

Only one character in the plot is unaware of what is being concocted: the fiancé of the murder victim's daughter. At one point he tries to find out what's wrong and reiterates his desire to get her away from the house (hence his being kept in ignorance: without the daughter, the charade cannot possibly succeed). There ensues the following conversation in which the fiancé speaks first:

> "I want to know why you're acting this way. You're not yourself."
> "Forgive me for what I'm doing."

At this point in the film, the spectators cannot possibly interpret the word *acting* as meaning other than "behaving," as they cannot but adopt the same subject position as the young man. Nor can they interpret the reply as an address of the heroine-as-actress to a person ignorant of the charade rather than that of a distraught victim of a vampire trying to elicit the understanding of her lover. If we now place the conversation in the context of other exchanges between characters, the form of the film represents an unconscious desire that cannot say its name.

Almost immediately after this confrontation, the daughter breaks down, and the film reveals the truth: it's all an act to trap the baron. She gives as her excuse the fact that the actor chosen to play her dead father and convince the baron he has returned as a vampire bears too close a likeness to her father: "To act as if you were my father, alive and with me—don't you see the horror of it?" Earlier in the film she had played her role most convincingly, claiming that she had heard her father's voice and that she had to go to him. The inspector had played his part by dismissing this as "hysteria," adopting a skeptical attitude so that the baron would not become suspicious and could thus be led bit by bit to believe, just like the inspector, once the "evidence" became too substantial to be ignored.

Let us return to the daughter's remark just quoted, for it contains a nice Freudian slip: the word *alive*. This is most odd, for if the actor is very much alive, the father in the plot is one of the living dead. That is the whole point of the little play enacted for the baron's and the spectator's benefit. We are dealing with a confusion between statement and enunciation and hence between conflicting and incompatible subject positions. One could interpret the word as indicating a desire for her dead father to be alive, but this takes no account of the fact that her remark is illogical from the point of view both of her real relation to the actor and of the role he is being called on to play. I suggest we interpret "alive" as the manifestation of two contradictory unconscious desires: that she wants her father to be alive in order to continue her special (incestuous) relation with him; and that she wants him dead so that she can have a normal relation with the fiancé. The place of incest in the film is hence complicated by the fact that she is glad her father is dead.

To this we must add another unconscious element. If at some time in the past prior to his murder she wished him dead, then her most secret unconscious fear can only be that he will return, in the time-honored tradition of the living dead, to collect a symbolic debt and to punish her for her desire. Since incest flows in both directions, however, he could also be returning from the dead to carry on the relationship. This is precisely what the film shows: when she was play-acting and claiming to hear her father's voice, her unconscious desire was precisely that he should return and call her to him so that their forbidden relation could continue. Her words to the fiancé— "Forgive me for that I'm doing"—are thus a horrified attempt at an excuse that I propose to rewrite as follows: "Forgive me for deceiving you with another man, my father." Whether we interpret the conversation as an admission to play-acting on the first level, that enounced by the film, or as an admission to indulging in incestuous fantasies, then the conversation is a particularly complex example of Lacan's fundamental insight that human beings are the only creatures that can deceive by telling the truth. Whichever way the fiancé, the spectator, or the film's makers interpret the conversation, they are being deceived, for the unconscious desire will remain repressed.

This, however, is far from being all there is to the incest theme. Immediately after the sequence where she claims to hear her father's voice, the inspector, as we have mentioned, barks, "Hysteria!" Never a truer word was spoken, including in jest. For hysteria is certainly present in the film: at the moment where she breaks down. Her loss of control is the effect of a particular cause, that of the truth of her desire suddenly being revealed in the remark she makes to the actor playing her father. Her inability to control her words, gestures, and body movements is surely a sign of the repressed desire inscribing its traces on her body in the form of a symptom. No further displacement is possible at this point. If this was possible after the inspector pronounced the word that now returns to haunt the daughter, then this is due to the fact that in the charade the father-daughter encounter had not yet taken place. The film cuts to a large close-up of the daughter looking adoringly off-screen right, in the direction of Professor Zelin, the film's stern patriarch and obvious father substitute. If only she can convince herself that by admiring/loving him she will escape punishment; if only the symbolic debt can be collected in this displaced form, then she can rest in peace—and so can her father.

Yet another twist is added through the character of the baron. In the last segment of the film, just prior to the baron being hypnotized so as to repeat the murder, the actor playing the father (the audience, let us not forget, knows everything at this point) says to him, "You've spoilt her since the day she was born." What transpires here is that the baron was and is in love with the daughter and killed the father to as to have access to her and her fortune. In this case we can perhaps refer to another remark of Freud's in the work mentioned earlier: another way of undoing an act to obtain the desired effect is to *repeat* it, but in a different way.[42] The final section of the play is a repetition of the murder of Sir Karell, so if we now see how the baron killed him, then this is the acting-out of the desire of another person—namely, the daughter. She desired to kill her father, and the baron unconsciously assumed that desire as his own by identifying with it.

Information on the original script, made available by Bryan Senn, shows that the incest theme was present in the film at the outset, indeed until the last minute.[43] There was to have been an incestuous relationship between Count Mora and his daughter Luna. The parallel is striking, to say the least. What is not explained is what function this could have had in the film. I would suggest that the makers of the film came too close to realizing that this was the acting out of the incest theme underpinning the film and removed all traces of incest for that reason and not just to avoid conflict with Breen. All traces? Not quite, for in the original script the count kills his daughter, then commits suicide by shooting himself, suggesting that it was the actor and actress who were father and daughter: a vampire cannot die from a bullet wound. Yet the count in the final minutes of the film has a bullet wound on his temple, a sign that something escaped the attention of the makers: the unconscious has left its trace in an all-too-literal way, a surplus or excess of meaning within the film's signifying system.

And what about the vampire in all that, the vampire as a concept, not the vampire in the film? Surely we must see him not only as the locus of castration but also of its counterpart: the phallus. As such his return is that of the primal father, brutally punishing his sons for wanting to usurp his power and his daughters for questioning his phallic rights. Thus we can offer an explanation for the inconsistencies listed earlier. They are the text's unconscious manifestation of the power of the vampire as the condensatory signifier of repressed and forbidden desires, a manifestation on the mode of denial and inversion: one great big happy family protecting themselves from the feared return, while at the same time believing in the vampire as a supernatural being because that belief, passed off as knowledge, is preferable to the knowledge of what the vampire signifies. As the old joke has it: "Incest! The game the whole family can play."[44]

Mark of the Vampire is undoubtedly the most inoffensive film of the period if one sticks to the manifest content of the story, so it is all the more interesting to note that the film elicited a furious and disgusted letter from a doctor, one William J. Robinson of New York City, published on 28 July 1935 in the *New York Times* with the title "Concerning Horror Films": "Several people have come to my notice who, after seeing that horrible picture, suffered nervous shock, were attacked with insomnia, and those who did fall asleep were tortured by most horrible nightmares."[45] Strong stuff for such an apparently mild film, unless one chooses to read this, as I propose to do, as the return of the (good physician's) repressed. That a nameless desire is circulating can be adduced from the words of the heroine herself, evoking an attack on her by Luna, whereas, as Senn rightly points out, it is clearly the count her father who was responsible for the attack.[46] As Joan Copjec has reminded us, the *objet a* stands in, among other objects, for the breast.[47] This can have at least two consequences for the film. First, it suggests a desire on the heroine's part—rejected in the form of a displacement—to be attacked by Luna as mother substitute so as to enjoy an impossible reunion with the maternal breast, a case of *jouissance* that cannot but set off feelings of the most extreme anxiety: something "horrible," a word Robinson uses and then *repeats*. Had this attack taken place, then it would help to explain the count killing his daughter, then himself, inhabited and inhibited by the conflicting feelings of jealousy and horror. Second, it evokes a lesbian attraction on the part of the two young women, a theme taken up explicitly in *Dracula's Daughter* the following year and one to which we shall return in the next chapter.

Senn refers to an interview with Carol Borland (Luna), to the effect that her mentor, Bela Lugosi, warned her to keep away from Elizabeth Allen (the daughter) who "had a bad reputation."[48] Whether this refers to her sexuality or her politics is unclear. Apparently it concerned men, but that can mean two quite separate things: either addicted to them (which for the *doxa* connotes nymphomania) or repelled by them (which connotes lesbianism). I would suggest that the anecdote tells us something interesting about Lugosi's unconscious relation to his screen persona of Dracula.[49] His remark to

Borland is clearly a patriarchal and phallocentric attempt to keep her under his wing (pun intended) and to determine her desires and sexuality, as if she were his daughter, thus acting out in reality the repressed of *Mark of the Vampire*. Few horror films have produced such a surplus of signification. The extratextual factors suggest that repression has taken place systematically, leaving a surface incoherency attempting to mask the repeated "attacks" of the Real.[50]

If we now return to *The Mummy*, we may extend our remarks on *Mark of the Vampire*, for the very title of the film evokes the maternal, a fact that should, but certainly does not, go without saying.[51] Let us take the hypothetical case of a French patient undergoing psychoanalysis. During one session he mentions how he woke up that morning with a start and for some moments felt a profound sense of unease; all that he could remember of the night was a dream concerning a vast, unidentified expanse of water. His analyst, a sound Freudian, encourages him to identify this water and, faced with his hesitation, suspects it must be the sea, *la mer*, thus indicating a slippage from signifier to signifier to maintain repressed the patient's desire: *la mère*, the mother. Freud, of course, has given us a nice example—of a somewhat different kind—with the "Glanz auf der Nase," the "shine on the nose," which his intuition and experience—given the patient's English origins—enabled him to reformulate as a "*glance* auf der Nase" and thus to pinpoint a case of fetishism: seeing is believing, with a spatial displacement there to show and disavow it.

The plot thickens in the case of *The Mummy*, for if the signifier designates the maternal, the referent is unmistakably masculine. However, that is only to be expected and is rigorously logical, for the young assistant whose folly brings Imhotep back to life goes mad—or, to be more precise and to stick closely to what the film actually shows, falls victim to hysterics. "He went for a little walk," he says, laughing incessantly, to explain the disappearance of The Mummy whom we have seen come back to life and take the scroll. Such hysteria in a man can only designate an unconscious question structuring his being: "Am I a man or a woman?" Hence the Mummy becomes the condensatory signifier of a pre-Oedipal desire for both parents, a bisexual element likely, given society's tendency to demand from all of us a commitment to a specific and unwavering sexual identity, to trigger a traumatic reaction and its attendant defense mechanism, here hysterics leading to insanity as an extreme form of (self-)defense.[52]

Having the best of both worlds sexually supposes, however, a delicate balance to be maintained, but the assistant's choice here is surely clear. By referring to The Mummy's "little walk," he is really giving form to the pre-Oedipal

desire to see the father disappear, which is precisely what Imhotep does—
until the return of Sir Joseph eleven years later for what I suggest we call "a
repeat performance," for Sir Joseph is accompanied this time by his son who,
as I have indicated, replaces the assistant. Ardath Bey uses his supernatural
powers to provoke a heart attack that kills Sir Joseph. Shortly after, when in
the company of the young woman whom Ardath Bey sees as the reincarnation of his princess, the son is shocked to find that he is more interested in
making love to her than in grieving over his father's sudden demise. This is in
no way, however, an indication that he wanted his father out of the way in order to court the young woman; the film had made it clear that the father was
not hostile to the relationship. If, however, we analyze the characters not as
individuals but as structural functions, then the film corresponds to a fairytale
or a family romance where children turn their parents into kings and queens,
stalwart heroes and beautiful heroines, and so forth. The fact that the young
heroine is the reincarnation of an ancient princess endows her with a noble
status corresponding to the child's idealization of the *mother*. We can therefore see why the son is so shocked that he should be forgetting his father so
quickly.

Discussing *Mark of the Vampire* earlier I referred to the "living dead" and
the collection of a "symbolic debt." Both are represented in a horror film that
has nothing remotely supernatural about it: *The Crime of Dr. Crespi* (we further discuss this film later in the chapter). Having buried alive Stephen Ross,
his former sexual rival and now the husband of the woman he still loves,
Crespi celebrates in the solitude of his office by drinking toasts to his success.
Ross, however, has been saved by being dug up by colleagues of the mad
Crespi, convinced the man has been murdered. Suddenly, Ross staggers into
the office and collapses into a chair. The fact that Crespi is not surprised or
horrified shows just to what extent he has "gone over the edge," but this reaction demands some explanation. The script obligingly furnishes us with
one. Crespi eyes Ross and asks if he is a ghost come back to haunt him. Given
the fact that Crespi has a small skeleton in his office that he salutes every
day, like a friend, the film is patently referring to *Hamlet*, the skeleton standing in for Yorick. More to the point, however, is the status of Ross in relation
to Crespi. Zizek has pointed out that the ghost of Hamlet's father "represents
. . . actual death unaccompanied by symbolic death, without a settling of accounts."[53] This is precisely how Crespi reacts to Ross who must therefore be
seen as the father(figure) back from the dead to collect a symbolic debt and
punish the son. Crespi's obsession with the woman Ross married was the symbolization of an incestuous desire, the fusion with the mother and an insur-
mountable death drive: burying Ross alive is like literally condemning him

to that enclosed space that is the womb. Crespi's desire to be the phallus and to have it is represented in the film by his phallic body: bald head and an upright, rigid gait. His drinking alone is thus the equivalent of the "solitary pleasure" of masturbation, the only solution left to him.

Werewolf of London provides a variant on the incest theme, but it also turns on a linguistic element and the ambiguity of representation. The film opens in Tibet where an English botanist, Dr. Glendon, and his assistant have come to look for a unique flower that blooms only in the rays of the full moon. The Tibetans accompanying them refuse to go on into the valley where Glendon hopes to find the flower, thus indicating "typical" superstitious fear. This is compounded the next moment: they flee in panic when an unknown man on a camel comes over the crest of the hill. He addresses Glendon by identifying himself as a British priest who has been living in Tibet for forty years and warns Glendon not to continue: "there are some things it is better not to bother with." Like Van Helsing or the priest (also British) in *White Zombie*, he is meant to be the voice of wisdom and caution, but I wish to insist here on the parallel created with *The Mummy*: Glendon calls him "Father" and thereby hangs a (fairy)tale. Later in the film, in the course of a discussion with Dr. Yogami (the film's other werewolf; it was he who attacked and bit Glendon in the valley, thus leading the two men to be rivals for the possession of the flower, the only antidote to "werewolfery"), Glendon dismisses talk of werewolves (he has not yet undergone transformation) by saying he stopped believing in goblins and the like when he was six. However, just as Freud taught us that the primitive beliefs of childhood may be overcome but can still leave traces to be reactivated in later life, so he also taught us that there are beliefs that certain people never overcome. This, I shall argue, is what *Werewolf of London* turns on.

Glendon tends to neglect his young wife in favour of his work, a common trait among mad doctors and scientists.[54] This does not prevent him from experiencing suspicion and intense jealousy when an old childhood friend of his wife's turns up and Glendon sees that the two of them are getting on famously. During Glendon's first transformation into a werewolf, he retains at the outset sufficient lucidity and control to rush into his laboratory to pick a flower as antidote. But the two flowers are missing (we learn later that Yogami stole them for himself), and at the moment he makes this unpleasant discovery, the film superimposes onto the shot where Glendon is transforming a shot of his wife and her old friend (who has clearly been showing an interest in her). The film's conscious discourse is perfectly clear for the rest of the film: Glendon, now a werewolf, pursues his wife with the intent to kill her to punish her for showing an interest in the man. This, however, does not quite fit the real situation. As Glendon's jealousy is aimed at the man, why does he not kill his rival so as not to share his wife with him? Moreover, the superimposed shot occurs when Glendon discovers the flowers have gone, which surely creates a link between the flowers and the "couple." I suggest that this is the path we must pursue.

Glendon has two rivals in the film: Yogami and the other man, Paul. If Yogami is set up by the film's conscious discourse as his rival to possess the flower, then so is Paul in the film's unconscious discourse: the repressed meaning of the superimposed shot. Just as Yogami is consciously associated in Glendon's mind with Tibet, so Paul will become associated with the same country in his unconscious. And Tibet is where he met the priest whom he dutifully and correctly calls "Father." In this light we can see Glendon acting out with both men a form of "sibling rivalry," with the flower as the "prize" to be won. As such we have the structure of an Oedipal fantasy comprising four terms, as Lacan has taught us. The flower therefore fills the function of the phallus, the two "brothers" fighting for the right to possess it against the stern warnings of the "father." Glendon's aggressive behavior toward his wife stems from the fact that she fulfils the function of mother. Two forms of inversion are at work: the object of the child's first love is turned into that of hatred because she is inaccessible, and the fact that Glendon seems so much older than his wife symbolizes in reverse the difference in age between mother and child.[55] As Freud taught us, such a reversal to permit negation or denial is common in dreams. It is hardly surprising, therefore, that the "showdown" in which Glendon is killed by the police (symbol of the Law through displacement, especially as the man who kills him is the *uncle* of the wife's childhood friend) should take place in the house of the wife's parents, where Glendon came to court her and where the childhood friend "proposed" to her: she was six and he was twelve. Nor is it a coincidence that Glendon should tell Yogami that he was *six* when he stopped believing in goblins, for in the film's unconscious all the characters are involved in the acting out of childhood fantasies concerning their incestuous desires for the parents and the attendant rivalry. And the last shot of the film—a plane taking off—shows the phallus being restored to its "rightful" place: Paul is taking Glendon's widow off to California as his wife. The two unworthy "brothers" have been safely dispatched, and the film can deny setting the other man up as anything other than a "normal" solution to a purely marital problem. Proud possessor of the "real" phallus, he shows the "father" was right and that the latter can now safely be forgotten. Life goes on.

A rather special case is that of businessman Eric Gorman in *Murders in the Zoo*. Gorman travels the world looking for animals to stock a private zoo in which he is the major shareholder. The film opens with one of the nastiest scenes in horror films of the period: Gorman sewing up the mouth of a colleague whom he suspects of having an affair with his wife. We are treated to a close-up of the victim's face after Gorman has finished with him. As Gorman is quickly shown to be a raving paranoiac, we could sum matters up by stating that his blocking up the "hole" in his colleagues face represents his desire not to see the "hole" between his wife's legs and categorize him as a repressed homosexual who has become neurotic as a result of an inability to overcome castration. Things are somewhat more complicated, however. We learn soon after the scene just described that the colleague has been devoured by a tiger (he has been left to fend for himself in the Indian jungle where the opening sequences take place). It is hardly a simple coincidence that Gorman disposes of his wife later in the film by throwing her to the zoo's crocodiles. If paranoia and homosexuality are certainly part of the scenario, so is a regression to the oral stage where extremes of tenderness and aggressivity coexist. Gorman can be seen as one who was devoured in childhood by a loving and beloved mother, while at the same time seeking to devour her in an attempt to maintain his identity through bodily harmony and integrity. His later guilt at the incestuous nature of his attachment to the mother and his aggressive feelings toward her have been transformed into an extreme form of sadism against a man who, by threatening his relationship with his wife, represents the father who once forbade *jouissance*, fusion with the mother's body. *Murders in the Zoo* thus represents in a literal form what was experienced unconsciously in the same way at a period of life which now determines Gorman's actions. Significantly, he is killed by being crushed/suffocated by a huge python. The obsession with being devoured underpins the entire film.

It is necessary at this point to pause and point out that the theme of incest has been deemed central to the horror film since James Twitchell insisted on it in his admirable book *Dreadful Pleasures*. This in turn has drawn a disclaimer from Rhona J. Berenstein who rejects Twitchell's theory as paying insufficient attention to questions of gender. While I would tend to agree with her over this point, I feel Berenstein in turn has tended to overprivilege the dimension of homosexuality, just as Twitchell has been anxious to see incest everywhere at the expense of other matters while at the same time denying its function in adult life. The issue of homosexuality will be addressed in the next chapter. My concern here is with the incest question as part of a wider problematic which we must continue to define.

The Imprint of the Real

A presentation and discussion of certain factors common to a number of films will help us to make this definition, as will various comments to be found in critical reviews of the films. These factors are "slowness and/or immobility" and "silence." *Dracula* is particularly striking here, with such scenes as the count's three wives moving about in the crypt; the wives advancing on Renfield until Dracula insists on his male prerogatives; Dracula advancing on Lucy; and Mina and the usherette at the theatre moving in a trance. Another scene shows Renfield on all fours moving slowly and deliberately toward a nurse who has fainted. It is interesting to note that, in the original version, he was shown to be after a fly, but the excision of this—for reasons of "bad taste," no doubt—only helps to reinforce a certain unconscious logic at work elsewhere, in both *Dracula* and other films. In *Mark of the Vampire*, the first time we see Count Mora and his daughter Luna, they are moving very slowly indeed, and in the sequence analyzed earlier where the daughter hears her father's voice, her descent of the staircase is similarly slow and deliberate.

Silence is created in a variety of ways and occurs especially in scenes where characters are under the control of the film's representative of the supernatural: the zombies in *White Zombie* or the supposed reincarnation of the princess in *The Mummy* suddenly abandoning her escort at a dance, wandering off in a trance, getting her coat and leaving. Such silence is made all the more insistent by juxtaposing it with a sound, such as the grating of the coffin lids when Dracula and his three wives rise from their resting places in *Dracula*, or the assistant's hysterical laughter following the silent return to life of Imhotep and his going "for a little walk." A combination of slowness and silence accompanies the last shot of *Dracula*: the hero and heroine mounting a huge staircase after Van Helsing has staked the count. This rather sudden conclusion indicates the persistence of those traits linked to characters under the control of some force, whereas the film calls for a happy end. The logic I have discussed above is persisting against the prevailing ideology of true love and triumph over evil.

Bryan Senn points out pertinently that *Dracula* has always been found wanting by critics, ever ready to accuse the film of being static or theatrical; he himself calls it "lethargic."[56] The author of the chapter on *The Mummy* in the collective volume devoted to Boris Karloff refers to Ardath Bey's "slow dignity," and the chapter on *The Black Cat* in the same work evokes the slow movements of Hjalmar Poelzig, the character played by Karloff, going so far as to call him "one of the undead at twilight," a most felicitous expression.[57] I would claim that if, on the conscious level, the film is exploiting the actor's performance in *The Mummy*, something else is at work. For it is also quite clear that Poelzig is obsessed by death to the point of multiplying actions and rituals—a chess game, a Black Mass—destined to keep at bay the inevitable. His slow movements therefore indicate the unconscious reasons determining what can only be termed an obsessional neurosis.

A uniquely chilling sequence in a uniquely unpleasant film, *The Crime of Dr. Crespi*, visualizes what is at stake in a particularly direct fashion. The "crime" referred to in the title is that of burying alive the man who was preferred to Crespi by the woman the latter loved. Crespi deliberately bungles an operation meant to save the husband's life in order to leave him in a state akin to death (no breathing, eyes closed, yet capable of hearing), whereas he is in fact in a drug-induced state from which he will emerge only after he has been buried.[58] The man is quickly dug up, however, by colleagues who leave his "corpse" in a room. The sequence in question comes next. The door of the room is situated in the far background. In the foreground, close to the camera and the spectators, is a desk behind which sits a nurse, her back to the corridor and therefore the room. Suddenly the door opens and the form of the man buried alive appears. It advances slowly, staggering under the effort, until it finally appears to the nurse out of the corner of her eye. This approach of the "living dead" has been recorded by the camera without any movement or change of POV, thus rendering the scene unbearable. For, if the audience knows that he has not died, they can also understand that he has been treated as one dead. More to the point is the situation of the nurse. Not knowing the real fate of the victim, her reaction on seeing him can only be compared to that of the assistant in *The Mummy*: the Real has her in its grasp. And this time there is nothing supernatural in the film to displace the effects. This did not prevent displacement from occurring. *The Hollywood Reporter* of 27 September 1935 wrote, "Stroheim [Crespi] gives the ultimate in repression," but this refers to his dictatorial running of his private hospital. The bandying around of such epithets as "disgusting," "nauseating," and "revolting" suggest that other sources were less duped.[59]

The victim's moving closer and closer, slowly, ever so slowly, takes us back to *Dracula*. Referring to Dracula's first attack on her, Mina cannot be sure whether it really happened or whether she dreamed it. What is important, of course, is how she describes the "visit," first saying how he came "closer and closer," and then referring to how she feels now, the following morning: "the life drained out of me." This comment surely indicates the aftermath of the equivalent of orgasm, or "*la petite mort*," and can thus only refer to the text's repressed: the impossible *jouissance* of union with a figure representing the incestuous dimension of desire, for characters of both sexes.[60] All these manifestations of slowness and silence are instances of the Real, a too-close proximity to which will trigger feelings of anxiety. Certain films, by a careful manipulation of POV shots, implicate the spectator in the Real in more direct and less displaced ways. The dimension of identification involved surely implies a feminine trait in the male in the way he relates to the mother figure and a masculine trait in the female in the way she relates to the father figure. Hence the excessively defensive strategy of seeing this in terms of homosexuality and lesbianism.

In one strikingly written description, Senn reveals how the interdependent opposites of movement and immobility coexist and are overdetermined semantically by POV shots. He is referring to the sequence in *Mark of the Vampire* where two servants driving their carriage toward the castle suddenly find Luna in front of them:

> While the rate of approach is smooth, [James Wong] Howe wisely jostles the camera as it tracks closer (just as if it were riding on the bumpy cart), creating a sense of immediacy and an air of realism. Luna simply stands still, performing no action whatsoever. The elevated camera angle and rushing, unsteady movement place the viewer in the driver's seat and so create the terror as we move inexorably toward this frightful figure.[61]

What must separate the subject from the Real, a sort of invisible barrier that cannot be broached, has "evaporated," as it were, by the presence, blocking the way, of the vampire, the impossible fusing of the Symbolic and the Real, two "spaces" that cannot coexist except through the effects of the latter, here represented by Luna. Thus we come face to face with the concept of the vampire as unstoppable drive, in a literal, verbal fashion on the mode of inversion: the frenzied "drive" of the two servants stopped in their tracks by the "irresistible" vampire. Once again, we find a film literally representing the "death drive."[62]

Both *Dracula* and *Freaks* contain tracks destined to bring us into close proximity with the impossible Real, although they are not filmed in an identical fashion. *Freaks* opens with a sequence in a sideshow where spectators are being told of what happened to a certain Cleopatra who, in injuring one freak, injured them all and was duly punished. The camera tracks in to a sort of pit set in the ground. There now occurs a break in the narrative through the introduction of a cut. We then see Cleopatra as she was, and the entire film unfolds until we return at the end to the sideshow and a shot of the wretched Cleopatra, transformed by the freaks into a cross between a human and a hen. Rather than see this impossibility as a simple addition of the *fantastique* to a film whose realism has, from the outset, been too close for comfort—hence the hysterical rejection from which the film has always suffered—I suggest we take it as the textual manifestation of the Real, the unbearable realization that any of us might have been in the place of the freaks. As the religious denial of the Real has it, "there but for the grace of God go I." The freaks are the unbearable "grimaces of the Real" analyzed and theorized by Zizek.[63] At the end, it is precisely a very human and direct intervention that has reduced Cleopatra to something even "worse" than the freaks themselves: she is a spectacle and incapable of speech. As Dracula said, "there are worse things than death," and *Freaks* gives us a resolutely nonsupernatural look at the truth of this, a truth to be repressed. The cut brings us, with a sort of jolt, that much closer to her, thus underlining that unbearable proximity mentioned earlier.

Referring to the sequence where the freaks crawl through the mud and slime to finish off Hercules, Senn, while finding the shots "effective," complains that Tod Browning has unwittingly transformed the freaks "into inhuman monsters and objects of terror."[64] I could not agree more, except that this should be seen as a compliment, not a criticism. Let us take the remarkable sequence where Cleopatra and the midget Hans are celebrating their marriage, Cleopatra continuing to play her part; her real concern is to get her hands on his fortune. At one point the freaks pay her the ultimate compliment: they welcome her into their inner circle, chanting "one of us, one of us." This is seen by them as an exceptional privilege, but Cleopatra takes it literally: she suddenly sees herself as being a freak, as if she had already been transformed. The Real becomes manifest through the presence of the freaks. Aghast at the truth of which she is suddenly an effect—anyone could have been born a freak—she rises to her feet and calls them "slimy monsters." The shot that so upsets Senn is therefore a case of the freaks taking Cleopatra and people like her literally: they quite simply become what prejudice says they are and behave in the appropriate fashion. They inscribe the Real into reality by enacting the discourse of the Other which has interpellated them: by crawling through the slime to kill Hercules they literally become "slimy monsters." As Joan Hawkins rightly points out, "the entire revenge sequence can be read as a systematic reversal of the pastoral scene (the scene that attempted to establish the freaks as harmless children) earlier in the film."[65] Having been "identified" as harmless children, a role that they have only partly accepted, the freaks now accept their new identity as monstrous "things" within the system of the ideological Other and act accordingly.

Near the beginning of *Dracula*, just prior to Renfield's arrival, is a scene in the crypt of the count's castle. The camera tracks slowly up to the coffins of Dracula and his wives, and then it stops as a lid rises and a hand emerges. The slowness of the movement creates a sensation of expectation and anxiety that a cut from a long shot to a close-up would not achieve here. The audience must be led to await the outcome of the camera movement eagerly, while at the same time fearing what they will discover.

Another form of the Real is communicated to us by POV shots in *White Zombie*. At one point Murder Legendre (Lugosi) looks into the camera, and then his face blurs and seems to disintegrate. Far from translating his state, however, this shows the spectators theirs and is explicitly linked to death itself. When the heroine is buried—prior to returning as one of the living dead because she has been poisoned by Legendre—we are inside the tomb as her coffin is slid into the niche awaiting it, a device exploited later when the heroine, now a zombie, looks at the camera and us, and then starts to blur and disintegrate like Legendre. It is as if we had encountered Death herself and thus experienced our own "appointment in Samarra."

Three other films broach the question of the Real by making it a sort of "absent presence" or absent cause, once again by point of view shots: *Supernatural*, *The Ghoul*, and *Island of Lost Souls*. The first of these films concerns a young woman whose brother dies suddenly and her attempts, with the help of a phony spiritualist, to get in touch with his spirit. In the scene that interests us here, she is moving disconsolately around his room in the presence of his dog. Senn describes the scene thus: "the almost continual camera movement creates a definite sense of presence—as if a third party were in the room and moving alongside the other two, effectively making the viewer a part of the unseen spirit world."[66] Now the film has shown the "spirit" of the dead brother looking on just prior to this moment. If the spectators are in the same "place" as he, then they are in an impossible and nonexistent place, that of the Other.

This placing of the spectator is achieved with great effect in the opening sequence of *The Ghoul*. An unidentified man watches as a second unidentified man arrives and goes to open the door of a house at the dead of night (an appropriate expression). The camera has panned to watch the second man, thus placing the audience as subject of the gaze of the first man, then pans back to show us the first man still watching. The film then cuts to a high-angle shot at the top of the stairs as the man enters and closes the door. I would argue that we cannot interpret this as simply representing the eye of the camera, for the film, by moving back to show us the first man looking, has created a certain logic of the look: someone looks as we look on, and then we are shown what he is looking at. This can only mean that the shot from the top of the stairs represents someone's look. As there is nobody there, the spectator adopts the look of the Other. This is repeated toward the end of the film when the hero and heroine sit down in a room to talk. Instead of the camera being placed beside them—they are alone—it first takes up a position across the room behind a sort of open bookcase. Here, too, there is a look corresponding to no person's look; the couple are being looked at from somewhere and this representation of the Other inscribes the Real into the text.

Similarly, in *Island of Lost Souls*, when Moreau is escorting to his house the man who has become an unwilling guest to his island, we see the two men being observed by various "natives" of a nondescript kind, later to be revealed as the "manimals," the products of Moreau's scalpel. As Moreau and Parker enter the house, a long shot intervenes where the camera observes the two men from the jungle. We are thus in the place of the "Things," and the fact that this shot is superfluous as far as the story goes puts into motion the blurring of boundaries that makes the film so disquieting. If it has not aged in more than seventy years, this is due both to Kenton's brilliant direction and the fact that the film is touching on something to be kept out of sight and out of mind.

The nature of this "something" is most forcibly realized in the articulation of two sequences from *Dr. Jekyll and Mr. Hyde* (the 1931 version). The opening of the film is now justly famous, with the audience being placed in the position of Jekyll as he comes to give a talk on his research; the other characters address him and look directly into the camera. In the first transformation scene, Rouben Mamoulian has recourse to a mirror to let us see Hyde, but what we see first is the image of Hyde in the mirror, without the presence of the character before the mirror. As such the film places the audience in the place of Hyde and has his hideous image look back at us.[67] This remarkable identification tactic decenters the viewing subject, since we know that Hyde represents an unconscious and inaccessible part of Jekyll. Similarly, the massive close-ups of Moreau's creations starring into the camera at the end of *Island of Lost Souls* put us in the place of something radically external to experience yet representing unconscious desires that have no other way of communicating their effects.

Lest the reader suppose that this phenomenon is limited to a handful of movies from the 1930s (which would already make it worthy of attention), I shall turn for more sustenance to the work of those intrepid vampire hunters Alain Silver and James Ursini. In their substantial and remarkably documented volume *The Vampire Film*, they resort to precisely the same discursive elements enumerated here. They describe one sequence from *Nosferatu* thus: "Orlok watching Mina's room from the window of a house across the street stands rigid and unblinking; while she paces frenziedly . . . and prays for strength to sacrifice herself to end the chain of vampiric killings."[68] Thus is created a parallel between immobility and movement, the latter implicitly indicating a sort of unconscious ritual resorted to in order to keep the Real at bay (garlic and crosses, of course, have the same function). Such rituals are neurotic in nature for Freud and we can see a link between them, hysteria and the bisexuality of the subject. The description also parallels that used by Senn when discussing *Mark of the Vampire*. Hysteria is also hinted at, the movement indicating that the body communicates, beyond the control of the subject, the inscription of the Real of desire. A second example draws attention to the television series *Night Gallery*, one episode of which "dealt with a siren-like female vampire imprisoned by the still water surrounding her barge (a bit of Eastern European mythology referred to in Stoker's *Dracula*)."[69] Here the imminent presence of the Real is negated by having the vampire immobilized by a supposedly uncrossable threshold, another way of denying the meaning of vampirism by resorting to superstition (it is, of course, the episode in question doing this, not Silver and Ursini). In their discussion of *Son of Dracula* (Robert Siodmak, 1943), however, the authors reveal the meaning of the vampire through the language they use. They refer to a crane shot that "stops abruptly on a high angle medium shot of Alucard gazing at the house, a revelation which is sudden and startling *despite* the anticipatory camera movement, *almost as if* the figure had drawn attention to itself or *somehow intruded into the frame while remaining immobile*."[70]

I have emphasized portions of this passage to draw attention to what is going on in this description: a disavowal of the conflict between technique and signification overdetermined by a precise description of the impossible Real. Similarly, when describing the look and the point of view, Silver and Ursini reveal discursively what we have seen at work in *The Ghoul* and *Supernatural*. The film under discussion is *Brides of Dracula* (Terence Fisher, 1960): "Eventually, the disturbingly 'objective' travelling shots which explore the upper corridors after the visitors have retired—objective because they represent no character point-of-view, although the viewer may again be deceived into suspecting that it is the vampire moving down the halls—cedes [sic] to a subjective perspective."[71] The use of *disturbingly* and the placing of *objective* between what are appropriately called "scare quotes" underline the effects of the Real as absent cause, to which we should add that *objective* is to be taken literally as representing an object that cannot become manifest, except in symbolic forms, which is why the absent "observer" is as invisible as the vampire in a mirror.

Werewolf of London brings together the elements analyzed here in a context allowing us to draw a further conclusion. After the encounter with the Father mentioned earlier, Glendon and his assistant set off for the forbidden valley ("forbidden" by superstition and the Law represented by the Father). At one point the assistant suddenly stops dead in his tracks (another appropriate expression) and says he cannot move. When asked by Glendon what he means and what he is experiencing, he repeats what he said, adding it was like the sensation of immobility you get in a dream. If we turn to Freud for help, we shall not be disappointed: the dreamer who has the sensation of a movement inhibited in some way is in fact representing in the dream a *conflict* between two incompatible desires.[72]

We are, according to the young man himself, certainly in the presence of a "sensation," and the "conflict of will" is overdetermined: consciously by the opposition of the Father who has warned them not to go on; unconsciously by the incestuous nature of the repressed desired behind the search for the flower, as we have seen. The warning of the Father on both the conscious and the unconscious levels—the condensation of religious law and the effects of the Name-of-the-Father—is located in the assistant as a further displacement, a new warning to Glendon not to pursue his folly. He continues and at once finds himself inhibited, as if someone had struck him. If this can be interpreted as the paternal superego punishing his refusal to obey the Law or as an effect coming from the place of the Other, what happens next is most revealing. Glendon is suddenly attacked and bitten by a werewolf. Repelling the creature, he crawls toward the flower that he has been seeking all along and stretches out his hand to pluck it. The camera cuts to show us his bleeding forearm, symbol of his contamination by the werewolf, but this cut to a close-up serves a far more radical unconscious function. Glendon's hand stretches out, stretches, stretches, but does not succeed in reaching the flower. The hand just remains there, motionless. Then the camera dissolves to his laboratory in London, and a shot of Glendon's arm holding the flower in his hand.

This is an appropriate point at which to offer a theoretical interpretation of the dissolve as a cinematic device. The pertinent trait of the dissolve is the copresence on the screen, however fleeting, of two images, one superimposed on the other. The first of these images—"first" from a linear and chronological point of view—is destined to give way and to disappear before the second image that replaces it and allows the story to move forward. As such, one of the two images looks back into the past, the other forward into the future. Fleetingly, therefore, the spectator is put in the position of being able to experience in the present a moment destined to become past and another about to become present in its turn. Unconsciously this position, which belongs to the Symbolic, then shifts to the Imaginary where the spectator, faced with the copresence of the two images, fantasizes the possibility of *choice*. From a strictly psychoanalytic standpoint, the dissolve therefore reproduces on the level of the cinematic signifier the situation that Freud describes and analyzes in "The Three Caskets," where a work of art affords us knowledge which is denied to us in reality: the knowledge of death.[73] The dissolve therefore becomes a way for the spectator to deny the significance of that knowledge by imagining him- or herself in a position where the film will be dictated, not by its own logic, but by the spectator's, the choice extending unconsciously to all that follows, based on the spectator's desire having been put in place by what has gone before.

It is also clear from this analysis that a particularly long and drawn-out dissolve, where one gets the impression that the two images are going to "last for ever," is nothing other than the textual manifestation of obsessional neurosis and, within the framework adopted here, corresponds to the slow movements and repeated acts of the Boris Karloff character in *The Black Cat*.[74] More to the point as far as *Werewolf of London* is concerned is the sense of the flower: it can only be interpreted as the textual manifestation of the *objet a*, especially as the flower is referred to explicitly as "the only one of its kind." As such, the dissolve partakes of the structure of fantasy in the film, where Glendon holds in his grasp something that cannot be reached—which the film shows on the mode of denial by having him fail to reach it in the first shot—but that, if grasped, reveals the truth of the Real itself. As this can be attained only in death, death is the inevitable fate of Glendon, a fact that he has unconsciously grasped all along; his last words after being shot are "in a few moments I shall know why all this had to be."[75] If we remember that the *objet a* can stand in for the maternal phallus, Glendon's gesture is an unconscious attempt to believe in that which permits the neurotic to repress the signification of the Symbolic Order.

Werewolf of London is of particular interest for the way it brings together a representation of *objet a* and the recurring theme of boundaries and transgression. Andrew Tudor has this to say on the latter topic:

> Only where the boundary between disorder and order is rigorously sustained is it possible to imagine successful human intervention. . . . Boundaries can be clearly drawn in relation to an external threat. Internal threats, precisely because they are internal, often blur the distinction between known and unknown, allowing the one to conceal the disturbing co-presence of the other.[76]

From what we have shown up to now, it must be evident that this is ultimately unsatisfactory, a positivist approach forbidding any of the slippages that occur regularly in horror. If the vampire, for example, is seen as simply an "external threat"—which is how films represent it—then all possibility of analysing how the subject is the effect of its presence (or its absence) is closed off. A cut-and-dried opposition between internal and external is precisely what horror films show to be a nonstarter and is surely belied by the existence of vampires, which are just as unknown as the psychological aspects presumably being referred to by Tudor under the heading of "internal threats." Once again language shows an unconscious force making its presence felt. When referring to the "known/unknown" paradigm, Tudor resorts to the formula "disturbing co-presence," an indication of the proximity of the Real and, at the same time, a confirmation of what we have already discussed about the paradigm "immobility/movement" in its various (dis)guises. What, for instance, are we to call the transformation of the werewolf in this light: an "external threat," since Yogami comes from Tibet and attacks Glendon; or an "internal threat" as the film explicitly makes a link between Glendon's behavior when transformed and the psychological problem of jealousy and revenge? I have already proposed an answer to this question, but the fact, as Freud never tired of pointing out, that children did not make this clear distinction between animal and human (taken up in the script of *Werewolf of London* where Yogami suggests to Glendon that he should not make too clear a distinction between animal and vegetable) is surely testimony to the infantile fears being reactivated and the meanings we can glean from them.

One film that successfully blurs the boundaries between external and internal in a way that makes Tudor's opposition inoperative is *The Monster and the Girl*, which is but one of the numerous films where a mad scientist carries out experiments such as mingling human and animal blood (*Murders in the Rue Morgue*), turning animals into humans (*Island of Lost Souls*), grafting the limbs of one man onto the body of another (*Mad Love*), or putting one man's brain into the body of another (*The Man Who Changed His Mind, Black Friday*, and the Karloff/Grindé trilogy shot in 1939–1940, *The Man They Could Not Hang, The Man with Nine Lives*, and *Before I Hang*). *The Monster and the Girl* harks back to Robert Florey's controversial film by introducing the notion of placing the brain of a dead man into the body of a gorilla. In the film, Scott Webster is executed for a crime that he did not commit. Mad scientist Dr. Parry (George Zucco) carries out the transfer of the brain from human corpse to simian body (already a scandalous refusal to recognize that certain boundaries cannot be crossed), but the "human ape" escapes and systematically murders the gangsters who had framed him (this recalls Karloff disposing of the gangsters in *The Walking Dead*).

The interest of *The Monster and the Girl* lies in the way it represents incest and the Real (apart from its genuine qualities as a piece of film making). Webster and his sister Susan are shown as being very close, a proximity that the brother does not want to lose. He has a regular but uninspiring job, whereas she is frustrated by life in a small country town and wants to "be alive." She refuses to be "buried alive," as it were, in the traditional role of the woman looking after the home, especially as she has none of the compensations (socially and ideologically speaking) of family. Already this indicates the death drive motivating her brother as having its effect on the words she uses, thus the suggestion that life with him is a sort of living death. He begs her to stay—"just the two of us," as he significantly puts it—but she leaves and gets involved in a phony marriage arranged by gangsters looking for naive young woman to blackmail into becoming "hostesses." Searching for his sister, Webster is also tricked: he is framed for the murder of a man who refuses to pay what he owes the gangsters; the gun used is thrown at Webster's feet by the gangster and the brother is duly condemned and executed.

The fact that Webster, disillusioned with life and his sister, makes no attempt to defend himself means that, when she pleads with him in court to tell the truth, he cannot: behind the truth of who killed the victim there is another truth that cannot speak its name. Two sequences will suffice to represent this truth. At one juncture, the gorilla with Webster's brain (explicitly represented as functioning as a human) comes to see the sister; she is sleeping in bed, and a close-up shows her contented face. This shot takes up exactly a shot of her sleeping in bed the morning after her marriage: Larry Reed, the man she married, is absent but there is a dent in the pillow beside her, so the marriage has been consummated and brought her pleasure and happiness. The fact that she looks the same in the second shot draws a parallel between Reed and the brother to the point of indicating that the brother would like to share the bed with her and that she would have found the same pleasure with him as with Reed. The second sequence is the confrontation between sister and brother/gorilla. The latter has now killed all four gangsters and, fatally wounded by bullets, has come to see her one last time. The way the sequence is shot is eloquent. The sister is manifestly more shocked by the killings (she is in the home of the gangster leader) than terrified by the ape, which is surely not "logical." She simply averts her gaze and then turns to look at the creature; their looks meet. Comprehension dawns as she looks at the eyes and then relief as it/he dies.

That the gorilla's eyes are so obviously human can, of course, be put down to the simple fact that it is an actor in an ape skin, which is a truism. Another logic is at work on the level both of the *mise en scène* and the dialogue. At a point in the film where she is ignorant of who or what is carrying out the killings, the sister says to the leader of the gangsters, "Something's in your way now, something you can't stop, something I can't stop." This is not just a jeer aimed at the man she knows framed her brother, a jeer of satisfaction faced with his fear. The fact she says "I can't stop" means that she reads her own desire in the acts of murder: the gorilla killing not just for revenge but to get back to her.[77] This simply indicates that the film is criticising her for leaving home and is suggesting it is more noble for a woman to submit to male desire (however taboo) than to strike out on her own. Her fate at the hands of the gangsters implies that it is a "fate worse than death," although the film's ending casts incestuous love in that role.

Inasmuch as the gorilla makeup in *The Monster and the Girl* insists on the eyes and the look, it functions as a sort of mask, a theme given considerable prominence in *Dracula's Daughter*. When Countess Zaleska moves in on her victim Lily, the image—we see the countess approaching looking off-screen left—blurs and we hear the young woman's cry. There then follows a rapid pan up to a shot of a mask hanging on the wall above the spot where the victim has just been vampirized. Both Berenstein and Harry M. Benshoff have drawn attention to the lesbian connotations of the film in general and this scene in particular.[78] It is certainly a revealing instance of one of Berenstein's theses: By eliminating an aspect of the film that upset them, the Hollywood censors merely succeeded in creating an absence into which meaning could be read, although that meaning could now be more diffuse, less tied to its representation. A proper discussion of this and related matters must wait until chapter 2. The question I wish to ask and try to answer here is, Why a mask?

The blur introduces on the level of the cinematic signifier the connotation both of an attack (which we have: the cry proves that) and of a fade to black (or to white, the case here), which is precisely what we find happening when the countess advances up to a man in the street. We find ourselves faced therefore with an enigma: why show the mask? Clearly this apparently superfluous surplus shows that the attack on Lily is *not* identical to that on the man. That the mask on the wall—we have already seen it hanging there at the beginning of the sequence where Lily has been ushered into the countess's studio—will summon up fantasies concerning primitive peoples, savagery, and the like, seems certain. It is hardly a simple coincidence that the title of that most racist of movies, *The Mask of Fu Manchu*, should be ambiguous: it refers both to the mask of Genghis Khan that Fu Manchu wants to own in order to wield power and wage war on the West and to the face of Fu Manchu himself. Thus, at one point his leering features are isolated in the center of the screen (thanks to little lighting and a black background) so as to give the impression of a mask hovering in mid air. In the case of *Dracula's*

Daughter, the otherness of the countess is being assimilated to an unconscious representation easy to circumscribe and, supposedly, easy to explain: her unnatural lust comes from afar, is a form of bestiality, and so forth. The boundary between the "civilized" and the "primitive" is thus safely drawn and rendered hermetic.

At the same time, however, her power can be assimilated to that animal magnetism referred to by Freud in *Group Psychology and the Analysis of the Ego*, associated as it is with people of noble rank enjoying social power.[79] Even this point must be tempered by the fact that such animal magnetism would be applied positively to, say, a movie star but negatively to someone like the countess.[80] Inasmuch as the mask stands in for precisely nothing, or is, rather, the signifier of a radical absence, the presence of the mask on the wall—which, it must be stressed, exists *exclusively* for the spectator—symbolizes the Real and is as such a stand-in for *objet a*. Clearly, then, the unconscious of the text is declaring that the countess possesses the phallus, while at the same time showing the phallus not to exist. She refuses to be passive, to submit to an exclusively male logic represented by psychiatrist Dr. Garth and her manservant Sandor who preaches submission to the Law of the father. The mask is also the signifier of contemporary superstition and functions to inscribe the structure of disavowal into the text. It is hardly surprising, then, that there should be so many contradictions at work within this film.

Just as Dracula draws his cloak around him when advancing on a victim, so the countess draws a sort of veil over the bottom part of her face, leaving only her eyes visible. We can thus see the mask as a way of showing that, as the harbinger of death and the Uncanny, the countess's eyes reveal, while hiding it, the void of the Real. This finds its most terrifying filmic representation in the look as *objet a* that fixes Lila Crane (Vera Miles) and the spectator in the cellar sequence in *Psycho*: that of the dead Mrs. Bates, embalmed, it might be added, like a mummy. This veil sets off an association of ideas rendered explicit by both Hollywood publicity and the complacent discourse of reviewers that overdetermines it. Thus the Arab connotations of the veil find expression in the claim that Theda Bara's name—one carefully chosen for publicity purposes—was an anagram of "Arab Death." And in his review of *Dracula* in the *Los Angeles Examiner* (28 February 1931), Marquis Busby wrote that the film "is all about vampires. Not the Theda Bara sort, but people who are dead."[81] The parallel between "vampires" and "vamps" is thus made explicit, yet another example of the fear instilled by the active female.[82]

This must not let us lose sight of the significance of the veil, which, as Lacan has pointed out, is what art or "le Beau" draws over the object to mask death or the Real. The word was systematically used by Freud's most famous patient, the Wolfman, to represent the way he felt cut off from the world. Freud points out, in a remark that bears what I can only call an "uncanny" resemblance to the horror film, that the Wolfman did not necessarily use the explicit term *veil* but the more vague one, *ténèbres*, or what we would now call "the twilight zone."[83] In *The Devil Commands*, the daughter of the scientist played by Boris Karloff relates the events after his death and tells how "he tore open the door to whatever lives beyond the grave." The horror film that brings together most of the topics addressed hitherto, with remarkable efficacity, is *Mystery of the Wax Museum*, whose French title is more explicit: *Masques de Cire*.[84]

Addressing her editor, Florence the journalist asks him, "Have you ever heard of a death mask?" which receives the answer "I used to be married to one." It is not the misogyny underpinning such wit that will retain us here but the parallel the exchange sets up between this scene and an earlier one in the morgue where two attendants are cleaning up among an array of corpses covered by sheets. Suddenly one of the corpses rises up, provoking the horror of one of the attendants. His colleague, however, is not impressed; this movement, he assures him, often happens with people who have just died, adding, "Ain't that just like a woman? Always has to have the last word." The woman, of course, has said nothing; it is her *body* that has "talked." This symptom, suitably displaced by another example of wit, suggests, yet again, male hysteria at work. The body, by suddenly sitting up erect, has clearly "said" something that the attendant does not want to recognize: that the erect woman could, after all, be endowed with a phallus and, if she is not, then it is men who have to endure the blow to their vanity. They could be castrated, too. This structure of disavowal is what has determined the existence of Igor the sculptor (Lionel Atwill), at least since the fire that destroyed his creations and left him monstrously disfigured and incapable of creating. That other characters are also fetishists and that the spectators are inscribed into this fantasy can be seen from what follows: an unknown individual (Igor, as we learn at the end of the film) penetrates into the morgue to steal the body of the deceased woman. As he lowers it from the window, it recalls yet again a Mummy and, by its stiffness, represents an erection, thus showing how, in culture and everyday life, the male organ comes to stand in for the phallus to assert male superiority: nothing missing, as it were.[85]

Various scenes are there to show that Igor is a pervert, a fetishist who refuses to recognize the lack in the big Other. He refers to his waxworks as "his children" and to the heroine (Fay Wray) as "my child," despite the complete lack of intimacy between them. Any and every person bearing a resemblance to a real-life character is thus always already a waxwork, transformed into a phallus so that the Real of castration can continue to be denied. Igor has only just met the heroine Charlotte, an encounter recorded in three remarkable shots Raymond Bellour reproduces in his article: a long shot of Charlotte looking at Igor; a medium close-up of Charlotte looking at Igor; Charlotte transformed into Igor's long-lost masterpiece, Marie-Antoinette. All these shots are from Igor's point of view, and the audience is thus left in no doubt as to what fate awaits the heroine. The fact that the third shot is a fantasy means that it is also there to defuse its meaning for Igor, for it repeats what we have already seen: the shot of Igor looking off-screen right at his waxwork Marie-Antoinette at the opening of the film is a look that is not returned, for she, too, is looking off-screen right. The fact that Charlotte, a woman, returns Igor's look fixedly at once turns her look into one emanating from the place of the Other and thus, as *objet a*, inscribing the fantasized lack in her body onto Igor's. This, as a good pervert, he cannot tolerate and prepares to transform Charlotte into a suitably "phallic" form, an object within the fantasy his life has become.

Not only Igor's look partakes of this dialectic of desire but also his speech. Berating a sculptor whose work he finds unsatisfactory (his hands being useless, Igor gives instructions so that pupils can carry out his work; their handiwork, of course, is always "lacking"), Igor wields sarcasm as deftly as Dr. Moreau does his scalpel: "Are you so beautiful that you make everything in your own likeness?" The sculptor thus taken to task is ugly and his work, by implication, equally so. The perfection that Igor seeks can be found only at the point of death or during that early period when a belief in the maternal phallus brought plenitude to the child's world. His art must therefore strive to attain the Sublime. Hence, his mask, but also the thin film of wax covering the dead bodies he now uses, is the veil drawn over the Real that his obsessive search signifies. We can also interpret his words as a nice case of the Truth returning to the subject in an inverted form. For Igor is not really addressing the sculptor—who, significantly, is deaf and dumb—but himself and the audience, except that he cannot know that.[86] He makes everything "in his own image" because that reminds him of the past when he was not disfigured. It also reminds him of a far more distant and radically repressed past, that of the pre-Oedipal stage where the (m)other was assimilated to the subject's own image. Certainly Igor's obsession with beauty suggests an inability to overcome this imaginary structure: the narcissistic aspect of his perversion follows the same logic of a refusal to recognize the lack in the Other. The woman breaks down this logic and enables the man to accept castration, but this is not operative in the horror film. Nor should we forget that the face we see in the second part of the film, eleven years after the fire that destroyed the Museum in London, is not the face of Igor but a mask itself. Significantly, when Florence catches a glimpse of him (without knowing who he is) while trying to get information for a scoop, she describes him to the police as wearing an African mask. What has become Igor's real face is taken for a mask, whereas the mask he wears is taken for his face. This is literally a case of a veil drawn by art over the Real. Igor's face is "impossible," too horrible for words, another "grimace of the Real."

The death drive is hence insistent in Igor's case. Toward the end of the film, Charlotte penetrates into the wax museum and is terrified when one of the five heads she looks at suddenly moves: it is the head of the deaf-and-dumb sculptor, flanked by two wax heads on each side. Although it could be argued that this inscribes Charlotte's castration into the film via its opposite—Freud suggested that, in dreams, a multiplication of certain elements indicated castration and the entire film, as Bellour has pointed out, turns on the equation "decapitated heads = castration"—surely more relevant here is the return of the theme of the breakdown of boundaries. *The Ghoul* provides an excellent example: one character strokes a cat, only to find the animal is stuffed, an uncanny moment evoking the collapse of the opposition animate/inanimate and the notion of death: the stuffed animal is a variation on embalming. I have already indicated that *The Ghoul* recalls *The Mummy*, as does the woman's corpse being lowered from the window in *Mystery of the Wax Museum*.

This breakdown of barriers finds its clearest expression in *Mystery of the Wax Museum* through the juxtaposition of eyes and a mask. A montage sequence of waxworks shows them all apparently looking at Charlotte, which means Igor's "children" are avenging their "father" by returning the heroine's look so as to inscribe her into the same place occupied by Igor in the sequence analysed above. Charlotte is thus castrated, but this parallel is an imaginary one, for the problem is Igor's and that of the dominant representation of the sexes, not Charlotte's, except as victim of that representation, just as she is meant to be Igor's victim. Suddenly a pair of real eyes comes into view behind a mask. Clearly this is Igor getting his own revenge and acting thus as the stand-in for the ideological big Other determining spectatorial desire. As such, it functions on the mode of reversal, for behind the masks, be it a case of Igor's or the waxworks's, is death—death, not as something we know to exist, but death as an unconscious desire revealing that "*Kern unseres Wesens*" Freud referred to, the kernel of being that is the death drive. Igor's wish to give Charlotte immortality (she will live "a thousand years" as a wax effigy) is his own desire speaking. Charlotte will be a fetish/phallus that will never melt away—or "wilt"—like the other figures in the film's opening sequence set eleven years in the past.[87] Charlotte will thus become the body of perfection, the maternal body that Igor has never given up. That he should refer to himself, as a result of his accident, as "a living dead man" only serves to render manifest that he has considered himself dead for the past eleven years. From this standpoint, *Mystery of the Wax Museum* is a variation on the theme of the "living dead."

The film's uncanny atmosphere stems not simply from the systematic representation of fetishism and death as intimately linked but from certain cinematic devices. I have drawn attention to the transformation of Charlotte into Marie-Antoinette, but there is a sort of "glow" around her that foregrounds the status of the image and how we see it. The film itself helpfully provides us with an answer to this. Replying to a remark about how realistic his figures are, Igor says, "Lighting came to my aid," which makes of *Mystery of the Wax Museum* a metaphor for cinema as a narrative and representational medium.[88] What we see depends on how we see it and, far more important, how desire—desire as a collective fantasy—determines our vision. There will always be a lack or an excess, something not corresponding to desire or something that cannot be reduced to the formulas we manipulate consciously but of which we are the unconscious effect. This the film shows in its most uncanny moment. At the end of the film, when Igor confronts Charlotte, he rises from his wheelchair to show his infirmity is false—he stands "erect"— and grasps her in his arms. For the first time his look does not meet hers; it seems to pass over her head. It is as if his eyes were sightless, as if he were already as dead as the subjects of his artistry; significantly, Marie-Antoinette always looks elsewhere. More than that, however: we see that the eyes are not the look. It is not his eyes that are sightless, as we can see them move, like the eyes behind the mask. It is rather his *look* that is not functioning. The *objet a* is not where he/we expect it to be, which sums up its status and thus enables the Real to insist through a network of representations.

We have seen how critical and institutional discourses, in a variety of linguistic forms, disavow the anxiety triggered off by horror films, an anxiety which we put down to castration, the maternal phallus and the excessive proximity of the Real. Such disavowal heralds at once a masculine refusal and the numerous forms of libidinal compensation sought. One of these is a rejection of the independent woman, of even a desire for independence on a woman's part. To counter such a refusal to submit to patriarchy, the films can suggest the woman is subjected to a fate lying outside her control, such as in *Dracula's Daughter*. In which case the film assumes the Real but represents it as a female problem, whereas the repression of the Real is basically a male problem.

Countess Zeleska is expected to accept "a fate worse than death" as imposed by the Law, the Name-of-the-Father as represented ideologically on a purely repressive mode by her servant Sandor. *The Monster and the Girl* presents a refusal of the home and an implicit incestuous relationship as leading to consequences far worse for the unhappy and frustrated heroine. What is at stake is therefore a radical imbalance between men and women, the stigmatising of any woman challenging the social order and, crucially, of any man refusing to take his "natural" gendered place within that order. This is but one of the examples of the "blurring of boundaries" that we have evoked periodically in this chapter. Yet, paradoxically, it is precisely by concentrating on male desire that the films start to deconstruct the patriarchal order they strive to maintain. This will concern us, in its multifarious guises, in chapter 2.

Notes

1. *Bride of Frankenstein*, Production Code Administration (PCA) file, Special Collections, Motion Picture Academy of Arts and Sciences, Margaret Herrick Library, Beverly Hills. Hereinafter referred to as MHL.

2. *Bride of Frankenstein*, PCA file.

3. In its review of the film (15 May 1935), *Variety* points out that the word *mate* figures in the film's credits. Both the *Motion Picture Herald* (20 April 1935) and the *Los Angeles Examiner* (22 April 1935) use the term in their reviews. This goes to show that censorship had, to a certain extent, an ideological form rather than a repressive function. *Bride of Frankenstein*, clippings file, MHL. I wish to thank Ned Comstock (Doheny Memorial Library, University of Southern California) for providing me with photocopies of reviews from the *Los Angeles Examiner*.

4. *The Old Dark House*, clippings file, MHL.

5. Clippings files for all the films referred to, MHL.

6. *The Monster and the Girl*, clippings file, MHL.

7. Sigmund Freud, "The Theme of the Three Caskets," in *The Standard Edition of the Complete Psychological Works of Sigmund Freud*, trans. and ed. James Strachey (London: Hogarth), XII: 291–301. Hereinafter the main work is abbreviated as *SE* and the volume number.

8. *King Kong*, Special Collections, MHL; italics in the original.

9. *Bride of Frankenstein*, PCA file, Special Collections, MHL.

10. *The Mask of Fu Manchu*, Special Collections, MHL.

11. Gregory William Mank, "*The Mummy* Revisited," *Films in Review* (August/ September 1984): 419.

12. "The Uncanny," in *SE* XVII: 241.

13. *The Raven*, PCA file, Special Collections, MHL.

14. Clippings files for both films, MHL.

15. *Murders in the Rue Morgue*, PCA file, Special Collections, MHL.

16. Clearly history itself is involved, as we shall see in chapter 4.

17. Slavoj Zizek, *The Sublime Object of Ideology* (London: Verso, 1989), 97.

18. We shall return to the questions of time and history in chapter 4.

19. Bryan Senn, *Golden Horrors: An Illustrated Critical Filmography of Terror Cinema, 1931–1939* (Jefferson, N.C.: McFarland, 1996), 311.

20. Senn, *Golden Horrors*, 347, italics in the original.

21. Senn, *Golden Horrors*, 207, 140, 142.

22. "The Mummy," in *Boris Karloff*, ed. Gary J. Svehla and Susan Svehla (Baltimore: Midnight Marquee, 1996), 60.

23. *Boris Karloff*, 61.

24. See Zizek, *The Sublime Object of Ideology*, 43.

25. See that obscurantist movie *Stargate* (Roland Emmerich, 1984).

26. See Slavoj Zizek, *Enjoy Your Symptom! Jacques Lacan in Hollywood and Out* (New York: Routledge, 1992), 123.

27. Director Robert Aldrich is on record as saying that Whale "was the first guy who was blackballed because he refused to stay in the closet." Vito Russo, *The Celluloid Closet: Homosexuality in the Movies* (New York: Harper & Row, 1987), 50. Russo himself refers to Whale's death in his swimming pool, adding that "there has never been a full investigation of the circumstances surrounding the event" (50). Although this can be interpreted as a desire (on the part of the authorities? Hollywood?) to cover up Whale's sexuality, it also regrettably reinforces the idea of "mystery" so often evoked when mentioning his premature demise.

28. Author of a short study on the horror film of the 1930s published in 1962 by the review *La Méthode*.

29. Randy Loren Rasmussen, *Children of the Night: The Six Archetypal Characters of Classic Horror Films* (Jefferson, N.C.: McFarland, 1998), 173.

30. We shall have cause to return to this formula in chapter 3.

31. Senn, *Golden Horrors*, 217, italics in the original.

32. Zizek, *The Sublime Object of Ideology*, 76.

33. See James Donald, "The Fantastic, the Sublime and the Popular, Or, What's at Stake in Vampire Films?" in *Fantasy and the Cinema*, ed. James Donald (London: BFI Publishing, 1989), 233–51. This important volume also includes a translation of Roger Dadoun's fundamental text "Fetishism in the Horror Film" (39–61), first published in French in 1970. My work is indebted to these studies.

34. Zizek, *Enjoy Your Symptom!* 126.

35. Reynold Humphries, "'The Horror! The Horror!' Mr. Kurtz and the Uncanny," paper presented at the Second International Conference of the European Society for the Study of English, Bordeaux, September 1993. A different version has been published in French: "Conrad avec Freud et Lacan: Les enjeux de la représentation dans *Heart of Darkness*," *Les Lettres Modernes*, Joseph Conrad I (March 1998): 7–19.

36. For a detailed discussion of the vampire and the mirror, see Jean-Claude Aguerre, "Si la chair n'était pas faible," in *Dracula*, ed. Jean Marigny (Paris: Autrement, 1997), 141–51. Aguerre is a Lacanian psychoanalyst.

37. Van Helsing, for no apparent reason, is now called Von Helsing. We shall comment on this little "slip" in chapter 4.

38. We shall have the occasion to return to this in the next chapter.

39. Jacques Lacan, *La Relation d'objet*, Le Séminaire Livre IV (Paris: Seuil, 1991), 408.

40. For a detailed discussion of the film, see Reynold Humphries, "The Semiotics of Horror: The Case of *Dracula's Daughter*," *Interdisciplinary Journal for Germanic Linguistics and Semiotic Analysis* 51, no. 2 (Fall 2000): 273–89.

41. *SE* XX: 119, italics in the original.

42. *SE* XX: 120.

43. See Senn, *Golden Horrors*, 268.

44. That the theme extends far beyond the film to society finds eloquent testimony in the presence of insects, a "leftover" from *Dracula*. Freud has suggested we see insects in dreams as manifestations of brothers and sisters. This can help to explain the bizarre presence of armadillos in *Dracula*, a sort of foreign body in the text having no logical place there. See *Group Psychology and the Analysis of the Ego*, in *SE* XVII: 82, n. 2.

45. *Mark of the Vampire*, clippings file, MHL.

46. Senn, *Golden Horrors*, 276, n. 1.

47. Joan Copjec, "Vampires, Breast-Feeding, and Anxiety," in *Read My Desire* (Cambridge, Mass.: MIT Press, 1995), 128.

48. Senn, *Golden Horrors*, 272. The quote is from the interview with Borland referred to by Senn.

49. I do not use the words *addicted* and *repelled* idly. Lugosi later became addicted to drugs, and a vampire can be repelled only by garlic. This suggests that Lugosi's screen persona and his real-life persona overdetermined each other and were themselves determined by the Other of representation in the fields of sexuality.

50. A film that offers a particularly condensed (in all senses of the word) version of the issues under discussion here is *The Shining*. I am thinking of the sequence in the bathroom where the beautiful young woman emerges naked from the bath and advances, ever so slowly, toward Jack. He advances toward her and they embrace, slowly but passionately. Suddenly, to his horror, she is transformed into a raddled, decaying, cackling old hag: the ideal woman or mother and the obscene, impossible *jouissance* structuring (the child's) desire. Perhaps this is why Hollywood movies tend to avoid actresses performing beyond a certain age, as if their getting old were a reminder of that which cannot be represented, except in a purely grotesque form, such as Bette Davis in *Whatever Happened to Baby Jane?*

51. James Twitchell has drawn attention to this polysemy of the word *mummy*. See *Dreadful Pleasures* (New York: Oxford University Press, 1985), 177.

52. I refer readers to what I wrote earlier concerning Lily in *Dracula's Daughter*. We shall return to the question of hysteria in chapter 2.

53. Zizek, *The Sublime Object of Ideology*, 135.

54. It is not, of course, a trait limited to the horror genre, as Todd Haynes's exemplary *Safe* (1995) shows.

55. As with *Mark of the Vampire*, this finds a parallel in real life: actor Henry Hull (Glendon) was forty-five when he played the role, while Valerie Hobson (Glendon's wife) was only seventeen.

56. Senn, *Golden Horrors*, 16.

57. Svehla and Svehla, eds., *Boris Karloff*, 71, 100.

58. Left alone with his victim, Crespi bends over the body and, in loving and sadistic detail, recounts what is going to happen to him and what it will be like to experience the earth being thrown onto the coffin. It is surely not irrelevant to note that Tod Browning, prior to his career as a director, gained his living (so to speak) by being buried alive. David Skal has this to say: "The first time had been the worst. 'When I heard the dirt come crashing down on that coffin, I actually shivered,' Browning told a reporter many years later. In time he almost came to enjoy the confinement." *The Monster Show: A Cultural History of Horror* (London: Plexus, 1993), 26. That the word *confinement* (Skal's, not Browning's) also applies to a woman in labor is not irrelevant, either.

59. In a letter to Will Hays (15 January 1935), Joseph Breen refers to the film in such terms. *The Crime of Dr. Crespi*, PCA file, Special Collections, MHL.

60. In a review of *Dracula* the *Village Voice* (22 April 1997) refers to "death as a sexual climax." *Dracula*, clippings file, MHL.

61. Senn, *Golden Horrors*, 267.

62. For an application of this notion to a different aspect and period of the horror genre, see Reynold Humphries, "On the Road Again: Rehearsing the Death Drive in Modern Realist Horror Cinema," *Post Script*, Realist Horror Cinema, Part II: Serial Killers, ed. Steven Jay Schneider, 22, no. 2 (Winter/Spring 2003): 64–80.

63. Zizek, *Enjoy Your Symptom!* 113–16.

64. Senn, *Golden Horrors*, 54.

65. In the admirable chapter devoted to the film in Joan Hawkins's *Cutting Edge: Art-Horror and the Horrific Avant-Garde* (Minneapolis: University of Minnesota Press, 2000), 157.

66. Senn, *Golden Horrors*, 199.

67. A particularly useful and detailed analysis of the film is to be found in William Luhr and Peter Lehman, *Authorship and Narrative in the Cinema* (New York: Putnam, 1971), 229–80.

68. Alain Silver and James Ursini, *The Vampire Film* (New York: Limelight, 1993), 64.

69. Silver and Ursini, *The Vampire Film*, 51.

70. Silver and Ursini, *The Vampire Film*, 69.

71. Silver and Ursini, *The Vampire Film*, 85.

72. Sigmund Freud, *The Interpretation of Dreams*, in *SE* IV: 337, italics in the original.

73. See Freud, "The Theme of the Three Caskets."

74. We shall analyze this aspect of *The Black Cat* from another standpoint in chapter 4.

75. In a memo to Joseph Breen (15 January 1935), it was suggested that this speech be added to the script that had been submitted as an indication that Glendon estimated he deserved to die for violating God's law. *Werewolf of London*, PCA file, Special Collections, MHL.

76. Andrew Tudor, *Monsters and Mad Scientists: A Cultural History of the Horror Movie* (Oxford: Blackwell, 1989), 214.

77. Clearly the incestuous relation between brother and sister came too close to the surface at the end for some, with *The Hollywood Reporter* (6 February 1941) referring to the gorilla's "kind eyes" as the element of the film that was "hardest to take." I presume the reviewer meant "ridiculous," but the formula can also mean "unbearably painful." *The Monster and the Girl*, clippings file, MHL. It is not the fact that an ape acts in a human fashion that causes rejection of this sort. As part of its publicity campaign to sell *King Kong* when reissuing the film in the 1940s, RKO did not hesitate to tell how a copy of the film was shown to a bull gorilla in captivity, named Gargantua. At first "puzzled" by what it saw, the creature finally settled down to watch the film with interest. *King Kong*, Special Collections, MHL.

78. Rhona J. Berenstein, *Attack of the Leading Ladies: Gender, Sexuality, and Spectatorship in Classic Horror Cinema* (New York: Columbia University Press, 1996), 24–27; Harry M. Benshoff, *Monsters in the Closet: Homosexuality and the Horror Film* (Manchester: Manchester University Press, 1997), 77–81.

79. *SE* XVIII: 125.

80. Hollywood was partial to setting up parallels between women and animals, particularly cats. See *Bringing up Baby* and *The Cat People*.

81. It was not uncommon for reviews of the period to use *vamp* for *vampire*.

82. Antonia Lant has also drawn our attention to the use and abuse of Theda Bara in her study "The Curse of the Pharaoh, or How Cinema Contracted Egyptomania," *October* 59 (1992): 109–10.

83. Sigmund Freud, "From the History of an Infantile Neurosis," in *SE* XVII: 75, 99.

84. On this film, see Raymond Bellour, "Symboliques," in *Le Cinéma américain: Analyses de films*, vol. 1, ed. Raymond Bellour (Paris: Flammarion, 1980), 184–92.

85. As we know since Freud, the unconscious could not represent an absence or a negation.

86. We can perhaps see in this address, apart from its value for the audience, the sign of psychosis on the part of Igor: addressing the empty place of the Other as if it were filled by someone capable of a conversation with him and ignoring the fact of the Other's indifference.

87. It is pertinent to point out here that the anxiety felt by Dr. Glendon and Yugami in *Werewolf of London* stems in part from the possibility of the flower wilting.

88. I am reminded here of that extraordinary moment in *Vertigo* where Madeleine pauses as she passes behind Scottie seated at the bar at Ernie's, her face giving off a glow, with the red wall behind her literally highlighted.

CHAPTER TWO

~

Mad Doctors in Love

The title of this chapter is not purely descriptive. Dr. Jekyll is in love, but is he mad, except in the eyes of his future father-in-law and the conservative Dr. Lanyon, for both of whom society as it exists is sacrosanct? Many of the doctors are scientists—Frankenstein, Mirakle (*Murders in the Rue Morgue*), Moreau (*Island of Lost Souls*), Rukh (*The Invisible Ray*) and Blair (*The Devil Commands*)—but by no means all: Gogol (*Mad Love*), Crespi (*The Crime of Dr. Crespi*), and Vollin (*The Raven*) are surgeons and are not engaged in scientific research. Moreover, the eponymous central character of *The Invisible Man* is a research chemist and not a doctor, while the Mummy is driven by an insatiable desire. Characters such as Count Zaroff (*The Most Dangerous Game*), Murder Legendre (*White Zombie*), Eric Gorman (the murderous, paranoid business man of *Murders in the Zoo*), and Hjalmar Poelzig (*The Black Cat*) are neither doctors nor scientists. The mad doctor/scientist of *The Monster and the Girl* plays a minor role, the main characters being a brother and sister and a group of gangsters. The eponymous central character of *Dr. Cyclops* is not in love, except with himself through his experiments.

This chapter raises the question of the representation of love and sexuality in the films of the period and of who, precisely, incarnates the socially and ideologically (un)acceptable forms of both. This in turn highlights the nature of the acceptable forms: heterosexual love and marriage. However, as we shall see when discussing *Dracula's Daughter*, the "abnormal" love of Countess Zeleska exists, at least in part, to hide and displace the problems raised by a whole battery of codes of representation that leave little of accepted norms intact. It will also be necessary, for reasons that will be explained in due course, to make a detour via the most famous "lover" of the 1930s: King Kong.

A major source of contradiction in classic horror is that which both demands the "happy end" consisting of a bourgeois marriage and proposes so insipid a hero that it is difficult to take such an ending seriously. Rhona J. Berenstein has summed up the situation neatly: "Classic horror movies may close with the reunion of the heterosexual couple, but that conclusion is usually forced and inadequate. . . . Girl gets boy at the conclusion but her best times, the moments that give her free rein to throw all caution to the wind, are spent with the monster in the narrative middle."[1] As the representation of love and sexuality depends on the various possibilities open to the characters according to their sex, I propose to devote this first section to the way critical and institutional discourses attempted to set up rigid codes of behavior for both male and female characters and to determine their expression in the films. The second section will address the question of gender disturbances and homosexuality in an attempt to go beyond the work already accomplished in this domain by suggesting an alternative reading whose purpose is to complement and not to reject the conclusions reached by authors such as Berenstein. The third section will extend this debate to a discussion on hysteria in the films directed by Ernest B. Schoedsack: *King Kong, The Most Dangerous Game,* and *Dr. Cyclops.* The fourth section will address the various ways desire and power become manifest. I have chosen to analyze the special role of hypnosis and the gaze in a separate section, given the relation between particular films and publicity material in the representation of this theme, which is central to the genre.

The Biological Phallusy

A consistent discourse within *Variety* concerned the setting up of the categories "men" and "women" as if biological difference determined every other form of difference. This discourse was a mixture of a paternalist protection of the "weaker sex," of a tongue-in-cheek attitude which acted as a cover for laughing at both the films and women spectators at the same time and of simple contempt. Reviewing *Dr. X* (9 August 1932), the trade paper talks of "women folks scared to death in future of doctors." *The Return of Dr. X* elicited the following point of view: "Average drama femme customer won't cotton to the theme." *Murders in the Zoo* allowed *Variety* to go to the heart of the matter concerning its ideology: "Main question will be the women, though they like to shiver too, but the snakes in this one are apt to be more than some can stand."[2] Elsewhere a more explicit opposition between male and female spectators is set up. One critic opined that "masculine audiences should be particularly interested in *Frankenstein*, but surely it is no women's picture."[3] The publicity material accompanying the 1947 reissue of *Dracula* and *Frankenstein* claimed that the scene where the monster comes to life in the latter film "has made strong women faint and courageous men turn pale."[4] Men, of course, cannot faint—it is biologically impossible. This sort of rhetoric is actually inscribed within a given film. In *The Invisible Ray* a newspaper recounts how a statue on a church suddenly and inexplicably melted. The spectators of the film are presented with a close-up of the front page of the newspaper where they can read that "a huge throng stood by in utter bewilderment at the sight. Women fainted, men were baffled." We are left in some doubt as to whether the fainting was due to fear or religious fervor, but the different reactions point clearly to a certain ideological notion of how the sexes are expected to (re)act in given circumstances.

That every woman, whether character or spectator, was also expected to be virtually a holy virgin can go some way in explaining the insipid male hero of the David Manners variety. It is hardly surprising therefore, in a society that at one and the same time venerates and debases everything female, that prostitution should be both an obsession and an object of systematic repression.

Two examples will suffice: *Dr. X* and *Werewolf of London*. In a letter to Jack Warner (16 May 1932) Lamar Trotti asked that the studio eliminate suggestions that Lee Tracy enters a "bawdy house" to make a phone call by cutting the line about it being too early for the "girls" to be there. That way the brothel would appear to be a speakeasy.[5] Apparently a journalist entering an establishment forbidden by law caused the Hays Office no qualms, though whether this indifference stemmed from a contempt for journalists or a belief that alcoholism is preferable to extramarital sex remains unclear. What is clear is that the Law in the Lacanian sense is stronger than the law. Either way, Warner wisely took no notice, for the scene in question is unmistakably set in a brothel.

Werewolf of London presents a more complex state of affairs, due in part to the increased severity of censorship in 1935. In a memo dated 15 January 1935, one of Breen's associates refers to the scene outside the zoo where Dr. Glendon the werewolf kills a soliciting prostitute and asks that she be represented as a beggar. Poverty and homelessness are therefore more acceptable than (illicit) sex. More intriguing is an exchange of letters between Breen (28 January 1935) and Universal. On 30 January, Robert Harris replied to

Breen and referred to the first killing, that of a young woman in a side street, in the following terms:

> The girl, being of the lower class, is wearing a skirt which is not too lengthy, possibly having shrunk when she herself washed it, being quite without money to send it to be regularly cleaned, and carried [sic] a handbag such as is carried by millions of respectable people today, large enough to hold the miscellaneous vanities which women carry today.[6]

This tortuous attempt to pass off the girl's presence as due to chance and the length of the skirt as the result of incorrect cleaning (not to mention the contempt exuding from the formula "miscellaneous vanities") suggests a battery of unconscious value judgments at work; only a woman of easy virtue could possibly be walking down such a street at so late an hour. In other words, the displacement from prostitute to beggar in the zoo sequence led the Breen Office to resort to a rhetoric of disavowal that connotes the girl walking down the street as a prostitute, whereas nothing in the film justifies such an interpretation. This assumption stems from a particular discourse of the ideological big Other overdetermined by Hollywood's codes of representation: an unconscious belief that a woman walking alone at night cannot be up to any good. How little it takes for a "virgin" to be transformed into a "whore"!

Thus, the return of the sexual repressed is overdetermined by that of class and social problems. This is an issue that we will address in detail in chapter 3, but the way it is linked here in critical discourse to the social function and cinematic representation of women is worth a moment's reflection. Reviewing *White Zombie*, a critic in the *New York Times* (29 July 1932) wrote that zombies "make good servants. They can carry off blondes without getting ideas in their heads, which helps in these mad days."[7] What exactly the critic had in mind is unclear, but posters of vampires, zombies, mummies and assorted creatures carrying off helpless or unconscious heroines have proliferated since the early 1930s.[8] This image also sums up perfectly the way the dashing hero either sweeps the smitten heroine off her feet or else rescues her from a fate worse than death. In this light, we can see the ending of *The Ghoul* imposing a solution that is totally at odds with what we have seen before. When the hero and heroine, who have shown nothing but hostility toward one another throughout the film, emerge from the tomb in which they have been locked, he is carrying her in his arms in a wholly unmistakable fashion. *Variety*'s remark (30 January 1934) that "the film overlooks the romance angle"[9] is both correct and a reminder that such an oversight was unacceptable. This is why the last shot introduces a theme completely absent from the film up till then—absent from the manifest content, I should add, for we can offer a psychoanalytic reading of the ending. The Boris Karloff character returns from the dead—which is the film's theme until catalepsy is evoked just as suddenly and unconvincingly as the love angle—because he has a debt to collect and a score to settle. Once this debt is seen as a symbolic debt, his chasing the heroine through the house takes on other implications and helps to explain the ending. His return to collect this debt points to the heroine's stubborn refusal throughout the film to submit to patriarchal Law, and the hero carrying her in his protective arms is thus the manifestation of her "natural" submission to that Law within the unconscious logic structuring the film. Audiences must be shown the woman functioning according to this logic, even if she is designated as a victim by the manifest level of the script.

Exactly the same narrative sleight of hand is at work in *Dr. Cyclops*. The young woman scientist is constantly chiding the young male scientist in such a way that it is clear that she is fulfilling a maternal role that aligns her with the paternal superego represented by the elderly head of the scientific expedition. Moreover, she shows bravery and initiative when faced with danger: it is she who saves her male companions from an alligator when the group—shrunk to the size of dolls by the film's mad scientist—is threatened. The young scientist in question shakes her heartily by the hand, which makes her "one of the boys." More subtly, she is in fact being congratulated for thinking of something that is normally part and parcel of male prerogatives. Thus, the handshake is the way the film gives back to the infantilized and castrated male the "natural" right to distribute praise or criticism, a right that the young woman has consistently claimed for herself since the outset of the film. The fact that the elderly scientist agrees with her creates within the film a contradiction that must be dispelled. And it duly is at the very end, where suddenly the two young scientists inform their companion and guide they are to be married, and the film promptly comes to an abrupt and unconvincing ending.

Publicity material used to sell *Dr. Cyclops* makes it crystal clear that the nonexistent romance was what mattered. A display ad shows a terrified woman and a protective man, dutifully described as "a beautiful woman and the man she loves." The frame contains the following remark, carefully placed within quotes:

"Hold me closer, Darling . . . *and I'll be brave*"

Another ad portrays the sinister doctor looking threateningly at the couple (I shall return to this aspect of the publicity material in the last section of this chapter) to the accompaniment of the question:

Can he destroy their LOVE?

From what I have just said about the film, it will be understood that nothing in this material remotely corresponds to the film, the ads functioning therefore to "correct" the ideological "imbalance" in favor of a woman—who also happens to be a scientist—and to prepare the audience to accept the spurious and unmotivated (by the script) happy ending.[10] Perhaps it would be more accurate to talk of an unconscious displacement rather than a lack of motivation. When the hero shakes the heroine by the hand, he is putting them on the same level socially, whereas her role up to that point had been more that of a mother chastising an irresponsible child than that of a woman scientist treating a colleague as an equal. His treating her as an equal in circumstances no longer belonging to the world of science thus enables the film to terminate as if the scientific aspect were secondary, even irrelevant, and thus to foreground what life is "really about": love and marriage. I shall offer a complementary reading later and analyze *Dr. Cyclops* from another standpoint in chapter 4.

The hypocrisy of the Breen Office, real though it was, must also be seen as a complex network of unconscious responses to what Berenstein has nicely called "the unspeakable terrors endured by men,"[11] a theme that is central to this chapter. The attitude to the female body is eloquent in this respect. Writing to Harry Zehner of Universal about the way the script of *The Invisible Ray* was evolving (6 September 1935), Breen pointed out that a dance sequence suggested that the women were naked from the waist up.[12] Since the scene in question does not appear in the film, it can be assumed that Universal decided it was simpler to eliminate it (we shall see other instances of this self-censorship in the following section). Given the film's story, the dancers were clearly black women, which makes things worse: there is nothing quite like the overdetermination of sex by race to trigger hysterical reactions leading to repression.

However, it is necessary to insist on an evolution on the part of the PCA over the years. Let us take the case of *Murders in the Rue Morgue*. In a memo dated 13 October 1931, objection was taken not to the theme of blood mingling (a woman and an ape) but to the scene with dancing women (this time they survive censorship) and the shot of the future victim of Dr. Mirakle strapped to a cross.[13] Five years later, however, Breen showed himself to be more alert than his predecessor to the implications of the film's main theme. On 2 October 1936, he wrote to Harry Zehner about Universal's plan to reissue the film and pointed out that the seal of approval would be given only if the entire sequence on the cross was cut. In this sequence Mirakle is ranting and raving over the girl's "bad blood," and it is clear that she is a prostitute. What has suddenly come to the fore is the unconscious male fear of contamination—a prostitute standing in usefully for women in general—overdetermined by the common belief that women are "closer to nature": they are somehow more likely to be the object of attention by apes, for example. *King Kong* partakes of this fantasy, among others. It is as if the fear of the female body and female sexuality was temporarily sufficient for the true significance of the theme of blood mingling to be repressed and displaced. Mirakle's sadistic behavior and the blasphemous implications of torturing a woman tied to a cross thus led to demands for cuts.

This theme of cross-breeding or cross-fertilization is explicit in *Island of Lost Souls* and implicit in *The Most Dangerous Game* via the tapestry of the centaur carrying a woman: the centaur is half-man, half-beast. Nowhere is this crossing of (forbidden) boundaries more disquieting than in *Freaks*, for the simple reason that we are dealing with real beings, not fantasies. Metro Goldwyn Mayer Studios (MGM) chose to sell the film as the direct opposite of what Browning had made.[14] Their publicity department evoked the "uncanny plot" of "the marriage of a normal woman to a midget" and referred to the freaks as "nameless things" and "creatures from the void."[15] It all reads like an attempt to sell a film based on H. P. Lovecraft. There even exists a cartoon showing Hans standing on a chair and trying to kiss Cleopatra. Such material is insulting to midgets and the deformed but also most revelatory. What we are being shown is that Hans is too small, which at once allows us to see that what is at stake is the male fear of not being able to satisfy the female, of being inadequate or too "small." This quality is then defused through displacement and inversion: a midget is too "small" for a "normal" woman, whereas the very concept of "normality" is one that the film deconstructs in a variety of ways that can leave no viewer indifferent.[16] Such advertising is also an unpleasant throwback to a particularly obscurantist aspect of Christian ideology: "In a world created by a reasonable God, the freak or lunatic must have a purpose: to reveal visibly the results of vice, folly, and unreason, as a warning (Latin, *monere*: to warn) to erring humanity."[17] Furthermore, the discrepancy in size between Hans and Cleopatra suggests a mother-child relationship that further downgrades and degrades the midgets as being incapable of looking after themselves. Wittingly or unwittingly, MGM therefore justified Cleopatra's robbing of Hans.[18]

The matter of "normality," of setting up certain physical, moral, and intellectual boundaries that must not be transgressed, is one that will be addressed later in this chapter and also in subsequent chapters, so multifarious are its ramifications. We shall, however, broach the subject briefly here in order to give an outline of the issues at stake. In its review of *Island of Lost Souls* (17 January 1933), *Variety* wrote about Lota the panther woman that actress Kathleen Burke was "too much like a girl to even suggest transformation from a beast."[19] A revealing remark. We can note at work the unconscious fear of proximity analyzed in chapter 1: "too much like" indicates rather that the experiment has been too successful and that this uncomfortable fact is being negated. As long as the "manimals" are neither men nor beasts but "things" (to quote the Sayer of the Law played by Bela Lugosi), they can be classified as some monstrous perversion due to Moreau's insane desire to play God. Once humanity dominates, however, the theme of evolution returns with a vengeance, carefully prepared by Erle Kenton's highly intelligent direction: Lota approaching the hero in a way that suggests the feline. A word of warning is perhaps opportune here, for such a representation could simply be interpreted as designating woman as closer to animals than any man. While this factor doubtless plays an unconscious role, the foregrounding of an apparently successful transgression of boundaries is, I would argue, more likely to set off anxiety at the very thought of humanity's proximity to another world normally deemed radically other. As Freud pointed out, children do not make such a difference between animals and humans, and the horror film systematically realizes infantile desires, as we shall see.[20]

The Breen Office's depressingly orthodox, repressive, and philistine approach to sexual and social "norms" does at times give a revealing glimpse into unconscious fears and prejudices and the sorts of priorities being taken for granted. On 24 May 1939, Breen wrote to Jack Warner about the studio's production *Return of Dr. X*, where Humphrey Bogart plays a mad doctor sent to the electric chair for "child slaying" in the course of his experiments. Brought back to life by another mad scientist, he now lives off human blood to stay alive. Breen urges Warner to avoid giving the Bogart character a "high voice" so as not to suggest "the gentleman is not perfectly normal."[21] We can assume that the juxtaposition of the reference to children and a high voice evokes hints of pedophilia, but this point is not made explicit, and the identity of the victims could have been removed from the script. What is at stake, therefore, is the censorship of homosexuality in general. One can express either amusement or stupefaction over the prejudice that considers it far worse to hint at the character's sexual proclivities than to represent him as a sort of vampire, but this is the sort of inanity that studios had to contend with. As

Berenstein has amply demonstrated throughout *Attack of the Leading Ladies*, writers and directors cultivated the noble art of innuendo and the double entendre, both at the level of the script and, especially, the performances of certain characters. Keeping this in mind, we shall now turn our attention to questions of gender.

Can Heterosexuals Behave with Gay Abandon?

I propose to start the ball rolling by examining *Dracula's Daughter*, a film much discussed not only by Berenstein but also by Harry M. Benshoff.[22] Benshoff describes the vampire countess as "butch," her manservant Sandor as "fey" and "a nay-saying bitchy queen."[23] If this interpretation of the countess as lesbian and Sandor as gay is perfectly justified in the case of Sandor, I would suggest things are less clear-cut in the case of the countess. During her nonvampiric appearances in posh salons, the film concentrates on her feminine attributes and does not question the sincerity of the sexual influence she exerts on Dr. Garth (and vice versa). Even if we allow, as Benshoff suggests, that her "butch" aspects are clear when she is on the prowl at night, a problem remains, for, like the count, she vampirizes both men and women. I shall argue here that the film's problematic representation of gender difference and sexuality is to be found less in the character of the countess than in those of Sandor and Dr. Garth and that the situation in *Dracula's Daughter* is far more complex than Benshoff and even Berenstein have allowed.

Breen and his associates were clearly very worried about the script of the film submitted to them in 1935. A memo from Breen himself (13 September 1935) evoked "countless offensive stuff," and in a six-page letter addressed to Harry Zehner of Universal (23 October 1935), he demanded that, as the vampire was portrayed as "a beautiful creature," it had to be made clear from the outset that she was a vampire.[24] A memo dated 6 February 1936 evoked the need "to avoid any suggestion of perverse sexual desire on the part of Marya or an attempted sexual attack by her upon Lili." Yet, just three weeks later (27 February 1936), Breen wrote to Zehner again, asking him to omit Sandor's remark to the countess: "You promised there would never be anyone else," on the grounds that it suggested "a possible sex relationship between Sandor and Marya." Clearly the possibility of sex between a female aristocrat and her male servant is out of the question, although this would just as clearly help hide the fact that the countess is sexually attracted to Lili.[25] As one of my arguments throughout this book is that class, politics, and history are far more massively repressed within horror and critical discourse thereon than sexuality of whatever persuasion, I feel this is an appropriate point to draw attention in passing to its role in *Dracula's Daughter*.[26]

What was clearly the bone of contention was any form of sexual interest between vampires, on the one hand, and nonvampires, on the other, overdetermined by the film's evocation of homosexuality, both male and female. This helps to account for the unconvincing performance of Otto Kruger as Dr. Garth. It is less a question of his talents as an actor than that of the fascination manifested by the filmic text for other forms of desire. As far as the countess and Lili are concerned, the fact that the film does not content itself with a fade to black as the vampire launches her attack (as it had done when she vampirizes an upper-class man in the street) but sees fit to pan up to the mask on the wall (see chapter 1), indicates that the attack may have been first and foremost a case of lesbian seduction. As the mask tends to connote both something hidden and something monstrous, the film reinforces the theme of lesbianism and hints that this form of vampirism is worse than the "simple" heterosexual kind. Once again, we must get our priorities straight!

This, however, is only part of the picture and not necessarily the most pertinent. Gary Don Rhodes and John Parris Springer have drawn our attention to a review of the film published in the *New York Times* describing the countess as Dracula's "red-lipped daughter."[27] We are surely entitled to ask why a critic should have recourse to this expression when writing on a film shot in black and white. Because women of the upper class are expected to wear lipstick? Or because much is made of red lips in Bram Stoker's original novel *Dracula*? Or for other reasons? This line of thought needs to be taken further.

At no point in the film is particular attention paid to the lips of the countess, only to her eyes and her ring, both used as means of hypnosis. Such, however, is not the case with Sandor, whose lips are full and fleshy. It is a characteristic he shares with Charles Laughton's Dr. Moreau in *Island of Lost Souls* and Warner Oland's Dr. Yogami in *Werewolf of London*, both of whom are vaguely "effete" and "nonvirile" in appearance, talk, and behavior.[28] We can turn with profit here to Christopher Craft's analysis of Bram Stoker's novel where, having coined the felicitous formula "semiotic wandering," he goes on to discuss the famous scene where Dracula opens a vein in his chest for Mina to suck on. The following comment is central to our concerns here:

> But if the Count's sexuality is double, then the open wound may be yet another displacement (the reader of *Dracula* must be as mobile as the Count himself). We are back in the genital region, this time a woman's, and we have the sug-

gestion of a bleeding vagina. The image of red and voluptuous lips, with their slow trickle of blood, has, of course, always harbored this potential.[29]

If we apply this idea to Sandor, then we have an example of a displaced representation of male castration anxiety, embodied, of course, in the film's homosexually connoted character who thus becomes at one and the same time the signifier of that anxiety and its repression: heterosexuals have nothing to fear.[30] This, however, fails to take into account other manifestations of "semiotic wandering" involving Dr. Garth himself.

I have chosen to describe Garth as he is represented in the movie as "effete," in the senses of "weak and ineffectual," "spent and worn out" and "effeminate." His curiously passive character, his immaculately groomed hair (something he shares with Sandor), his rather weak and precious voice, added to his inability to vanquish the countess and to his need to be authoritarian toward women (particularly his fiercely independent young secretary) all go toward connoting a definitely atypical heterosexual hero. What I wish to avoid is the claim that Garth is gay; he is simply connoted as not being as "straight" as one might expect from such a character as a psychiatrist presented (unconvincingly, as we saw in chapter 1) as occupying the empty, ideological place of the "Subject Supposed to Know." My concern here is to show that, as from the moment censorship prevents certain forms of representation from obtaining conscious approval and taking on explicit textual form, there can be no end to the disturbances, both verbal and visual, wrought on gender (and class) boundaries. Take, for instance, the commissioner of Scotland Yard. Represented as a "dithering old maid"—scare quotes de rigueur—he is shown at one point in bed with his collection of stamps, while his butler "fusses" around. The dialogue becomes quite obscure and merits our attention.

The commissioner, who has not quite made up his mind as to whether he believes in vampires or not,[31] makes a facetious remark to his butler about vampire hunting, which elicits this bizarre reply: "I thought you chased after them with checkbooks." The signifiers here are not so much wandering as leading us a merry dance. Given the Slav origins of the countess, we must rewrite the end of the sentence as "Czech books," especially as the countess's studio is situated over a bookshop in London's Chelsea district, renowned (at least outside Britain) for eccentric (= gay?) artists. The comment also foregrounds sexual and economic exploitation, central to the way the countess pursues Lili. I shall propose a more detailed interpretation of class in the horror film in chapter 3, but it is necessary to insist here on the relations between Garth—who is upper class and goes grouse shooting in Scotland with aristocrats—and the aristocratic milieu in London. Toward the end of the film, he has a conversation over the phone with an aristocrat whom we have already encountered and who is connoted as markedly effete and downright cretinous. Garth intimates he is unavailable that evening, to which the other man replies, "Have you found a better party?" As *party* can also signify "partner" or "companion," the remark brings us back to who is in love with or attracted to whom in this film.

Berenstein has pointed out that the whole film can be seen as an "exploration of Garth's journey toward Oedipal adulthood,"[32] citing his inability to tie his bow tie and the way he counts on his secretary to do so. I could not agree more, but if the bow tie as a symbol of male genitals is firmly in place by the end of the film (as we have seen in chapter 1, this is hardly the case with Garth as symbol of phallic mastery), Berenstein is also right to point out how Garth nearly succumbs to the countess. It is only thanks to Sandor killing her for preferring Garth to him and the film repressing all we have been shown concerning Garth's ineffective "science" and his responsibility for the death of Lili that the psychiatrist's social status as patriarch is secured. The British class system and law and order have been saved by the intervention of the jealous gay Sandor.

Garth himself, with his sartorial elegance, looks ahead to Hollywood's most famous gay character, Waldo Lydecker (*Laura*, 1944), whose sartorial elegance and verbal mastery serve to hide his hysteria, whereas Garth's need for a mother figure to "fix" his own narcissism is displaced onto his contempt for women.[33] For both Garth and Sandor, the countess is the (m)other of the mirror stage, the image they identify with narcissistically and the absolute otherness they cannot accept. When Sandor tells the countess he sees death in her eyes, this remark must not be read as symbolizing her "soul" or the future demise of both characters, but rather as an example of *forclusion* (foreclosure), his rejection of castration in the Symbolic returning in the Real in the form of a hallucination represented as doom-laden destiny—that of the male, however, not of the female. Leaving Garth at the close to look after his secretary who has steadfastly looked after him throughout is just the film's way of redrawing the boundaries that it has constantly refused to recognize in the first place: those closing off the feminine component of Garth's being.

It is worthwhile pausing here to reflect on a sartorial aspect of the countess's appearance. When she vampirizes the man in the street, she uses her ring and her look to draw his attention, to hypnotize him, then draws a veil over her face before advancing on him. It is at this point that the image fades to white. What is surely being represented by the cinematic signifier is the annihilation of the subject's being faced with the Real, and it is necessary to remark that this is experienced as much by the spectator as by the character or, rather, that what is meant to be an experience on the level of the story is in fact a representation of this experience for the spectator.

Lacan has drawn our attention to the function of the veil, to the structural relation between it and what lies beyond, "beyond" being taken in the sense, not of what lies physically behind the veil, but what that physical position represents for the subject.[34] What is represented as the beyond of the veil is the maternal phallus. By exciting the man's/spectator's fascination and curiosity when drawing the veil over the bottom half of her face, the countess turns the piece of cloth into a fetish. Immobilized, the victim keeps the anguish of the Real at bay via the fascination provoked. By the time he/we realize what is happening, it is too late. The cinematic fade-out is the unconscious representation of *aphanisis* or the "fading" of the subject/spectator, which Dylan Evans defines as "the fundamental division of the subject . . . which institutes the dialectic of desire."[35] This "fading" is itself a manifestation of the anxiety attendant on the notion that, if the countess is active (= masculine), then the man is passive (= feminine), a notion that subverts precise and immediately discernable boundaries concerning sexual identity and, by implication, ideologically gendered social roles.

If, to conclude, we take up Benshoff's description of the Countess as "butch," then a further and quite unexpected meaning emerges from her behavior and representation. It should be clear that at no point in the film will the countess divest herself totally, as far as the unconscious effect on the spectator is concerned, of the signifiers connoting her "masculine" side; the traces will remain whatever the circumstances, whatever the codes of representation deployed. In this case we must interpret Lily's scream as polyvalent, all the more so as we see nothing. If we take the masculine connotations literally— which is precisely what the spectators' unconscious will do—then what is important is less the lesbian implication than the attack itself. The countess thus functions as a displaced manifestation of her own father, the Father of Enjoyment having access to bodies both male and female,[36] the anxiety produced by the proximity of the Real overdetermined by the presence of an impossible desire, of a drive that cannot be stopped.

Let us return briefly to Waldo Lydecker and the opening sequence of *Laura* where he attends so painstakingly to the details of his appearance: adjusting his trousers, tying his tie, folding a handkerchief, and choosing a flower for his buttonhole. It is this last gesture that I wish to expand on here, in the light of the role of flowers both in certain horror movies of the 1930s and in the various critical and institutional discourses surrounding them. On 12 September 1935, Maurice Revnes of MGM sent Breen a script entitled *Witch of Timbuctoo*, destined after numerous fundamental changes to become *The Devil-Doll*. The very next day Breen replied, objecting to a scene where a character reacted like a "pansy." This is missing in the final version of the film,[37] where the character no longer exists. Reviewing *The Son of Kong*, a critic for *Variety* wrote that the "offspring is just on the verge of being a bit of a pansy."[38] Jason Joy wrote to Darryl Zanuck on 27 September 1932, asking him to eliminate from the final version of *Mystery of the Wax Museum* the line "he made Frankenstein look like a pansy." Zanuck respected the letter, if not the spirit, of this request, and thus the Glenda Farrell character in the film now says, "He made Frankenstein look like a lily." This, of course, fools nobody (except, perhaps, the censors), but this sort of metonymic slippage takes over the discourse of Jerry Hoffman who, reviewing the same film for the *Los Angeles Examiner* (10 February 1933), wrote that, in comparison with the hideous features of the unmasked Lionel Atwill character, Frankenstein and Hyde were "orchids."[39] We also find the same rhetoric at work in *Mark of the Vampire* where the police inspector, referring sarcastically to the doctor's cowardly refusal to go out at night, says to him, "You're not a moon flower; you're a morning glory." Thus the flower becomes the signifier of femininity and cowardice when linked to a man.[40] Not surprisingly, the doctor is played by actor Donald Meek, but more pertinent is the fact that the inspector is wearing a carnation in his buttonhole as he addresses him. Thus, the social code that allows a man of a certain social standing to wear a buttonhole without his masculinity being questioned reveals itself to be a sign functioning as a signifier. The effect of the latter is to question the clear boundaries between virile and nonvirile men and to highlight the well-attested fact that details in a text mean something, but not necessarily the same thing at the same time to the same addressees.

This point takes on a specifically linguistic and syntactic form in reviews of *The Mad Genius*. Evoking the male-female relationship in *Svengali* (to which *The Mad Genius* is a sort of follow-up later in the same year), the review in the *New York Times* (24 October 31) stated, "Yet Tsarakov's influence over a youth never calls for hypnotism."[41] The implications of this male-male relationship become even more ambiguous in Marquis Busby's review of the film in the *Los Angeles Examiner* (20 November 1931): "The boy becomes famous, but the great master's control ends when he falls in love." For anyone who has seen the film, the personal pronoun *he* can only refer to the boy (coached by the John Barrymore character—the "mad genius"—to become a great dancer, the boy starts to show independence when a girl comes into his life), but the laws of syntax demand that *he* refer to the closest male person designated in the sentence: the "great master." In that case the implications are that the "influence over a youth" is of a decidedly sexual nature and that the master can exert this control only when he is able to sublimate his homosexual tendencies. I am not arguing for a minute that this is the subtext that "explains" *The Mad Genius*. My point is that once questions of homosexuality are censored, every trait of representation, every discursive and rhetorical device deployed to evoke a signified that dare not say its name, becomes detached from its "normal" frames of reference and starts to float or wander, setting up networks of signification that can only produce excess meaning, or meaning that is never where the discourse of the ideological big Other wishes to fix it. We are rather in the realm of desire where a certain thrust running counter to norms and fixed boundaries makes its presence felt in things going wrong, never being quite in the "right" place.

Berenstein has argued that, "although most monsters are coded male, they are also more-than-male and different-from-male."[42] Clearly, this can also be said of characters who are not monsters or mad doctors, suggesting that "monstrosity" applies to any male not conforming to the various unconscious traits that are meant to represent the biological specimen designated as a "man." Such a trait, as we know from Lacan, defines the subject without being conscious. Berenstein reproduces a publicity still for *The Crime of Dr. Crespi* and stresses that "Crespi wears a very delicate, feminine bracelet on his wrist throughout the film."[43] On closer inspection, the still reveals an interesting visual element that is discursive. It shows Crespi and a small skeleton—that of a very young child? Of a dwarf? Impossible to tell, but what is clear is that the bracelet referred to appears to be a continuation of the skeleton, as if the two existed in some symbiosis, thus "defining" Crespi. That a mad doctor who buries a former sexual rival alive (Crespi has never forgiven his fiancée for marrying Dr. Ross, whom he submits to the ultimate horror) is an obsessional neurotic who has projected his death drive onto his other is clear.

This is fairly explicit in the scene where Crespi prepares the now drugged and paralyzed Ross for the premature burial that awaits him. Sitting by the motionless body, he describes, in what can only be called a "loving tone," what Ross will experience as the coffin is lowered into the ground. Unquestionably one of the most chilling moments in all horror, classic or contemporary, the sheer nastiness of it must not make us forget the way the scene is shot, any more than the way Crespi speaks: softly, as if to a lover. "You will experience such horrors as you have not dreamed of in your wildest nightmares," says Crespi, which has the merit of informing us that Crespi is talking of his own repressed nightmares of death and castration. To eliminate this angst, what better way than to make it real for the other, who is his unconscious self? Thus, burying Ross alive is a form of suicide.

This sadistic tenderness is strikingly represented in *The Mask of Fu Manchu*, most notably in the scene where the eponymous character submits the English archeologist, Sir Lionel, to the torture of the bell. To begin with, Fu Manchu regresses to a form of infantilism, the anal stage, wallowing by proxy in the excremental: he graphically informs Sir Lionel that, after several weeks, he "will be unspeakably foul." This, I would suggest, is why Fu Manchu later takes to smoothing the hair of his wretched victim and speaking to him in dulcet tones, like a devoted father—or mother. For the stern patriarch and famous man of science, Sir Lionel functions as the father to Fu Manchu as son, notably in the sequence where he sarcastically casts aspersions on Fu Manchu's doctoral degrees. Fu Manchu needs to reverse the roles to show who is master. For what is Sir Lionel doing if not *retaining* something, the information Fu Manchu wants and that Sir Lionel refuses to give up, to expel verbally from himself? Fu Manchu becomes the stern but benevolent paternal superego coaxing the stubborn child to relinquish what he wishes to keep to himself, and the loving maternal superego offering endearing terms in exchange for the gift of the turd/phallus. Sir Lionel becomes thus the two sides to Fu Manchu's desire: to retain and to expel, to control and to give.

It would be unwise therefore to see Fu Manchu as predominantly homosexual, despite the plethora of material seemingly pointing in that direction only.[44] The critical determination to brand Fu Manchu as a monstrous homosexual fiend is too insistent to be innocent, especially in the light of the film's racism and that of much criticism surrounding it. That an Asian group should have protested against the reissue of the film in 1972 on the grounds that the character "is an ugly, evil homosexual"[45] should inspire caution. Surely *The Mask of Fu Manchu* gives in to the worst sexual and racial prejudices in order to lead us to assume that "Orientals are like that," for precise political reasons to which I shall return in detail in chapter 4. Suffice it to state here that one cannot analyze the function of Fu Manchu without taking into account his daughter, never averse to a bit of torture herself. At one point she reacts quite clearly to the sight of handsome, virile Westerner Terrence Granville: she finds him sexually attractive. Her next action is to have him stripped to the waist and flogged! "Faster! Faster!" she screams, as if on the point of having an orgasm; the film clearly represents things thus.

What is happening here, beyond yet more fantasies about Eastern cruelty and nymphomania? Incestuously attached to her father, she experiences guilt and a need to be punished that she projects, in an inverted sadistic form, onto the prisoner: the desire she feels for him replaces that impossible desire for Fu Manchu. There is clearly also a problem for the spectators who, by identifying with the male victim, adopt a masochistic subject position that they can only reject by identifying with the daughter and thus adopting a sadistic position. Either the spectators accept their helplessness, or else they adopt the active role and thus find themselves occupying the position of the negatively connoted Orientals. This reproduces in a most interesting fashion what we see systematically in the film and that the film avoids by a sleight of hand extricating the Westerners from the traps they systematically fall into: it is not the West that acts and the East that submits, but rather the reverse.[46] Similarly, just as Fu Manchu denigrates his daughter as worthless because she is not a boy, so attempts are made (unsuccessfully) by Nayland Smith to prevent Sir Lionel's daughter from accompanying the men to the East in an attempt to rescue her father. So she, too, is not considered worthy (of trust and admiration). The film displaces its own racism and phallocentrism on to Fu Manchu and his daughter and overdetermines this via fantasies of Eastern cruelty. Just as Fu Manchu was referred to at the time as "positively effeminate"[47] (doubtless because he does "queer" things such as wearing a long "dress"), so at one point there is a close-up of the daughter smoking a cigarette and looking decidedly masculine.[48] Thus "abnormal" gender positions are imposed on Eastern characters to hide the repressive implications of "normal" heterosexuality: the woman must obey, in this case the surrogate father represented by Nayland Smith.

To attach the epithet "homosexuality" to such representations is both to try to fix into position something that is inherently mobile and labile—unconscious desire—and to suggest that homosexuality is somehow "different," therefore abnormal. If Benshoff tends to fall into the former trap, the discourse of *The Mask of Fu Manchu* clearly sets the latter trap for its spectators, only to fall into another trap of its own unconscious making, due to the "polymorphously perverse" dimension of pre-Oedipal desire. A revealing test case would be the cinema of James Whale, which has been the occasion for much comment. Some caution is surely called for. Just as unconscious homosexual desires do not mean that the characters are necessarily repressed homosexuals, so the openly gay life of Whale and the presence of explicitly homosexual characters in his films—Dr. Pretorius in *Bride of Frankenstein* is the most blatant example—should not lead us to assume that Whale was anxious to turn his films into militant gay tracts. If I would agree absolutely with Berenstein that it is what we now have on the screen that matters,[49] a consideration of certain elements of *The Old Dark House* will hopefully help to clarify a most complex issue.

In its presentation of the film—shown in a retrospective in 1971—the Museum of Modern Art in New York City wrote that the Charles Laughton character (Sir William Porterhouse, a wealthy young industrialist) is "accompanied by a chorus girl, who is loved in turn by a sensitive young man who thinks his malaise can be cured by marrying her."[50] The juxtaposition of *malaise, sensitive,* and *cured* immediately connotes a serious sexual problem. However, nobody on the critical scene seems to go on the assumption that the Melvyn Douglas character is homosexual, but this quote takes on other resonances if juxtaposed with the remarks made by the chorus girl about the Laughton character. She informs Douglas that "he doesn't expect anything" and "just wants people to think he's gay." Things have got to the point between the two that Sir William just sits on the bed at night with her and boasts of what he's done during the day.

Benshoff understandably, but perhaps unwisely, leaps on the word *gay*, especially as Laughton was known to be homosexual, and attributes all this to "the sly gay humor that defines Whale's ironic sensibility."[51] We have therefore a gay married actor playing the role of a man who cannot get over the death of his wife and who has learned to do without sex. The problem with this is located in the Melvyn Douglas character and in the attempt to sum up both his place in the film and his relation with the female companion of the Laughton character. He behaves toward the young woman in a similar manner, talking to her as if she were a soldier (= a man) and saying, during their trip outside to get a bottle of whisky from the car, "I shall drop you in the mud and go on alone." Given the film's explicit references to the aftermath of World War I and to the return of socially imposed rituals, I would argue that what is being represented is an attempt to rise above repressive and reactionary norms of a precise sexual nature, represented in the film by Rebecca Femm. If homosexuality exists in the film, then it is surely she who incarnates it. Her sadistic desire to see her late sister die in agony as the result of an accident suggests a projection onto her of guilt arising from repressed desires that Rebecca, as a religious bigot, cannot possibly accept. In such circumstances, we are surely justified in considering the relationship between her mad brother, Saul, and Morgan, the family servant, as a further unconscious attempt to circumvent the neurotic rituals that make up the pathetic existence of Rebecca and to which the infantilized Horace submits, like the little child he has become again (afraid of the dark, etc.). The desire to destroy others on the part of Rebecca has been exteriorized into an obsessional neurosis that leads her to multiply rituals destined to keep death at bay for herself, while wishing it on everyone else. The way she gobbles her food as if each mouthful were her last is eloquent testimony to this. Rebecca is represented as the repressive superego of a conservative and right-thinking social order, and the persistent representation of sexual ambiguity needs to be interpreted as an unconscious rejection of that order by the filmic discourse.

That one critic can find it "disturbing" that an actress should play the part of the ancient father of the family must certainly be seen in the context of anxiety faced with the blurring of male and female boundaries, which un-questionably occurs in *The Old Dark House*.[52] The fact that Morgan beats Saul to cover feelings of tenderness and affection echoes *The Mask of Fu Manchu*. Both Fu Manchu and his daughter are victims of a certain debased form of representation, wherein they act out in, the form of sadism, feelings which are the reverse to the point of being incestuous. Father and daughter desire each other, but not even a racist Western film can render that explicit and perforce displaces the issue onto one of hideous cruelty toward helpless Western victims. As we have seen, it is, rather, the East that is historically the victim. The polemical and progressive thrust of *The Old Dark House* is that in a hostile environment role-playing becomes the only form of defense, the only way to forge an identity that, however alienated, can at least be claimed as authentic when all values are inauthentic and imposed by the Other. Rather than see Sir William Porterhouse as homosexual because of the word *gay* or because he has sublimated libido, we should perhaps deplore the fact that it is in the pursuit of money that he has done so.

I would suggest that two intimately connected misconceptions are at work when critics come to discuss homosexuality in the horror film (and in other genres too): a confusion between *textual* codes and *social* codes; and the be-lief that homosexual characters exist in a film for the sole purpose of repre-senting "sexual perversion" and, by extension, of denouncing it. The first misconception simply forgets that no character in a text functions without other characters, which means that we are dealing with a system of signifiers, not signs with a pregiven referent. The second tends to pay lip service to psy-choanalysis but in the last instance brackets off the unconscious and the dis-course of the Other in favor of an interpretation that smacks of the alien-ation Lacan saw as stemming from binary oppositions. In an attempt to think these points through, I shall turn to *Murders in the Rue Morgue*.

Two of the characters in the film are medical students, Pierre and Paul. Referring to the latter as "the usual gay stereotype," Robin Wood continues: "His relationship with Pierre (they share an apartment, he wears an apron, cooks the dinner, and fusses) is a parody of bourgeois marriage."[53] Anyone who has seen the film cannot but agree that Paul is connoted as gay: the script gives him a girlfriend to circumvent censorship. The question that surely needs to be asked is, Why make him gay in the first place? My argu-ment will be that critics are reversing cause and effect. They are going on the assumption that it was decided to represent Paul as gay, which led to him do-ing such "feminine" things as cooking, while at the same time functioning as "straight," thanks to the presence of his girlfriend. But what if all this is, precisely, an *effect* in its own right, with an unconscious *absent cause* that it is our task to explicate? Let us proceed from there.

Wood has provided us with the answer in his formula "a parody of bourgeois marriage." For that is precisely what the whole film is heading toward: Pierre's union with Camille after saving her from Eric, Dr. Mirakle's ape. The film's story tries to keep separate two strands that are in fact unconsciously intertwined: the relationship between Pierre and Paul; and the parallel between Pierre and Dr. Mirakle. If Paul cooks for Pierre and fusses about with an apron on, he is clearly filling the role that Camille will be called on to accept at the end. One might surely ask, in this day and age, why we should continue to accept the notion that only women wear aprons and do cooking, why we do not wonder whether the film's unconscious discourse *is not already asking that very question. Murders in the Rue Morgue* is portraying, in the form of a parody of marriage resorting to stereotypes taken from a completely different and supposedly unrelated domain, the sort of fate that awaits Camille if she marries so self-centered a young man as Pierre. As Berenstein points out, he moves from ignorance to knowledge, a situation that makes him unique in the film. Moreover, his behavior toward Paul augurs ill for Camille: just as Pierre refuses to talk to Paul, he never answers her questions, each time preferring his experiments to a genuine relationship (whatever its sexual nature). Camille suffers the same fate as Paul: Pierre refuses to tell her anything, which explains her rather bizarre desire to know what is going on in other flats in Paris. Less a manifestation of prurient curiosity, it is surely akin to the curiosity of a child—here, a young woman is treated like a child, as Paul is, groping her way toward knowledge that is denied her on the grounds that children are and must be kept ignorant of sexuality. Significantly, Pierre makes the even more bizarre remark, "Perhaps it's just as well that we don't know," a sign of repression in which both enunciator and addressee are the unconscious victims. In our society sexuality cannot but be experienced as traumatic, given the repression it suffers from the outset. Which brings us to the parallels set up between Pierre and Dr. Mirakle.

Mirakle is a doctor; Pierre is studying to become one. Mirakle is carrying out experiments in an attempt to advance knowledge in a way that will force the world of science to recognize his genius. Pierre is carrying out classical experiments on human bodies so as to be recognized by the medical authorities and allowed to practice. Both of them are acting illegally, Mirakle because he wants to mingle the blood of an ape with that of a woman to prove his theory about evolution, Pierre because he has to bribe the morgue attendant to have access to corpses. However, this illicit dimension is displaced in Pierre's case by turning him into an amateur detective determined to uncover the secret of Dr. Mirakle; it is no coincidence that the script gives him the name of Poe's famous detective, Dupin, who is absent from the film. This is necessary to cover up the unpleasant implication of this network of parallels: Pierre's narrative and symbolic function is that of Mirakle's son.

Once we move into that particular realm, another parallel—equally unpleasant ideologically—becomes clear: one between Camille and the young prostitute tortured for her blood. Both are objects of exchange, circulating in the body of the text like blood in the human body, used for the benefit of science/men. Significantly, Pierre spends what money he has bribing the morgue attendant to obtain corpses, which places Paul in the unfortunate position of having to live in straitened circumstances and look after the flat. Both men are "active" in one way or the other, but from a purely ideological standpoint Paul is "passive." After their marriage, Pierre will impose the same economic logic on Camille. Much more is at stake, however, if we take up the parallel between Pierre and Mirakle, and it is here that we can understand the various displacements at work to prevent the repressed returning in a recognizable form, in a way that would cast doubts on Pierre's virility.

Raving hysterically when he discovers that the blood of the prostitute is useless for his experiments, Mirakle reveals a peculiarly puritanical side to his character: "Blood as black as your sins," he screams at the victim, adding, "Will my search never end?" This remark is most odd indeed, for there is no reason why every prostitute he picks up should be so "contaminated," no reason why he should not look for blood elsewhere. After all, mad doctors of the 1930s are nothing if not determined and take all sorts of ingenious initiatives.[54] Mirakle even goes so far as to accuse her of cheating him, which is meaningless unless we see the unconscious at work. For it is rather he who has cheated her by tricking her into accompanying him to his laboratory, which suggests sexual impotence on his part: he tries hard but cannot get things to work. Clearly this unconscious logic can contaminate the whole film by suggesting that Pierre neglects Camille and ignores Paul for similar reasons. Pierre must therefore be allowed to do things his way and discover the secret of Mirakle's experiments so that he can be granted the proper status of the loving and virile hero. The film's unconscious logic has therefore connoted Paul as effeminate and possibly gay in order to displace another interpretation which questions Pierre's motives, both scientific and sexual. If Pierre corresponds much of the time, particularly toward the end, to the dashing young hero, this is simply the effect of the absent cause of unconscious desire that has been working its way through until displaced in the time-honored tradition.

The massive anxieties that find such distorted expression, as I have tried to indicate, come to the surface in no uncertain fashion in *Freaks*, that realization of one of our worst nightmares. The film's opening sequence—various freaks being looked after like children in the woods and meadows of the property of a wealthy landowner—was doubtless intended by Browning to put audiences at ease, to show them that the freaks are human beings first and foremost. One can admire the director's progressive stance, while at the same time regretting how naive he was concerning audiences. For this bucolic setting and the childlike innocence and friendliness of the freaks only serve to bring to the fore the notion that such "accidents of nature" are as natural as any of us. The hysterical reactions should not have come as a surprise and explain the desperate attempt by MGM to regain control of the situation via its thoroughly disreputable press and publicity campaign, destined to ridicule and vilify the film's "freakish" heroes and heroines. I would suggest that it is this state of affairs, rather than Browning's alcoholism, that compromised his later career.

It is arguable—and I present this as a working hypothesis—that what set the cat among the pigeons for spectators of *Freaks* was the androgynous character of Joseph/Josephine. The fact that (s)he has two names while being one person is eloquent and can be seen as the film's literal representation of the bisexual drives Freud saw as forming the basis of pre-Oedipal libido. (S)he is, of course, the object of contempt and prompts the character of the stutterer to say to Hercules, "*She* likes you but *he* doesn't." The question immediately arises: How does he know? Clearly the remark functions to designate precisely those clearly delineated boundary lines the film challenges, but to say "*he* likes you but *she* doesn't" would be to transform discursively a literally split *biological* position into an explicitly split *subject* position and therefore to question the sexuality of the male characters concerned. Such contempt on the character's part is only another form of those aggressive narcissistic tendencies existing since the mirror stage—which Joseph/Josephine incarnates most uncannily and which return here in the form of designating a scapegoat, the butt of sadistic laughter. This, of course, rebounds with a terrible vengeance on both Hercules and Cleopatra. Significantly, just as Cleopatra exploits Hans by planning to steal his fortune, so Hercules robs the young woman who had been staying with him. *Freaks* therefore has the merit of showing how economic exploitation is an unconscious social manifestation of the desire to eliminate the other in order to settle, on the imaginary mode, all questions concerning one's own identity.

The character of Phroso the clown enables the film to reinforce its progressive discourse on sexuality, desire, and representation. At one point, he adopts what society is wont to call "effeminate mannerisms." As he is the only male character in the film who refuses to insist on masculine preroga-tives, this must be interpreted as a readiness to put himself literally in the place of the other without the wish to humiliate, asking that the spectator— of the film, at the circus that is its setting—do the same. Thus, when he con-gratulates one female freak on her dress, this is experienced both by us and by the addressee of his compliment as an act of solidarity (Phroso is *not* a freak) that places the subject above any consideration of self-interest, whether financial, social, or sexual. This eloquent acceptance of the right to difference is represented through the Siamese twins. When one is pinched, the other feels it, but they do not kiss in the same way, and there is no jeal-ousy on the part of one when her sister gets married. It would be difficult, es-pecially given such delicate material, to find a neater expression of the in-evitable and necessary coexistence of individuality and intersubjective desire. *Freaks* is as courageous as it is exemplary.

I wish to conclude this section with a detailed discussion of *Frankenstein* and *Bride of Frankenstein* that foreground both textually and extratextually a number of issues pertaining to gender, sexuality, and difference as social phe-nomena. Benshoff writes of

> the mad scientist, who, with the frequent aid of a male assistant, sets out to cre-ate life homosexually—without the benefit of heterosexual intercourse. . . . To-gether the mad scientist and his sidekick become a major generic convention that is easily read as queer: the secret experiments they conduct together are chronicled in private diaries and kept locked away in closed cupboards and closets.[55]

This situation, I shall argue, can easily be read as something else that does not so much eliminate the homosexual subtext as suggest another frame of reference that displaces matters considerably. If we pay close attention to cer-tain shots, situations, and elements of dialogue in *Frankenstein*, we shall be able to propose a quite different reading that will also help us to suggest that *Bride of Frankenstein* is more than just the gay text it is so frequently claimed to be.

The problem with Benshoff's reading is that it not only sets Whale up as sole author of *Frankenstein* but suggests that the homosexual elements have been deliberately and carefully planted. My concern, here as elsewhere in this study, is not with some latent preconscious content to be extracted and thus be rendered fully conscious, but with an unconscious desire that deter-mines a certain number of elements that are otherwise inexplicable. Prompted by a letter Henry Frankenstein has sent to his fiancée, Elisabeth, in which he writes, "My work must come first, even before you," she and Henry's friend Victor go to see Dr. Waldman, Henry's former teacher. There then follows a lengthy discussion between the three, shot in the following way: from right to left we see Victor, Elisabeth, Dr. Waldman, and a skull. Rather than give a traditional symbolic meaning to the skull—sign of the dire consequences of tampering with life, of Henry's "monstrous" vanity—I suggest we read the shot as a representation of Lacan's version of Freud's Oedipal triangle that Lacan recasts as father, mother, child, and phallus. Dr. Waldman, the stern, conservative, and repressive father figure, functions to fulfill the role of phallic father figure in the Symbolic, leading the future spouse to accept her passive position in the "normal" social order: thanks to him she will be able to marry Henry and have children. Victor's function is to overdetermine this "correct" choice. To accept that the maternal phallus is an illusion is to resolve the Oedipus complex, enter the Symbolic Order, and hence to accept one's mortality.

The next shot confirms this by framing, from right to left, the skull, Elisabeth, and Dr. Waldman. Victor is temporarily eliminated as he is not in a position to fill the role of father figure; that will come later, first during the visit to Henry's castle/laboratory, and second during the wedding celebrations. Dr. Waldman takes charge, gaining Elisabeth's trust so that they can control the unruly Henry, who is treated as if he were a child. Waldman as signifier of the phallic order leads the operations. The trio that finally gains entrance to the castle is therefore very much the image of a young couple led by the determined patriarch, with Henry as someone whose enthusiasm must be properly channeled into acceptable activities. However, if Henry is treated as a child, he behaves very much like an independent adult, even more determined than Waldman. Once in the laboratory, he puts everyone literally in their place and brings the monster to life.

It is when Henry's father, Baron Frankenstein, makes his entrance that things start to take form. The father is even more conservative and repressive than Waldman, but he is presented as doddering and stupid. His feeble intellect can only assume that, as something is clearly wrong, there must be another woman, and he decides to go to visit Henry himself, with Elisabeth and Victor tagging along. Waldman has stayed with Henry to help him control the monster, who thus becomes the stand-in for the unruly "child" Henry. An interesting displacement is taking place here from Henry onto the monster, one that goes some way in explaining the attested fact that critical discourse—and even the title of the following film, *Bride of Frankenstein*—confuses Frankenstein and his monster. Since both function as children who must be controlled and, in the case of the monster, punished, this confusion is as revealing as it is inevitable. Before leaving, however, the baron receives a visit from the Bürgermeister who wants to know when the marriage will take place, then calls Henry "the very image of his father," to which the irritated baron replies, "Heaven forbid!" Clearly we are expected to see this as a sign of his intense disappointment at having such an eccentric and unruly son,[56] but we are surely entitled to read it otherwise: as the manifestation of the text's unconscious desire, namely that Henry liberate himself from the control of so stuffy, shortsighted, intellectually feeble, and intolerant a father.

What is so fascinating about the following scenes in Henry's castle is the way the various male figures join forces. Henry, Victor, and Waldman hide the monster from sight before the baron and Elisabeth arrive. Then Henry staggers up the steps leading to the interior of the castle, leaving Victor and Waldman alone. When the baron and Elisabeth arrive, she escorts the old man up the steps—he is far less robust and active than Waldman—and Waldman persuades Victor to leave them. The two men exit. As we shall see, it is important that they join forces at this point. The film then cuts to Elisabeth, the baron having conveniently disappeared, and she rushes in to look after Henry, who faints, a feminine trait if ever there was one as far as the doxa is concerned. (See my remark on *The Invisible Ray* in the opening paragraph of the first section.) Elisabeth is very much the devoted fiancée *and* the worried mother figure at this point, as can be judged from a most odd remark she makes: "My dear, what have they done to you?" Who are "they"? She cannot be referring to the monster and Fritz and we can only interpret this remark as that of a woman—particularly a mother—anxious to protect her child from excessively stern and zealous father figures: in other words, from Victor and Waldman. Elisabeth, I would argue, is showing signs of independence, of a determination not to allow the men to take the decisions and impose their order on Henry. Whether we see her as fiancée or as mother figure, she clearly is not going to renounce the phallus so easily, particularly in the sense of wanting to play an active—read: masculine—part in saving the man she loves.

It is the wedding celebration that brings the various threads together, through certain remarks made by the baron. He gives Victor a flower for his buttonhole, with the words "This will make the best man even better," an indication of his desire to see the more conservative and reliable Victor as his son and husband to Elisabeth.[57] Then he handles a sort of crown of jewels, saying that he had placed it on the head of Henry's mother, wants him to do the same to Elisabeth, and hopes that in thirty years the couple's son will carry on the tradition. The camera cuts to Henry looking anything but happy and smiling uneasily. We can, of course, read this as a sign of his (repressed) homosexuality being revealed to him: he cannot possibly have a son. We can also suggest that what Henry is unconsciously refusing is not heterosexual marriage but a certain kind of imposed social convention that forces husband and wife into the mold fashioned by the big Other, where having children is taken for granted and where the male must, if not earn his living—Henry's family has private means—then at least bow to certain ancestral customs. He can become a respected academic like Waldman (who owes his position to his self-proclaimed conservatism), or spend his time organizing mindless festivities for the peasants,[58] or go hunting and have grandiose receptions, or pursue any of the other essential activities of the moneyed classes. *Frankenstein* may well be implying that Victor, and not Henry, is the "ideal" husband for Elisabeth, but the film is surely also suggesting that, in a different sort of society where the Symbolic Order is conceived otherwise, the fact of carrying out experiments would not be regarded with the suspicion that Victor patently manifests when Elisabeth talks to him of her fears (in the sequence where she reads Henry's letter). If Henry places his work before her, it is not because of some homosexual impulse but because he is trying to reconcile love and intellectual activity in a society where such an endeavor is doomed. For that society, the "pleasure principle" is constancy with a vengeance, and the sort of *jouissance* to which Henry unconsciously aspires and actively seeks is out of the question.

A structural parallel created between one shot in *Frankenstein* and one in *Bride of Frankenstein* strengthens this reading, despite the overtly gay elements of the latter film, too overt, I would suggest, for us not to suspect they are a cover for a discourse that is even more unacceptable. When the monster comes to life, Henry is beside himself and becomes "hysterical," shouting, "It's alive!" Victor and Waldman rush to restrain him, and an extraordinary shot follows of Henry all rigid and taut, with Victor grasping his left arm and Waldman's right hand clutching at his chest. In *Bride of Frankenstein*, after the creature has been brought to life, it is she who is held in a similar fashion by Henry and Dr. Pretorius. In other words, she occupies the same physical place in the second film that Henry does in the first one, which we must surely interpret symbolically as showing Henry occupying a feminine subject position. This in no way means that Henry "is" a woman but that he refuses to fill the "normal" male subject position. It also indicates that the triumphant cry of Pretorius—"the Bride of Frankenstein!"—must be taken literally, especially as the creature detaches herself from Pretorius to go toward Henry who then takes her by the hand and escorts her to a couch in a grotesque parody of a tango. The clearly phallic form of Henry's hysterical body in *Frankenstein* and of the creature's in *Bride of Frankenstein* would suggest, from a juxtaposition of the two films, that what is at stake is an impossible desire—not a homosexual wish to procreate without woman but rather a need for intellectual activity, as such, to be recognized and not rejected when it takes on forms that refuse God, social convention, and procreation. It also suggests the more or less overt contempt in our societies for intellectual activity as nonvirile, therefore feminine. Henry-as-phallus further creates a parallel between his life as scientist and that of an active woman, Elisabeth, refusing conformist and rigid gender roles.

In light of this reading, the explicitly gay elements of the second film constitute not a celebration of the right to difference but a reactionary blind, for they can only confirm that *any* manifestation of a desire that is not rigidly patriarchal will be proscribed. After all, Dr. Pretorius is portrayed as a dangerous madman, which can hardly advance the cause of gay rights. I remind readers of my remarks on Fu Manchu's "homosexuality." *Frankenstein*, I would therefore argue, is more progressive and convincing, inasmuch as it sets up an opposition, not between heterosexuality and homosexuality as *Bride of Frankenstein* does, but between a phallocentric heterosexuality and a more "Utopian" version whose vision moves rather in the direction of an understanding of hitherto unacceptable masculine and feminine positions that are not necessarily occupied rigidly or unquestioningly by a man or a woman. The ending of the film, with an enfeebled Henry in bed in the background, suitably domesticated, and his ridiculous father droning on contentedly in the foreground, suggests the price a man like Henry has to pay in such a repressive society. That Pretorius visits Henry in bed in *Bride of Frankenstein* only serves to show that the latter has remained incapable of asserting his rights. Ultimately, then, the baron in *Frankenstein* and Pretorius in *Bride of Frankenstein* fulfill equivalent ideological roles.

Thus, Henry's hysteria—which I can now refrain from placing between scare quotes—is literally that he is asking, "Am I a man or a woman?" or "What is a woman?" less because he is a repressed homosexual than because he refuses a certain kind of masculine subject position occupied socially by people like Waldman and Victor. It is to the question of hysteria that we must now turn our attention.

The Case of the Overwrought Ern[59]

In its review of *Mystery of the Wax Museum* (12 February 1933), the *New York Times*, contemptuous as ever of horror movies, evokes "Glenda Farrell sharing the feminine hysteria with Fay Wray."[60] Anyone who has seen the film will surely have to agree that, although the woman journalist played by Farrell is frightened at one point, she has every logical reason to be so and tends to act with the sort of bravery and self-control "normally" reserved for men. She is therefore less "hysterical" than the character of the male journalist played by Lee Tracy in Dr. X, but the latter's profoundly irritating "comic" performance is denounced solely as that: he is not referred to as suffering from hysteria. If we can put this down to unconscious male prejudice concerning women and men, it is perhaps not insignificant that the reviewer chose to add the word feminine when referring to the reactions of two female characters, an indication that male hysteria is unconsciously recognized, if not accepted; the doxa "female hysteria" is a pleonasm. Equally pertinent here is the reference to Fay Wray in the review. Just one month after this review appeared in the New York Times came the premiere of the film in which Fay Wray became famous overnight for her screaming: King Kong. The fact that Wray also starred with Tracy in Dr. X and was saved by him at the end of the film is certainly not incidental to the whole question of fear and hysteria. As we shall see later, in both films she is saved by a courageous male from "a fate worse than death."

In a stimulating and thought-provoking study of King Kong, R. C. Dale has written that the film "does succeed in dreaming for us, and we are swept along with the dream as helpless spectators, as if the dream were our own. Every viewer's reaction is obviously his own, but few can resist completely the involvement that the picture offers."[61] Dale also evokes the phallic imagery of the scene on board the ship in which Denham gets Ann Darrow to imagine she sees something terrifying and encourages her to scream, which she does, under the gaze of the crew.

If I reject absolutely Dale's view that each spectator reacts in a purely individual fashion to the film, what interests me here is the use of the word dream, in the light of the later sequence on Skull Island where the sacrificial victim Darrow finds herself face to face with Kong and screams bloody murder. Dale also writes that the narrative must "remove Ann from Denham's control" and pass through the gate "leading into the land of unsuppressed desire." He goes on to describe Kong's attempts to recover Darrow after she has been saved by the Bruce Cabot character in these terms. The ape shatters "the huge phallic bolt that is meant to keep him in his own element. With that symbolic act of castration, he bursts into civilization and his downfall."[62]

If we take Dale literally—which, for the purposes of my argument, I intend to do—then it is clear that what Ann "sees" off-screen as a result of Denham's promptings as a most persuasive film director can be assimilated to an image in a dream that represents something too unpleasant for the subject to contemplate (in every sense of the word). From a narrative point of view, the scene in which she screams at the sight of Kong is surely the film's response to the unconscious spectatorial desire triggered and put in place by her look off-screen with which the spectator identifies. What she sees and is terrified by is thus the visual manifestation of what the spectator does not see, yet desires to see, despite the clearly horrific implications. As there is—and can be—no reverse shot, the spectators hallucinate an image, a presence where there is none. In that case, the celebrated scream of *fear* functions as a displaced form of *anxiety* for the spectator faced with the intolerable proximity of the Real. In Lacanian terms, Ann is reacting with anxiety to something foreclosed in the Symbolic that returns in the Real. There is surely a parallel to be drawn here with the difference between phobia and anxiety:

> Even a phobia is preferable to anxiety; a phobia at least replaces anxiety (which is terrible precisely because it is not focused on a particular object but revolves around an absence) with fear (which is focused on a particular object and thus may be symbolically worked-through). . . . [A]nxiety appears first, and the phobia is a defensive formation which turns the anxiety into fear by focusing it on a specific object.[63]

Unconsciously, the sight of Kong is less traumatic than the absence determining Ann's first scream, although the film (re)presents Ann's scream as the result of the fear Denham is calling on her to simulate. We can duly interpret this as follows. Kong represents the return of the Father of Enjoyment to take full advantage of the predicament of the heroine, appropriately unable to run away from something she desires and responds to hysterically at the same time. Kong bursting through the phallic bolt representing the prohibition of such pre-Oedipal desire is thus the pure, unstoppable drive determined to obtain immediate satisfaction.

Let me now propose another interpretation. If Ann is calling for the males to save her, she is unconsciously granting that they have the phallus she does not. This, however, must be seen in the context of a male discourse overdetermined by a male vision of the roles the two sexes are meant to fulfill in society. Her scream faced with Kong on the island takes up her scream at the "sight" of something off-screen. As such, Kong functions as a fantasy for the spectator, deprived of the reassuring maternal phallus and forced to confront the Real via the off-screen. Inasmuch as Ann screams "for" the crew, she functions to displace onto a woman's fear the castration anxiety summoned up by the extraordinary sequence onboard the ship and duly kept at bay by Kong, the real creature from which the males will be able to save Ann. Thus, the Real has been kept at a safe distance by the Imaginary. The giant ape is therefore the signifier of the male phallus because he is "King Kong" and of the maternal phallus for which his huge frame is a reassuring stand-in.

Such an interpretation can be justified, however, only if one accepts a premise that, I shall now argue, is dubious. To do so, I shall turn to another article in *The Girl in the Hairy Paw*, Kenneth Bernard's "King Kong: A Meditation." In the course of this most witty and fascinating study, the author poses the pertinent question, "How big is King Kong's penis?" Having entertained us with a discussion of the anatomy of real-life male gorillas—who apparently have very small penises—he suggests that spectators could not possibly accept such a small organ for so splendid and awe-inspiring a creature as Kong: "So we are left with this fact: that the penis Kong ought to have is insufficient to cause the terror and anxiety he inspires. Therefore the penis Kong has is the one he *ought not* to have. . . . *It is obvious that Kong must exceed the estimates of comparative anatomy to inspire the universal dread that he does.*"[64] I want to call attention to the ambiguity of the formulation "the one he *ought not* to have" (the italics are Bernard's throughout). Clearly Bernard is stressing the level of fantasy in which we all assume Kong has a long dong and need to believe such a thing, however intimate our knowledge of primates and their private parts may be. After all, *King Kong* is a fantasy, so why not go all the way, as Kong is meant to do with Ann Darrow?[65] Bernard is obviously right about this, and the question of penis size is also part and parcel of racist fears: Kong as black rapist, which tells us far more about the castration fears of white racists than about the real endowments of black males. But to follow up this avenue of approach would lead us to sidetrack a more fundamental issue that I want to address here and one that is implicit in the remark by Bernard I have chosen to foreground. In order to tackle the issue frontally (so to speak), I shall make what will doubtless be considered an outrageous statement: *There is no textual evidence that Kong is male.*

Bernard would obviously disagree with me, for he states that "he is not called King for nothing."[66] I could not agree more, provided you interpret the statement literally: it is not for nothing that Kong is called "King" because there are several perfectly good reasons why it is necessary to have audiences consider the ape to be male. Now let us not get confused: the title of the film only tells us how the filmmakers conceived the film in general and the ape in particular. We are under no obligation to take them at their word, especially as the natives refer to the ape as "Kong" and do not have any more say in the matter. It is only because God is male in all "recognized" religions that we assume that all gods are male, despite proof to the contrary—those of ancient Greece, for example. Writing on *King Kong* shows a massive and unconscious anthropomorphism at work that consists of attributing to an ape the desires of heterosexual males: as Ann Darrow is a female, only a male ape could want to carry her off to meet a fate worse than death. It is surely a moot

point whether a real-life male ape from the African jungle could tell the difference between a male and a female human, but Kong is meant to understand that Ann is desirable by males, which inverts cause and effect: because
Kong desires her, "he" is male. What is functioning here surely is our old
friend the "absent cause," which passes effects off as causes so as to hide the
Real.[67] So where does this get us?

Three clues have been given us, one by Dale, the others by Bernard. The
former refers to "the phallic bolt" that bursts asunder under pressure from the
ape, while the latter writes that "the penis Kong has is the one he *ought not*
to have." He also evokes the motherly affection and tenderness with which
Kong carries Ann around. A case of mother and daughter removed from all
male interference, perhaps? All this adds up to *King Kong* as a protofeminist
text concerned with matriarchal, as opposed to patriarchal, culture; and with
a form of "female bonding," which certainly makes a change from its male
equivalent. Once again, it is not my intention to present this as an alternative reading, but to insist that the proliferation of meanings stems from the
very sexual ambiguity of the subject positions being created by the film's narrative and representational strategies. What is at stake therefore is quite simple: it is not Ann Darrow who behaves as a "typical" hysterical female but *the*
film itself that is hysterical, inasmuch as its discourse asks the hysterical question about Kong: Is it male or female?[68]

Here a most pertinent parallel can be drawn between *King Kong* and *Son*
of Kong, on the one hand, *Frankenstein* and *Bride of Frankenstein*, on the
other. Kong's son comes into existence through some miracle: there is no
mate, the baby just appears. Thus the filmmakers have indulged in exactly
the same fantasy as Frankenstein in Whale's two movies. If *King Kong* is
"about" something, then it is the ambiguous nature of sexuality, the fact that
subject positions are sexed and social, not biological and natural: "hysteria is
conceived by psychoanalysis as a challenge to the subject's social identity:
hysteria is the first analyzed instance of the subject's essential division, its
questioning and refusal of social dictates."[69]

We can perhaps now suggest another dimension to the exhibition of Kong in
New York. Ann in bonds finds a parallel in Kong in chains, just as Ann surveyed
by the crew finds a parallel in Kong gazed at by the New York audience. The
theme of "female bonding" is therefore to be taken in more than one sense and
the film literally equates Ann and Kong, not simply by unconsciously assimilating the woman to the monster but by suggesting Kong is female.

Let us pause here for a moment. The skeptical reader—meaning the reader
ready to question rather than simply to disbelieve—may argue that I am doing
no more than juxtaposing different interpretations, which is correct to the

extent that I am arguing, on the one hand, that readings of *King Kong* assume something that cannot be taken for granted, and on the other hand, that the lability of the unconscious has cut loose the signifier to the point of the latter no longer being tied to any signified whatsoever. One scene in particular shows the theme of sexual ambiguity and hesitation being inscribed into the text at the precise point where symbolism of the "X symbolizes Y" kind seems to be functioning in a traditional fashion. I am referring to Kong's second great fight to protect Ann, threatened this time by some creature from a black lagoon. After a struggle, Kong vanquishes the amphibian and then shakes its elongated neck to make sure it is dead. The phallic aspect of the neck and head are unmistakable, and the ape is clearly represented as intrigued. I suggest that the creature stands in for the phallus Kong does not have, and it is precisely this element that shows the film's discourse to be hysterical.

Why? When I refer to "the phallus Kong does not have," I am not saying that Kong is a female ape and therefore does not have a penis; the sequence in question has nothing to do with "penis envy." What I am claiming is that, whether Kong be male or female, he or she cannot have the phallus, for the simple reason that it does not exist: the phallus Kong does not have is a phallus no creature can have, for the simple reason that it is the maternal phallus, the phallus the women wants, the phallus the male wants to (continue to) believe in. At this particular juncture, therefore, it is literally impossible to decide which sex Kong is, which comes down, yet again, to asking the question, Is it male or female? This can only bring us back to the arguments already proposed.

Another, but related, approach is suggested via a remark by Dylan Evans: "Distinguishing religion from magic, science and psychoanalysis on the basis of their different relations to truth as cause, Lacan presents religion as a denial of the truth as cause of the subject, and argues that the function of sacrificial rites is to seduce God, to arouse his desire."[70] If we take up this notion in relation to the scene where the native girl is being prepared to be sacrificed to Kong, then something interesting is taking place, for the girl in question is clearly presented as a virgin: young and "demure." In this case, by putting Ann in her place, the natives attribute to her the same sexual status. The film, however, can hardly be said to represent Ann thus; the opening sequence hints that Ann is being "saved" by Denham not only from starvation but, possibly, prostitution, too. The natives are thus acting out the unconscious of the text where certain male fantasies are being represented. One of these is patently rape.[71] Another is scopophilia as displaced rape: the voyeur wonders what happens during a particular act of sex that he is incapable of carrying out himself. Yet a third would be the primal scene. What links these possibilities—and others—is the central fantasy concerning female sexuality as such and hence the whole question of a form of knowledge the male subject cannot have. This in turn can lead the male hysteric to desire a female position in order to "know" what the woman experiences. Once this happens, however, and our hysteric puts himself in Ann's place, there then arises the situation discovered by Freud when analyzing the case of President Schreber: the male subject occupying the position of the female to copulate with a male figure. This in turn coexists, given my line of thought, with another male fantasy that is a displaced form of the one just formulated: watching two women having sex. Once again, the stress must be laid on the copresence of these fantasies in the subject's unconscious and, thus, the possibility of activating them in succession in a doomed attempt to arrive at the imaginary absolute knowledge of what female sexuality is. We find these notions at work in different ways in the film Schoedsack codirected while *King Kong* was in preparation: *The Most Dangerous Game*.

What should be obvious is the fact that, far from being simply Zaroff's adversary and rival, Rainsford is surely also his mirror image. The concept of rivality is therefore to be read in Lacanian terms, the image of the self taken as that of the other and the ensuing narcissistic wound that can be cured only by eradicating that other. The parallels set up by the film—both consciously and unconsciously—are sufficiently numerous to be meaningful. First, both men are hunters. Second, just as Rainsford is trapped in Zaroff's castle by the servant who hides behind the door and closes it when Rainsford enters, so Zaroff is trapped by Rainsford who hides behind the same door and closes it prior to their final and fatal confrontation. Third, just as Zaroff breaks the "contract" existing between the two men—Rainsford will be free if he survives till dawn—by drawing a gun on his rival because he cannot accept being beaten, so Rainsford stabs Zaroff in the back (with an arrow). This literal manifestation of a metaphoric expression—"to stab someone in the back"—indicates the unconscious at work and suggests that Zaroff and Rainsford occupy the same subject position. What are the implications of this logic?

I wish to draw attention to two aspects of the film in particular: Zaroff's temple wound, the result of a near-fatal encounter with a buffalo, and the pursuit through the jungle where the film cuts between him rushing through the tall grass and Rainsford and the heroine fleeing desperately. The placing of the camera in successive shots puts the spectator explicitly both in the position of being the object of Zaroff's pursuit and as the pursuer of the man and the woman. This dual subject position occupied by the spectator represents the duality and the interdependence of sadism and masochism, a factor that we shall also see at work in *Dr. X*. (I shall return to this point later when analyzing *Dr. X.*) More to the point, however, is the question, Who is Zaroff pursuing?

The film has it both ways. Zaroff is chasing Rainsford to kill him in order to carry the woman off as the spoils of the hunt. In the light of the concept of hysteria, however, things are far more complex, and I would claim that Zaroff is pursuing Rainsford and *him alone*: the heroine is a decoy for the unconscious of the film and the spectators. Once again, I refuse to see this as a matter of homosexuality. Rather, I suggest we read the pursuit as a continuation in the form of an act of the opening sequences aboard the boat in which "men of the world" belonging to the moneyed class discuss matters without the presence of women, suggesting that all important decisions—or all decisions considered important by men—are made by men in secret, closeted as they are in order to be free from female interference.[72] Thus, *The Most Dangerous Game* unites Rainsford and Zaroff in "male bonding" just as *King Kong* does Ann and Kong in "female bonding." The "gentlemen's agreement" existing between Zaroff and Rainsford, however, is not a simple matter of two men fighting over who is going to possess the woman's body, especially as Zaroff may be impotent. Hence the temple wound that he caresses bitterly, the "narcissistic wound" of castration.

However, this head wound is too blatant to be taken at its face value as referring solely to Zaroff himself. It is the signifier of the film's hysteria that has been displaced and that is to be located in the character of the dashing and virile hero, Rainsford. Zaroff in pursuit is the discursive manifestation of the *desire of Rainsford to be pursued*. Rainsford, the spectators' representative in the fiction, wants to know what it is like for a woman to be pursued by a man. We find represented in *The Most Dangerous Game* what we have already located in *King Kong*: the hope of the male hysteric that he can find an answer to the question, What is a woman? in order to reassert his own problematic (and diminished?) virility. Thus, *The Most Dangerous Game* offers the traditional ending in which the active male saves the passive female, which is easy to represent, since Rainsford is a typical Hollywood hero. We might remember, however, that there is a passive, weak and ineffectual male in the film: the heroine's fatuous, drunken brother. And that the actor who plays the role, Robert Armstrong, returns in *King Kong* as none other than Carl Denham, the virile and active explorer who is ideologically and socially the spitting image of Rainsford. *King Kong* is also a remake of *The Most Dangerous Game* in the sense of a repetition of the same in a different form: repeating in the form of an act a desire that cannot speak its name.

A somewhat different approach is needed to understand how hysteria figures in *Dr. Cyclops*, the third film directed by Schoedsack in our corpus, for it will be necessary to have recourse to advertising used to promote the film, in particular the poster to which reference has already been made. As we have seen, this is a throwback to *King Kong*, with Thorkel (Dr. Cyclops) playing the part of Kong, holding a helpless young woman in his hand. That she should be scantily clad is indicative of an attempt to sexualize the encounter, although the mad doctor in the film is totally indifferent to sexuality. That, however, is on the level of the film's manifest content. That he should have shrunk the characters to a fraction of their normal size and that Joseph Breen should have expressed anxiety over the way the "little folks" in the film were dressed suggests something less innocent taking place.[73]

Unconsciously, Breen had understood that we are dealing with a sort of fairytale in which Thorkel is the giant or primal father and the other characters as the brothers deprived of all access to women. It must be remembered that the heroine is treated like a man and does not function as a woman until the last seconds of the film.

At no point in the film does Thorkel pick up the heroine; he only treats thus the elderly head of the expedition in order to examine his evolution now that he has been shrunk. This physical handling of one male character by another character disturbs somewhat socially acceptable codes where such touching is looked on as a trait of homosexuality. I would argue therefore that the publicity material quoted is an unconscious attempt to show that Thorkel is a good heterosexual at heart, lewdly manhandling a nearly naked female. It is therefore the juxtaposition of the textual and the extratextual that suggests a hysterical reaction to what the film is really representing: the anal father enjoying having a helpless *male* at his disposal, using his body as if he were the typical helpless female. We are back in the company of Fu Manchu and Sir Lionel.

We shall have cause to return to this publicity material at the end of the chapter. The next section will enable us to address the question of other ways in which desire can become manifest in distorted forms and its relation to power.

Just What the Mad Doctor Ordered

Island of Lost Souls opens with a man adrift at sea being rescued by a passing ship; it is the film's hero Edward Parker, destined to play a role in Dr. Moreau's experiments. The second sequence shows Parker lying in bed in a cabin, the ship's doctor tending him. Suddenly he sits up and looks with increasing horror in the direction of—what? His look off-screen right is virtually into the camera and is accompanied by inarticulate cries that draw the doctor's attention. Presumably intended to show the spectator how a man's mind can become affected under extreme duress, it also looks ahead to a film being made at the same time and which would be released some two months later: *King Kong*. For Parker's look and cries correspond too closely to Ann Darrow's look and screams while being filmed by Denham for us to dismiss the parallel as a simple coincidence, especially in the light of what the off-screen will soon serve up on-screen to the spectator once Parker finds himself on Moreau's island.

Parker's reaction in the ship's cabin is that of a subject suddenly confronted with the Real, as surely as Ann's was, and what the film reveals of Moreau's experiments confirms the film as the realization of what Parker experienced (we cannot write "saw," as there was nothing to see). Moreau is a sort of master of ceremonies, directing a series of "operations" going from literal vivisection to the ritual of "What is the Law?" and to the attempt to mate Lota the panther woman and the still ignorant Parker. Just as Kong becomes the visual representation of spectatorial desire to have a reply to the question, What did Ann Darrow see?, so the encounters between Parker and Lota realize the desire that lies behind such a question, a desire inscribed into the film by another look, that of Moreau himself as he watches with anticipation to see how the "couple" will react to each other. This look is the condensation of Moreau's various symbolic functions in the film. It is the signifier of the primal scene for the spectator, the displacement of our look onto Moreau's and his morbid yet "scientific" curiosity defusing the scandalous because forbidden nature of the hoped-for mating. It also represents Moreau's status as "primal father," which is less obvious.

Moreau's Law is a series of prohibitions and can be seen as both his triumph and his downfall. He has simply proscribed desire or, rather, thinks he has. By assuming that the speeding up of evolution is as automatic with the "manimals" as with plants, he has privileged animal instincts and repressed the human dimension, the Symbolic Order. His belief in control and mastery is total; because he has sublimated his own desire and channeled it into playing God and creating a new race, he fails to appreciate the existence of desire. For him sexuality is purely physical, and the concept "subject" is nonexistent. He cannot even read the signs when one of the manimals shows a clear sexual interest in Lota, but more to the point is the way Parker reacts to Lota: he finds her attractive, kisses her, and then notices her long nails and realizes she is yet another of Moreau's experiments. By rounding on the doctor and calling him a "criminal," he is in fact revealing a truth about himself. Just what was Parker attracted to? This sort of ambiguity makes the film profoundly unsettling and is more pertinent and interesting than the question of

Moreau's homosexual attraction to Parker. Or, rather, this male-male dimension of desire is simply a less scandalous version of the radically forbidden and impossible attraction felt by Parker for Lota, especially as Moreau discovers that she is slowly but inexorably reverting to her animal origins.

I would suggest, therefore, that *Island of Lost Souls* is in fact the realization of an impossible desire that can only instill a sense of horror in the subject who becomes aware of it. This is the meaning of Parker's reaction onboard the ship. The unconscious logic of the film has worked backward from the sequences on Moreau's island to "contaminate" an early scene that takes place before Parker sets foot on the island but whose meaning is already determined by the role of other looks and other encounters worked through later. The shot without a reverse shot, held for an excessive time when one reflects on the fact that there is nothing to see and that it cannot be interpreted, is a condensation of the desire to witness something forbidden and of the inevitable horror that must arise when the subject places itself within the (primal) scene at the expense of one of the actors of the scene. One possible interpretation of the last shot, in which Parker is told by Moreau's assistant, Montgomery, not to look back at the island as they escape, would therefore be an attempt to repress all knowledge of what one has seen and experienced—repress or, rather, foreclose. For the early shot of Parker in the cabin, picked up when he was drifting helplessly at sea, seems to form with the last shot a narrative circle, as if he has been picked up *after* witnessing the horrors of Moreau's island. The film therefore sets in place a form of endless repetition that is surely nothing other than that of desire itself, of which the spectator is as clearly an effect as he or she will be of the similar device deployed in *King Kong*.

Much attention has been paid to the opening of *Mad Love* in which Dr. Gogol religiously attends the Grand Guignol spectacle where the object of his love, an actress who in real life is the wife of famous pianist Stephen Orlac, is tortured by her husband to discover who the other man in her life is. That her alternating screams and cries of "Yes! Yes!" are intended to represent orgasm is abundantly clear; I refer readers back to my comments on *The Mask of Fu Manchu*. The sequence therefore foregrounds the important theme of pleasure in pain and, by cutting to the audience in the theater, shows how the spectator can occupy simultaneously a sadistic and a masochistic position. This, of course, is the point being made about Gogol, but more needs to be said on this score. When he closes his eyes in empathy with the suffering heroine, he is also experiencing orgasm. The question is, Whose? Given Gogol's infantile behavior toward Yvonne Orlac in later sequences, we can interpret the sequence as a beating fantasy and as the primal scene. In this case, Gogol simultaneously experiences orgasm in the imaginary position of the father, identifies with the position of the victim as mother figure (which makes of Gogol a genuine hysteric), and identifies with the sadistic husband deriving intense pleasure from having his unfaithful wife branded. Thus, Gogol derives simultaneously from the torture sequence the pleasure of not having to decide whether he is a man or a woman, the masochistic pleasure of being punished for his own guilty incestuous desire, and the sadistic pleasure of punishing the person "responsible" for the existence of this desire and whom he resents for being inaccessible. At the same time he can also occupy the absent place of the wife's lover, thus enabling him to fulfill a socially normal heterosexual function and behave in an active fashion (the athletic lover who leaps on and off balconies like Douglas Fairbanks Sr.). This last subject position is, as we shall see presently, important for the film's ending.

Unlike many other mad doctors, Gogol is not engaged in insane experiments; on the contrary, he is a famous surgeon who devotes himself to operating on accident victims and to forming future surgeons. He occupies a socially respectable position. However, his libido has undergone massive sublimation and then finds an outlet in an arrested infantile form once he witnesses Yvonne Orlac's performances in the theater. As the film is clear on the fact that he has never had sex with a woman, we can only conclude that the wife is the incarnation of the most ideal of women: the mother. If she does not reciprocate his love, it is because she has unconsciously understood what role she is being called on to play, thanks to a remark where he tells her, "You are cruel, but only to be kind"—the little boy misbehaving so as to draw the mother's attention exclusively to him and away from the legitimate object of her love and to be deliciously punished at the same time, thus confirming for the child his narcissistic impression of his own importance.

A quite remarkably perverse scene occurs when Gogol checks the progress of the operation he has performed: successfully grafting on to Orlac's arms the hands of the recently executed murderer Rollo. Freund insists on the way Gogol massages/caresses Orlac's fingers, the phallic symbolism and hence masturbation being patent. Thus the scene apparently turns into one of homosexual seduction. But matters are not that simple, for Gogol occupies successively or simultaneously the positions of son, spouse, and Yvonne herself. Freud has insisted on the polysemy of a hysterical symptom: on the one hand, a compromise between the libido and repression; on the other hand, the condensation of a male and a female fantasy.[74] In which case, the film is representing incest (the son lovingly masturbating his father) and onanism: if Gogol is Orlac, then he is masturbating himself; if he is Yvonne, then it is a case of a woman masturbating her husband. This scandalous logic is, however, doomed to remain unexploited in the face of other, more reactionary values. Europeans are seen as effete, passive art lovers, whereas Americans love action and the outdoors: rather a murderer like Rollo who is proud of America's achievements than an impotent like Gogol who worships a wax statue of Yvonne Orlac!

The Hollywood guardians of morality were clearly disturbed by the film's sexual implications. Breen wrote to Louis B. Mayer on 22 April 1935 to warn him about any "suggestion of perversion" between Gogol and the wax figure of Yvonne he buys from the theater.[75] More intriguingly, the *Motion Picture Herald* dated 6 July 1935 evoked the central character's "bestiality" in connection with the statue.[76] This term functions as a signifier condensing a variety of facts and fantasies. A conscious recognition of the existence of heterosexual copulation a tergo is transformed unconsciously into the image of animals copulating. This in turn is overdetermined by the homosexual implications of Gogol caressing Orlac's hand of which the viewing subject becomes an effect through fantasizing the act of sodomy. The copresence of heterosexuality and homosexuality on the one hand, and of animal behavior on the other hand, evokes that other copresence referred to earlier via the coexistence of human and animal attributes: bisexuality with its masculine and feminine components. As if this were not enough, there comes into play the hoary old chestnut of the female being "closer to nature" than the male, with its "bestial" connotations.

Such a blurring of boundaries must be displaced in order to reassert phallocentric ideology and fixed gender positions at the end. Orlac has come under Gogol's influence to the point of identifying with the latter's masochistic and passive position in the theater sequence; thus, he weakly agrees to go along with the police, who accuse him of murdering his father, telling his wife, "There's nothing you can do." Seeing Yvonne in the process of being strangled by a demented Gogol, Orlac is suddenly galvanized into action and kills Gogol by throwing a knife into his back. Thus it is the hands of executed murderer Rollo that stop Gogol and not a suddenly active Stephen Orlac. This point, however, is passed over in favor of the rebirth of the legal couple, but it solves nothing as far as Orlac's career and future behavior are concerned. When he has Orlac under his control, Gogol is occupying a sadistic and active position. When Orlac throws the knife that kills Gogol, he certainly becomes active suddenly, but this is because he has the hands of a convicted murderer. This also goes some way in explaining why Rollo is portrayed as positively as a murderer can be (which is not difficult as he pays the supreme penalty that placates the censors). For when Orlac observes, through the opening in the door, Gogol in the act of strangling Yvonne, he is occupying the same passive, masochistic position as Gogol in the opening sequence in the theater. This in turn means that Gogol is occupying the place of the vengeful and sadistic husband and Yvonne, once again, the place of the tortured and helpless wife. This subverts the phallic prerogatives of the legitimate husband, so Orlac/Rollo leaps into action to save the day. At the same time, however, this sudden activity places Orlac in the position of the active lover in the opening "Grand Guignol" sequence. The contradictions set in motion by creating parallels between Orlac and Gogol, as the film has done, cannot be solved. It is surely significant that Gogol attempts to strangle Yvonne with her hair. Turning it into plaits to wrap around her throat, he gives it phallic shape so as to maintain until the end a belief in the maternal phallus and "to expel the phallus as the signifier of paternal authority and sexual difference."[77]

If Gogol is one of the decade's most truly demented loonies, then Bela Lugosi's Dr. Vollin in *The Raven* is even more over the top. What is most interesting in this underrated and neglected film is the way director Louis Friedlander manages, by a careful use of cutting and close-ups, to introduce the theme of an incestuous father-daughter relationship that puts Vollin's sadism and paranoia in a new perspective, to the point of making him virtually a victim, although his behavior toward the father and victim Boris Karloff tends to shunt this aspect onto a dark siding. On the level of the storyline, *The Raven* has in common with *Mad Love* and *The Crime of Dr. Crespi* (all made in 1935) the theme of the character who turns in desperation to a doctor to convince him to operate on a loved one: he and he alone can save the person in question. Thus, Crespi's former fiancée turns to him to save her husband; Gogol accepts to undertake the hand graft; and Vollin, after first refusing to operate on Judge Thatcher's daughter, changes his mind when the father tells him that all the medical experts consider that he is the best specialist. Having been refused that recognition in the past, Vollin smiles triumphantly and accepts, saying, "So I am the only one." The film thus indicates both his megalomania and his paranoia.

Unlike Gogol and Crespi, however, Vollin has no ulterior motive: it is not until after the operation, when his young patient has recovered, that he realizes he has feelings for her that are not simply professional. And it is here that the film's direction clashes with the script, and even aspects of the acting, to produce an intriguing subtext that only the extreme nature of Vollin's later behavior works to repress. The victim of the accident, Jean, is a dancer and stages a composition of her own, "Lenore," to celebrate her return to health. The sequence at the theater where she dances before an admiring audience indicates without any ambiguity that Vollin is captivated by her, but also that her father is disturbed by this attraction. He and Vollin are sitting

side by side in a box, and a cut to the father's face shows the truth of the situation dawning on him. After the performance, Vollin comes to the dressing
room to congratulate Jean, and a shot frames him on the right, her on the left
and the increasingly anxious father in the middle, looking from one to the
other. Clearly the film is presenting the father as the only force that can
come between the two of them, a fact that allows for more than one interpretation.

The father, who is a judge, comes to see Vollin at his home shortly after and
makes the following remark: "I questioned Jean and she made a confession:
she's in danger of becoming infatuated with you." This comment is strange indeed, as no indication has been made of this, and the father manifestly—
through the precise and subtle direction of Friedlander, as we have just
noted—considers the infatuation to be on Vollin's side. As the conversation
continues, Vollin's infatuation is made evident in the dialogue—"Jean torments me; she has come into my life, into my brain"—and soon the men become aggressive, with Vollin demanding that the judge send his daughter to
him and the father calling him mad. The sudden and violent change in Vollin
incites the spectators to consider this to be the case, but in reality Vollin is
condensing at this point two extremes: love, where the subject renounces the
self in favor of the object, and the narcissistic megalomania characteristic of
paranoia.[78] However, the behavior of the father, who places the discussion on
the terrain of his daughter's infatuation with Vollin, suggests that he cannot
accept his daughter entering into a relationship with a man who is much older
than she when a suitable fiancé is at hand. This in turn suggests an excessive
attachment on his part to his own daughter, a potentially dangerous development hinting at incest. This is given some credence by the refusal of the father to take Vollin's feelings seriously, whereas he takes his daughter's very seriously indeed. However, the film has already introduced an element that
enables it to disavow what it is in the process of representing in the course of
the confrontation between the two men.

During Jean's dance number, the camera cuts twice, the first time to show
us her fiancé watching her, and then to show Vollin doing so. Most of the
time the camera places the film's spectators with those in the theater, but a
further cut has the action framed from the stage, behind Jean dancing, in
such a way as to show her looking in the direction of the box containing her
father and Vollin, the guest of honor. I propose to read this shot as the discourse of the Other momentarily taking over that of the film. For Jean is
presented here as a "flirtatious female," especially as she is wearing a sort of
transparent veil assimilating her to Salomé. In this way, the film justifies in
advance the attitude of the father who, as guardian of not only the law but

the Law, must impose a certain choice on his daughter: the fiancé already designated, and not someone like Vollin.[79] Moreover, the presence of the father and Vollin in the box together could suggest that the father's overprotective attitude toward his daughter is reciprocated by the daughter's over-attachment to him. By representing her as potentially "flighty" and not "knowing her own mind"—a way of both justifying the paternal superego and admitting to unconscious desire—the film hedges its bets. The linguistic dimension of the dance number overdetermines this hesitation. Jean dances to Poe's poem "Lenore," which is recited as she performs, and the presence in the verbal text of the expression "forgotten lore" foregrounds the patriarchal aspect I have just referred to. For *lore* is a homophone of *Law*, indicating that Jean has "forgotten"—read: repressed—her father's—and hence her fiancé's—phallic rights. Vollin's obsessive behavior and his rapid descent into madness and sadism do the rest: the subtext is duly repressed in favor of a daughter knowing that her place is designated by the father.

What impossible desire is Vollin projecting? There are any number of clues. Long fascinated by Poe, Vollin has constructed beneath his mansion a torture chamber straight out of "The Pit and the Pendulum."[80] Having invited Jean, her father, her fiancé, and other guests to spend the weekend with him, he seals the house off from the outside world by means of steel shutters and, with the help of his servant/henchman Bateman (of whom more in a moment), takes the judge down to the torture chamber where he will be slowly sliced in two by the blade of the pendulum. Gloating, he says to his victim, "I tear torture out of myself by torturing you." The hideous act he is preparing will enable him to retrieve the *objet a*; just as it was "torn" from him by the never-accepted separation from the mother, so he will now literally "cut" into the body of the judge. When the latter told him he was "the only one" capable of saving his daughter, he unwittingly gave Vollin the satisfaction of being the phallus for the mother, a satisfaction all the more cruelly crushed by the father asserting his own phallic rights and thus forcing Vollin to relive the castration trauma. The judge's paternal role thus makes him an ideal object of Vollin's sadism, for it allows Vollin to punish his real father for forbidding his desire to be the phallus for the mother. Vollin's jubilant and sadistic laughter also shows him to be another instance of the obscene Father of Enjoyment.

Vollin's relation to Bateman contains elements that make things more clear. A murderer on the run who has behaved very much like Vollin—he turned an acetylene torch on a customer in a bank who did not obey his orders during a hold-up—Bateman persuades Vollin to change his face by plastic surgery. Seeing a way to turn Bateman into an invaluable ally in his plans for Jean, her father, and her fiancé, Vollin deliberately botches the operation, leaving Bateman looking like a monster, with one sightless eye and one side of his face paralyzed. Long ago Bateman had been told that he was ugly; he identified with this image of himself and put into practice literally the common prejudice that ugly people do ugly things. We have already seen how this is represented in *Freaks*, in which the freaks behave at the end exactly as society represents them. To put it another way: The discourse of the Other triggered in Bateman that aggressivity against the other that exists potentially in every subject since the mirror stage.

The Raven exploits literally this aggressivity of the mirror stage in a remarkable and unpleasant sequence in which Vollin reveals to Bateman how disfigured he is. After removing the bandages, Vollin leaves the room—whose walls are covered with mirrors—and watches, laughing sadistically, as Bateman discovers what he now looks like and how he is under Vollin's control: if he does what he is told, Vollin will mend his face.[81] Bateman cannot escape his hideous image; wherever he turns, he sees only that. In a scene that looks ahead strikingly to the "Hall of Mirrors" sequence at the end of *The Lady from Shanghai* (Orson Welles, 1947), Bateman shoots the mirrors to pieces. I would suggest that the film is showing us here what Vollin's madness is all about. Just as Bateman cannot escape his ugliness, so Vollin is under the control of something he cannot escape: the object-cause of his desire. Vollin's mutilation of Bateman is due to the same absent cause as his planned cutting up of the judge, and Bateman's shattering the mirrors literally mirrors Vollin's desire to destroy the other in an attempt to deny the lack in the big Other.

Here we return to the question of the place of the woman in patriarchy, for Vollin has offered the fiancé an important position as his assistant "to take the place of what he's losing." This odd remark condenses remarkably the various themes of the film. The fiancé will lose the daughter, but an exchange will take place whereby he gives her to Vollin and receives a job in return. At the same time, Vollin is acting out his refusal of the Law: the fiancé will renounce the phallus just as Vollin was forced to do, while the latter will retrieve it in the form of a newfound authority where he is "the only one" (to have it). Both Vollin and the father are anxious faced with a loss, but whereas Vollin's is psychic, the film can pass the father's anxiety off as social and highly commendable. Thus, a genuine disturbance of the patriarchal function is once again repressed by its displacement onto the case of an individual madman.

Both *Son of Frankenstein* and *Dr. X* have real and not symbolic parent-child relationships, but more intriguing is the fact that they have in common an element that extends the meaning of these relationships to the domain of desire: the ambiguity of their titles. Thus, the "son" referred to designates both Wolf von Frankenstein, who returns twenty years later to the place of his father's experiments, and Wolf's young son, Peter. However, another textual logic sets up between the monster and the little boy a relationship that complicates matters.[82] In the case of *Dr. X*, the title at once designates the leading character Dr. Xavier (Lionel Atwill) and implies the existence of an unknown doctor whose identity will be revealed at the end. The film is indeed constructed like a detective story, a fact that has led one critic to refer to the Atwill character as a "red herring."[83] This is perfectly accurate, and the film is an excellent example of Lacan's reminder that a subject can deceive by telling the truth. For, as we shall see presently, "X" not only refers to Xavier as doctor, but to Xavier as signifier having a certain effect on the spectators, thanks to the displacement at work via another doctor who is one of his collaborators. Thus, by really referring to Dr. Xavier, the title leads the spectator astray as to the film's unconscious themes of incest, male bonding, and voyeurism, all of which imply the subject positions the spectator is led to occupy.[84]

Let us turn first, however, to *Son of Frankenstein* and to the question of the referent of "Son." We shall soon see that the word is not a sign but a signifier whose signified is far removed from what seems to be the case. The film explicitly (just how explicitly will soon be apparent) presents itself as part of the continuing saga of Dr. Frankenstein, with the character of Wolf von Frankenstein (Basil Rathbone) filling the function of the son of the infamous scientist. However, Wolf in turn has a son of his own, Peter, who is about five years old. This fact in itself introduces an ambiguity into the title that we would be advised to take very seriously indeed, especially in the light of what *Frankenstein* has shown us concerning the creation of the monster. Much has been made of the intimately connected notions of "creation" and "procreation," and it is on this question that discussions of gender and homosexuality focus. It is necessary here to point out that Frankenstein's hysterical cry "It's alive!" looks ahead some forty years to Larry Cohen's film *It's Alive*, which concerns a baby that is a monster. If we take literally the notion that Frankenstein brings into the world a monster that has been "conceived" without the participation of a woman, then the signifier "son" also refers to the monster in *Son of Frankenstein* as the film turns on the survival of the creature and its activities.

Given this state of affairs, it might be more accurate and pertinent to use the term *polysemy* rather than *ambiguity*, all the more so as an incoherency is introduced by the third film in the series: the very *existence* of a son. This, of course, can be put down to the need to justify a third film but is such a crashing banality that it gets us nowhere. Rather, we should interpret it as a disavowal of the fact that Frankenstein did not have a son in either of the preceding films, and as a repression of the implications—that go far beyond homosexuality—of the relationships set up between male and female characters, on the one hand, and between male characters, on the other. We must therefore pay the closest attention to the way *Son of Frankenstein* refers to the past.

In the train transporting the family to the village where his father carried out his experiments, Wolf refers to his childhood in England and the stories his mother told him about his father's experiments and the monster. Even more to the point is a remark he makes on their arrival: he informs the mayor and the villagers that he never knew his father. Rather than simply attribute this to a question of explaining to the audience that the son did not appear because he had been sent to England (totally in conflict, moreover, with what the earlier films both said and showed), we must surely be struck by a structural parallel: just as Frankenstein brought a monster into the world without the participation of a woman, so Wolf was brought into the world in such a way that he never knew his father, *as if the latter had nothing to do with his birth.* This indicates patently the absence of an ego ideal for Wolf, who has nevertheless internalized the Name-of-the-Father in certain ways.

Let us pursue this reasoning, starting with this comment on *Son of Frankenstein* by Bryan Senn: "Everything is huge, oversized, on a massive scale. . . . Even the furniture is oversized. It's as if the castle were made not for ordinary mortals, but for beings of monstrous size and form, subtly reminding us of what this story revolves around."[85] This text echoes uncannily remarks made by Freud in his study "Family Romances." Just as Senn evokes literal size, so Freud does figurative size: the child replaces his parents with people belonging to a higher social category who in fact represent how the child actually saw his real parents early in those childhood days forever lost.[86] When we remember that the monster comes to visit Peter during the night thanks to a secret passage that only it/he and Ygor know, and that Peter refers to these visits as those of a "giant," then the film's status as a sort of "Grimm" fairytale becomes obvious. Peter, it must be noted at once, is in no way frightened but pleased and fascinated by the presence of the "giant," a fact whose implications are obvious in the light of the remarks quoted in the preceding paragraph. For it is not only the signifier "son" that does semantic overtime but the characters, too. We are therefore justified in claiming, first, that the monster is Wolf's "brother" and therefore Peter's "uncle"; second, that, as such, it/he functions as a surrogate father figure. Senn's most pertinent comment implies that all the characters seem to be inhabiting an enormous "doll's house," with the monster appearing as he must to the little boy: as "larger than life." I would argue in the light of these observations that we can refer to another film that would not have seen the light of day without *Frankenstein*, namely Mel Brooks's *Young Frankenstein*, which comes to the witty conclusion that, if the monster is built on such a huge scale, then all parts of him must be "larger than life," which means that it/he is "well endowed." In psychoanalytic terms, this can be construed as indicating, on the one hand, that Peter's desire is to be the phallus for his mother and, on the other hand, that he sees his own father as "inadequate." This in turn suggests that, just as Wolf never knew his father and therefore could identify with an ego ideal only by creating a fantasy figure, so the little boy Peter feels neglected by his own very self-centered father and turns to a substitute for compensation. Wolf has, in fact, found the ideal "fantasy figure" to identify with: himself as scientist and inheritor of his father's knowledge. Certain other aspects of the film tend to stress this narcissistic element in unexpected ways.

Let us begin with the artificial limb of Inspector Krogh, whose arm was torn out by the roots by the monster when he was a boy. As he points out, in a quite sublime euphemism, this is not the sort of event one tends to forget! If the castration imagery hardly needs to be stressed—the limb as stand-in for the *objet a* that the subject must renounce to enter the Symbolic order, the maternal phallus—what is less obvious is the parallel between the inspector and Peter, for Krogh lost his arm *when a boy*, a detail that hints at a form of displacement indicating the metonymy of desire. Peter at the same time wishes to be the phallus his mother desires and installs the monster in the place of his father, not simply to be able to identify with a more "adequate" ego ideal, but also to ward off the sort of hideous punishment meted out to Krogh. By turning his real father into someone far bigger and more powerful, he endows him with that strength and phallic power he finds he lacks and that he desires to exercise himself. This helps to explain why Wolf takes the visit of the "giant" seriously; it is less because he is afraid the monster will hurt his son than because he feels so inadequate himself as a father, a fact hardly independent of his unconscious grudge against his own father, Henry Frankenstein, for having neglected him.

Before trying to understand the psychoanalytic implications of the monster's attack on Krogh, we need to investigate the other aspects mentioned earlier. *Son of Frankenstein* sets up in the most systematic way a visual parallel between Wolf and Ygor. Just as we see Wolf and his wife looking out through the compartment of the train or through the windows of the castle, we see Ygor looking in, first through the same window, second through a secret panel in the wardrobe in Peter's room. Ygor, too, visits the little boy, but does not announce his presence. I propose to read these looks in terms of the primal scene, so central to a series of films based on (pro)creation and entangled sexual functions. Perhaps more pertinent for the film under discussion is the suggestion, via the function of the act of looking, that Wolf and Ygor are mirror images of one another, a manifestation of Wolf's narcissism: his identification with his own image as his ego ideal.[87] In which case, he and Ygor are each other's ego ideal, a notion that demands some explanation.

Just as the monster is the element that creates a semantic bridge between *Frankenstein* and *Son of Frankenstein*, so is Ygor. For he was once sentenced to death for grave robbing and hanged. However, although his neck was broken, he survived and therefore cannot be hanged again as he was actually pronounced dead. The magic of the verb has therefore made of Ygor a dead person, so he now functions as an example of the "living dead," back from the dead to get his revenge on those who sentenced him. And the monster, of course, is his weapon. It is impossible to contemplate this aspect of the film and not to recognize the parallel with *Frankenstein*, where Henry and Fritz cut down a hanged man in order to have material to work on to create the monster. If we take literally the notion of the dead being transformed into a new body that is then brought to life by the scientist, then we must see the various corpses as participating in the creation of a new "man." In other words the monster is just as much their "offspring" as it is Frankenstein's. At the risk of sounding ghoulish, the corpses function as the woman Frankenstein was able to do without.[88] From the standpoint of the social functions filled by the characters, Ygor steps into the shoes of Henry Frankenstein, especially as he turns the monster into a tool—"He does things for me," as he significantly puts it. We are therefore obliged to conclude that Ygor, too, is a father figure. But of what kind?

If Ygor's remark, within the conscious logic of the text, means that he gets the creature to carry out his murders for him—Ygor and the monster thus function like the aptly named Murder Legendre and his zombies in *White Zombie*—we can also see the metonymy of desire at work, this time on the level of a preposition. I propose to rewrite this statement as "He does things to me." Once again, I refuse to interpret this in the simplistic terms of homosexual male bonding, but rather to see Ygor as the obscene Father of Enjoyment returning from the dead, unheeding of any law or Law, to satisfy his drives. For we must not forget that, if Ygor represents Henry Frankenstein, then the monster is Ygor's "son." The monster ripping Krogh's arm out by the roots is repeated in the monster murdering Ygor's persecutors one after the other; after all, Henry Frankenstein was also a grave robber! This in turn means that the monster, in killing and maiming once Henry had lost control of him/it, was really carrying out Henry's unconscious desire to punish society for trying to force him into a masculine mould he refused. Dead, yet not dead, excluded from the daily life of the community, Ygor returns in the place of the dead Henry to collect a form of "symbolic debt," an act and a function duly displaced and disguised as simple vengeance.

We are now perhaps in the position of being able to offer one explanation for the completely unconvincing ending of the film in which the villagers suddenly acclaim Wolf as their savior despite the fact that his behavior has shown him to be far more ambitious and unscrupulous than his father. For the monster, by turning the unfortunate Krogh's body into an object of obscene enjoyment, also functions as the Father of Enjoyment, hence the film's need to defuse the ideologically intolerable connotations of the monster visiting little Peter. By eliminating the creature and killing Ygor, Wolf has done more than save lives: "Since the primal father is the principle of *jouissance*, of excess enjoyment, the signifier of his absence will be the son who promises to protect society from the trauma of *jouissance*'s return. The son stands for the evacuation, or drying up, of excess enjoyment and thus for the possibility of pleasure's even apportionment."[89] By transforming Wolf's paranoid and narcissistic determination to carry on in his father's footsteps—which creates a further parallel between Wolf and Ygor—into a heroic act, the film in turn transforms him into "Jack the Giant Killer" and thus reinforces his function as phallic patriarch that the film's unconscious discourse, true to the spirit of Whale's two movies, had sought to deconstruct. The fact that one critic has referred to Rathbone's excellent performance as "embarrassingly hysterical,"[90] thus foregrounding the way the series of three films upset gender conventions, only goes to show the role of disavowal on the part of both films and critics alike. Incoherencies are always interpreted as aesthetic flaws, never the presence of some "absent cause" determining the effect they have on us.

My reading of *Dr. X*—one of the most "unhealthy" and disturbing movies of the period from the point of view of orthodoxy in matters of gender and sexuality—owes much to Rhona Berenstein's cogent analysis.[91] Evoking the film's "homosocial encounters among men," she goes on in these terms:

> Homosocial desire—social bonds underscored by an erotic thrust—is a significant narrative attribute in the majority of 1930s mad-doctor movies. In one sense, then, this is a subgenre that celebrates male homosexuality by ensuring that a repressed component of dominant culture returns with a vengeance.
>
> These movies also figure homosexuality as the culmination of misogynistic impulses, the ultimate in patriarchal power, and a sign of the oppression and elision of women.[92]

If Berenstein also raises the question of incest, I shall insist on this factor. By so doing, I am in no way attempting to substitute one reading for another but simply to extend the argument to embrace other aspects.

Dr. X is an early "serial killer" movie about a murderer referred to by the press as "the moon killer," as he has killed six people in as many months, always at the time of the full moon. The murders are committed "by means of strangulation and an incision with a strange surgical knife," in the words of the police commissioner to Dr. Xavier, owner and director of a private research laboratory where just such knives are used. This is yet another red herring, to which must be added the four researchers working under Xavier.[93] These are Professor Wells, presented as a "student of cannibalism"; Professors Haines and Rowitz, who, with a third man, survived a shipwreck but who were alone when picked up; and Professor Duke, a club-footed cripple who can move about only in a wheelchair or on crutches. Already referred to as a red herring, Xavier is in fact doubly so: as Bryan Senn has pertinently reminded us, the film finds him "complaining at one point about the 'ghastly' moonlight bothering him."[94] Other factors lead us to suspect Xavier, according to the codes of the detective thriller rather than to those of the horror movie (which should, I might add, incite us to use a certain amount of caution). First, Xavier has a theory about the killer, which is a way of suggesting that a character is trying to deceive by telling the truth. Xavier sees the killer as victim of a "fixation," a "past experience," adding for the benefit of the spectator rather than the more than skeptical commissioner: "The madness only comes at certain times when the killer is brought into contact with some vivid reminder of the past." If we remember that an "experience" in the unconscious can designate a desire that is striving for realization, it is clear that the film is putting forward a Freudian interpretation, confirmed immediately afterward when Xavier taps his head, saying, "Locked in the human brain is a little world all its own," adding that "the full moon, anything" could act as such a reminder, thus making of the moon a signifier, a clue we would be advised not to forget.

Tapping one's head is, of course, a way of indicating madness in some person under discussion, so this can be interpreted as yet another red herring inviting the audience to suspect Xavier. To this must be added another element: Xavier's clothes and diction. He is wearing spats and a coat with a large fur collar, the former being a signifier of "Englishness."[95] Atwill, of course, was English, with a rich, upper-class accent. Xavier is thus in a position to be transformed into the paradigm of the English homosexual, just as my favorite example—Waldo Lydecker—will also function in *Laura*. Lydecker may be an American, but he is just as removed from the America represented by detective Mark McPherson as Xavier is from the world of the commissioner. Once we take into account that gay director James Whale and gay actor Charles Laughton were English and that most of the actors incarnating mad doctors and the like in the 1930s were from Europe, then we should be very much on our guard when it comes to "queer" connotations in these films.[96] The matter goes far beyond homosocial relations. I suggest that this element is displaced in the film and finds a most unusual form of representation: when journalist Lee Taylor (Lee Tracy) arrives at Xavier's home to do some snooping, he drives up in a horse-drawn carriage! This suggests London at the end of the last century, the London of Oscar Wilde and Jack the Ripper, for instance, and shows how the institutionalized censorship of the Hays Code and the discourse of the ideological big Other can overdetermine each other in filmic texts.

Two key scenes in the film put a certain number of factors in place. Berenstein concentrates on the second, relegating the former to a footnote. I wish to accord equal weight to both: their articulation is essential to grasp what is going on. In the first scene, Xavier's daughter comes across him in his library; in the second, she disturbs him in his laboratory during the night. I shall describe the scenes shot by shot, attempting to place them as accurately as possible in their context. Between the two scenes Xavier has carried out an experiment (which I shall discuss later) in an effort to determine the killer. It misfires, and Professor Rowitz is murdered. It is his body that is lying in the laboratory during the second sequence.

A1: A shot of a plaque bearing the inscription "Academy of Surgical Research."

A2: A dissolve to a medium close-up of Xavier on a ladder, looking for a book.

A3: A long shot of Xavier, then pan to a closed door; it opens and a young woman enters. She looks up to the right, off-screen, and screams.

A4: A cut to a clearly frightened Xavier: "What is it?" he cries.

A5: A cut to the young woman, who runs to the window and throws up a blind to let the light in. "Father!" she cries.

A6: A medium close-up of Xavier: "It's you, Joanne. What is it, dear?" As he descends the ladder, she replies (off-screen left), "Nothing. I just came in here to say good night to you."

A7: Xavier walks up to her. "Father, what are you doing here in the dark? You frightened me!"

A8: He pulls the blind down again, making the remark (already referred to) about the moonlight being "ghastly."

A9: He admits to being "a little nervous."

A10: They kiss.

A11: Xavier leaves by another door, turning to give Joanne a "strange look."

A12: She exits by door she came in, turning to give him an equally "strange look."

B1: A long shot of the daughter in bed, asleep, and muttering "Father."

B2: A cut to a door opening, throwing light on the floor, and a man wearing spats coming through; we cannot tell if he is leaving or entering the room.

B3: A cut back to the daughter, who wakes up at the sound of a door slamming; she puts on the light and gets out of bed.

B4: A cut to her in the corridor trying the handle of her father's bedroom, crying, "Father!" but the door is locked.

B5: She starts to descend the stairs; cut to the inside of a laboratory where a man is doing something behind the sheet covering an unidentified body. Joanne appears in the background and opens the door.

B6: She is framed alone in the shot, looks off-screen right and screams.

B7: A return to the same framing as in B5; Xavier emerges from under the sheet.

B8: "I just wanted to make sure the incision was made by a brain scalpel"; the audience now knows the body is that of Professor Rowitz.

B9: They are about to leave when Professor Haines appears, claiming he wanted to make a more thorough examination of the body.

B10: Daughter to father: "Will you please come to bed?" He says he'll be right up, escorts her to the door, where they kiss. He walks back toward Haines.

B11: A shot of the sinister butler, hiding and watching.

B12: Haines: "Professor, since we retired, this body has been . . . it's been . . . ." Xavier: "I know, but I don't want her to know."

I believe that it is futile to analyze the second sequence without placing it in the context of what the first sequence shows. Certain remarks must be made about the sequence in the library. First, Xavier was not in the dark as Joanne says: there were two lights burning, one at the top of the ladder, the other on a table at the foot of the ladder. Second, if Joanne came into the library to say goodnight, then she obviously expected him to be there, so why be so terrified at the presence of a figure on the ladder, as it can logically only be Xavier? Third, Xavier wanting to avoid the moonlight is certainly significant, but so is Joanne's fear of the dark. It would be more precise to say she is afraid of the *dark*, while he is afraid of a certain kind of *light*.

Similarly, certain points need to be made about the sequence in the laboratory. First, Xavier is in the dark. Second, Joanne opens the door, looks off-screen right, and screams in a way that repeats exactly the earlier sequence. Third, Xavier escorts his daughter to the door and they kiss; this is another exact repetition of the earlier sequence. Fourth, Joanne saying "Father" in her sleep leads to a shot where we cannot tell if the character (obviously Xavier because of the spats) is leaving *his* room or entering *hers*; the cause-effect of Hollywood editing can suggest either, but the fact she is saying "Father" lends weight that he comes in answer to her call/desire. Fifth, the dialogue between Xavier and Haines does indeed suggest something "unspeakable" between men, as Berenstein has suggested, especially as the woman is got rid of so that the men can discuss matters. Where does all this lead?

My argument is the following, although it will be tempered later. Joanne's fear of the dark and terror at the presence of her father stem from the sequence representing for her the revival of the primal scene and her desire to occupy the mother's place, a "fixation" in which the repressed returns when the circumstances are favorable. Hence my wish to insist on the juxtaposition of the first two shots of the second sequence in which I suggest that it is her calling "Father" in her sleep that calls up the shot of his feet: it is as if he is entering her room as an answer to what can be seen as desire becoming manifest during sleep. No wonder she wakes up with a start: the Real of her desire has come too close for comfort. The articulation of the two sequences clearly foregrounds the young woman's incestuous desire. After all, she does ask her father to "*come* to bed," whereas we would have expected her to say "*go back* to bed." "Come to bed" is a form of sexual invitation, whereas "go back to bed" is an order. However, this incestuous dimension certainly does not rule out the possibility of something else nasty going on under the sheet. The fact that Xavier and a dead man are involved, that Haines comes in to, as it were, take over from Xavier when the latter has to comfort his daughter, quite clearly suggests a social order where men are accomplices to keep women "in the dark" and where it is women who come across as the neurotics. I am not unaware that my reading risks categorizing Joanne thus. However, there is evidence aplenty that Xavier is not just the *object* of incestuous desire but its *subject*, too. In order to clarify the situation, we shall have to turn to the sequence where the killings are acted out in what is an even more remarkable example of metacinema than *King Kong*.

The sequence is a reprise of an earlier one where Xavier's experiment goes wrong and results in the murder of Rowitz. Another element changes too, for the film shows who the moon killer is: Professor Wells. He has created, with the help of the flesh he has cannibalized, synthetic flesh which has enabled him to replace his artificial hand. After making himself up as the moon killer, he puts his synthetic hand in place and brings it to life via that stalwart, electricity. What must be retained here is the clearly phallic nature of the hand: as the electricity gives it life, the look on Wells's face indicates clearly that he is having an orgasm. He then kills the butler who is about to repeat his performance and takes the man's place. In the place of a murder victim, killed in her hospital bed by the moon killer, is none other than Xavier's daughter. The sequence continues as follows:

C1: The camera is placed behind Xavier, Haines, and Duke, strapped into chairs as before; the three men are watching a sort of raised stage, with Joanne on a bed in the middle and figures representing the earlier victims in the background.
C2: A cut to a medium shot of the killer advancing towards the bed.
C3: A huge close-up of Joanne looking off-screen right.
C4: A huge close-up of the killer about to strangle her.
C5: The truth dawns on Joanne, who screams, "It's the killer!"
C6: A cut to a close-up of Xavier: "It's the killer!"
C7: A cut to a close-up of Haines: "It's the killer!"

There then follow shots of the men struggling to free themselves and of general shots that are a reprise of C1.

C8: A shot of the killer bending over Joanne and covering/straddling her body as if about to have sex with her.

The insane Wells tells Xavier he has given everything to science, except one thing, and now he is going to give that, too: his daughter. The three men can only struggle with their bonds and look on helplessly. Suddenly one of the figures comes to life: it is Lee Taylor who tackles the moon killer. A struggle ensues during which Taylor throws a lamp at the killer and then pushes him through a window. He falls to his death on the rocks below.

The sequence described is not simply a *mise en abyme* of the act of going to the cinema and watching a spectacle. It also reproduces the passive, masochistic position of the spectators (both those of the film and those in the sequence) who, having identified with the hapless victim, cannot do anything to help and suffer with her. Or, as Berenstein puts it, "Men are as profoundly victimized as she is in this sequence. . . . While male spectatorship has a sadistic reputation (which the professors put into effect by vicariously enjoying the *sight* of the heroine's attack), it is profoundly masochistic as well (they are as helpless as she)."[97]

This was nicely given to us in the form of a clue early in the film where, referring to Wells's artificial hand and his inability to kill by strangulation, the commissioner says, "That lets him out of the picture." Wells returns (like the repressed), but not just as the moon killer: he returns as Xavier's representative to carry out on Joanne's supine body what Xavier would like to do.[98] If I have concentrated on Joanne's incestuous desire for her father, I have left until now the corollary: the reciprocity of such desire. The notion of "acts between men" is taken literally in the film, where each of the professors can act as a stand-in for the others. Thus, Haines is seen spying on the daughter and the journalist as they lie on the beach. This clear, if displaced, representation of Xavier watching the couple finds other forms in the film. We see an eye looking through a hidden hole in the wall and watching the couple: is it the butler, Wells, or Xavier? It matters little, for the dominant structure is one of the control of the young woman by the men, representing Xavier's desire to possess her. The virtual copulation on stage is eloquent testimony to this.

And it is here, perhaps, that the homosexual element can be seen to return. The sequence where the doctors are tied to chairs and forced to watch as the killer makes his attack on Joanne can surely be seen as a literal form of "male bondage," a reworking of the flogging scene in *The Mask of Fu Manchu* and the scene where Fu Manchu administers both torture and caresses to the helpless Sir Lionel; or the scene in *Mad Love* where Gogol massages/caresses Orlac's hand. In this reading, the attack on Joanne is a displaced form of a male desire to enjoy the bodies of the doctors, held firmly in place by their bonds. We can also interpret the sequence as the staging of an infantile fantasy of union with the father duly transformed into the masochistic desire to be tied up and beaten. The formula "working under" Dr. Xavier has become decidedly polysemic.

What, then, is being represented in *Dr. X*? I would argue that, if Wells is a stand-in for Xavier, this is to displace onto the insane killer an aspect of Xavier's character that cannot be admitted. Wells is halfway between a cannibal and a vampire; as such, his return on stage as the moon killer is the film's representation of the Real, but in the form of a monster that we cannot consciously identify with Xavier. Yet the cuts from Wells onstage to Xavier in the audience make it as plain as possible that Wells is acting out Xavier's impossible desire for his daughter. Wells, monstrous and hideous, is surely the obscene Father of Enjoyment, come back to have his way with the daughter's body. As such, he is another early version of the character of

Freddy Krueger in *Nightmare on Elm Street.*[99] If Xavier is helpless in the audience, then it is also because he does not want to stop what is happening onstage: it is the literal enactment of his desire. His unpleasure stems both from the fact of being helpless (a feminine position) and an understanding of what is happening. The sudden and unheralded appearance of the journalist is also the manifestation of desire, the response of the superego to this impossible obscene enjoyment, the triumph of the discourse of the Law represented by the Other. The young man at once vanquishes the moon killer, exorcises the obscene father's desire, and weds the grateful heroine, saved from a fate worse than death, a fate all the more horrific as she desired it. But the true ambiguity of this fascinating movie lies primarily in the male figure designated by the title, which just as clearly means that "acts between men" also entail choosing which partner will be chosen for the passive heroine. Joanne can no more save herself without male help than Ann Darrow can get back to civilization alone. Which nicely removes all the contradictions set up by the tensions existing between desire and socially acceptable gender positions and functions, while enabling the spectator to forget how cowardly the hero was shown to be prior to the spectacular ending.

Good Lookers

The look is arguably the element that most clearly links the various themes brought to the fore in *Dr. X.* We have both the female look off-screen that seems to evoke some nameless horror without anything being made specific, and the sadistic look of the male spectator that is suddenly transformed into a passive, masochistic look by the circumstances and the modes of identification. Another kind of look, however, is central to horror: the hypnotic look.[100] I wish to approach the question in three ways: first, by analyzing *White Zombie*; second, by discussing publicity material used to sell *The Devil-Doll* and *Dr. Cyclops*; third, by describing posters used to advertise other films belonging to our corpus. I shall conclude with an analysis of *The Walking Dead* by way of the material used to advertise the film.

Freud has stated how hypnosis both resembles and differs from being in love. After insisting on the absence of sexuality in the hypnotic relation, he refers to the sensation of paralysis induced by this special relation between a person endowed with power and one reduced to a state of helplessness.[101] As far as the storyline of *White Zombie* is concerned, these remarks correspond to the situation in which both Madeline and Beaumont find themselves. We need to keep the plot in mind. Madeline and Neil are in Haiti to be married, and Beaumont falls under the spell, so to speak, of the young woman whom he has met on the boat. Murder Legendre, a voodoo expert with uncanny hypnotic powers, agrees to help Beaumont by arranging for Madeline to take a poison that will result in her being reduced to a state akin to catalepsy and thus pronounced dead. After the burial, she will be removed from her tomb and delivered into the hands of the obsessed Beaumont. Once he has Madeline and Beaumont in his castle, however, Legendre reveals he has other plans for the young lady and reduces Beaumont to a state of near paralysis by poisoning his wine. When Neil, who has followed the trio to the castle with missionary Dr. Bruner (an expert on voodoo), finds his way into the castle, Legendre locks his hands together in order to concentrate and to impose his will on Madeline so that she will kill Neil. Needless to say, love triumphs. What does need to be stressed, however, is who is in love and the nature of that love.

Beaumont's love for Madeline is presented as more intense than Neil's, another example of the rather insipid hero; "mad love" is far more interesting and intense in the horror film than conventional heterosexual love leading to marriage:

> Surprising as it may seem, given the genre's reputation, most of classic horror's heroes are feminized men. Yet the genre does not let all gender codes run amuck. In the final moments of most film, the hero gets the girl and clasps her to his chest or lips to make sure that she does not get away again. His prior failures are seemingly forgotten and he takes his place as a real man. The hope is that since the monster is believed to be dead, ontological and gender instability evaporate, and traditional roles are firmly in place.[102]

The scene where Beaumont escorts her down the staircase of his home to be wed to Neil gives the distinct impression that she is already a zombie, which suggests her unconscious attitude to her official husband-to-be and her future state as a zombie in which she will belong to Beaumont. This notion is taken up at the end of the film in such a way that it is impossible to attribute her state to some literal-minded dimension of incompetent acting. The way she relates to the three men in her life when under the influence of Legendre's poison—Neil, Beaumont, and Legendre—indicates that other matters must be taken into consideration.

In one strikingly filmed sequence Madeline comes out onto a balcony of Legendre's castle and stares vacantly into space. Neil, down with a fever and resting on the beach while Bruner goes in search of a way into the castle, suddenly rises to his feet, staring off-screen left, and mutters "Madeline!" The screen is divided into two, with Madeline on the upper left and Neil on the lower right of the screen. However, she is much too far away for him to be able to pick her out, so the image cannot but indicate that particular state to which Freud referred on several occasions in which one mind enters into communication unconsciously with another mind. Moreover, Madeline's zombielike state prevents her from indicating any awareness of Neil's presence, and all we can conclude at this point from this visual reworking of *Romeo and Juliet* is that the film is attempting to indicate "true love" may still triumph. It is the sequence that follows, after Neil has managed to find a way into the castle and is spotted by Legendre, that enables us to propose a less conventional interpretation of what we have just seen to demonstrate that the mutual love existing between Neil and Madeline is not that powerful.

Legendre approaches Neil's unconscious body, turns toward the camera, and gives a smile worthy of Count Dracula. His staring eyes look directly into the camera as it zooms in on his face. Cut to a shot of Madeline rising from the bed where she has been lying motionless, then making her way into the hall. Legendre has returned to the table where Beaumont, helplessly paralyzed but conscious, watches as she picks up a knife under Legendre's influence and moves in the direction of Neil. There then ensue the following shots:

Shot 1: Madeline raises the knife to stab Neil.
Shot 2: A medium close-up of Beaumont clearly trying to cry out to stop her, but his state prevents him from uttering as much as a sound.
Shot 3: She lowers the knife and looks around her as if wondering what is happening.
Shot 4: A huge close-up of Legendre's glowing eyes fills the screen.
Shot 5: A hand appears from behind a curtain to stop her blow.
Shot 6: A close-up of Legendre's locked hands working madly.
Shot 7: Madeline runs away from Neil's body.

The point to be retained from this sequence of shots is that the juxtaposition of shots 2 and 3 suggests that Beaumont has entered into communication with Madeline and momentarily stopped her from stabbing Neil. That this lasts only a moment and that Legendre regains control with an effort does not detract from the only valid interpretation: Beaumont has managed to rival Legendre's hypnotic power via the strength of his own love for Madeline, a love that is thus patently far stronger than Neil's, for the latter failed to enter into contact with Madeline in the sequence described earlier. The representation of events in the hall of the castle therefore only goes to show that Madeline is far more sensitive to Beaumont than to Neil, so the ending where Beaumont throws Legendre over the cliff and falls/leaps over after him—the possibility of suicide is unmistakably present—is simply a way of presenting a typical happy ending that flies in the face of what the film has shown. More than that is at stake, however.

The character of Neil has been shown to be not only insipid but as having the usual racial prejudices: when told by Bruner after they have discovered Madeline's body is missing from her resting place that she may be in the hands of the natives, he cries out, "Better dead than that!" In other words, Madeline may be suffering "a fate worse than death." This formula, whether used solemnly or flippantly, indicates that the heroine's virtue is under assault, and in the context of the film's setting we can see at work the old fantasy of white maidens raped by blacks. Neil's remark must, however, be seen in the context of another remark made twice by Beaumont: "No, not that!" No further information is afforded the spectator. The first time it is uttered, Beaumont is distraught at the idea that Madeline will soon be married to another man. Legendre whispers something into his ear and, aghast, he speaks the enigmatic formula. We assume later that he is referring to turning the young woman into a zombie, but this is by no means the only meaning possible if we take into account other details.

At one point during the final sequences in the castle, as Legendre is sitting at a table with the partially paralyzed and now-speechless Beaumont, the latter's hand advances painfully and tremulously across the table to grasp Legendre's; Legendre pats it with his other hand, saying, "You refused to shake hands with me once." Legendre's poisoning of Beaumont precedes the *Romeo and Juliet* sequence already discussed. Unseen by his victim, Legendre slips something into a glass of wine, and they drink. Beaumont's failure to see what Legendre has done is due to his state over Madeline being a zombie: he has her but she cannot respond, a point to which we shall return in a moment. Beaumont suddenly realizes from the smell what Legendre has done, and the latter makes the following remark: "I have other plans for Madeline, and you may not agree. I have taken a fancy to you, Monsieur." Horror-stricken, Beaumont asks the butler to help him, and the man raises a tray to strike Legendre, who turns and stares at him. There is a cut to a POV shot of Legendre staring at the butler/the camera and the image going out of focus. The camera cuts to a shot of the butler, as horror-stricken as Beaumont. Legendre's zombie servants enter and carry the butler off.

At this juncture, the vulture that heralds Legendre exercising control over an unsuspecting victim appears screeching at the window, and Beaumont, for the second time, cries, "No, not that!" The spectators can interpret this as an indication of Beaumont's realization that he is about to suffer the same fate as Madeline. But there is a problem with logic and continuity here. Beaumont has already, by the look on his face, shown that he knows he is poisoned, and Legendre confirms the fact by repeating the expression "only a pinpoint," already used when planning the fate of Madeline with the same Beaumont. Another meaning to the relationship Legendre/Beaumont is coming to the surface, one that is intimately linked to the concept of "a fate worse than death." The film appears to have given us more than a clue when Legendre says that he has "taken a fancy" to Beaumont. This comment, it will be claimed, indicates overt homosexual advances on Legendre's part—so overt, in fact, that one wonders why censorship did not take place. However, we should pay closer attention to what Legendre also says: "I have other plans for Madeline, and you may not agree."

This is hardly a limpid statement. Just as it can indicate that Legendre intends killing Madeline in order to have Beaumont to himself, so it can suggest something quite different and, I would argue, more likely to trigger anxiety than a verbal attempt at homosexual seduction. Beaumont has just admitted to Legendre "I thought beauty alone would suffice" to describe his feelings for Madeline. We must surely see this as an unsuccessful attempt at sublimation on his part, stemming from a fear of not being able to function as a husband to Madeline: unable to satisfy her sexually, he nevertheless wants her near him for always. But he now realizes that being in the company of "a living doll" is not compensation enough. Beaumont is clearly bisexual, a fact he represses by sublimating all sexual desire and seeking satisfaction in the proximity of the loved but unattainable object, exactly as Gogol does with the wax figure of Yvonne Orlac in Mad Love. This homosexual component to his sexual constitution turns Madeline into the ideal but inaccessible woman, a sort of maternal figure he can worship but never possess physically. Where does Legendre fit in?

We have left aside until now an element of the story that seems to indicate a breakdown of conscious logic. Whereas Madeline is reduced to a zombie by Legendre's poison, Beaumont is paralyzed but remains perfectly conscious of what is going on and what is happening to him. As Legendre's powers can be seen as a variant on those of the hypnotist, I suggest we shall find an answer to this by turning again to Freud, who compares the relation between the compliant subject of hypnosis and the hypnotist to that between a member of the primal horde and the primal father.[103] I propose, then, that we see White Zombie as a working-out of a pre-Oedipal fantasy where Legendre plays a father figure of a very particular kind: the obscene Father of Enjoyment whose sole interest is to dispose sexually of the characters he desires, without any concern for their sex. His drives must be satisfied, Beaumont and Madeline functioning indifferently as the means to that end.[104]

Moreover, as far as Beaumont's unconscious desires are concerned, we have a sort of obscene parody of the Oedipal triangle, where the three characters enjoy one another indiscriminately under the aegis of the obscene Father who orchestrates everything. These, then, are Legendre's plans, and both Beaumont and the butler seize on the implications of his remarks at the same time, which means that the butler could also be about to suffer the same "fate worse than death" as Beaumont and Madeline did when carried off by the zombies. This, I would suggest, is why Legendre's face goes out of focus for the butler/for the spectators. The cinematic device functions as the signifier of the disintegration of the character's very being as the Real becomes manifest through Legendre's pursuit of his drives. At the same time, there is a displacement onto the butler of the anxiety at the heart of Beaumont's being— caused by his bisexuality but represented in terms of being turned into a zombie—and a recentering of the truth of desire by having the spectators identify with the butler's vision, a vision that corresponds to the proximity of the impossible Real. When Beaumont says of Madeline that he would rather see hatred in her eyes "than that dreadful emptiness," he is at once admitting guilt over the nature of his desire for her—she would hate him for it—and revealing through language the meaning of the Real, a form of living death.

Various documents pertaining to how the studios themselves conceived the films they produced (press books, posters, lobby cards, etc.) bring to light prejudices and ideologies that are eloquent inasmuch as they both reveal those unconscious forces that are our concern here and contradict the films in question. I shall proceed in stages: (1) a comparative analysis of material used to advertise *Dr. Cyclops* and *The Devil-Doll*, then an analysis of the films themselves; (2) a brief discussion of posters reproduced in Bryan Senn's *Golden Horrors*; and (3) a study of material used to advertise *The Walking Dead* that will enable us to draw certain conclusions.

I have already referred to publicity material concerning *Dr. Cyclops* at the start of this chapter, but I wish to turn now to the place occupied by the central character, Dr. Thorkel, in the sales techniques. What I have had to say above is enough to show that the distance separating the film from the publicity material at hand[105] is far more than a simple case of poetic license. Two separate posters concentrate on Thorkel's spectacles with their thick lenses and pronounced rims; the first shows his right eye in shadow and the left eye lit up; the second has a beam of light emanating from the left eye and pinpointing the heroine lying prostrate on the ground. The link with the film's story is tenuous indeed, although we could assimilate the eye to the microscope he uses periodically. Far more to the point, however, is the question of the all-powerful, all-embracing look and the presence of the beam of light. On a straightforward level of symbolism, it represents the woman as spectacle, lit up on a stage—or represented on the screen by the cinema projector—and subjected to the male character's sadistic gaze.[106] Within the logic of the documents, she is manifestly the object of his desire, although Thorkel shows no interest in her as a woman whatsoever. She is a guinea pig like all the others, but this was obviously considered insufficient to pull the crowds in. As already stated, the ending of the film confirms this ideological ploy blatantly by seeming so obviously tacked on.

I propose the following interpretation. At one point in the film, Thorkel says to the victims of his experiment, "So, you would spy on me!" Given the fact that they can, at least at this juncture, do nothing to harm him, we might be justified in seeing this as a case of paranoia, brought on by the return of the repressed. There is a reactivation of the primal scene by the character's being reminded of a very particular act of spying. This reading would in turn allow us to see his experiments as a perfect manifestation of sublimation, but not simply in the context of the film. From a censorship standpoint, such experiments do indeed enable the film to displace the question of sexuality, so the total absence of any love interest and the unconvincing way it is dragged unceremoniously onto the scene in what is literally the film's last sequence is the unconscious representation of censorship stemming from both the production codes and Thorkel's real function in the movie: that of primal father, for his experiments represent his complete control over the bodies and activities of his victims, thus inscribing the theme into the film via a thematic displacement overdetermined by sublimation. The advertising material, however, represents the situation differently, as we have seen earlier in the chapter. One poster has Thorkel holding the scantily clad heroine in one hand. Such a situation does exist in the film, but it is the elderly scientist who is so treated, prior to being suffocated (I refer the reader back to the remarks made earlier). What we have here is a throwback to director Schoedsack's *King Kong.* By putting Thorkel in the place of the giant ape, the poster is suggesting that he is about to inflict the customary "fate worse than death" on the hapless heroine. What the unconscious of the publicity discourse is also saying is something that cannot be expressed consciously— namely, that the woman is and should be subjected to the man's point of view for the correct functioning of society and its attendant ideologies. Thus, the heroine is placed metaphorically in her male colleague's hands in the last shot, just as she is placed literally in those of Thorkel in the advertisement.

When we turn to the discourse of publicity accompanying *The Devil-Doll,* things become even more complex. A whole series of posters aimed at the press concentrates on two details: the head of the Devil, complete with horns and surrounded by flames, and eyes (always both eyes) from which emanate the same intense beam we have referred to in connection with *Dr. Cyclops*. Clearly reference is being made to the original script that turned on voodoo until various censorship problems nipped the theme in the bud.[107] More to the point is the explicit link between a remark made in the film itself and this visual representation of a form of hypnotic power. The main character, Lavond, has escaped from Devil's Island with an elderly scientist who has succeeded in reducing animals and people to a fraction of their normal size and hopes to use this power to help humanity.[108] Once so reduced, both humans and animals take on the appearance of dolls, but they can be reanimated by the application of the mental powers of a person of normal stature. The scientist's wife refers at one point to "the beam of his thought," which, taken literally, is transferred via the publicity material to the look, which is then privileged as the locus of power and control. Thus, just as the count's look in *Dracula*, that of Ardath Bey in *The Mummy*, and Legendre's locked hands in *White Zombie* result in a character being henceforth completely under their control, so in *The Devil-Doll* Lavond, after the death of the scientist, has only to concentrate his mental powers while looking in the direction of his victim for the dolls under his control to come to life and carry out his murderous designs.

I shall propose a political reading of these and other phenomena redolent in the movies under discussion in the following chapters and shall limit the discussion here to a more explicitly psychoanalytic approach. A few comments are in order on publicity material relating to *The Invisible Man*, *Werewolf of London*, *Mad Love*, and *The Walking Dead*.[109] The poster for Whale's film looks ahead to both *The Devil-Doll* and *Dr. Cyclops*, particularly to the former as beams of light emanate from both of the eyes of the central character. Once again this betrays a cavalier disregard for the story, indicating that something repressed is becoming manifest via the publicity. The sexual angle is rendered explicit in the poster for *Werewolf of London* where "WARNING!" is accompanied by the following revealing text:

TO HYSTERICAL WOMEN!
SHUT YOUR EYES!

Presumably nonhysterical women can be trusted enough to be allowed, like all men, to keep their eyes open and actually watch the movie, but as we shall see presently, such warnings function less to titillate than to represent something that cannot find expression in the films themselves.

The *Mad Love* poster is even more interesting in that it shows both Dr. Gogol and the feminine object of his obsession looking out at the potential spectator, she appearing terrified, he mad and intense. It is as if the two were contemplating themselves/one another in a mirror, but another reading is possible, and it is here that we move into the uncanny territory opened up by the publicity campaign for *The Walking Dead*.

Given the look on the heroine's face, which on a literal level can be attributed to Gogol's firm grip on her shoulders, it is as if she were facing something too horrible to contemplate. It is precisely this dimension that is systematically exploited by a series of posters for *The Walking Dead*. Senn reproduces one of these, a shot of a totally bald Boris Karloff as John Elman (the innocent man sent to the electric chair who is brought back to life by scientist Evan Beaumont (Edmund Gwenn) and who proceeds to hunt down the gangsters responsible for his execution), looking out at us, with the figure of a young woman in an evening dress superimposed on his grim face. Other posters represent the Karloff character as having a full head of hair, which corresponds to his actual appearance in the film. What these posters have in common, however, is the presence of a woman staring out at the spectator in horror and throwing up her hands as if to protect herself or, more pertinently, to hide her eyes. At the same time we must notice that the posters suggest that it is the Karloff character of whom she is terrified and that she is protecting her look from his. Yet both he and she are looking *out* at the spectator. It is this element of the publicity material that needs to be addressed.

The posters encourage the spectators to believe that the young woman depicted has seen the horror represented by a man, irrespective of aspect or intent, returning from the dead. There is a certain logic to this interpretation, but it is surely the logic of the supernatural and does not explain the literal form of the posters that I propose we take at their face value. In that case, the gaze of the Karloff character does not coincide with the gaze of the terrified woman, who is the spectator's representative within the posters and, by extension, within the filmic text. The fact that there is no terrified woman in the film, however, has strictly nothing to do with the matter; it is how the film was conceived that concerns us here. Either we interpret the terrified gaze as being due to the woman seeing us, which makes no sense; or else we conclude that the fact that the two gazes within the posters do not and cannot meet means that the young woman is terrified precisely because she sees nothing at all, that there is a gap, an absence at work that the Karloff character is meant to fill. An object that instills fear is far less unnerving than a nonobject that can only trigger anguish: Lacan's *objet a*. We must then conclude that we are in the domain theorized by Joan Copjec—namely, that the subject is "cut off" from the gaze that does not see it by being assimilated to the terrified woman: "it is what the subject does not see and not simply what it sees that founds it."[110]

By a most useful coincidence, Senn reproduces a poster from a film that does not belong to our corpus but that can be assimilated to it via the presence in it of a mad killer. Titled *Terror Aboard*, it shows a number of characters all looking out of the poster with looks of terror on their faces. What draws the reader's attention is a square located in the bottom left-hand corner. Clearly intended to "represent" the killer whose identity must be kept secret, it literally represents nothing and corresponds to the remarks made by Slavoj Zizekon about the paintings of Mark Rothko: the presence of a "black hole" that is "the change of the status of the real into that of a central lack. All late Rothko paintings are manifestations of a struggle to save the barrier separating the real from reality, that is, to prevent the real (the central black square) from overflowing the entire field."[111] The Karloff character in the advertising material has thus completely "taken over," swallowing up characters and spectators alike, a sort of "Blob." This is a disturbing factor that the film attempts to get around via its religious ending: we cannot know anything about life after death because "the Lord our God is a jealous God." The whole point of the film, however, as personified by the scientist who brings Elman back from the dead, has been precisely to know what cannot be known, what by its very nature cannot be represented: the Real itself. Such posters come close to representing Lacan's notion of *ex-sistence* where "the subject is decentered, his center is outside of himself."[112]

This nonrespect of barriers is precisely what we have seen at work in the various films analyzed in this chapter, whose ambiguous and conflicting elements merely point to the failures of representation and, hence, to the inability of the spectators to constitute themselves by simply gazing at the screen in the hope of having their image thrown complacently back at them. The violent, sadistic, and "unmotivated" behavior of so many characters mirrors spectatorial narcissism, if we see narcissism as "the source of the malevolence with which the subject regards its image, the aggressivity it unleashes on all its own representations."[113] In the following chapter we shall consider the social implications of these conclusions, merely hinted at until now, as they are inscribed in various displaced and distorted forms into the films in question and how they address the spectators as subjects within that social field so constituted.

Notes

1. Rhona J. Berenstein, *Attack of the Leading Ladies: Gender, Sexuality, and Spectatorship in Classic Horror Cinema* (New York: Columbia University Press, 1996), 31, 90.

2. Clippings files on the films referred to, MHL.

3. Whitney Williams (no source given), the Audrey Chamberlin Scrapbooks, vol. 2, Special Collections, MHL.

4. Special Collections, Doheny Memorial Library, University of Southern California. Hereinafter referred to as DML.

5. *Dr. X*, PCA file, Special Collections, MHL.

6. *Werewolf of London*, PCA file, Special Collections, MHL.

7. *White Zombie*, clippings file, MHL.

8. A poster for *Forbidden Planet* (1956) shows the robot with a scantily clad and unconscious young woman in his arms, much as if he were abducting her for nefarious purposes. Given that she is the unsuspecting object of her father's unconscious incestuous desire, the poster is telling the truth precisely in the way it deceives us: the robot is in fact obeying the father.

9. *The Ghoul*, clippings file, MHL.

10. *Dr. Cyclops*, Paramount Special Collections, DML.

11. Berenstein, *Attack of the Leading Ladies*, 7.

12. *The Invisible Ray*, PCA file, Special Collections, MHL.

13. *Murders in the Rue Morgue*, PCA file, Special Collections, MHL.

14. For more details on this and other matters concerning the production and reception of the film, see David Skal, *The Monster Show: A Cultural History of Horror* (London: Plexus, 1993), 145–59.

15. *Freaks*, Special Collections, MHL.

16. *Freaks* was reissued in a double bill with *Mad Love*, a coupling that is highly suspect ideologically, for it could imply that Hans is as sick as Dr. Gogol in the later film. The representation of Hans as a child in publicity material creates a further link, since Gogol regresses to the stage of pre-Oedipal drives.

17. Chris Baldick, In *Frankenstein's Shadow: Myth, Monstrosity, and Nineteenth-Century Writing* (Oxford: Clarendon, 1987), 10.

18. This kind of "argument," of course, was also applied to blacks, both in Hollywood and in society generally.

19. *Island of Lost Souls*, PCA file, Special Collections, MHL.

20. If David Cronenberg's *The Fly* is one of the most truly horrific movies ever made, it is precisely because the transformation is slow and inexorable and, up to the bitter end, insists on the humanity of the scientist as a *subject*: the fact that the film opens with a shot of Jeff Goldblum's eyes and closes with the "appealing" eyes of the fly is a major contributing factor.

21. *Return of Dr. X*, PCA file, Special Collections, MHL.

22. Harry M. Benshoff, *Monsters in the Closet: Homosexuality in the Horror Film* (Manchester: Manchester University Press, 1997), especially 77–81.

23. Benshoff, *Monsters in the Closet*, 49, 78.

24. *Dracula's Daughter*, PCA file, Special Collections, MHL.

25. I would suggest that Breen's remark "countless offensive stuff" is an unconscious pun betraying sexist prejudices. If we rewrite "countless" as "count-less," it indicates

that the count's sexual tastes pose no problem, whereas the same cannot be said of those of his daughter. Apart from a brief appearance as a corpse, Dracula plays no part in the film, a fact that highlights female sexuality.

26. I shall return to these questions in chapters 3 and 4.

27. Gary D. Rhodes and John Parris Springer, "They Give Us the 'Weird Feeling': Vampiric Women in Films of the Thirties," in *Bitches, Bimbos, and Virgins*, ed. Gary J. Svehla and Susan Svehla (Baltimore: Midnight Marquee Press, 1996), 24–49. I assume the formula "Weird Feeling" is put between quotes as it is used in a poster to advertise the film. This poster is reproduced in Berenstein, *Attack of the Leading Ladies*, 25.

28. Berenstein makes much of Laughton's gayness and the homosexual implications of the character he plays in the film. I shall return to this later. She also draws attention to a contemporary review of *Mad Love* where the critic referred to Lorre's "thick lips." *Attack of the Leading Ladies*, 155. I have placed *effete* and *nonvirile* between scare quotes in anticipation of my discussion of Garth.

29. "'Kiss Me with Those Red Lips': Gender and Inversion in Bram Stoker's *Dracula*." Reproduced in the *Norton Critical Edition*; quotes on 452, 458.

30. The fact that Sandor is connoted as a "queen" tells us more about the film's makers and the dominant ideologies of representation than about the character himself. This is a question that requires an answer, and I shall take it up when discussing *The Mask of Fu Manchu* later in this section.

31. As we shall see in the next section, not "making up one's mind" can have other, more ideologically disturbing implications for characters and spectators alike.

32. Berenstein, *Attack of the Leading Ladies*, 93.

33. In 1946, ten years after *Dracula's Daughter* and two years after the film *Laura*, Otto Kruger appeared in a stage version of *Laura*. It is quite clear that he played Waldo Lydecker! Thus what was repressed in the first film and represented via the codes of voice, gesture and clothes in the second converge in a given performance. See Gregory William Mank, *Women in Horror Films, 1930s* (Jefferson, N.C.: McFarland, 1999), 99.

34. Jacques Lacan, "La Fonction du voile," in *La Relation d'objet*, Le Séminaire Livre IV (Paris: Seuil, 1994), 151–64.

35. Dylan Evans, *An Introductory Dictionary of Lacanian Psychoanalysis* (London: Routledge, 1996), 12.

36. The most notorious modern manifestation of this notion is Freddy Krueger in *Nightmare on Elm Street*. See Slavoj Zizek, *Looking Awry: An Approach to Jacques Lacan through Popular Culture* (Cambridge, Mass.: MIT Press, 1991), 23. More generally on the Father of Enjoyment and the "anal father," see Zizek, *Enjoy Your Symptom! Jacques Lacan in Hollywood and Out* (New York: Routledge, 1992), 124–28 and 143, n. 20.

37. *The Devil-Doll*, PCA file, Special Collections, MHL.

38. *Son of Kong*, clippings file, MHL.

39. It is interesting to note that in this review, not much more than a year after the release of *Frankenstein*, the creator and the monster have already become confused.

40. The French term for "morning glory" is *belle de jour*, which foregrounds the feminine. See Luis Bunuel's film of that title (1967).

41. *The Mad Genius*, clippings file, MHL.

42. Berenstein, *Attack of the Leading Ladies*, 23.

43. Berenstein, *Attack of the Leading Ladies*, 132 (quote), 135 (still).

44. See Benshoff, *Monsters in the Closet*, 57–58.

45. Benshoff, *Monsters in the Closet*, 58.

46. On this representation of the active West and the passive East and the far-reaching ideological and political implications of such a representation, see Edward W. Said, *Orientalism* (London: Penguin Books, 1985).

47. *Pittsburgh Post-Gazette*, 12 November 1932. The Jean Hersholt Collection, vol. 10. Special Collections, MHL. The name of the reviewer is not mentioned.

48. Or "butch" like Dracula's daughter.

49. Berenstein, *Attack of the Leading Ladies*, 136.

50. *The Old Dark House*, clippings file, MHL.

51. Benshoff, *Monsters in the Closet*, 44–45.

52. David J. Hogan, in *Boris Karloff*, 87.

53. "Return of the Repressed." Quoted by Berenstein, *Attack of the Leading Ladies*, 150.

54. This situation can be interpreted in political and historical terms, as we shall attempt to show in the last chapter.

55. Benshoff, *Monsters in the Closet*, 48.

56. Or "worthless." I refer the reader to my earlier comments on *The Mask of Fu Manchu*. A detailed examination of such matters as class and economics will be proposed in chapter 3.

57. In light of my earlier discussion of flowers and of signifiers determining unconscious subject positions, it is perhaps pertinent to point out that a flower can indeed function as just that and nothing else. This seems to me to be the case here.

58. The representation of peasants, here and in other movies, looks ahead with uncanny prescience to the never-never land of Walt Disney amusement parks. We shall return to the function of peasants and villagers in chapter 3.

59. Berenstein uses the term *overwrought* at least twice. She links "female gender behavior to an overwrought performance" and has recourse to the word, hardly surprisingly, when discussing *King Kong*. *Attack of the Leading Ladies*, 73, 188.

60. *Mystery of the Wax Museum*, clippings file, MHL.

61. R. C. Dale, "Narrative, Fable and Dream in *King Kong*," in *The Girl in the Hairy Paw*, ed. Ronald Gottesman and Harry Geduld (New York: Avon, 1976), 117–21.

62. Dale, "Narrative, Fable and Dream," 119, 120.

63. Evans, *An Introductory Dictionary of Lacanian Psychoanalysis*, 146.

64. Ronald Gottesmann, and Harry Geduld, eds., *The Girl in the Hairy Paw* (New York: Avon, 1976), 126.

65. It is worthwhile noting that fantasies concerning the size of penises are not limited to homosexuals and are an integral part of the heterosexual libido, as obscene jokes attest.

66. Gottesmann and Geduld, eds., *The Girl in the Hairy Paw*, 128.

67. And, of course, history itself, a matter that will be addressed in chapter 4.

68. I would suggest that the werewolf is at the center of this question, inasmuch as his transformation takes place once a month, like menstruation. I shall return to this when analyzing *The Wolf Man* in the last chapter.

69. Joan Copjec, *Read My Desire* (Cambridge, Mass.: MIT Press, 1995), 51.

70. Evans, *An Introductory Dictionary*, 163.

71. There is no contradiction between this argument and my claim that Kong is female. Totally incompatible notions and desires can coexist in the unconscious.

72. It is hardly a coincidence that the ship's lounge and the discussion resemble a boardroom and businessmen discussing company policy. This and related matters will be addressed in chapter 4.

73. In a letter to Luigi Luraschi of Paramount, dated 8 June 1939, PCA File, Special Collections, MHL.

74. Sigmund Freud, "Hysterical Phantasies and Their Relation to Bisexuality" in *SE* IX: 165.

75. *Mad Love*, PCA file, Special Collections, MHL.

76. *Mad Love*, clippings file, MHL.

77. Frank Krutnik, *In a Lonely Place: Film Noir, Genre, Masculinity* (New York: Routledge, 1991), 102. Krutnik is discussing the masochistic hero of *The Dark Corner* (Henry Hathaway, 1946).

78. Sigmund Freud, "On Narcissism: An Introduction," in *SE* XIV: 76. As we see later in the film, Vollin has transformed his mansion into a sort of fortress totally cut off from the outside world, as if the latter has already ceased to exist: shutters sealing windows hermetically, rooms transformed into lifts. The significance of this aspect of the film is discussed in chapter 4.

79. That so many fathers or father figures are soldiers, lawyers, judges, scientists, or doctors is hardly coincidental.

80. Hollywood's use and abuse of Edgar Allan Poe in the period under discussion does, however, set up interesting links between films. Thus, *The Crime of Dr. Crespi* is inspired by "The Premature Burial." The horrible and lingering death that Crespi plans for Ross and the fate Vollin has prepared for Judge Thatcher are both perfect examples of a remark by Freud, to the effect that the conscience no longer applies to acts carried out for the love object. The subject is blinded to the point of remorselessness, indeed of committing crimes. *Group Psychology and the Analysis of the Ego*, in *SE* XVIII: 113.

81. This desire for total mastery and control over others is characteristic of paranoia.

82. The film also includes an example of "male bonding" between the monster and the vengeful Ygor (Bela Lugosi), to which I shall return in chapter 3.

83. Stephen Jones, entry on Lionel Atwill in *The BFI Companion to Horror*, ed. Kim Newman (London: Cassell and the British Film Institute, 1996), 28.

84. Benshoff has pointed out that *Dr. X* is one of a group of films turning on "Voyeuristic sado-masochism." *Mad Love* is also cited. See his *Monsters in the Closet*, 57.

85. Bryan Senn, *Golden Horrors: An Illustrated Critical Filmography of Terror Cinema, 1931–1939* (Jefferson, N.C.: McFarland, 1996), 389.

86. Sigmund Freud, "Family Romances," in *SE* IX: 237, 240–41.

87. See Freud, "On Narcissism," in *SE* XIV: 94.

88. We shall return to the political and economic aspects of these social relations in chapter 3.

89. Copjec, *Read My Desire*, 154–55. In the same chapter, Copjec evokes the ripping apart of the body of Damiens in a way that sets up uncanny parallels with *Son of Frankenstein*.

90. Paul Jensen, *Boris Karloff and His Films*, quoted by Senn, *Golden Horrors*, 390.

91. See Berenstein, *Attack of the Leading Ladies*, 123–29.

92. Berenstein, *Attack of the Leading Ladies*, 128–29.

93. This formula "working under," as we shall see in due course, takes on new meanings in the light of Berenstein's reading.

94. Senn, *Golden Horrors*, 92.

95. "Clothes make the man, or the woman, as the case may be." Berenstein, *Attack of the Leading Ladies*, 36.

96. I shall return to this question from another perspective in chapter 4.

97. Berenstein, *Attack of the Leading Ladies*, 125.

98. The fact that Joanne looks off-screen right here, as she does in the two sequences analyzed above, is a clear indication of Wells' symbolic role.

99. I remind the reader of the writing of Zizek on this subject. See, for example, *Enjoy Your Symptom!* and *Looking Awry*.

100. Berenstein deals with this aspect of the genre in a chapter appropriately entitled "Looks Could Kill: The Power of the Gaze in Hypnosis Films," in *Attack of the Leading Ladies*, 88–119.

101. Sigmund Freud, *Group Psychology and the Analysis of the Ego*, in *SE* XVIII: 115.

102. Berenstein, *Attack of the Leading Ladies*, 5.

103. Freud, *Group Psychology and the Analysis of the Ego*, 127.

104. Tanya Krzywinska has put it slightly differently: "Like Freud's bad father, Legendre aims to prevent anyone but himself from achieving the object of their desires." *A Skin for Dancing In: Possession, Witchcraft and Voodoo in Film* (Wiltshire, England: Flicks Books, 2000), 167.

105. Special Collections, DML, for the three films under discussion here.

106. I refer the reader back to the *mise en scène* in *Dr. X* analyzed earlier.

107. *The Devil-Doll*, PCA file, Special Collections, MHL.

108. The ecological dimension of the film will be discussed in chapter 4.
109. Senn, *Golden Horrors*, 217, 290, 310, 351.
110. Copjec, *Read My Desire*, 36.
111. Zizek, *Looking Awry*, 19.
112. Evans, *An Introductory Dictionary*, 58.
113. Copjec, *Read My Desire*, 37.

CHAPTER THREE

~

The Road to (Dis)enchantment

Let us stand back for a moment and attempt to sum up the main characteristics of the central figures of the corpus in question. *Narcissism, paranoia, megalomania,* and *sadomasochism* are terms that come readily to mind. This being said, we must not lose from sight the fact that the main characters cannot be placed in a single category enabling us to describe them all as exhibiting in an identical fashion one or another of the traits in question. The spectators are manifestly being invited to feel great sympathy for Dr. Jekyll, to consider that Dr. Frankenstein is well intentioned, and that Dr. Blair (*The Devil Commands*) has the advancement of knowledge and humanity at heart, at least until his morbid obsession with the "spirit" of his dead wife engulfs him.[1] At the same time, the single-minded and totally self-centered behavior of megalomaniac Carl Denham (who is portrayed positively) and Eric Gorman (the paranoid and sadistic businessman of *Murders in the Zoo* who is portrayed negatively) allows us to place them alongside, for instance, Drs. Mirakle, Moreau, Crespi, Gogol, and Vollin, Count Zaroff, and the Invisible Man. An unconscious schizophrenic attitude is being adopted on the part of the filmic texts toward science and individualism, an attitude shared by us, the spectators, as subjects coded ideologically. The films are appealing to early, indeed archaic, drives whose conflictual nature we have seen at work throughout the previous chapters and whose more properly social and political nature we must start to appreciate in detail.

Generally speaking, I would argue that we can see in the behavior of the "mad doctor" and his relations with the world and the other characters vestiges of childhood, with its enchantments and inevitable (just how "inevitable" is a question this chapter will be addressing) disenchantments. To a great extent, then, the films (re)enact the tensions between the pleasure principle and the reality principle, provided that one grants some political and economic dimension to Freud's use of the latter term. A consideration of his brief but dense and suggestive study "Family Romances" proves instructive.[2]

Freud's concern in this study is with the need of the child to pass through the painful stage of liberating himself from the authority of his parents. I have no intention of drawing a simple parallel between the child and the central male characters of the horror film. Rather, it is a question of highlighting the tension within these characters and our identification, however negative, with those characteristics that belong to a child and to an authoritarian parent. Freud stresses the child's evolution from a position where it identifies solely with its parents to one where those of other children come to play a role. Thus, the child can no longer maintain the pleasurable belief that his parents are unique and perfect.[3] Indeed, they tend to be downgraded by the child who is now anxious to replace them by adults belonging to a superior social category.[4] Since Freud inscribes this tendency within the twin aims that he designates as erotic and ambitious, I propose we extrapolate by positing that the child's narcissistic belief in his own omnipotence and homogeneity, cruelly wounded, is maintained in the mad doctor in the form of an arrogant conviction of his inherent superiority and his right to satisfy his drives at will. At the same time, we can see at work the crucial fact that the mad doctor tends to take himself as his own superego and ego ideal. Moreover, the matter of social standing enables us to pinpoint the interesting fact that the mad scientist seems to be completely without any problems of a financial kind, as if he had the world in his arms in much the same way as he was once in the arms of the all-protecting mother. The latter's tenderness and affection are duly transformed within the scientist's psyche into its opposite via the further narcissistic wound of the mirror stage.

The extreme self-centeredness of the central characters partakes of the child's displeasure when forced to share with its siblings its place at the center of the world. The child's desire for revenge and retaliation, which takes the form of fantasies toward parents who have punished it for naughty behavior, becomes manifest in a literal form in the various acts of sadism and torture, sequestration, and sexual exploitation paraded lovingly before us in film after film. I wish now to extend these remarks and open the discussion out to embrace, by stages, elements of a more precisely historical nature, prior to showing in chapter 4 how history itself comes to be represented in the horror film. I shall turn first to two of the most decisive contributions to (dis)enchantment, the meeting on the common ground of radical theory of a political conservative and a political militant: Freud's *Civilization and Its Discontents* and Marcuse's *Eros and Civilization.*

Freud with Marcuse

I shall simplify somewhat Freud's argument by presenting it as a conflict between the pursuit of happiness and the need for (self-)restraint within a community; between the single-minded satisfaction of drives and the repression of those drives in the name of social order; between selfishness and altruism; and between the individual and society. This set of binary oppositions belongs, at one level, to the Imaginary Order of misrecognition, yet to a certain extent it sums up how the mad doctor/scientist or his surrogate is represented in the films under discussion. If we now take two further pairs of "opposites"—namely, freedom and control, and good and evil—then we can, indeed must, ask, To which element in each of the above-mentioned pairs does each of the terms proposed correspond? This should allow us to see how profoundly ideological the various binary oppositions are. "Freedom" and "the individual" tend to be synonyms in Western society, yet they are hardly represented positively in the case of the mad scientists who tend to take them too far—too "literally," as it were. At the same time, much sympathy is elicited for, say, Frankenstein: to whom, or to what, are "good" and "evil" attached in the films in which he appears? Unlike other mad doctors, he survives. In *King Kong,* Carl Denham, whose megalomania and single-mindedness are typical characteristics of mad doctors, is a symbol of courage, initiative, and free enterprise. He, too, survives. These are not exceptions or accidents but symptoms of a far wider and more complex problem in which tensions and contradictions are rife and in which totally conflicting positions are present, not simply within a given film but within the very representation of a single character. This has been the thrust behind the delineation of subject positions as we have analyzed them until now.

I propose first to draw attention to a number of remarks made by Freud in *Civilization and Its Discontents* and to suggest how appropriate they are for understanding the films in question, and then to take the arguments a stage further by addressing Marcuse's reading of Freud in *Eros and Civilization.* This in turn will highlight certain weaknesses in Freud's arguments—what he repressed, if you like—and enable us to give a more precise sociocultural dimension to the matter.

Freud identifies one of "the sources from which our suffering comes" as "the inadequacy of the regulations which adjust the mutual relationships of human beings in the family, the state and society."[5] We obtain here a clear picture of the notion of a lack of harmony inherent in the subject's place in a community, whatever the nature of that community may be, and of the various rules and constraints determining the subject's behavior within the community. This is a (relative) banality I wish to insist on in the light of the mad doctor's rejection of such rules and his implicit seeking for a return to some form of harmony. Toward the end of his study, Freud insists on the chasm between "the process of individual development" and "the process of civilization." In the former case, a tension is set up between "the urge toward happiness" and "the urge toward union with others," between what we are wont to call egoism and altruism. In the case of civilization, however, if the tension exists, it is heavily weighted toward one side:

> It is true that the aim of happiness is still there, but it is pushed into the background. It almost seems as if the creation of a great human community would be most successful if no attention had to be paid to the happiness of the individual. The developmental process of the individual can thus be expected to have special features of its own which are not reproduced in the process of human civilization.[6]

If what Freud wrote in 1930 is taking place in the last stages of global capitalism—the word *almost* has now become superfluous in the second sentence of the above quote—I would suggest that his remark has much to tell us about the behavior of characters in horror films, and not simply those fulfilling the function of mad doctor. As we shall see, the films (re)enact the pursuit of happiness on the part of both individuals and communities as something positive, while at the same time stigmatizing any action or desire that does not correspond to the most conservative, repressive and benighted vision of what happiness and the collective are. In which case, genuine happiness enters into open conflict with society, a conflict that can only be solved in the time-honored fashion: with the elimination, in one way or another, of the "foreign body" representing a lack of harmony that an ordered society cannot tolerate. Exactly what "society" and what "order" are involved will become plain as we progress, but I refer the reader back to the previous chapters, in particular the matter of male-female relationships and the subject positions the films simultaneously put into place and put into question.

Two concepts that return repeatedly in *Civilization and Its Discontents* are of the utmost importance for our topic: guilt and sublimation. Implicitly or explicitly, they are discussed and analyzed along with the concepts of the superego and the ego ideal, inasmuch as they concern both the individual and the community. Let us turn our attention first to the question of guilt. It is present in the individual as a result of the earliest stages of development where the child sought the immediate satisfaction of its vital needs and where demand set desire in motion. The Oedipus complex and its dissolution attest to the existence of a pleasure principle and its counterpart, the reality principle, in which the child must submit to castration and the Law forbidding incest. Freud ceaselessly insisted on the fact that former desires, once overcome, never cease to leave their traces in the unconscious, and this is a point to which we shall have to constantly return in the course of this chapter and the next. That such an impossible desire can be reactivated, given a "new lease of life" as it were, at any moment of the subject's subsequent existence as an adult gives rise implacably to an incomprehensible feeling of guilt, the pleasure principle and its aims being unconscious. The narcissism of early childhood—a determining factor for later development—and the self-centered demands of the ego go hand in hand with an aggressivity both mental and physical: Lacan's theory of the mirror stage eloquently makes the stakes clear. Freud has summed up the situation of how civilization has defused such aggressivity on the part of the individual:

> His aggressiveness is introjected, internalized; it is, in point of fact, sent back to where it came from—that is, it is directed toward his own ego. There it is taken over by a portion of the ego, which sets itself over against the rest of the ego as super-ego, and which now, in the form of "conscience," is ready to put into action against the ego the same harsh aggressiveness that the ego would have liked to satisfy upon other, extraneous individuals. The tension between the harsh super-ego and the ego that is subjected to it, is called by us the sense of guilt; it expresses itself as a need for punishment.[7]

Before making these remarks, Freud had returned briefly to the coexistence within the subject of Eros and the death drive, the latter being a most controversial topic over which Freud worried on more than one occasion. Here he returns to the notion of a portion of that drive being directed toward the external world. Something outside the subject would be destroyed instead of the subject's own self, a fact that shows an intricate interdependence of the erotic drives and the death drives:

> In sadism, long since known to us as a component instinct of sexuality, we should have before us a particularly strong alloy of this kind between trends of love and the destructive instinct; while its counterpart, masochism, would be a union between destructiveness directed inwards and sexuality. . . .

It is in sadism, where the death instinct twists the erotic aim in its own sense and yet at the same time fully satisfies the erotic urge, that we succeed in obtaining the clearest insight into its nature and its relation to Eros. But even where it emerges without any sexual purpose, in the blindest fury of destructiveness, we cannot fail to recognize that the satisfaction of the instinct is accompanied by an extraordinarily high degree of narcissistic enjoyment, owing to its presenting the ego with a fulfillment of the latter's old wishes for omnipotence.[8]

From our discussions of the various manifestations of desire in chapter 2, it will be obvious that Freud had horror films and mad doctors in mind when making these comments. It now remains to see in what way.

The mad doctor's death drive has been directed outward so that his desire for self-destruction—or suicide—can be misrecognized by him and turned into the elimination of some real or imaginary enemy. The precise political and historical dimension of this drive will be made clear in the last section of this chapter and throughout chapter 4; here I simply wish to suggest various lines of approach. In The Black Cat, Hjalmar Poelzig's death drive is represented as an obsessional neurosis, made concrete in the film by his keeping the body of his dead wife embalmed in a displaced attempt to ward off his own death, and by the chess game to which he challenges Vitus Werdegast, a game that symbolizes his unconscious belief that he can control the future, including, therefore, death itself. That the eponymous central character of The Crime of Dr. Crespi commits suicide at the end cannot be simply put down to censorship, especially as the censors frowned on suicide as an escape from the due processes of the law. Another, unconscious, logic is at work that, for once, got the better of the Breen office, particularly horrified by this grim and unrelenting movie.[9] Crespi's existence depends on the long and lingering death by premature burial of his sexual rival. The failure of his scheme—the victim literally returns to confound him—and the discovery of the truth by the doctors working under Crespi in his private clinic remove the last barrier between the character and death. He is now forced by desire to turn on himself the destructiveness that, transformed into chilling sadism, had been intended to send the other to the grave in his place.

Generally speaking, we can interpret the mad doctor's sadism as an unconscious reaction to the guilt that is meant to derive from aggressive tendencies: he "desocializes" these tendencies, refuses to submit to the communal superego, and turns in on himself, functioning in a purely narcissistic fashion. Hence his arrogance, his feeling of superiority and of an omnipotence that will help him to become "master of the world." The mad doctor refuses to give up on this desire: "The effect of instinctual renunciation on the conscience then is that every piece of aggression whose satisfaction the subject gives up is taken over by the super-ego and increases the latter's aggressiveness (against the ego)."[10] By refusing such renunciation, the mad doctor rejects the community and its values, a situation which, by constant repetition, can only increase his aggressivity. The existence of a community presupposes a certain lack of attention being paid to the particular needs and desires of each individual member of that community, a fact unacceptable to the narcissistic mad doctor. He seeks happiness in his own way, regardless, a regression to pre-Oedipal drives. His libido is turned in on his own ego, with objects proving of no interest, except where an appropriate female can replace the mother. Thus, Dr. Gogol in *Mad Love* revels in the torture meted out on the young actress he yearns for; via masochistic identification, he is both atoning for an impossible desire and punishing the image of the mother whose love he could never obtain. The fact that we are dealing with a play, a spectacle, enables the film to present the play as a metaphor for its own social function and Gogol as the signifier of spectatorial desire, suitably displaced and, hopefully, defused.

Dr. Vollin in *The Raven* is perhaps the most extreme and unalloyed example of such drives in the horror films of the 1930s. Torture for him is an art resembling that of his hero Edgar Allan Poe, except for one detail. Whereas Poe found an outlet for his tortured mind in the art and act of writing, Vollin functions according to the literal meaning of the signifier "tortured." Like a very young child taking words for things, he exteriorizes his mental "torture" and indulges in real torture, thus unconsciously recognizing in the art of Poe a perfect case of sublimation and of the existence of the death drive. It is to the concept of sublimation that we must now turn.

Freud is prompted to evoke sublimation in the context of his reflections on human suffering in *Civilization and Its Discontents*, the mental suffering that results from a drive not finding satisfaction due to the resistance of the outside world or the reality principle. He sees the sublimation of drives as "an especially conspicuous feature of cultural development" and as a means of avoiding a pathological situation.[11] Earlier he had spelled out in detail what was entailed:

> The task here is that of shifting the instinctual aims in such a way that they cannot come up against frustration from the external world. In this, sublimation of the instincts lends its assistance. One gains the most if one can sufficiently heighten the yield of pleasure from the sources of psychical and intellectual work. When that is so, fate can do little against one. A satisfaction of

this kind, such as an artist's joy in creating, in giving his fantasies body, of a scientist's in solving problems or discovering truths, has a special quality which we shall certainly one day be able to characterize in metapsychological terms. At present we can only say figuratively that such satisfactions seem "finer and higher." But their intensity is mild compared with that derived from the sating of crude and primary instinctual impulses; it does not convulse our physical being. And the weak point of this method is that it is not applicable generally: it is accessible to only a few people. . . . And even to the few who do possess them, this method cannot give complete protection from suffering.[12]

Lacan has written that Freud considered that, once carried out, sublimation was permanent, but this hardly seems the case on the strength of the above passage. Freud's final remark surely implies that a constant rechanneling of the drives is necessary if the subject is to be able to function socially as artist or scientist and find in artistic output or experiments the satisfaction that a particular drive could not obtain. Thus, a breakdown of the new order imposed by the subject on the world is possible at any moment.

We can see here the beginnings of an explanation for the behavior of mad doctors. Their refusal to bow to the values of the society in which they live, their paranoid craving for omnipotence and recognition as geniuses, and their sadistic behavior all need to be analyzed, not only in the terms used here, but also as unconscious manifestations of the failure of sublimation, or, to put it differently: an unconscious refusal to see in scientific or artistic activity an acceptable and bearable displacement for socially proscribed drives. In that case, not only does sublimation succeed only if there is a constant expenditure of energy to defuse the drives by finding another outlet, but this expenditure is insufficient, since the subject's desire is to satisfy the drives. If the constant regression to the stage of infantile narcissism can help to explain the excessive behavior of the mad doctor, his need to feel omnipotent, and to have his slightest whim satisfied at once, and his belief in the power of thought and the word, we still need to look for some explanation for the failure of sublimation, for what such failure means.

Lacan has opened for us certain avenues of approach. First (from a chronological point of view), he has stated that sublimation enables the subject undergoing a given experience to find a compromise with death. The stronger the drive, the greater the need to sublimate in order to protect the ego. The latter is constantly torn between a desire for peace (i.e., death) and a fear of its own finitude. Thus the vampire functions in fantasy as a figure that has overcome this conflict, while remaining its privileged signifier: the vampire is dead yet immortal. Second, Lacan has extended such remarks in his theory of "la Chose" ("the Thing"), elaborated in the greatest detail in his

Ethique de la psychanalyse.[13] In the Lacanian system, "la Chose" corresponds to Freud's "*Kern unseres Wesens,*" that kernel of our being that is radically inaccessible to conscious thought; we can interpret it as the impossible desire of incest, of union with the maternal body. Sublimation, then, is the new channel into which the pleasure principle flows. Artistic and scientific endeavors are thus substitutes elevated to the dignity of the Thing and endowed socially, culturally and ideologically with everything that is noble and worthwhile. As Dylan Evans has reminded us, for Lacan, there is no change of object involved, only a change in its function, in its place within fantasy.[14]

Things are not that simple, however, for the desire exists to go beyond the pleasure principle, which entails the conversion of pleasure into pain and suffering, which in turn can reach an unbearable point. That point, which by definition cannot be reached as no subject can endure such pain, is the Thing and here we have an intimation of the pathology of the mad doctor. The various forms of suffering inflicted on diverse victims—Dr. Mirakle's torturing the prostitute in *Murders in the Rue Morgue,* vivisection in *Island of Lost Souls,* burial while alive in *The Crime of Dr. Crespi,* Dr. Vollin's recreation of Poe's torture chamber in *The Raven*—are manifestations of *jouissance,* going beyond the pleasure principle to the point of actually reaching the Thing via a substitute: the wretched victim. The mad doctor becomes the obscene Father of Enjoyment, with the victim's body replacing that holy (and wholly inaccessible) body, that of the mother. Incest is conceived unconsciously as so monstrous and hideous that to achieve it in one's wildest fantasies must be accompanied by the monstrous and hideous disfiguring of the body of the person designated as substitute (or animals, in the case of Dr. Moreau).

Retribution in horror films is, of course, seen in religious terms, with the mad doctor being punished for his hubris: seeing himself as God. Of particular interest in this context is Lacan's contention that the Ten Commandments exist, not to be taken literally or even seriously—especially as they are consistently broken—but as a system of laws and interdictions whose existence denies what they in fact reveal: the impossibility of breaking the Law, the only law that counts, that forbidding incest. It is amusing to note here the real—that is, unconscious—meaning of censorship concerning religious matters. Exception was always taken to mad doctors openly comparing themselves to God, such as Frankenstein and Moreau. Playing God means, of course, playing (God) the Father, which brings the films uncomfortably close to admitting that the mad doctor is acting out the impossible desire. By repressing the truth, censorship obligingly reveals it at the same time, in the only way the Real can be symbolized: in the form of a displacement that maintains the veil in place over the Thing.

If we return now to *Civilization and Its Discontents*, we find Freud making a remark that goes a long way in helping us understand the unconscious logic behind the representation of mad doctors:

> The work of civilization has become increasingly the business of men, it confronts them with ever more difficult tasks and compels them to carry out instinctual sublimations of which women are little capable. . . . What [a man] employs for cultural aims he to a great extent withdraws from women and sexual life.[15]

What interests me is less the manifestation of an ingrained prejudice about women—if Freud had thought further, he might have seen that women are compelled by social pressures not to sublimate precisely because this "noble" task is reserved for the male—than the notion of the mad doctor as homosexual, in other words: "really" a woman incapable of sublimation.

I shall now take up again certain arguments of chapter 2 because of the second sentence of the prior quote that clearly helps to explain the central character in *Frankenstein* and *Bride of Frankenstein*. In particular, I wish to return to the theme of his hysteria, in light of another remark of Freud's, concerning bisexuality:

> If we assume it as a fact that each individual seeks to satisfy both male and female wishes in his sexual life, we are prepared for the possibility that those [two sets of] demands are not fulfilled by the same object, and that they interfere with each other unless they can be kept apart and each impulse guided into a particular channel that is suited to it.[16]

We saw in chapter 2 that Frankenstein's hysteria cannot be put down simply to his being a repressed homosexual, but to the ideological force behind the notion that certain activities are not really "masculine," to the hero's refusal to submit to certain representations of masculinity, and to fulfill his patriarchal function in conventional and conservative ways (a refusal to identify with his idiotic father). I would argue that *Bride of Frankenstein* takes up the question of homosexual drives in a most particular way, and that Pretorius should also be seen less as a "gay" doctor in his own right than as the unconscious manifestation within the filmic text of that "feminine" side to Frankenstein's character that produced the symptom of hysteria in *Frankenstein*. In other words, the two sides to the character are literally "kept apart" by being represented in two distinct characters. I would suggest *Bride of Frankenstein* is on this issue an obscurantist and reactionary film, pandering unconsciously to repressive views of homosexuality by showing that the "feminine" within the male is nothing other than effeminate homosexuality. It is as if the biological were taking precedence over the social.

This reading could, however, be challenged as insufficient, and I shall suggest at once two other ways of considering the matter. The entry "Sublimation" in *L'Apport Freudien* traces the term back to alchemy, to which Pretorius is explicitly linked.[17] The striving to create life ex nihilo (a characteristic of sublimation for Lacan) is a form of displacement, a drawing of the veil over the Thing. Moreover, the representation and function of Pretorius can be taken as a Utopian strain within the film, the textual unconscious being split into a reactionary side and a progressive side that coexist in a state of conflict. *Bride of Frankenstein* is not representing homosexuals as they "are"—as "bitchy queens" —but is advancing the notion that homosexuals have the right to present themselves thus to the world, without opprobrium. The film is thus presenting not a real state but a potential one where the effeminate homosexual will not be compelled to sublimate the feminine drive and behave as if he were a heterosexual. The text's unconscious is saying "If only things could be like that," but, as Freud taught us, hypotheses and wishful thinking cannot be represented as such by the unconscious, but only as having taken place. It is to this crucial Utopian thrust that I wish to turn now via Herbert Marcuse's *Eros and Civilization*.

The juxtaposition of the names of Freud and Marcuse must not lead readers to assume I am suggesting Marcuse rewrote Freud in order to introduce a social dimension to his work; for Marcuse, that social dimension, radical and subversive, already existed in Freud's text. What Marcuse did do in his work was to pinpoint a particular prejudice of Freud's that the latter was unable to overcome, if only because no historical subject can live outside ideology.[18] That prejudice concerned work, obviously a major theme in a study that turns on questions of sublimation. Just what Freud meant by the term is, however, open to dispute, and it is this aspect that will concern us now.

Eros and Civilization can be seen as an extension of the insights of *Civilization and Its Discontents*, an extension of an explicitly political nature. Here is the opening paragraph of Marcuse's study:

Sigmund Freud's proposition that civilization is based on the permanent subjugation of the human instincts has been taken for granted. His question whether the suffering thereby inflicted upon individuals has been worth the benefits of culture has not been taken too seriously—the less so since Freud himself considered the process to be inevitable and irreversible. Free gratification of man's instinctual needs is incompatible with civilized society: renunciation and delay in satisfaction are the prerequisites of progress. "Happiness," said Freud, "is no cultural value." Happiness must be subordinated to the discipline of work as full-time occupation, to the discipline of monogamic reproduction, to the established system of law and order. The methodical sacrifice of libido, its rigidly enforced deflection to socially useful activities and expressions, *is* culture.[19]

Marcuse's reminder that Freud considered "the process to be inevitable and irreversible" led post-Freudians to decide that Freud was wrong and that something radical had to be done to "liberate" people. This, as Russell Jacoby has shown in his splendid book *Social Amnesia*, led to "conformist psychology" aimed at "the forgetting of psychoanalysis."[20] He points out in his introduction to the new edition:

> In a crowded market no American psychologist could advertise Freud's therapeutic goal, transforming hysterical unhappiness into everyday unhappiness. Yet it was Freud's therapeutic pessimism that was radical; his refusal to inflate therapy kept alive the possibilities of real social change that later psychologists surrendered in confusing normal functioning with liberation. In conflating therapy and politics the radical psychologists ill served both.[21]

Marcuse would have agreed with Jacoby's insightful remark that Freud was a political conservative but a theoretical radical. This can be seen clearly toward the end of *Civilization and Its Discontents* in which Freud is berating the Christian notion "Love thy neighbor as thyself":

> I too think it quite certain that a real change in the relations of human beings to possessions would be of more help in this direction than any ethical commands; but the recognition of this fact among socialists has been obscured and made useless for practical purposes by a fresh, idealistic misconception of human nature.[22]

Such an observation brings together succinctly the blindness and insight that structured Freud's thought when considering social and political matters: on the one hand, a dislike, stemming from a pessimistic view of humanity, of socialism in general and the Bolshevik Revolution in particular; on the other hand, an uncanny prescience concerning the increasing role of commodities in modern society and the attendant reification of social relations under capitalism.[23] What Freud was unable to do—for reasons of a precise historical nature—was to see past the functions, both narcissistic and social, of these "possessions" to the circumstances that led to their production in the first place. Which brings us back to the notion of work.

At one point Freud makes the following observation:

> After primal man had discovered that it lay in his own hands, literally, to improve his lot on earth by working, it cannot have been a matter of indifference to him whether another man worked with or against him. The other man acquired the value for him of a fellow-worker, with whom is was useful to live together.[24]

Earlier, in a footnote, Freud had had this to say:

Professional activity is a source of special satisfaction if it is a freely chosen one—if, that is to say, by means of sublimation, it makes possible the use of existing inclinations, of persisting or constitutionally reinforced instinctual impulses. And yet, as a path to happiness, work is not highly prized by men. They do not strive after it as they do after other possibilities of satisfaction. The great majority of people only work under the stress of necessity, and this natural human aversion to work raises most difficult social problems.[25]

Placing these two quotes side by side, one can only be struck by the disavowal at work. It is granted that Freud in the first quote is thinking of the earliest forms of collective existence, but his reference to the unpleasant aspects of work—which we should perhaps baptize "labor" or "toil"—surely indicates an awareness of a continuity over the millennia as far as most people are concerned. More to the point, at least for the present time, is his juxtaposition—a classic example of miscognition—of two different kinds of work: manual and intellectual, or, as Marcuse points out succinctly when quoting another remark from *Civilization and Its Discontents*, "between alienated and nonalienated labor."[26]

The vocabulary Freud uses when discussing "professional activity" indicates that he has in mind the medical and legal professions; he also just as surely implies artistic and scientific activities. Just how "free" one's choice is lies beyond the scope of our investigation here, but it is hardly beside the point that most of the mad doctors in horror films have *private means;* even the rare doctor who works for a fee—Gogol, Crespi—does so within the private sector. If we shall have to return to this not irrelevant question later, what must be stressed at this juncture is the fact that Freud evokes work and sublimation in terms that show an unconscious readiness to privilege the professions over less "noble" and more "degrading" activities, hence my remark that Freud is disavowing what he is so manifestly stating. On the one hand, he values collective labor, which makes of him a sort of "closet" socialist; on the other, he gives pride of place to intellectual work. At the same time, he adopts a somewhat moralizing tone about those who do not prize work as the route to happiness, while openly admitting, by stating that most people work only because they have to, that there are constraints over which people have no control. For Freud, intellectual labor enables sublimation because it produces results society needs and prizes highly. But what of manual labor? There is no sublimation possible as it is systematically denigrated. There is no way out for the subject obliged to sell his or her labor; he never derives any satisfaction, not even a pecuniary one. And leisure—the time given over to reading and visiting museums for an intellectual like Freud—belongs exclusively to the professional or moneyed classes, the product of surplus value. Given that Freud also raises, albeit via the euphemism of "difficult social problems," the question of social unrest, it is patent that he is thinking of his own day and age, not of the earliest cultivation of the land. In other words—and to anticipate somewhat—there is a specter haunting Freud's text that leads him to say more than he wants to say. We shall return to this point later.

The mad doctor, by insisting on the individual pleasure and psychic benefits to be derived from experiments and intellectual labor, is the condensation of several elements: (1) he foregrounds the lack of collective satisfaction meant to be found in sublimation; (2) his pleasure and satisfaction signify, on the mode of reversal, the lack of pleasure and satisfaction experienced by the manual worker; (3) his endless labor shows he has all the (leisure) time in the world, unlike the person subjected to dull, hard and repetitive toil; and (4) his striving for *jouissance* dislocates the collective social fantasy, unveils the Thing and triggers anxiety and horror. For the spectator, this fascination with an impossible beyond must terminate with the death of the mad doctor. If not, society collapses.

Marcuse made the essential point that alienated labor "is by its very nature repressive of human potentialities"[27] and goes on to refer to a remark by Freud that staggers by its insight into the real forces at work in alienated labor. Marcuse does so in a precise context that I take the liberty of changing, along with the thrust of his reasoning because of his insistence on the potential that is repressed (but not necessarily destroyed: what is repressed leaves traces, as we shall see in due course). The remark by Freud to which Marcuse refers to is taken from *Group Psychology and the Analysis of the Ego*. Freud asserts that collaboration between workers can lead to the creation of relationships that can live on in circumstances other than those destined to be profitable.[28] We must not lose sight of the fact that Freud had admitted that most people work because they have to, not because they want to. Although he may have been thinking of working in order to feed oneself and one's family, we are entitled to interpret the remark in the context of the manual worker constrained to sell his labor in exchange for a wage. In such a case, the earlier-cited quote reveals a factor insisted on by Marcuse and denied by Freud: things can change and are not inevitable because they are determined historically. In other words, and despite himself, Freud is admitting to the possibility of a Utopia.

Marcuse's critique of capitalism is that, for it to function, any possibility of such a Utopia must be dispelled to the point of being driven from conscious collective memory; and it is surplus repression that is called upon to assist in this task. Surplus repression consists of "the restrictions necessitated by social domination": the domination of one class by another.[29] In capitalist society, the prime "achievement" of surplus repression is to pass off the social division of labor as natural rather than historical:

> Society emerges as a lasting and expanding system of useful performances; the hierarchy of functions and relations assumes the form of objective reason: law and order are identical with the life of society itself. In the same process, repression too is depersonalized: constraint and regimentation of pleasure now become a function (and "natural" result) of the social division of labor.[30]

In that case, the reality principle—such as selling one's labor for someone else's profit—is shown to be profoundly ideological, which in turn must modify the representation of the pleasure principle:

> The pleasure principle was dethroned not only because it militated against progress in civilization but also because it militated against a civilization whose progress perpetuates domination and toil. Freud seems to acknowledge this fact when he compares the attitude of civilization toward sexuality with that of a tribe or a section of the population "which has gained the upper hand and is exploiting the rest to its own advantage. Fear of a revolt among the oppressed then becomes a motive for even stricter regulations."[31]

All Freud had to do when evoking the "collaboration" between "fellow workers" was to postulate a society where the social division of labor was not only not "natural" but would no longer exist, or in other words: a classless, communist society of the kind Freud could not contemplate.

Freud's remark cited by Marcuse in the previous quote highlights perfectly the sort of madness we are concerned with here. Dr. Moreau's "Law," which he forces the "manimals" to repeat whenever they threaten to get out of hand, is a paradigm of those "stricter regulations" that become necessary when a form of domination that is cultural and historical is questioned. This must not prevent us, however, from seeing things from the point of view of the mad doctor. The films can be, and need to be, interpreted as representing a form of reaction on the part of the mad doctors who refuse to have their labor alienated and who therefore "revolt" against the society in which they live and its attendant "reality principle" in order to assert their identity. As Marcuse pertinently reminds us: "The memory of gratification is at the origin of all thinking, and the impulse to recapture past gratification is the hidden driving power behind the process of thought."[32] However, for the ego to give way to such gratification would be to destroy it, to give in to the death drive determining the pleasure principle. When Marcuse describes the death drive as "an unconscious flight from pain and want . . . an expression of the eternal struggle against suffering and repression,"[33] I would suggest we see this as a valid comment on the behavior of the mad doctor. The latter strives to overcome the alienation inherent in labor in capitalist society, the only problem being that his unconscious memory of past gratification is narcissistic and individualistic, thus leading him to use and abuse others in his striving for self-realization. The universe being as hostile to him as to any other worker, and the mad doctor functioning under the sway of reified social relations, his need for self-preservation can be satisfied only at the expense of the other/the others. As John Brenkman has stated:

> The subject, in order to find sustenance in a world organized by capitalist social relations, is in effect expelled from the community, in that the bourgeois mode of self-preservation sets the individual against others. The total life of society cannot appear to the subject as the interconnected whole of human activities but instead appears as the calculable relations between things. . . .
>
> Self-preservation is organized as a destructive assault on the body, on others, and on nature. And it positions the homogeneous subject, whether entrepreneur or producer, as the agent of this destruction. . . . *Self-preservation, in the capitalist form, manifests the death drive.*[34]

To conclude, I would like to draw attention to two other aspects of the mad doctor that help to highlight the contradictions within the "reality principle" as now taken for granted in a capitalist society and the fact that their "competitive" nature allows of no reconciliation, except through the destruction of the individual doctor, which we must perforce interpret as the imaginary solution to a real contradiction. The first of these is the fact that, whatever his behavior, the mad doctor is fundamentally refusing the profit motive. Scientific or medical research is, for him, a question of knowledge, and only certain mad doctors wish to use that knowledge for a reason other than narcissistic self-aggrandizement, revenge, or a hysterical refuge from the Thing: for sheer, naked power (one such case is the Lionel Atwill character in *Man Made Monster*, of whom more in chapter 4). The second aspect is that the mad doctor harks back to that mythical time of the primal father. His desire to control everyone and everything leads the other characters—colleagues, wise elders, peasants formed into a mob—to hunt him down and destroy him. Yet it is not necessary to go back so far; we can interpret this in the light of modern families and their values. The mad doctor is a father figure representing older, archaic values, a figure that must be cast down like a false idol lest his insistence on his prerogatives prevent society and science from "progressing" toward an ever more economically efficient reality principle.

Theodor Adorno has some pertinent observations to make here:

Our relationship to parents is beginning to undergo a sad, shadowy transformation. Through their economic impotence they have lost their awesomeness.
Once we rebelled against their insistence on the reality principle, the sobriety
forever prone to become wrath against those less ready to renounce. But today
we are faced with a generation purporting to be young yet in all its reactions
insufferably more grown-up than its parents ever were; which, having re-
nounced before any conflict, draws from this its grimly authoritarian, un-
shakeable power. Perhaps people have at all times felt the parental generation
to become harmless, powerless, with the waning of its physical strength, while
their own generation already seemed threatened by the young: in an antagonistic society the relation between generations too is one of competition, behind which stands naked power.[35]

In the context of the real family, Marcuse sees the son as representing "the
mature reality principle against its obsolescent paternal forms."[36] If we see
the young hero or the wise elder as fulfilling the function of the son, then the
often unconvincing defeat of the mad doctor suggests an unconscious refusal
of the new values, without necessarily constituting a defense of the archaic.
The young hero, insipid and passive, cannot possibly "measure up to" the
phallic father/mad doctor.[37]

In an attempt to bring together and extend the above remarks and the notions of desire and subject positions elaborated in the previous chapters, I
shall now propose a comparative reading of the versions of *Dr. Jekyll and Mr.
Hyde* made in 1931 and 1941.

The Very Strange Case of Dr. Jekyll

We shall see that the representation of character and action in the version of
1931, through both dialogue and the use of the camera, corresponds strikingly to Freud's view of the dream as having a manifest content, a latent content and an unconscious content, which we shall call "desire." It will not
therefore come as a surprise to find that what the film "means" and what it
"says" are not only different but radically opposed, to the point of running
counter to certain dominant interpretations of the "Jekyll and Hyde" myth.

Superficially, the argument that Hyde represents the release of those aspects of Jekyll's personality that cannot find a socially acceptable outlet finds
ample confirmation in the film from the very outset in which Jekyll outlines
his theories to an audience composed of students and colleagues, including
his friend Dr. Lanyon. He insists that man is not one but two, that there is a

good element that is striving to be separated from an evil element so that the former may scale new heights; in that case, the evil side "would trouble us no more." This clearly means that Jekyll in no way believes in an unconscious in the Freudian sense, inasmuch as he implies that the person's good side will be able permanently to dominate penchants toward evil. The fact that the use of certain chemicals will achieve this separation further stresses the biological basis for his arguments and eliminates any need to entertain the notion of unconscious conflicts. At the most, therefore, evil would be preconscious and thus susceptible to control by the good, conscious element that would henceforth dominate the personality. In a discussion with Lanyon after his talk, Jekyll makes it clear that his determination to separate the two sides to human personality stems from his wish to be "clean," implicitly placing the doctor squarely within the ideology of sexuality as something dirty but necessary. And if his remark about sexuality being like a "thirst" that must be quenched suggests a contradiction within his own discourse—sexuality is perfectly natural and therefore not dirty—the remark also lends credence to the notion that sexuality is a natural force leading just as naturally to marriage and procreation. Jekyll spends his time trying to have the date of his marriage put forward by his future father-in-law.

The religious dimension of such arguments is patent and underscored—literally—by the use of organ music as the film's opening credits appear on the screen. References to the human "soul" and the fact that at one point Jekyll prays to God to forgive what Lanyon has denounced as "the ultimate blasphemy" serve to strengthen this ideological presupposition. Given other elements of the dialogue and certain remarkable uses of the camera implying a far less conservative latent content, it is feasible that the scriptwriters chose this approach both to make the film fit in with the dominant ideology of the Victorian era and to placate the censors.[38] Moreover, the symbolic weight lent to the skeleton in Jekyll's laboratory and to the flames behind which the camera is placed for the last shot where Jekyll pays for his hubris with his life underlines the notion that man must not tamper with God's work, a favorite refrain in horror films of the period under discussion, as films as different as *Frankenstein, Island of Lost Souls, The Walking Dead,* and *The Devil Commands* bear witness.

The articulation of dialogue and image, camera and cutting also tends to stress this dual aspect, but in a way that moves simultaneously in the direction of a more psychoanalytic approach. Three quite remarkable—and authentically Freudian—instances illustrate this point. During the first transformation we are shown elements of recent discussions and meetings Jekyll has just had with other characters: his future father-in-law expressing his idea

that it is "indecent" to rush into marriage, his fiancée, Muriel, begging him
to marry her soon, and Ivy, the prostitute, cooing seductively "come back" as
he leaves her bedroom after examining her injuries. Thus the hostility of
General Carew to any view of marriage that considers that sexuality might
extend beyond procreation is linked in Jekyll's mind as he turns into Hyde—
by means of a montage of superimposed faces of characters uttering words we
have just heard—with his desire to get married as quickly as possible, with
Muriel's complete agreement and, especially, with a vision of sexuality that
foregrounds pleasure rather than duty. The second example occurs when Ivy,
reassured by Jekyll that she will never be bothered by Hyde again, returns
home and has a drink to celebrate, expressing aloud the hope that Jekyll—
with whom she has fallen in love—will spare a thought for her. At this point
the door opens—and Hyde walks in. So her wish has come true, albeit in the
form of a dimension of Jekyll's desire that is starting to disturb the manifest
meaning of the film and to which we shall return.

The third instance is crucial for showing that Jekyll has now reached the
stage where he transforms into Hyde without the benefit of his potion. This
lends credence to the notion of the unconscious as something escaping conscious control, while still presenting it in terms of a split creating two sides
to a person's personality; the notion of good and evil dominates, the crucial
shift lying in the awareness that, far from no longer being troubled by evil,
good is now failing. It is here, of course, that the explicitly religious dimension of the film is important for trying to rectify matters. Jekyll walks through
a park on his way to the dinner party being given by General Carew to announce the impending marriage. At one point he hears a bird singing and sits
on a bench to listen. Suddenly he begins to turn into Hyde. The brilliance of
this scene lies in a simple fact that the film does not stress; it is one of the
many examples of the way Mamoulian counts on the intelligence of his spectators. Hyde frequently calls Ivy "my little bird" (we shall see another meaning of this later). Thus, the bird's song evokes unconsciously in Jekyll the verbal expression his "other self" is fond of, which in turn indicates that Jekyll
cannot get Ivy out of his mind. And the only way he can satisfy that desire
socially is to become Hyde.

Clearly much of what I have just outlined works against the manifest content, as I have chosen to suggest possible ways of going beyond a simple di-
chotomy Jekyll/Hyde. However, the film is still sticking to its ideological
guns, inasmuch as it maintains that there is an individual called "Jekyll" who
has succeeded in creating a separate individual called "Hyde" who represents
evil. The fact that Hyde is now stronger than Jekyll only goes to show that
Jekyll underestimated the force of evil in man, which keeps us essentially

within the manifest Christian ideology of the film. As already indicated, we shall have cause to return to certain elements outlined here when considering the way the film represents desire as the desire of the Other. First, however, we must address the latent aspects of the text.

One of the most modern elements in the film lies in the way it shows Muriel ready to support Jekyll and oppose her father. This support and opposition have a clearly sexual basis and are not just a question of being in love. The way she stands up to her father at the end of the film, where he refuses to allow Jekyll to enter his house on account of his failure to turn up to the dinner party and to excuse himself later, indicates an openness of mind and a determination not to submit to paternal authority. This independence of mind may have struck a chord in some women spectators at the time, but it is hardly in keeping with the representation of male-female roles and relationships, either in Hollywood or in society in general. *Dr. Jekyll and Mr. Hyde* is in many ways a remarkably progressive film. Even more to the point—and even more subversive—is the fact that, in supporting Jekyll against her father's wishes that they not marry immediately, she makes it clear that she is "unhappy," too. Given that the film goes as far as it can, without becoming explicit, to suggest that Jekyll has sexual needs that cannot be sublimated any longer, it is also surely clear that she also has the same sexual needs and refuses to await her father's pleasure to satisfy them. As we shall see, however, it is only via Ivy that the film shows that the apparent equality between Jekyll and Muriel is, in fact, a case of imbalance and inequality, but the film is already making an important claim: sexuality is not something that can be turned on and off like a tap. Here the latent content of the film—sexuality as desire, not a social duty—contradicts neatly Jekyll's remark to Lanyon about sex being like a thirst, a remark that represses desire in favor of simple physiological needs. Not surprisingly, therefore, it is through the character of Lanyon that we see the doxa starting to come unstuck.

Lanyon is perfectly in tune with the ideas of General Carew and, despite being a good friend of Jekyll's, is presented from the outset as being impatient with his experiments.[39] We shall analyze in due course the social mould which has produced Carew and his clone, Lanyon, but it is necessary to point out here that Lanyon manifestly shares the General's concept of sexuality as something to be kept for the marriage bed and procreation. Moreover, his acute sense of tradition and etiquette and his benighted opposition to the very idea of change have led him to reject out of hand, without benefit of argument, anything that threatens the status quo, a subject massively overdetermined in the film. However immune he may be to ideas, Lanyon is certainly not immune to something whose existence he denies: desire itself. The look on his face when he enters Ivy's bedroom where Jekyll is examining her and catches a glimpse of Ivy's captivating leg and thigh shows just to what extent he is fascinated.[40] As the two men descend the outside staircase down to the street, Lanyon gives vent to his feelings: "I thought your conduct was disgusting!" We hardly need to insist on the displacement taking place here, where Lanyon is berating Jekyll for what he himself has felt but cannot admit to. More to the point is what ensues. Jekyll dismisses his remark: he was kissed by a pretty girl and admits he liked it. Outraged, Lanyon commands him to control his instincts. Mamoulian has the brilliant idea of accompanying the shot of them outside with the superimposed image of Ivy's leg, swinging seductively to and fro. It is present during the conversation, then suddenly disappears as Lanyon utters his remark about "instincts." This communicates beautifully the fact that Lanyon is also under the sway of Ivy's charms and that, unable to countenance this, he represses again that which has long been repressed but which is in the process of returning. Incapable of questioning himself or society, of even listening to Jekyll's arguments, Lanyon is a paradigm of that particular intimidation of the intelligence that Freud saw as resulting from a submission to religion.[41]

As I have pointed out, it is not until Ivy makes her appearance and is firmly established as a character in her own right that the full implications of Muriel's attitude to her father's refusal to bring forward the date of the wedding start to take shape. Mamoulian's oft-mentioned use of the split screen sets up parallels between the characters that in turn create meanings that exceed even the latent content of the film. The systematic linking of Ivy and Muriel is the most productive manifestation of this. When Jekyll and his fiancée are talking about their future in the garden of her father's home near the beginning of the film, Mamoulian suddenly changes from a shot in which we see them sitting looking at each other to a shot-reverse-shot in which a huge close-up of Muriel as Jekyll talks to her off-screen is followed by an identical close-up of Jekyll talking to her (Muriel is now off-screen). This finds a revealing equivalent in the music hall where Hyde, having met and forced himself in no uncertain fashion on Ivy, starts to kiss her: a huge close-up of her face submitting unwillingly to these advances is followed by the same close-up of Hyde bending down toward her upturned face. We can notice in passing that Hyde's physical superiority echoes the fact that Jekyll talks while his adoring fiancée listens. Before addressing this particular parallel, however, let us observe certain uses of the split-screen technique.

In each case, Mamoulian introduces a wipe so as to divide the screen into two halves. Only two examples interest us for the moment; we shall analyze two others at the appropriate point. Both concern Ivy and Muriel. In the first, a shot where Ivy is being advised by her landlady to seek help from Jekyll, who has just sent her fifty pounds (of which more shall be said presently), is replaced by a wipe that eliminates the landlady and shows Muriel sitting on a sofa in her father's home; Ivy is seen standing on the left, Muriel on the right, the wipe dividing the screen diagonally. In the second, a shot of Muriel sitting on a chair at her father's dinner party and engaged in conversation with an elderly gentleman is replaced by a wipe that eliminates the man and replaces him with a shot of Ivy standing sipping a glass of champagne (the scene, discussed earlier, where she thinks she is celebrating her freedom from Hyde, thanks to Jekyll). In the case of the first shot, Ivy then disappears to be replaced by Jekyll; in the second, it is Muriel who disappears, leaving Ivy alone prior to Hyde's dramatic entrance.

What is being implied in these two shots? Muriel is complaining about Jekyll's unexplained absences, and he is reassuring her of his love—nobody ever needed another person as he needs her. At the dinner party, Muriel is worried at Jekyll's failure to appear (he is in the process of turning into Hyde in the park after hearing the bird sing). The elderly gentleman is trying to comfort her, pointing out that Jekyll is not late—she is simply being impatient. These are exactly the words used by her father, irritated at being asked to allow the couple to marry earlier than planned. If we consider these shots in light of those in which Jekyll talking to and then kissing Muriel is echoed by Hyde talking to and then kissing Ivy, we are surely justified in suggesting that, just as Hyde takes the place of Jekyll, Ivy takes the place of Muriel, and vice versa, inasmuch as in the first shot we move from Ivy and the landlady to Ivy and Muriel, in the second from Muriel and the male guest to Muriel and Ivy. In other words, there is an imbalance: Hyde takes the place of Jekyll, while Ivy and Muriel are literally interchangeable. This imbalance is meaningful in more than one way.

We have seen that both Jekyll and Muriel have sexual needs that cannot wait and that cannot be satisfied, as they are both coded by the discourse of the Other to refuse to have sexual relations until they are married. This discourse does not address men and women on equal terms, however. If Muriel is forced to do without sex, Jekyll can find an outlet if he so desires: he can visit a brothel. To put it more explicitly: If a man cannot sublimate his sexual desires, he can take a lover or find a prostitute; a woman can either take a lover or become a prostitute. This, perhaps, is why Ivy is a member of "the oldest profession," except that there are precise class elements involved that we shall address later. What is interesting here is that, on the level of the text's conscious, it would have been possible for Jekyll to find an outlet for his sexuality by returning to Ivy, not as Hyde but as Jekyll. Let us, for sake of argument, accept that, being a gentleman pure in heart and clean in body, he could avail himself of her charms only by turning into Hyde. After all, it is Jekyll himself who says to Lanyon how "clean" he wants to be. That in no way explains why Hyde is a brute whose libido is sadistic. To return, then, to the question of the latent content of the film, it would have been feasible to present Jekyll's "dual personality" in coherent psychoanalytic terms without resorting to making Hyde so cruel and, crucially, so *ugly*. The critical accusation that Hyde is unconvincing because he is like a Neanderthal man is a nonstarter but indicates the beginnings of an awareness that something is wrong, although, as so often happens, such "awareness" gets nowhere as the reasons for it are unconscious. Such ugliness may fit in with the film's manifest content—the evil side of man belonging to the "animal" in him, as Jekyll says during his public lecture—but it is excessive as far as the psychoanalytic dimension of the film is concerned. I am not interested here in the original story that no film is forced to respect, and Hollywood was notorious for the liberties it took with even the most illustrious works of fiction. *Something else is at stake.* To ascertain why Hyde is so hideous and cruel and what the narrative functions of Ivy and Muriel really are, we need to go back to the scene in the garden where Jekyll and Muriel are talking of their love for each other.

To prove his love, Jekyll says to her, "You've opened a gate into another world," and then admits, surely somewhat incongruously, that this frightens him. Evoking the "unknown" of science, he adds, "Now the unknown looks at me with your eyes." Cut to a huge close-up of Muriel looking into the camera, followed by a close-up of him looking into the camera. We have discussed one level of meaning of these two shots, but now we must look at them in a different context, for the fear that Jekyll feels can only have one coherent meaning: an excessive proximity to the Thing. During the same sequence, Jekyll tells Muriel that she can "chide" him, very much as if he were a little boy. In the previous sequence her father complains that she does not spoil him as she spoils Jekyll, thus placing himself in an identical infantile position. Both men, then, maintain an unconscious quasi-incestuous fixation on Muriel who thus finds herself in the unenviable—and impossible—position of being mother, daughter, and future wife, all at the same time. This unconscious position, be it said, is a *social* one and betrays the way men see women in the society portrayed in the film. For both Jekyll and General Carew—and, we shall see, Lanyon—Muriel is the inaccessible woman who must be raised up to the status of the Sublime to avoid them coming to terms with their desire, facing up to the real role a woman plays in society: a Madonna or a whore. Enter Ivy. Incapable of understanding how women are exploited—reduced to receptacles for procreation or objects with which to assuage male lust—men like Jekyll and Carew fetishize them as manifestations—or objects—of perfection. Just as Hyde refers to Ivy as "my little bird," so Jekyll refers to Muriel as "my little bride," the slippage from one signifier to the other, overdetermined by homophony, representing the metonymy of desire, the impossible signified: Muriel and Ivy as interchangeable objects.[42]

We must be careful, however, not to overstate the similarities between Jekyll and Carew nor to neglect what separates them. Jekyll has reached the point where the contradictions are such that he is breaking loose, hence Carew's impatience and irritation with him. Jekyll's desire to break out of the vicious circle represented by "polite society" is to admit to something that cannot be said. He is a sexual being, and this is why, despite his quasi-religious fervor over Muriel, he is reaching the stage where he can free himself from the discourse of the Other when it comes to representing women as either chaste or whores. It is not, however, possible for Jekyll to liberate himself openly, although liberation is what he is striving after. Thus, when he talks of liberating evil during his lecture, a massive displacement is going on. Another form of "evil" is being referred to: the existence of poverty and his commitment to the poor, whom he treats for nothing, even to the point of giving them precedence over his private patients and, especially, over the dinner parties organized by Carew. Not only does Jekyll refuse to fetishize money, but there is a whiff of class betrayal in the air.

This is a major problem for the general, especially as the fetishization of Muriel transforms her into a commodity. It is for this reason that a certain textual logic represents her and Ivy as interchangeable, circulating like goods, with money as the common factor. For people like the general, Ivy is a necessary evil; she is a commodity that can be bought and hence enables him to repress the real role of women in society and their place in maintaining that role. With Freud, we can see Carew as the condensation of authority and the superego—it is hardly an accident that he is a soldier.[43] He has learned repression and submission to authority the hard way and is a paradigm of the subject an aspect of whose ego has regressed to the anal stage. Congratulating Lanyon for being punctual and claiming that he himself always has been "for forty years," which he puts down to "training," and evokes an incident that occurred when he was four without saying what it was. "Training," not "discipline," just as adults talk of "training" young children to go to the toilet, either when they need to or when they are told to. What the general submitted to he is now demanding that Jekyll submit to, aided and abetted in this by his stand-in, Lanyon. Jekyll and Lanyon have certain things in common: both doctors, they live in huge, luxurious homes and have servants. Both therefore are wealthy, although the film does not say whether their wealth comes exclusively from private practice or also from property. Clearly Carew lives on the income from wealth accumulated or inherited. The theme of money is insistent in the film.

Why, for instance, does Jekyll send Ivy fifty pounds, a considerable sum at the time? On the manifest level of the film, he is anxious to compensate for the wrongs Hyde has done her; on the latent content, which the film cannot render explicit, he is expressing a desire to keep in touch with her. On the unconscious level, things are much more complex. Ivy comes to see Jekyll, who acts surprised; the conscious meaning of his act returns to him in the true inverted form of his desire. Ivy says, "I'll slave for you," so desperate is she to free herself not only from Hyde but the role imposed on her by a patriarchal society, or, in other words, rather a relationship of a feudal nature where the lord accepts his obligations to his serfs than life in a capitalist society where all relations are mediated by money and where women, particularly but not exclusively those of Ivy's class, are commodified.

Let us return to Carew who, as we have said, has regressed to the anal stage. To be more precise, we should have said that mnemic traces of the anal stage lead him to punish Jekyll as he himself was punished for acts—or refusals—that ceased to exist after early childhood: accepting or refusing to relinquish his feces. Carew is the authoritarian superego that "enforces not only the demands of reality but also those of a *past* reality."[44] By not recognizing the real forces at work in society, Carew can see the present in terms of the past and appeal to tradition as if it were something natural and ahistorical. Having been obliged to behave in a certain way and to accomplish certain tasks in order to exist and function, he now assumes everyone to be concerned in an identical manner—everyone, that is, of his own class, something that is also taken for granted, like the place of women. Carew therefore cannot understand that Jekyll can work without payment, in what are called the "free wards" in hospitals. Since everything is mediated by money, that Jekyll should not exchange his knowledge of medicine for money is literally unthinkable; to ask why would be to question the entire economic basis of society where the "performance principle" is seen as an "economic authority."[45] Paternal authority and economic authority overdetermine each other, functioning in a closed circuit that eliminates history and ensures domination.

Just as the general had to wait five years before being able to marry, so he wants to delay the wedding of Jekyll to Muriel. Significantly, the date he has chosen is the anniversary of his own wedding. With one fell swoop he not only hopes to bring Jekyll to his senses—force him to abandon his charitable work and get on with the "normal" business of making money—but also expects Jekyll to submit to what I would term a "repeat performance principle," reinforcing society and paternal authority alike. Lanyon has a particular function to play in this "game." Like Carew, he punishes Jekyll by denouncing him to the police. If this can be justified on the grounds that Hyde is a murderer (he has just killed Carew, as symbolic an act as one could ask for!), another unconscious logic is at work. Lanyon is, as it were, carrying on the good work of the patriarch, while at the same time getting his revenge on Jekyll for the latter's superior social position (he has fame as well as money) and, arguably, for Jekyll obtaining the love of a woman, Muriel. Interestingly, he is as sadistic toward Jekyll as Hyde is toward Ivy, except that it does not appear so because, although cold and calculating (money is at stake), he is carrying out the desire of the ideological big Other, the social status quo. Lanyon, who is not a mad doctor of the Moreau or Vollin variety, surely reflects Lacan's notion of the sadist as the mere instrument of the Other's *jouissance*.[46]

Immediately after Jekyll's lecture, Lanyon expects his colleague to accompany him to a dinner engagement at the house of a duchess, but Jekyll has other things in mind: the patients in the free ward. Since this choice on his part takes place in the context of a discussion on the need to separate good from evil, with Jekyll anxious to allow the good elements to elevate man even further, a fascinating opposition is set up between an evening in polite society and looking after the poor. Good versus Evil? We need to address two questions: What is the meaning of Jekyll's desire to split good from evil, and what is the meaning of his commitment to helping the poor when they are sick? A number of strands of the story need to be followed through before we can hope to see them converging.

Critics have been quick to seize on the symbolism of "the front door" and "the back door" to Jekyll's abode and to interpret this in clear-cut terms: Jekyll versus Hyde, the conscious versus the repressed. The only problem with this is that it assumes that neither Jekyll nor Hyde is the locus of contradictions as a character in his own right, which we have seen to be a nonstarter. Perhaps we can approach the question by taking Hyde's name as a signifier, indicating not only something hidden but also "a hide" in the sense of "a home," where the notion of the secretive is already contained in the word *hide*. Hyde thus represents both what is "homely" and "familiar," and that aspect of it that has become unfamiliar and susceptible to produce anxiety through repression. Hyde is therefore the locus of *das Unheimliche*, the Uncanny. Early in the film, protesting at the way the general dictates things to his daughter and, by extension, to him, too, Jekyll exclaims, "I don't want to marry your father." If we take this statement as a form of unconscious denial, we can interpret it as indicating a desire on Jekyll's part to have the right to be both an upright bourgeois citizen and a person indulging his drives at will at the expense of others: the Father of Enjoyment. Strictly speaking then, something in Jekyll presents an aspect of the general's character that the latter has repressed and cannot give vent to: the naked and unhindered exercise of class domination untrammeled by bourgeois rules and regulations.

To sustain this argument, I shall point out a strange "inconsistency" on the level of the image. At one point Carew, beside himself at Jekyll's absence from his dinner party, says to his daughter, "I forbid you to see this man again." There follows a wipe that eliminates Muriel from the shot and reveals—Hyde, so that the two men are "facing" each other within the frame. It would be difficult to indicate more clearly that the general "knows" Jekyll is Hyde and therefore recognizes in Jekyll/Hyde something about his own social position that he cannot have access to: the Real of an impossible desire. We shall soon see other aspects of this class element coming to the surface.

Hyde's behavior at the Variety Music Hall is an instance of this split within desire itself. He is simply a brute, threatening and even beating up anyone who gets in his way or, by a look or a remark, seems to be questioning his God-given right to use others as he wishes. The "feudal baron" aspect of Hyde—who, significantly, remains dressed in the clothes that signify his belonging to the upper class—marks an interesting link with Dracula who was a product of the Middle Ages and who brings to the foreground the notion of "bleeding people dry," an obvious case of class exploitation.[47] What needs to be remembered in this sequence is the fact that Hyde does not simply brutalize and terrorize the unfortunate Ivy. At the beginning of their encounter, Hyde is clearly overcome by Ivy's beauty and says she deserves better than the hovel in which she lives, to which she replies sarcastically, "Buckingham Palace, I suppose." Hyde roars with laughter and cries, "That's the spirit!" His pleasure is clear, as is the class complicity between them at this brief moment, all too soon repressed in favor of Hyde's brutality and sadism.

But the point has been made, especially as the film contains an interesting parapraxis. Hyde refers to Ivy's address as "Baffin's Court," whereas the newspaper that announces her murder says she lived at "Diadem Court." The fact that Ivy's name is spelled in the credits as "Pierson" and in the newspaper cutting as "Pearson" draws attention to the first syllable of the name as a signifier in its own right: it can also be written as "Peer." And "Baffin's Court"—a decidedly odd name—can be seen as an unconscious deformation of "boffin," an English word for a scientist. That two parapraxes in as many lines can be seen as simple carelessness on the part of those responsible for continuity is a notion I refuse to take seriously, except as a desire on the part of critics to repress again what is coming to light: an unconscious desire on Ivy's part to "go up in the world" and the copresence within Hyde of brutal social repression and a desire for social progress—indeed, social upheaval.[48]

Now, *boffin* designates a scientist doing military research, which creates a fascinating link among Jekyll, Hyde, and Carew. If Hyde is brutal and contemptuous toward the proletariat, as we have seen, then he represents General Carew without a superego to watch over excesses, to control drives that have now become unacceptable to bourgeois society but that were once indulged freely. Hyde is a reactionary in the literal sense: putting the clock back to "the good old days" (what member of the proletariat would use such a formula?), to an epoch of limitless exploitation of the working class, an exploitation that continues but has been shorn of its most excessive and "unlawful" cruelty and brutality. Hyde behaves like a capitalist: he strives to obtain as much as possible from manual labor, craving limitless profit beyond what is necessary for survival. Hyde, in all his ramifications, represents both *plus de jouissance* and *surplus value*.

Hyde is thus also *objet a*, the surplus produced by Jekyll's desire: a thirst for knowledge and an attempt to go beyond good and evil to attain that knowledge. Jekyll himself is a wealthy bourgeois living off surplus value and doing acts of charity to make up for it unconsciously, as a form of "penance." This is just the word Jekyll uses when he goes to Muriel at the end and renounces her: "This will be my penance." He is not being noble, although this is how he sees his gesture. It is because the full implications of Hyde are having an effect on him: the total breakdown of values: sexual, social, and political. This can be interpreted as anarchy—or revolution. We must not lose from sight that Jekyll, in wanting to separate good and evil, considered this a way to free good and let evil perish. After the initial transformation, Hyde stands triumphantly before a mirror and cries, "Free at last!" Now it was good, not evil that Jekyll intended to set free, so Hyde's cry has surely a Utopian side to it: to free that element in Jekyll that calls out for radical social change, that puts the poor first and that, in the shape of Hyde, cheers Ivy when she evokes what is for her and her class the impossible social Real: the proletariat occupying Buckingham Palace. In the discourse of a communist (i.e., Marxist) Utopia, this remains an end to strive after.

Stevenson wrote *Dr. Jekyll and Mr. Hyde* not long after the Commune, at a time when the bourgeoisie thought it had laid to rest the specter of proletarian struggles (we address this topic later and in chapter 4). That this was to be a pious hope is represented in one of the most remarkable set pieces of the film. After the lecture, Jekyll and Lanyon walk back home through foggy streets discussing Jekyll's theories. What is striking is that, thanks to a rapid fade, they leave the fashionable neighborhood and find themselves in Soho, as if the two districts were as contiguous geographically as they become in the film. It is a nice instance of the cinematic signifier connoting desire and class at the same time. It is at this point that cries are heard and Jekyll rushes to help Ivy. These cries emerging from the dense fog, this abrupt eruption of a working-class neighborhood, surely herald the return of the (socially) re-pressed and present Jekyll with a reality Lanyon is anxious to keep at bay. Inasmuch as Lanyon and Carew represent an aspect of Jekyll that is domi-nant, albeit threatened by Jekyll's independent frame of mind, we can per-haps interpret Hyde's ugliness not only in terms of the Thing that turns from the Sublime to the monstrous when approached too closely, but he also con-denses the ugliness of the society that has secreted him and that of the pro-letariat in bourgeois representations of them: dirty, hirsute creatures. Hyde's hideousness and elegance is the signifier of the class struggle that is the film's "real" subject. As Jean-Jacques Lecercle has written so cogently of Hyde, there is a certain monstrous vitality about him attributed socially to the other in its various forms: the Jew, the black, and so forth. Hyde thus becomes for Lecercle a stand-in for the "dangerous classes" and a symbol of all that threat-ens the established social order. Ultimately Hyde is the revolutionary, whereas Frankenstein's monster is the "sans-culotte."[49] We shall keep this point in mind.

Turning to the 1941 version of *Dr. Jekyll and Mr. Hyde* is a dispiriting ex-perience, although we shall see that it does have something to teach us. The film is completely sanitized in a way that goes so far beyond the require-ments of Breen that these are simply irrelevant. In other words, if Ingrid Bergman does not exude the same sensuality as Miriam Hopkins, she does remarkably well, given the changed circumstances. No, other factors are at work, and they are infinitely more interesting and to the point. That the film reduces Jekyll's experiments to the releasing of that desire for the for-bidden fruit that is a sexually promiscuous working-class girl can be seen as a paradigm of what Metro Goldwyn Mayer Studios (MGM) had become un-der the aegis of the ultraconservative Louis B. Mayer. The film was in the hands of those who were soon to form the Motion Picture Alliance for the Preservation of American Ideals, ostensibly to combat communism in Hol-lywood. Thus, both director Victor Fleming and art director Cedric Gibbons were among the founding members of the Alliance, while screenwriter John Lee Mahin was from the mid-1930s one of the most active members of the Screen Playwrights, MGM's conservative "house union."

Gone from the film are the implications of the fifty pounds sent by Jekyll to Ivy; now the gift is anonymous, and it is Ivy's friend who suggests she contact Jekyll. Gone are all the marvelously inventive uses of the camera and cutting. By so blatantly reducing Jekyll's quest to a need to answer the call of the flesh, the film sets up a simple "good versus evil" equation that it never gets beyond, thus making of the story a cautionary tale in keeping with the ideology of its makers. There are, however, two new elements that merit our close attention. One of these—and here we must do Mahin justice—is a striking anticipation of Lacan's theory of the discourse of the Other in all its social and cultural implications. The other element only goes to show just to what extent the film is a profoundly reactionary and repressive enterprise.

Prior to trying out his formula on himself for the first time, Jekyll sits down to write a letter to his fiancée, Beatrice, informing her that he must go ahead, even if it should mean his death. As he writes the fateful word, Fleming cuts to a shot of Beatrice sitting up in bed, apparently wakened from a nightmare. She rushes over to Jekyll's house—in the middle of the night!—to see if he is still there, as she has had a premonition that he was "going away." As he comforts and reassures her, who should walk in but Sir Charles, the father of Beatrice and a *père sévère* ("stern father"), who puts even General Carew in the shade, at least in one domain we shall have cause to analyze presently. Finding her missing, he has concluded that she has gone to see Jekyll. The film has already shown that Sir Charles disapproves totally of Jekyll's experiments and is becoming increasingly dubious both of his conduct and of the prospect of having him as a son-in-law. This current "escapade" leads him to take his daughter abroad, out of Jekyll's way.

What is so interesting about this sequence? Freud mentioned on several occasions his belief that the unconscious of one person could enter into contact with the unconscious of another without becoming conscious. I would suggest that Beatrice's suddenly waking up is caused, on the one hand, by an unconscious "knowledge" of the nature of Jekyll's experiments and, on the other hand, by her desire for her father to "go away"—in other words, *die*— so that she can have free access to the man she loves. To this we must surely add that the equally unexpected and unmotivated arrival of Sir Charles is triggered by his refusal to give up his daughter, unless it be in circumstances that indicate that the man taking his place has totally submitted to the father and has recognized that he is right in all things (or has all the rights). The film can, at least on this issue, be read as an early and protofeminist work berating the inferior status of the woman in bourgeois society. The other new element in the film shows, however, that not only is this aspect a purely isolated phenomenon, but that the "real" meaning of the film has nothing to do with repressed sexuality at all.

The film opens with a sanctimonious sermon in church about moral values and the need for all and sundry to follow the example of Queen Victoria.[50] Suddenly a man of patently working-class origins starts to heckle him, evoking the Devil. Jekyll takes over as the man is escorted out so that he will not be thrown in prison but put in Jekyll's care, for Jekyll has seen in the episode the proof of his belief in the struggle between good and evil in man. The episode exists therefore to show that an apparently good man—a "solid citizen" as Jekyll significantly calls him—can be the prey to evil forces, those driving him to disrupt a sermon whose sole purpose is to defend the most self-satisfied and repressive status quo.[51] Thanks to Jekyll's questions, we learn that the man had been living a "normal" life until an explosion at work, following which he is prone to the sort of outburst we have just witnessed.

The film thus at one and the same time evokes the dangers inherent in certain forms of manual labor and denies that there is anything political or economic about them. Or, rather, it does evoke the political and the economic, but in such a displaced way as to repress their real function in society. The incident in church needs to be seen in conjunction with a later scene during the travels abroad of Sir Charles and his daughter. In order to hide from her father the content of a letter from Lanyon informing her that he has not seen Jekyll for some time and expressing his anxiety that she has not heard from him, Beatrice pretends that her fiancé has become interested in improving the housing conditions of the workers as a result of a visit to a poor neighborhood of London. Sir Charles welcomes this activity—it will occupy Jekyll's mind and turn him away from those useless experiments that keep him away from the important thing in life: building up his practice, making money, and forging a social reputation.

Now Mahin's script has the merit of denouncing the notion that doctors should be more interested in class contacts and their bank balance than in the health and welfare of the community, a point of view that might have caused him trouble after the war had he not been an impeccable conservative. There is, however, no reason to assume that a man of the Right will not be interested in social matters or will not have a pronounced sense of commitment to a particular social cause. For Mahin, a doctor's first concern must be with his patients. This, of course, is a moralistic discourse based on a conventional—but not wrong-headed—notion of duty. Politics and economics thus become strictly *irrelevant* in the film, as the matter is seen in a purely *individual* light. Unconsciously, however, Mahin has revealed the fundamentally conservative and repressive nature of such a discourse by introducing the theme of class, which promptly creates an excess of meaning in the film that escapes both his notice and his control. Jekyll's experiments have always been on animals, and we see him administering the potion to rats that become docile and to rabbits that become aggressive. The "morality" behind this is fairly clear, once one brings together the disturbance in the church and the role of money and domination. Evil is equated with working-class violence and bourgeois lasciviousness, both of which must be repressed. That Sir Charles should be delighted at the idea of Jekyll going in for a bit of charity work thus means that the film is suggesting that one only has to improve the living and working conditions of the lower orders for them to function perfectly according to the precepts of their social betters.

It should also be noted that one of the pertinent traits of "evil" in Mr. Hyde lies in his eating habits: he spits out grape seeds! When those who rule society can no longer behave themselves at the table, then it can hardly be surprising if the workers copy the "wrong" values. To put it another way: by spitting out grape stones, Hyde is behaving as if he were a member of the working class.[52] This is more in keeping with bourgeois fears. The sexuality of the working class is a force that must be contained, repressed at all costs, by force if necessary—as it might contaminate the established order, thus showing that the latter's representatives are not so sure about their right to rule or the solidity of their domination. Equating evil with, among other things, working-class "violence" surely means that the unconscious discourse of the film is that of a bourgeoisie that knows its domination can be challenged and where that challenge lies. Which brings us to the representation of class and labor in 1930s horror.[53]

The Peasants Are Revolting

There is an old joke about a faithful feudal retainer who runs panic stricken into his master's castle, shouting, "Sire! Sire! The peasants are revolting!" to which the baron replies: "Yes, they are rather, aren't they?" I suggest we see in this seemingly terrible pun an astute comment on the state of mind represented in a number of horror films: an awareness of the real situation at hand that is repressed in a desire to keep the Real at bay, in which the meaning of what is represented is treated in an offhand manner betraying a form of contempt, of social and intellectual superiority. Clearly the baron in the joke is living in a world of fantasy, untouched by any of the grim realities around him. The Master Signifier turns on feudal power and cannot therefore accommodate any signified that as much as questions let alone threatens it. Thus the terrible joke is really most astute: it reflects the psychic structure of the baron and of the absent subject of the enunciation of the joke, thus un-veiling the unconscious of class.

Peasants, villagers, and townspeople are represented in *Dracula*, *Mark of the Vampire*, *The Vampire Bat*, *Frankenstein*, *Bride of Frankenstein*, *Son of Frankenstein*, *White Zombie*, and *The Black Room*. In a very different way they appear in *The Mask of Fu Manchu* and *The Devil Commands*. The third film in the Frankenstein saga is superficially different inasmuch as the hostility of the villagers is aimed from the outset at the eponymous central character rather than at the monster, but we shall see that a link is forged between this film and the first of the series. For reasons that will become clear, I am mak-ing no attempt here to distinguish between peasants, villagers and towns-people. We shall pursue these investigations at length in the next section in which I shall show why "the peasants are revolting." To set the scene I shall restrict myself here to some preliminary remarks, sometimes of a descriptive nature, before proposing a reading of a special case: *White Zombie*.

The very opening of the very first film of the period, *Dracula*, sets the scene for the representation of peasants and villagers in these films. God-fearing and superstitious, they dress and behave quaintly, although their fear of vampires soon proves to be only too justified. Renfield the rationalist will have cause to regret his contempt for such fears.[54] Van Helsing's later remark about "the superstition of today" becoming "the reality of tomorrow" can be interpreted as follows: The film is suggesting that the villagers have a better grasp of things than their social and intellectual "betters." That Dracula is a sort of feudal baron living off the blood of the locals is an element that must not be forgotten, in the light of other films of the period, such as *Franken-stein*, *Dr. Jekyll and Mr. Hyde*, and *The Black Room*. It is significant that in Stoker's novel Van Helsing should regret that Dracula does not emanate from God, such is his potential for Good on Earth. In other words, if Drac-ula bled people dry figuratively, what a gift he would be to the ruling class![55]

In the case of *Mark of the Vampire*, it could easily be argued that the film's opening, with its terrified and superstitious villagers, is a simple irrelevance or the pandering to prejudice, given that the whole story is an elaborate plot to confound a murderer: there is no such thing as a vampire. However, in the light of what that plot hides the better to represent it in displaced forms—the little matter of incest—one could with more justification claim that these villagers, too, have a better grasp of things than the bourgeois charac-ters: they at least know that certain drives can be fatal if indulged in and, al-beit unconsciously, take the necessary precautions.[56] In *The Vampire Bat*, the village idiot, Herman, is the victim of a witch hunt because his fondness for bats is interpreted as proof that he is the vampire said to be terrorizing the neighborhood. We have here an example of peasants and villagers turning against a hapless outcast and destroying him in the name of security; we shall return to this theme in its various guises in the next section. Suffice it to point out that *Bride of Frankenstein* quite subtly shows how those who are transformed by a given community into "the other," who must be cast out to preserve an imaginary identity—in this case a family of gypsies, also need someone or something to expel to preserve their enforced identity, now experienced as natural. This is a classic case of miscognition. The gypsies, who are clearly forced to live alone in the forest, feel threatened by the monster, a reversal of roles whose significance we will make clear later.

In *Frankenstein*, the villagers are depicted as ever ready to don "traditional" garb—Hollywood's ideological vision of how people in "exotic" places dress—and frolic in a carefree manner in the village square to celebrate a great event such as Frankenstein's getting married. This is, of course, but a reflection of the importance given to the event by his father, the baron, who addresses the villagers from the window of his castle, very much like a monarch or head of state today, informing them generously that there will be as much beer as they need, a remark greeted by thunderous cheers. The situation is a perfect manifestation of what Slavoj Zizek, in a discussion of a remark made by Marx in *Capital*, has referred to as a "mandate":

> To the participants of this social bond, the relationship appears necessarily in an inverse form: they think that they are subjects giving the king royal treatment because the king is already in himself, outside the relationship to his subjects, a king; as if the determination of "being-a-king" were a "natural" property of the person of a king.[57]

The fact that Baron Frankenstein has nothing but contempt for his faithful subjects—turning away from the window, he remarks, "Tomorrow they'll all be fighting"—at one and the same time introduces the notion of irresponsible villagers and looks ahead to the fact that the villagers will unite to fight the monster and represses the class dimension of the remark. The baron behaves exactly like the feudal baron in our joke. Similarly, in *Son of Frankenstein*, the villagers, who have shunned the central character and his family since their return to the village where it all started, cheer him enthusiastically—despite the havoc his experiments have created—when, on departing, he leaves to the village his estate and the title to the castle.

A clear parallel is to be found in *The Black Room*, but the situation is more complex and contains sufficient inconsistencies to put us on our guard. The film relates the tale of an aristocratic family living under a curse: should twin sons be born, the younger (the one who comes second into the world) will kill the elder. When this happens, at the beginning of the film, the father seals up the room—the "black room" of the title—where the killings have taken place in the past so as to prevent a repeat performance. When the twins are adults, Anton, the second born, leaves in order to avoid the hostility of his brother, Gregor, and then returns at the latter's request when they are age forty. All this, however, is a plan by Gregor to overcome the implacable enmity of the villagers, due to his penchant for seducing and then murdering their wives. Gregor murders Anton and takes his place, having already abdicated to placate his restless and increasingly hostile subjects. This enables him to obtain from one Colonel Hassel the permission to marry his daughter. Forced to murder the colonel when the latter discovers the truth, Gregor frames the young soldier who wants to marry the daughter. In this way, he has disposed of all his opponents and the two houses can be united. Unmasked during the wedding ceremony, Gregor is trapped by the villagers and falls to his death into the same pit where he threw the body of Anton.

The inconsistencies in question turn on the character of the colonel. On the one hand he is represented as the figure of authority in the district, a sort of representative of the government. Yet he seems to have no power to intervene on behalf of the villagers: they have already appealed to the authorities, who have refused to answer. Now the colonel makes no attempt to hide his loathing of Gregor and his sympathy for the plight of the villagers, but the film cannot follow through the logic of an earlier scene where the desperate villagers have reached the point where they realize they can count on nobody but themselves. A genuinely collective attitude is in the process of taking shape, with the peasants literally revolting. However, it soon transpires that they are quite happy to be lorded over by Anton and are simply opposed to Gregor's cruelty. Thus, the film presents the rebellion as being devoid of any class element by reducing it, in the best Hollywood tradition, to a question of individuals, with Gregor filling the shoes of the mad doctor.[58] This is made abundantly clear by a low-angle shot of the colonel as he sallies forth from Gregor's castle to face the "mob"; the castle towers up behind him, lending him a symbolic authority that indicates that birth is everything, provided one has the power which goes with it. Which is the case here, as the colonel is just as anxious as Gregor to unite their houses and, by implication, to increase their wealth and power. It is therefore as fitting as it is revealing that the film should open with the villagers bringing gifts to celebrate the impending birth and close with them dancing in the square to celebrate the forthcoming marriage between "Anton" and the colonel's daughter, Thea. Ultimately, Anton occupies the same position as the baron in *Frankenstein*, as do the villagers: they know their place, and the "mandate" is safe.

White Zombie has drawn much comment thanks to its use of zombies as an extended metaphor for the exploitation of labor by capital, the unseeing, unthinking and unfeeling zombies functioning as a stand-in for alienated labor and the notion of having no control over either one's labor power or its products. They are the perfect manifestation, in a supposed fantasy setting, of Marx's remark that "Man has often made man himself, under the form of slaves, serve as the primitive material of money."[59] The zombies are the "desubjectivized living dead, frail specters deprived of their material substance."[60] As has been pointed out, the film "enacts quite literally what in other films is represented only by implication: the link between character alliances and property relations."[61] Just as the Haiti plantation owner Beaumont uses zombie master Murder Legendre to "own" the body of Madeline, whom he loves but who is about to marry Neil, so Beaumont in turn is "owned" by Legendre, who thus adds him to the "collection" of people under his control: both the black workers transformed into zombies and the members of the white ruling-class whom Legendre is thus punishing for their refusal to accept him.[62] If we apply to *White Zombie* Freud's remark that the hypnotist is occupying the place of the ego ideal,[63] then it becomes clear that Beaumont identifies with Legendre-as-colonialist because he is himself the signifier of colonialist drives.

This is the point to take up the analysis by Edward Lowry and Richard deCordova of the gaze of Legendre in the film's opening sequence in which he stands in the way of the coach bearing Madeline and Neil to the home of Beaumont. The first shot of the sequence is of the coach heading along a road at night toward the camera:

> Suddenly, two enormous eyes are superimposed across the frame, staring directly at the spectator. The shot of the coach fades out, leaving only the eyes against a black background. Almost immediately, another long-shot of the coach proceeding toward the camera begins to fade in, but this time Legendre stands in the mid-ground in the center of the frame, next to the road, facing the carriage, with his back toward the camera. The enormous eyes still fill the frame; but as soon as the new shot has faded in completely, the eyes shrink and move toward Legendre. When they reach the back of his head, they fade out completely, disappearing into him.[64]

As the authors rightly point out, the eyes are absent from the diegetic world set up by the film, but present as the dominant factor of the enunciation. They are (1) within the action; (2) in a space existing outside the action but within the frame; and (3) looking in from the outside, like the film's spectators. This means that the eyes will be "read as supernatural."[65]

Although I agree entirely that this is how the eyes will be read inasmuch as they are given a "life of their own" and cannot be simply assimilated to the eyes of Legendre, it seems to me that to leave things here would be to misread what is implied by the unconscious of the text. To begin with, it might be more accurate to refer, not to "the eyes," but to "the *look*," especially in light of the way the film later sets up the equation of Legendre's look and his relation, based on power and desire, with the other characters in the film. I would suggest that the film is representing, most subtly, the real nature of colonial exploitation, where the colonialist passes off his presence in the colonial country as going without saying, presenting himself as someone from *outside* who just happens to be living, working and making his living in the country colonized.[66] That *White Zombie* is a film dealing with the supernatural is patent. Yet Legendre's look in this sequence both extends and limits the notion of the control and exploitation of labor. It extends, as it shows Legendre attempting to exert total control over black islanders, the local ruling class, and Western visitors as well, a condensation of "global capitalism," as it were. It limits, as it tends to displace the theme of class and economic exploitation onto the more time-honored and conventional horror theme of hypnosis, on which the film's manifest content turns. Thus, the supernatural needs to be granted its political dimension, as it is nicely contained in Zizek's formula quoted earlier: the zombies as "frail specters." These "specters" are resolutely human, and it is to this theme and its attendant vocabulary and imagery that we shall now turn.

Specters of the World, Unite!

At one point in *Bride of Frankenstein*, a mob of incensed villagers pursues the monster through a wood, captures, and brings it/him—we shall return to this linguistic "split"—back to the village, where the creature is chained to a chair in a dungeon. Left alone, it struggles briefly, tears itself free from its chains, breaks down the door and escapes, sowing panic everywhere. As critics have fallen over one another to present the capture of Frankenstein's creation in religious—and therefore transcendental and ahistorical—terms by comparing the monster to Christ,[67] I suggest we see the shot of the creature freeing itself with remarkable ease as a reference to the exhortation of Marx and Engels at the close of *The Communist Manifesto*: the proletariat has nothing to lose but its chains—in which case the signifier has left its Marx on the filmic text.

The Communist Manifesto opens, of course, with the celebrated reference to "the specter of Communism." Chris Baldick entitles a chapter of his splendid book *In Frankenstein's Shadow* "Karl Marx's Vampires and Grave-diggers."[68]

Raising the question of why Marx should go back to something as archaic as "a Gothic phantom" to describe "the new, unashamedly self-interested bourgeois world," Baldick adds that, for Marx, the "specter" in question is really "a nursery tale or bogy," which in turn can only lead us to wonder why Marx should have been so anxious to show how the new, triumphant bourgeoisie could still be haunted:

> The problem repeats itself throughout Marx's writings, in which some of the most gruesomely archaic echoes of fairy-tale, legend, myth, and folklore crop up in the wholly unexpected environment of the modern factory system, stock exchange, and parliamentary chamber: ghosts, vampires, ghouls, werewolves, alchemists, and reanimated corpses continue to haunt the bourgeois world, for all its sober and skeptical values.[69]

This dense and succinct passage evokes perfectly the world of the horror film, but much more: it reminds us that a particular representation can be invaluable for throwing new, unexpected light on a question apparently totally removed from it. In an attempt to discover the meaning of the monster's energetic breaking of its chains in a village dungeon, I propose to look at a number of heterogeneous quotes, their very heterogeneity condensing nicely that of the monster's body parts.

Writing on *Frankenstein*, one critic has said that Frankenstein's servant, the hunchback Fritz, torments the creature (suitably chained in the dungeon beneath Frankenstein's laboratory) "for no apparent reason."[70] Summing up the story of *Bride of Frankenstein* and the collaboration between Frankenstein and Pretorius, Bryan Senn writes, "With the aid of a murderer-cum-graverobber named Karl . . . the scientists set about constructing their woman. (Karl comes to a sticky end when the monster *inexplicably* stalks up to the roof and hurls the little ghoul to his death during the experiment's climax)."[71] Baldick has drawn attention to the fact that Edmund Burke attacked "the French revolutionaries not just as cannibals, but as sorcerers, alchemists, and fanatical scientists" and goes on to quote Burke's reference to "a vast, tremendous unformed specter" rising "out of the tomb of the murdered monarchy in France."[72] In the course of a discussion of Derrida's *Spectres de Marx*, Fredric Jameson writes that "it is the absence of the problem of materialism, its occultation or repression, the impossibility of posing it as a problem as such and in its own right, which generates the figure of the specter," going on to suggest that the abandoning of the notion of class in favor of such issues as race, gender, and multiculturalism—a regrettable tendency that he sees as being systematic on the Left—has led to this state of affairs.[73] Let us step back and try to ascertain what is being rehearsed here.

The quotes on the two James Whale films have a rhetorical device in common: behavior is seen as taking place "inexplicably" or "for no apparent reason," which at once implies that something unknown is determining the action referred to, an element the critic disavows. This provides the basis for my analyses in what follows. If we now juxtapose Burke and Senn, while keeping Burke and Hare in mind, we shall note a strange but not inexplicable thing happening. To Burke's evocation of the revolutionaries in terms identical to Marx's representation of the bourgeois capitalist[74] corresponds an intriguing element in *Bride of Frankenstein*: the fact that the grave robber (who, perforce, is also a grave digger) is called Karl and is referred to by Senn as "the little ghoul." In other words, the unconscious of the filmic text is overdetermined by that of Senn to produce the following equally unconscious ideological semes: Karl (Marx) as someone exploiting the dead; the monster as exorcising this particular specter by killing him; the collaboration between two scientists and a member of the working class in creating life from dead tissue. What can possibly be going on here?

The alert reader will have noticed that I have had recourse twice to the term *collaboration*, once to refer to the experiment carried out by Frankenstein and Pretorius, then to the fact that they are aided and abetted by Karl. This is deliberate on my part, as what interests us here, among other related matters, is *class collaboration*, which, in a variety of guises, is a fundamental (unconscious?) theme of the horror film. It is necessary to return here to Jameson's study:

> Class consciousness turns first and foremost around subalternity, that is around the experience of inferiority. This means that the "lower classes" carry about within their heads unconscious convictions as to the superiority of hegemonic or ruling-class expressions and values, which they equally transgress and repudiate in ritualistic (and socially and politically ineffective) ways. . . .
>
> It should also be noted that everything that has been said here about subalternity holds for hegemonic or ruling-class consciousness itself, which bears within itself the fears and anxieties raised by the internalized presence of the underclasses and symbolically acts out what might be called an "incorporation" of those class hostilities which are built into the very structure of ruling-class consciousness as a defensive response to them. . . .
>
> This means in effect that each of the opposing classes necessarily carries the other around in its head and is internally torn and conflicted by a foreign body it cannot exorcize.[75]

I shall now suggest that the forms of transgression and repudiation taken by the peasants, villagers, and assorted "mobs" in horror films—the "lower classes"—can be highlighted, described, and analyzed only if we keep in mind Freud's teaching that conflicting and mutually opposed ideas can be represented simultaneously in the unconscious; and that the effects of ideology can—and do—lead people to turn against those who are their "objective allies."

That Frankenstein's monster represents the proletariat is patent, perhaps *too* patent. Let us, however, for the sake of argument, take this as "read," which will enable us to interpret the form of disavowal underpinning the quoted remarks about Fritz tormenting the monster "for no apparent reason" and the monster "inexplicably" killing Karl. In a world based on class antagonism where the wealth of one class depends on the systematic and never-ending exploitation of the labor power of the other class, what better way to "escape" exploitation than to throw one's lot in with the dominant side? This does not change the nature and existence of one's own exploitation but through a fantasy one believes it does. In other words, Fritz tormenting the monster is one member of the proletariat turning against another. Basically, Fritz nurses a grudge against his master Frankenstein, (mis)perceiving the latter as someone having access to endless *jouissance* thanks to his wealth and social status (i.e., power). Fritz appropriates some of that *jouissance* by behaving with a cruelty that is totally unnecessary (from the standpoint, that is, of conscious logic), thus reinforcing his servitude to Frankenstein and the social order he represents by becoming an instrument of the Other.[76] Similarly, the mob that pursues the creature in both *Frankenstein* and *Bride of Frankenstein* is acting according to the belief that it is safeguarding its existence, whereas it is in reality reinforcing its own exploitation. We are in that area Slavoj Zizek has called "trans-ideological."[77] The villagers are identifying not simply with the bourgeois notion of natural order but with that of a "foreign body" to be expelled: the monster-as-other must be cast out, for only in this way can a harmonious whole be maintained and defended. At the same time, the mob's behavior must be put down to alienation, "the surrender of your vital capacities to an "alien" force that ensures that your own powers are turned against you."[78] Misperceiving the monster's purpose and misrecognizing its own place in society, the mob turns on the monster, thus mirroring by its aggressivity the real aggression of which it is the daily victim. This helps to explain why the gypsies, the excluded other, turn against the monster who is as much a victim as they.

If *Bride of Frankenstein* has the merit of portraying the monster in even more sympathetic terms than does *Frankenstein*, then a clear regression is at work in *Son of Frankenstein* where the monster appears to be hardly less negative than Ygor. This, I would argue, is due to the collaboration between the two characters, which collaboration is manifestly of a class, and therefore proletarian, nature. The bourgeois fear of the proletariat, duly repressed in such films, thus returns in the form of anxiety faced with the activities of Ygor and the creature, who plot together. Hence, the real historical *victims* of economic aggression are turned into fictional and imaginary *aggressors* in a classic manifestation of that reversal at the base of alienation in its ideological form. Such alienation, which harks back to the mirror stage, is remarkably represented in the scene in *Bride of Frankenstein* where the monster drinks from a pool and then desperately strikes at the water with his hand as he sees his hideous features reflected there. The gesture is that of a subject who hurls an object at a mirror to break it in a doomed attempt to destroy the Other.[79] This recognition by the subject that he has no stable identity of his own helps to explain the behavior of the mob that hurls itself after the monster just as one hurls an object at a mirror. This, in turn, should bring home to us that the existence of a mob does not go without saying, that its presence and actions are meaningful and not just some regrettable return to atavistic tendencies: "For Freud, 'crowd' is not a primordial, archaic entity, the starting point of evolution, but an 'artificial' pathological formation whose genesis is to be displayed—the 'archaic' character of the 'crowd' is precisely the illusion to be dispelled via theoretical analysis."[80] The fact that the monster is a product of scientific experiments and technology means that he is as much a machine as a man—hence the critical tendency to refer to the creature as "him" or "it." Moreover, he is constructed out of "bits and pieces" of dead people, an assemblage of "spare parts," as it were. The fury of the mobs finds a parallel in that of the Luddites, destroying machines in a desperate attempt to save their jobs and way of life.

Another, but related, line of approach is suggested by certain remarks made by Fredric Jameson. Describing how capitalism breaks up "the older traditional forms of human activity" and restructures them "along the lines of a differentiation between means and ends," he highlights the paradox at work:

> It cannot be properly appreciated until it is understood to what degree the means/ends split effectively brackets or suspends ends themselves, hence the strategic value of the Frankfurt School term 'instrumentalization' which usefully foregrounds the organization of the means themselves over against any particular end or value which is assigned to their practice.[81]

I suggest that we interpret the monster as an "end" to this process, the end or fate of proletarian labor under capitalism. The creature is a huge, disfigured brute, vividly corresponding to Hobbes's remark that people's lives are "nasty, brutish and short." Thus the mob's attack on the monster is triggered by a return of the repressed of its real but misrecognized social conditions of life and labor. They wish to kill it to exorcise their unconscious feeling of being "the living dead."

Baldick has quoted Marx as referring to the "titanic" size of workers' political culture compared to that, "dwarflike," of the bourgeoisie, which helps to understand the unnatural size of the monster and to explain what class values Fritz unconsciously embodies: he is, of course, a hunchback, almost a dwarf. However, the monster's ugliness—like Hyde's—is surely a manifestation of conflicting ideologies and forces, representing both the real conditions in which workers toiled and the way the capitalist characterized those same workers: dirty and hideous. To maintain this, however, it is necessary to answer a possible objection: Are the films representing a "class society" in the sense meant by Marx in his analyses of the class struggle between proletariat and bourgeoisie?

I have already discussed *Frankenstein* and *The Black Room* in the context of the *feudal* dimension they clearly represent. To that must be added, concerning *Bride of Frankenstein*, the question, In what period is the film set? It brings together the current age (the time of the film's production), the early nineteenth century (the prologue representing Mary Shelley, Shelley, and Byron) and a far more distant past, that of alchemy as represented by Pretorius.[82] I would reject out of hand both the notion of "artistic license," as if this were "free" and totally conscious, and that hoary chestnut "artistic incompetence," the makers having no sense of such distinctions. Rather, I would turn to what Jameson has written about romance, of which horror is a generally unrecognized aspect if one sees romance as a series of Grim(m) fairytales "that are the irrepressible voice and expression of the underclasses of the great systems of domination."[83] Similarly, Jameson's comment on "two distinct modes of production" seems to me to encapsulate perfectly what I have just referred to: the uneasy and "irrational"—according to a linear view of history devoid of class antagonism—copresence of the modern and the archaic: "Their antagonism is not yet articulated in terms of the struggle of social classes, so that its resolution can be projected in the form of a nostalgic (or less often, a Utopian) harmony."[84] This Utopian dimension, be it said at once, is profoundly reactionary in the films of the Frankenstein saga and *The Black Room*, as it seems to look into the past without any notion of a potential change in the future: a past harmony as imaginary as the present is real and fragmented. We can perhaps take this point further by evoking again the "quaint" aspects of certain horror films, starting with *Dracula*, whose central figure is surely the paradigm of the cruel, feudal baron enjoying to excess, and without fear of reprisal, the bodies of his subjects. In their very different ways, Frankenstein and Baron Gregor are variants of this. For the peasants and villagers seem to do nothing except dance or sit around trembling with fear. This surely suggests a form of denial by the films of the very (f)act of labor. "Labor" or "toil," not work in the "noble" sense, unless the experiments of the assorted mad doctors be so dignified. What can we make of this "labor"?

Let us take a step backward to put matters in perspective and turn again to *Civilization and Its Discontents*:

> In the realm of the mind . . . what is primitive is so commonly preserved alongside of the transformed version which has arisen from it that it is unnecessary to give instances as evidence. When this happens it is usually in consequence of a divergence in development: one portion (in the quantitative sense) of an attitude of instinctual impulse has remained unaltered, while another portion has undergone further development.
>
> In mental life nothing which has once been formed can perish . . . everything is somehow preserved and . . . in suitable circumstances (when, for instance, regression goes back far enough) it can once more be brought to light.[85]

Once again, it is Marcuse who has attempted to historicize Freud's insights. In a reference to the failure of Eros to fulfill the subject's life he remarks, "The manifest forms of regression are unconscious protest against the insufficiency of civilization: against the prevalence of toil over pleasure, performance over gratification."[86] "Regression" must be interpreted, then, not just as the return to an early stage in the subject's psychic development but, crucially, a *collective* return to earlier periods of the evolution of society when life was not fragmented, rationalized in the name of the "performance principle." Marcuse sums up the current situation in these terms:

> Men do not live their own lives but perform pre-established functions. While they work, they do not fulfill their own needs and faculties but work in *alienation*. Work has now become *general*, and so have the restrictions placed upon the libido: labor time, which is the largest part of the individual's life time, is painful time, for alienated labor is absence of gratification, negation of the pleasure principle. Libido is diverted for socially useful performances in which the individual works for himself only in so far as he works for the apparatus, engaged in activities that mostly do not coincide with his own faculties and desires.[87]

This view raises several issues that we shall deal with in turn.

Baldick has stated that the monster's ugliness as an indication of "the unhealthy conditions of production in which he was assembled," pointing out that Frankenstein's activities "can be taken as embodying the socially irresponsible logic of private production itself."[88] This is a most productive notion, especially in light of what Baldick writes later—namely, that the bourgeoisie came to be terrified of the proletariat as the former depended ever more exclusively on the latter: "Marx insisted that the "monster" condemned by bourgeois society is the true maker of it, while the maker of this monstrous outcast is itself the true monster."[89] The monster on the loose abducting and killing can be interpreted as the reverse side of the coin: it is capitalism that is destructive and life-denying. Returning to Baldick's insight, we can also claim that *Frankenstein* and *Bride of Frankenstein* represent literally how capitalism functions. By having Frankenstein and Pretorius dig up dead bodies and use freshly hanged corpses, the films are surely making a comment on accumulation and the past. Not content with bleeding the proletariat dry while they are alive, capitalists make them work *after they are dead*. Thus the capitalist extracts surplus value out of the worker's living body, then out of his corpse, which, by the nature of things, works for nothing. We can now appreciate the full extent of the subtlety and subversive aspects of *White Zombie*.

This, however, fails to grant to the mad doctor what we have granted to the monster and the villagers: that he, too, might represent conflicting values that are meant to hide or cancel one another out in the negative representation of him. In other words, might there not be within the representation of the mad doctor a reactionary Utopian thrust that has been neglected, less a hope for the future than a refusal to accept the role laid down by capitalism? Lacan has called our attention to a simple fact, too often overlooked: the master-slave dialectic concerns every single social subject, and those generally referred to as "the exploiters" are mere servants of the economic order they believe they control.[90] Another answer to the question is provided in a remark made by Baldick:

> The pitiable condition of the capitalist consists in his frantic compulsion to accumulate exchange value which the laws of profit forbid him to squander as use-values in personal enjoyment. . . . Like the worker, the capitalist is reduced to an appendage of his own economic machine, driven by unquenchable and destructive cravings.[91]

It should be noted that financial profit is not high on the list of a mad doctor's priorities; rather, it is power and pleasure. I would claim that the mad doctor is represented as abnormal and dangerous for precisely that reason—that he puts pleasure and leisure before the accumulation of money, a "monstrous" perversion in orthodox capitalist eyes. This seems to enter into conflict with what I suggested: that torturing his victims was the way the mad doctor strove after limitless and never-ending *jouissance*, seeking in the martyrized body of the victim a *plus de jouissance* that corresponds to the surplus value extracted, ripped unceremoniously from the worker's weary frame.

However, we must remember that both *plus de jouissance* and surplus value are unnecessary for the subject's survival and can therefore be construed as a form of *personal* enjoyment. Moreover, the monster's "inexplicably" huge frame can be seen as a site of *resistance* to such exploitation. This conflict, however, obeys the laws of logic, of the secondary processes. If we insist on the unconscious desire being represented, the conflict condenses that between a purely repressive reality principle—power, success and money are the only things that count—and a very special form of Utopia, negative and reactionary without a doubt, but constituting a rejection of the mainstay of that reality principle on the part of the mad doctor or scientist.

It is here that Marxism and psychoanalysis converge in a most productive manner. How money comes into existence is the great "absent cause" within capitalist society: the nature and conditions of its creation must be absented from view, lest the subject—particularly the proletarian subject—get a glimpse of the real historical situation. In other words, a too-close proximity to the cause in question risks exposing the capitalist to the effects of the Real, which is precisely what is at stake here. We have already referred to Zizek's discussion of *Hamlet* where the ghost returns, as there has been no "settling of accounts."[92] I propose to take the word *accounts* in both its figurative, psychoanalytic sense and its literal, economic sense. The sudden manifestation of the monster can only be, from the capitalist's point of view, the return of the repressed of his fear of proletarian agitation in the form of strikes or insurrection: the specters of (the dead of) the Commune weigh heavily on the minds of the living.

The whole question of money as an absent cause and of the forces of labor rendered invisible is represented in an intriguingly literal fashion in the film Bela Lugosi made in England in 1939: *The Dark Eyes of London* (aka *The Human Monster*). Lugosi plays a dual role, as Dr. Orloff and the owner-director of an institute for the blind. Obstensibly a charity organization, it is in fact the locus of a double exploitation. In his capacity as director of the institute, Orloff obtains substantial funds by ingratiating himself with the wealthy, convincing them to include him in their wills and then getting his henchmen to dispose of them. Moreover, he has the inmates of his institute work for him without knowing what they are doing. In other words, they are unwitting victims of their own exploitation, charity not being high on the list of Orloff's priorities in the film. This notion of the senses unconsciously overdetermining ideology—what we do not see does not exist—is inscribed into the film in a way that rebounds on Orloff. To make sure one of his minions will be unable to reveal anything, he deafens the man—who is already blind and dumb—in a particularly harrowing scene. Retribution takes on an ironic form. The only person able to "converse" with the wretched victim is precisely the henchman who, under Orloff's guidance (for he, too, is blind), murders those who have left money in their wills. The man kills Orloff in the same fashion and dumps his body in the muddy banks of the Thames, a nice example of class solidarity, of the proletariat making history but without re- alizing it.

As we saw earlier, *White Zombie* depicts zombies working ceaselessly and repeating endlessly and unthinkingly the same tasks conceived to produce commodities for profit and, crucially, unlimited surplus value inasmuch as the zombies are dead and do not need to be paid, nor do they have to be paid overtime, which means that Humpty Dumpty is an enlightened capitalist compared with Murder Legendre.[93] *White Zombie* is, however, an exception, for the only work on display in horror films in general is that of the mad doc- tor or scientist, obsessively involved in experiments in his laboratory around the clock. There are no workers toiling in workshops, no peasants laboring in the fields, no exploited children.[94] It could certainly be argued that this nonstop activity on the part of the mad doctor condenses both the capital- ist's unquenchable thirst for profit and the result of this drive: the introduc- tion of night shifts, the better to get the most out of the proletariat.[95] Hence, the mad doctor, like the monster he creates, condenses capitalist and worker, albeit an intellectual worker. More fundamental, perhaps, is the way this im- age of the mad doctor condenses a repression overdetermined by an inver- sion: a repression of the very (f)act of labor, and an inversion of the real so- cial relations obtaining, which inversion suggests fetishism. The real social relations between people have been transformed into the imaginary social re- lations between things to the point where the only production of commodi- ties is to be found in the scientist's laboratory.

This situation is represented literally in *The Devil Bat* where inventor Dr. Paul Carruthers (Bela Lugosi) has created, in the usual secrecy of a laboratory (complete with hidden doors, just in case), a giant bat that he sends to kill those who have robbed him. Years before, one of Carruthers's inventions drew the attention of the businessmen he worked for. Needing money, he sold it for a modest fixed sum, thus being deprived of any share in the profits, which turned out to be enormous. The film is therefore a case study of an intellec- tual worker standing in for the usual manual worker and exacting his revenge on those who have exploited him for financial gain. Given the status of the Lugosi character—both middle-class and a scientist—the film turns on a purely individual action, but *The Devil Bat* deserves our attention for the way it highlights the lie of "free choice." The scientist employee is "free" to sell or not his invention, an argument that stands in here for the capitalist ideology of the worker being as free as his or her employer on the "free market."[96]

The Invisible Man invites us to take literally the Marxist argument that, under capitalism, all traces of labor disappear when the products of that labor are marketed: the research chemist literally disappears. All that is left are his clothes, which "take on a life of their own," the perfect signifiers of commodity fetishism, like Marx's example of the table to which Jacques Derrida devotes much reflection.[97] This in turn sheds new light on Inspector Krogh's artificial arm in *Son of Frankenstein*; it is at once part of him and strangely other. When the inspector says to Frankenstein's little boy, "This is not my arm," the lad takes him literally and asks, "Whose is it, then?" Given that Krogh has some difficulty controlling the limb and getting it to do what he wants—it is not, of course, controlled by his brain as his other limbs are—we are surely permitted to see Krogh as the extension of the arm and not the other way around. This limb, too, "takes on a life of its own," symbolizing the way the worker's body is "controlled" by the capitalist who exploits the worker's labor power to his own ends.

When Marcuse refers to "the mutilating dominion of the performance principle," he shows an uncanny understanding of the activities of the mad doctor.[98] His comments on labor and capital, private and public life, work and sexuality are most pertinent:

> Mankind was supposed to be an end in itself and never a mere means; but this ideology was effective in the private rather than in the societal functions of the individuals, in the sphere of libidinal satisfaction rather than in that of labor. The full force of civilized morality was mobilized against the use of the body as mere object, means, instrument of pleasure; such reification was tabooed and remained the ill-reputed privilege of whores, degenerates, and perverts.[99]

And, one might add, of mad doctors, except that capitalist exploitation is the most perfect institutionalization of precisely this proscribed reification.

Yet it would be unwise to try to pin the filmic text down to too narrow a reading. Marcuse provides the following quote from Friedrich Schiller's *Aesthetic Letters*:

> Enjoyment is separated from labor, the means from the end, exertion from recompense. Eternally fettered only to a single little fragment of the whole, man fashions himself only as a fragment; ever hearing only the monotonous whirl of the wheel which he turns, he never develops the harmony of his being, and, instead of shaping the humanity that lies in his nature, he becomes a mere imprint of his occupation, his science.[100]

Although this extraordinary passage, uncanny in its prescience, betrays its Romantic origins—the pre-Freudian conception of "the harmony of his being"—it nevertheless sums up perfectly the Utopian urge in its progressive form: a hope for the future. It also, surely, encourages us to see in its depiction of "man" a being who is not limited to the proletarian. The remark just as clearly applies to the mad doctor himself, incapable of recognizing his true social position and, in true capitalist fashion, contemplating his science as something that belongs to him alone, outside any social reality and consideration. As such he is a true fetishist and a victim of reified social relations. Georg Lukacs quotes here an important observation made by Marx:

> The property-owning class and the class of the proletariat represent the same human self-alienation. But the former feels at home in this self-alienation and feels itself confirmed by it; it recognizes alienation as its own instrument and in it, it possesses the semblance of a human existence. The latter feels itself destroyed by this alienation and sees in it its own impotence and the reality of an inhuman existence.[101]

A number of these points are worked out, in almost textbook fashion, in *The Vampire Bat*. Mad scientist Dr. Niemann (Lionel Atwill) has succeeded in creating life in the secrecy of his laboratory, which in itself condenses the notions of capitalist production and of intellectual labor: "The truth of capitalist production lies not in the open market but in the enclosed, secret lair or workshop, like all the best family skeletons and Gothic terrors."[102] As this life needs sustenance, he uses his hypnotic gaze to turn his assistant temporarily into a zombie and wander abroad, puncturing the necks of villagers to drain them of their blood. Peasants and villagers being what they are in horror films, they immediately jump to the conclusion that a vampire is on the loose and, as stated earlier, decide that Herman, the village idiot, is responsible, as he is fond of bats and collects them. Given the right circumstances—another death—they turn into a vengeful mob, hunt Herman down, and "stake" him in a cave where the wretch has taken shelter. This provokes the detective brought in to clear up the mystery to exclaim, "Are we living in the Middle Ages?" Things, however, are far from being so clear-cut.

The supposedly better-educated city fathers also believe they are dealing with a vampire and claim vampirism is a historic fact: records dating back to 1643 "prove" the existence of vampires. The detective (Melvyn Douglas) dismisses this out of hand by pointing out, with impeccable logic, that the records simply state what happened—they prove nothing. He, at least, can distinguish between history and discourse. For the villagers and the city father, through their spokesman, the Bürgermeister, the records function as the source of truth because of their "historical" status. The detective may react skeptically, rejecting vampirism as "peasant superstition," but he too is the effect of a Master Signifier. The film's script is quite sophisticated on this score.

Neimann lends credence to a document concerning a South American Indian who confessed to being a vampire, despite the fact that he did so under torture, a confession as valid as one extorted from a "heretic" during the Inquisition. We must not forget that the detective has made a horrified reference to the Middle Ages. Since Neimann must throw everyone off the scent, he goes along with the vampire explanation, which in turn leads the detective to start to change his mind: "It's impossible to believe, and yet it would explain their deaths, wouldn't it?" The structure of disavowal is written into the sentence he utters, which is all the more striking as the mad scientist has firstly stated, on examining a victim, "I doubt the evidence of my eyes." In other words, Neimann occupies the place of Master Signifier for the detective, an unimpeachable source of knowledge outside all considerations of class and history.

Everyone, therefore, is denying their senses or knowledge in favor of something that they know not to be true or that they claim to believe in as it furnishes a simple explanation that flies in the face of reason but which enables the ego to refind a momentarily decentered self.[103] This is surely the structure of fetishism, and it is hardly surprising that the social relations elaborated in the film show all the traces of displacement and inversion. Once Herman has been suspected, arguments must be found to justify the fact, or Herman must be turned into the image the villagers have of him in order for their world to function properly. In that case, we have an inverted example of the "mandate" we have discussed earlier in the case of the baron in *Frankenstein*. That such inversion can function to the bitter end—Herman's death, in this case—can be seen from the remark of one villager who points out the damning evidence of his guilt: "He never works and never begs, but yet he appears well-fed." More to the point, perhaps, is that this remark designates Herman as a capitalist, whereas it fits perfectly the character of the mad scientist who, having created life, must find food "for its continued growth." Thus, in much the same way as Fritz tormented the monster in *Frankenstein*, it is another character of working-class origins, the crippled night watchman, who is instrumental in turning everyone against Herman. Once again, ideology represses the "absent cause" of class exploitation by creating an imaginary cause/effect relation.

This exploitation is worked out in an unusual fashion in *The Walking Dead*, which, like *The Monster and the Girl* four years later, uses gangsters as symbols of capitalism, graft, and general corruption. In *The Walking Dead*, the gang frames a timid, out-of-work musician, John Elman (Karloff), for the murder of a judge they have eliminated for looking too closely into their business affairs. Executed before the truth can be made known, Ellman is brought back to life by the efforts of scientist Dr. Beaumont (Edmund Gwenn) and is driven to seek out and kill the gangsters.

Elman can be seen as a particularly naive member of the working class: he is used for a job, then paid off in no uncertain fashion by being executed by the state, which thus stands in for the capitalist gangsters. He then returns from the dead, like a zombie, to exact his revenge; much of the film's power derives from the fact that Elman is a genuinely tragic victim. The political implications of *The Walking Dead*, however, are made more explicit by publicity material used for the film. It shows Karloff, as bald as Nosferatu, about to lunge out of the frame at the spectator. Now not only does Elman have a full head of hair, he is in no way represented as being menacing for us, only for the gangsters.[104] I would suggest that a displacement is at work, one that is overdetermined by the film's ending where the scientist's attempts to find out what life after death is like are thwarted when Elman dies for a second time, shot by the gangsters before they too die in an accident. For if Elman is portrayed as a vampire in the publicity material, this is precisely what the capitalist gangsters are in the film according to the rhetoric resorted to systematically by Marx: it is not for nothing that they suck out Elman's life blood by using his labor and then discard him. Like the vampire, Elman in the publicity material is pure drive, stopping at nothing to get what he wants. As we have seen, this is precisely the dimension of surplus value in capitalism. This real aspect of capitalism is thus inscribed into the film, but in the inverted form of Elman-as-vampire in the publicity material and the very safe theme of religion. Elman has nothing to communicate about the afterlife, not because the Real cannot be symbolized, but because "the Lord our God is a jealous God."

Both *The Monster and the Girl* and *The Face behind the Mask* are negative portrayals of contemporary American society where enchantment turns rapidly to disenchantment. We have already seen in chapter 2 how the incest theme of the former film—the brother and sister are presented as if they were a courting couple—is followed through to its conclusion: the ape into whose skull the brother's brain is grafted after his execution for a murder he did not commit (a concept central to *The Walking Dead*) kills off the men who tricked his sister and engineered his own doom. The ambiguity of the film—just how critical is it?—stems from the fact that a man is there to comfort the heroine when the ape dies, an indication that she has indeed understood his/its look and must be comforted by the well-meaning journalist who has supported her all along. Also at the origin of this ambiguity is the fact that the film cannot make up its mind whether or not she was right to leave her brother and their small hometown for the bright lights of New York City. Given what happens, she was wrong. However, the film clearly indicates that something is pushing her to leave that she cannot formulate: "I want to be somebody. To go somewhere where things are happening." We can surely see here not simply a wish to extract herself from an incestuous relation but also a desire to find an identity for herself that life in such an environment as her home town—which turns on church services and acts of charity—refuses.

Although the film is hardly explicit on this score, it gives the overall impression that, whatever a young woman like her does, she will lose out, not exactly a positive way of looking at things. If she stays, all she can hope for is to play the organ in church like her brother and become an elderly spinster. Going to New York involves her in a phony marriage that leads to her becoming a call girl. In other words, the film works over the twin representations of Woman in the psychic and ideological Imaginary: Madonna or whore.

What must be stressed here is that the film explicitly shows that there are two frames of values functioning: one for women, another for men who have wealth and social standing. When she is being questioned by the district attorney at her brother's trial for murder, he implicitly has her condemned by the jury by asking what her profession is. She casts her eyes down and remains silent. Summing up, he makes this remark: "A woman who, by her own admission, is unworthy of trust." As she has said nothing, the district attorney—and the jury with him—is filling in the gaps according to the ideology that assigns social roles to each subject, and then condemns them if they fail to conform, while at the same time denying any influence the subject may have undergone, as if it were a question of free choice. One is reminded of Daumier's drawing of a proletarian suspect in a bourgeois court of law. Carefully gagged and held by police, he is addressed by the judge: "Speak up—you're free to say what you like." By refusing to speak, the sister simply corresponds to the image the jury already has of her.

This is all the more interesting as the judge has granted her the right to tell her story. As soon as she incriminates the character played by Paul Lukas, however, the judge overrules her testimony. The character in question is in court, listening attentively. Whatever he says and does is turned to his advantage; moreover, he has the law to defend him, without his asking. She, on the other hand, condemns herself whether she speaks or remains silent. The judge's decision and the obsequiousness of the porter at the luxury apartment where the Paul Lukas character lives simply show the role of money and the importance of class, going hand in hand, or hand in glove.

Money is central to *The Face behind the Mask*, a bleak and despairing film that follows its logic to the bitter end, without the slightest concession either to Hollywood or to the spectator. It is a negative portrayal of American society where enchantment can only result in disenchantment. The film tells the story of Janos Szabo, who comes to New York from Hungary, thinking he will find a job and earn enough money to bring his fiancée over. As a result of a fire, he is hideously disfigured and nobody will hire him. He writes to tell his fiancée he is going to marry an American girl in order not to impose his fate on her. Then he falls in with thieves and, thanks to his manual skills, becomes an expert safe cracker and finally head of the gang. When he meets a blind woman, however, he falls in love, realizes that crime is not for him, and leaves the gang. Believing themselves double-crossed—Szabo has kept the card of a detective he befriended on his arrival in the States—the members of the gang plant a bomb in his car, but it is his fiancée who gets killed. With nothing left to live for, Szabo plots the downfall of the four gangsters. He replaces the pilot who is to fly them to Mexico and lands the aircraft in the middle of the Arizona desert. The gangsters tie him to the plane and set off in different directions for help. Several days later the police, whom Szabo has informed by letter of where they can be found, discover the bodies of the gangsters and that of Szabo, also dead.

Thanks to a particularly subtle, complex, and carefully thought-out script, the film succeeds in showing that Szabo's vision of life and America is a question of taking the American Dream seriously, until it turns into a nightmare.[105] A firm believer in beauty—the Statue of Liberty, his fiancée, and New York are all beautiful—Szabos discovers that having one's face burned away means for others that beauty is literally only skin deep: remove the veil—beauty as the Sublime—and one is exposed to the Thing. This is clearly how everyone reacts to him after the accident, and it is what makes *The Face behind the Mask* akin to a horror film, closer in spirit to *Mystery of the Wax Museum* than to the gangster movies it resembles.

The film's political intentions are quickly made clear, however. It denounces quotas that limit entry into the United States and evokes the idea of a country open to victims of oppression. As we are in 1941, there can be no ambiguity on this score. However, such is not the America that reigns supreme. Walking around the streets of the city, Szabos approaches a man and tells him how beautiful New York is. The reply is significant: "Wanna buy it?" From then on there is no scene that does not turn on money, from the high cost of skin grafts to the simple fact that, unless you steal, you do not eat. One telling scene has a well-dressed man with a large cigar approach Szabos for a light. On seeing his face he flees in terror, dropping his wallet. A professional pickpocket befriends Szabos at this point and is furious when he discovers only twelve dollars: "These stockbrokers are all alike." Szabos cannot get a job because of his looks, whereas a stockbroker makes his living by speculating with the surplus value produced by people like Szabos who is presented as a manual worker.

However, *The Face behind the Mask* does not set up a straight opposition of bourgeois versus proletariat. Thus, the pickpocket has the capitalist's purely selfish and individualistic view of life: grab what you can. The film shows that he is not completely wrong, for without stealing both he and Szabos would starve, and nobody will give them credit. More to the point is that the film shows in this way that people are forced into situations they abhor for reasons of survival. It is here that *The Face behind the Mask* elaborates a genuinely ethical view of society and social relations. For Szabos, shocked at the idea of theft, states, "You can't do wrong and find happiness in life." The film shows this to be false, as from the moment you place money above all else: everyone is happy within a system based on theft. It is a remark by the blind woman he befriends that reveals the truth—and his own truth—to Szabos. She is concerned with what he is as a subject—kind and gentle—because she cannot see his face. She also considers the gangster (and therefore Szabos, although she is unaware of the company he keeps) as "blind and ugly inside," a remark that places Szabos in a position to see himself and life differently.

On the manifest level, the film is not saying anything other than the old cliché about the need to go beyond appearances. However, in the light of the way money is treated as a fetish by everyone, we are surely entitled to suggest another reading. Just as people treat Szabos as a dangerous monster because of his frightening appearance, they go about life as if having or not having money were a natural phenomenon, whereas the film insists on circumstances and the simple fact of being employed. Szabos decides to die at the end, not simply because the gangsters have killed the blind woman but because the disenchantment that has come from actually living in America has rendered existence too painful. "It won't hurt as much as being alive," he states when his former associates tie him to the plane and leave him to die. Moreover, Szabos has fallen into the trap of trying to turn the clock back: "I'm going back to where I came from, a long time ago" is his significant comment when breaking with the criminals. Not back to Hungary, but to the moment when he set foot, joyful and enchanted, on American soil. The loss of the blind woman, following on his decision to give up his fiancée, suggests that Szabos, having died once because his disfigurement led to abandoning his beloved, now dies for a second time with the blind woman in his arms. There is nothing left for him to do but to refuse to give in on his desire, to recognize that certain values have always been literally a matter of life and death for him and that, now that these values have ceased to exist, so has he on the level of his most intimate being.

Perhaps we can best sum up the thrust of the preceding pages and the desire at work in the films analyzed as follows. This desire is to lay to rest a particular ghost, that of class solidarity, of social agitation. The contradictions may be solved in an imaginary fashion, in the best tradition, but the fact that they live on, in however displaced or distorted a form, needs to be interpreted politically: to lay to rest the specter of class is possible *only in the future*, in a classless society.

Commenting on Max Weber's notion of "rationalization," Christina Britzolakis points to his claim "that the essence of modernity was the disenchantment of the world," to which she adds her own observation: "A distinctively modern temporal sensibility is characterized by a fragmentation of memory and of subjectivity which assumes a certain spectralization of subject-object relationships."[106] These remarks take up the analyses made by Adorno in his brief but devastating study, "Theses against Occultism," in which he writes:

> As a rationally exploited reaction to rationalized society . . . reborn animism denies the alienation of which it is itself proof and product, and concocts surrogates for nonexistent experience. The occultist draws the ultimate conclusion from the fetish-character of commodities: menacingly objectified labor assails him on all sides from demonically grimacing objects. What has been forgotten in a world congealed into products, the fact that it has been produced by men, is split off and misremembered as a being-in-itself added to that of the objects and equivalent to them.[107]

To conclude this chapter, I shall look at two films that, in varying ways, reflect the concerns made explicit by Adorno: *Supernatural* and *The Devil Commands*, both of which deal with ghosts and mediums, as well as boasting the necessary mad scientist.

From Beyond

The script of *Supernatural* introduces heterogeneous aspects that come together in striking fashion by the way the film locates the action in its characters. Ruth Rogen is condemned to death for murdering three of her lovers. Psychologist Dr. Houston, convinced that the personality can escape from the body after death and take over other living persons, persuades the prison warden to hand Rogen's corpse over to him so that he can carry out an experiment to prevent her "evil" living on. Roma Courtney is grieving the death of her twin brother John, who has just died at the age of twenty-four. A millionairess, she is engaged to Grant Wilson. Spiritualist Paul Bavian, who betrayed Rogen to the authorities, is anxious to prove to Roma that her brother is attempting to get into contact with her, as he hopes thus to get his hands on a sizeable portion of her enormous heritage. Houston's experiment fails and the "spirit" of Rogen possesses the body of Roma and seduces Bavian who, fleeing in horror when he realizes what has happened, is caught in ropes on board Roma's yacht and is strangled, thus fulfilling Rogen's "curse": she had strangled the other men in her life. Roma recovers and marries Wilson.

The film is a revealing example of how both script and direction produce a series of "excess" meanings that escape the manifest project of the film—there *is* life after death—to move into another sphere. It is Rogen's sexuality or libido that turns out to be the film's unassimilable "foreign body," for by attempting to make a clear distinction between the physical body and the mind, the film fails to take into account the sexualization of the body. Thus, a complex montage of newspaper articles, shots of the trial, and Rogen laughing fiendishly establishes the background to the case. A headline informs us that "Rogen killed the men who loved her," while an article states, "Ruth Rogen yesterday confessed she killed each of her three lovers after a riotous orgy in her sensuous Greenwich Village apartment." Two things are to be noted here: the fact that there is a displacement from Rogen onto her apartment, which only serves to highlight intense sexual activity and pleasure; and the implicit contradiction between her activity—killing men—and the representation of this in the headline. The men loved her, making of Rogen an object of masculine desire, fully in keeping with Hollywood's and society's representation of the female.

Rogen's "insane" laughter accompanies her unrepentant remark, "I'd do it again and again and again." In the context, this means she would kill other men after more orgies if she had the chance, but the insistence on some link between sex and murder allows us to interpret the remark as a compulsive desire to have sex, thus representing Rogen as a nymphomaniac. The fact that the word *again* figures three times in her remark and that she had three lovers lends to "it" in the formula "I'd do it" the dual meaning of "having sex" and "committing murder." It is here that the film's conscious project is overtaken—or "taken over" as it were—by another discourse. In the case of a nymphomaniac, sexual alienation and socioeconomic alienation overdetermine each other. When Houston proposes to Rogen that he use her body after she's dead, saying that she has nothing to lose, her reply is eloquent: "I've nothing to gain, either. My body's my own; the law grants me at least that much." It would be difficult to state the matter more succinctly: Rogen is considered an object for scientific research, an object that will be obtained for nothing. As such, she is a member of the proletariat, a fact she clearly recognizes in this remark. The psychologist functions as yet another Frankenstein. When she rejects the alienation of this, her only possession, Houston sanctimoniously replies that she should do it for "humanity," an argument that is rightly greeted with a healthy skepticism on her part. Represented as strong willed and strong fingered, Rogen is deprived of the chance to explain the killings, except for her ambiguous remark just discussed. No information is forthcoming about how the victims may have treated her. Just as Franken-stein's monster cannot talk (in *Frankenstein*) and therefore cannot defend it/himself, so Rogen as a woman—and a proletarian one at that—has no voice in the matter. Workers, women, and children are to be seen but not heard. As the newspaper talks of "*a riotous orgy*" as a result of which she kills the three men, we are surely entitled to interpret this as meaning she pol-ished all three of them off one after the other and not that three separate or-gies took place. An "orgy" surely indicates that a number of people are pres-ent, so the film pruriently dangles before us the tantalizing image of three men having sex at the same time with one woman. We only have to imagine the three men under the influence of drink for it to be easy to see how she could indeed have carried out a triple murder. In that case, it is clear that Ro-gen has acceded to *jouissance* against the desire of the patriarchal Other and must be punished.

I have insisted on this aspect in an attempt to show how the film, through dialogue and images, has let loose its own "monster" in the form of repressed desires and how the body—the female body: the male body is not concerned—is suddenly endowed with drives and desires it is not meant to have and which are not easy to contain. The situation also shows how the subject can be dis-possessed of his or her body in the name of established power or "disinterested" science. It is therefore not surprising that Rogen should choose Roma Court-ney as the "host" for her spirit so that she can strangle Bavian; the fact that it was he who informed on her without this being divulged at the trial suggests he may have been present at the orgy, too. I am, of course, going on the rea-sonable assumption, first, that what a script omits masks a contradiction and, second, that an ambiguity suggests an "excess" that conscious discourse cannot contain. It is in this context that the choice made by Roma cannot be said to coincide with some simple act of "chance."

Roma is still in mourning over the sudden death of her brother, but in its attempts to communicate her understandable grief the film gives information that exceeds what might be deemed necessary. Thus, at one point she plays one of the "home records" they made together, and we are treated to the brother singing a song that is an explicit declaration of love to his sister. The fact that she kisses and caresses his dog afterwards can be seen as a displace-ment of genuine affection or a grotesque example of unconscious irony, given the incest theme. Things are complicated, however, by the film's desire to eat its cake and have it. Bavian is a fake, but life after death does exist and this the film shows by the way John's spirit helps Wilson to guess that Roma is on her yacht with Bavian; via superimposed images, he participates in the events that confound the hoaxer and free his sister. The brother is there to make sure that his sister does the right thing and marry Wilson who has refused to propose, considering she is in no state to decide. By a sleight of hand, the film disavows the incest theme by displacing the brother's interest onto a "normal" marriage. We are perhaps entitled to see such a ghost as the signifier of Freud's concept of *Urverdrängung*, something that has never been conscious and always repressed. In other terms, the Real:

> Reality is never directly "itself," it present itself only via its incomplete-failed symbolization, and spectral apparitions emerge in this very gap that forever separates reality from the real, and on account of which reality has the character of a (symbolic) fiction: the specter gives body to that which escapes (the symbolically structured) reality.[108]

At the same time the film raises a question that is crucial: that of "possessions." Now that she is alone, Roma inherits the whole family fortune. This, again, is ambiguous: Does it mean she now has John's share, too? Or that she could not inherit while he was alive? This ambiguity disturbs the film's conscious discourse, as it suggests that the brother's "enjoyment" of his sister when they were both alive will not give way to her enjoyment of the money unless she marries. There is a remarkable parallel, in an inverse form, between the situations of the brother and of Rogen: just as she will be deprived of her body after death for the "benefit" of science, so John will possess his sister after his death until he is sure she has settled down in the correct, bourgeois fashion.

The incest theme foregrounds the dimension of "the symbolic debt." Rogen's desire to be a "free agent" leads to her breaking the law, and she is punished, whereas Roma's unconscious submission to the Law in the form of her brother is "compensated": she gets the handsome hero and the family fortune. Thus, the "spirit" of capitalism wins out, yet again, over the dangerous, independent "spirit" manifested by Rogen. Although not a member of the proletariat, as a woman she is its patent stand-in: "menacingly objectified labor" in the words of Adorno, quoted earlier. As one critic has pointed out, the Gothic and ghost stories "began by offering exclusive insight into inheritance as concurrently economic and psychic determinant."[109]

The Devil Commands also sports a mad scientist and a phony medium, but here the former is at the center of the plot through his experiments and the way he allows an obsession to destroy him. Dr. Blair (Karloff) considers he has proof that the brain gives off an impulse that can be recorded mechanically on a chart and that, with the help of donors capable of withstanding more than the usual dose of electricity, he will be able to converse with the dead. This notion becomes an obsession as a result of his wife's death in an accident and his unexpected discovery that her brain impulses can be recorded, whereas until then he had entertained the idea of living people conversing with one another via their brain impulses, even without speaking. Clearly this takes up, in a suitably disguised fashion, Freud's notion that the unconscious of X can communicate with the unconscious of Y without becoming conscious. In the context of our investigation, Blair's notion is an obvious unconscious manifestation in the film of a subject's anxiety produced by living in a society that fragments the subject and reifies social relations, all in the name of "easy" communication.

More intriguing, however, is the way the film concentrates on class and that favorite stand-by: the mob. This time, however, we are very much in the present and the United States, which, as we shall see, enables the film to move into the realm of politics. Blair has an assistant who, as the result of an accident when helping Blair get into contact with his dead wife, is transformed into a mental defective, moving around like a zombie and obeying Blair's every order. I beg to differ with Randy Loren Rasmussen, who finds this inexplicable,[110] and with David H. Smith, who considers Blair's device "anachronous" as it obviously resembles the electroencephalograph.[111] The unconscious of the text is dealing with something other than the supernatural. Thus, the wind that rises when Karloff tries to summon his dead wife's spirit, though clearly meant to be interpreted as a force from beyond the grave, is a striking representation of the Real: the wind from nowhere.[112] It is sufficient that the assistant be called Karl—hardly a common American name, although the character is presented as an average (i.e., stupid and easily influenced) American worker—and that, as a result of the accident, he be turned into a hunchback to note that he is the condensation of Fritz in *Frankenstein* and Karl in *Bride of Frankenstein*. This idea calls for further investigation.

If Karl does not turn against Blair, it is surely because he is *already alienated*, accepting his social situation as natural. He respects his intellectual and social betters and thus can make no connection between his new state and the fact that his mind and body have been exploited by Blair for purely selfish and individual reasons. Under the circumstances, the fact that the mob can make such a connection is surely an indication of superior understanding, a form of unconscious knowledge. As usual in such cases, however, this is simply displaced onto Blair as an individual, whose house they storm in an effort to prove he is responsible for the disappearance of the bodies of towns-people who have died since he arrived (which is true). In other words, just as Karl trusted Blair implicitly, the mob distrusts him for the same reasons. An inability to grasp their social situation as one of alienation—they are mani-festly working-class people, like Karl—leads them to blame it all on science, which again is partly true as Blair has now completely forsaken any pretence to be advancing science and is consumed by the idea that his wife will soon be able to speak to him. Putting the blame on science as such, however, is like blaming a meteorologist when there's a flood, an ideological subject po-sition determined by alienation.

The scene where the mob attacks shows Karl trying to defend his master and being buried beneath a tide of human bodies in an image that reverses that of modern zombie movies where the zombies overrun the survivors and consume them. The reversal is interesting, since Karl is a virtual zombie, and the mob venting its impotent fury on him returns us to the ideology of the two Frankenstein films, where the subject mistakes an objective ally for someone hostile to him instead of seeing him as just another victim. To that extent, the mob behaves like a sort of collective zombie. The fact that Blair and the medium who has thrown in her lot with him steal bodies puts them in the same category as vampires or Murder Legendre in *White Zombie*, the significance of whose acts has been discussed. The medium had understood perfectly how to exploit Karl's alienation: by convincing him that she can put him into contact with his dead mother. If this works, it cannot be put down to Karl being a dumb worker, although the film presents him as such. The mother, duly materialized, tells her son how wonderful the afterlife is: "No pain, no sickness." One can only add "No desire." The medium is quite simply encouraging Karl either to put up with his earthly lot, now that he can identify with a blissful state via his dead mother, or to die, which will suit her as he could then serve as a guinea pig for her and Blair's experiments. The "specter" of Marx's writings returns yet again to haunt the text. It should, however, be pointed out that there is a certain Utopian dimension function-ing here, albeit in a reactionary way. The medium is respected by her cus-tomers as a sort of all-powerful maternal figure, the séance setting "the scene for the creation and exploration of a new kind of collective bodily experi-ence."[113] Despite his being very much the "absent-minded professor," Blair at the outset is part of this collective logic by seeking to reinforce communica-tion between individuals.

Something else is haunting *The Devil Commands*: the specter of politics. Smith has referred to "the meaningless title."[114] And a poster does indeed portray a horned and fanged devil, indicating that Blair is in league with the forces of evil. The force that reaches out for Blair at the end of the film is not, of course, Lucifer, but the drive toward death that has motivated him since his wife was killed. However, if we listen carefully to the script and take into account the "demonic" performance of the medium (the excellent Anne Revere), we can detect another "force" at work. Apprised of Blair's experiments and his notion of giving people the opportunity to communicate with one another without going via speech, she tells him this power will enable him to rule the world. If we remember Freud's remarks on the psychology of the group, then the film is making a subtle reference to Nazism: people identifying unconsciously with the Führer and doing his bidding, as if they were acting in accordance with their own wishes. The film dates from 1941.

Another aspect of the film returns to "haunt" us today in the most uncanny fashion. The town sheriff is worried by rumors that threaten Blair's livelihood and wonders how he can calm the townspeople down, to get them to adopt a more rational approach to things. What is this if not a reference to the House Committee on Un-American Activities—already active in Hollywood in the year prior to the film being made—which exploited rumors when it did not actually invent them, in order to pillory those it considered as Communists and thereby to deprive them of work? If I say *The Devil Commands* returns out of the past like a specter, it is because the film's director, Edward Dmytryk, was to become one of the "Hollywood Ten" in 1947 and Anne Revere to be blacklisted in the early 1950s, after having been named.[115] This shows that history has its own way of representing itself, but we realize so only after the event. It is to the concept of history, implied in various forms throughout this chapter, that we must now turn to conclude our investigation into the "political unconscious" of the horror film.

Notes

1. Later in this chapter we discuss this film in the context of specters and the occult.
2. *SE* IX: 237–41.
3. Sigmund Freud, "Family Romances," in *SE* IX: 237.
4. Freud, "Family Romances," 239.
5. Sigmund Freud, *Civilization and Its Discontents*, in SE XXI: 86.
6. Freud, *Civilization and Its Discontents*, 140.
7. Freud, *Civilization and Its Discontents*, 123.
8. Freud, *Civilization and Its Discontents*, 119, 121. The *Standard Edition*, of course, is guilty of the disastrous mistranslation of "Trieb" as "instinct" instead of "drive."
9. See my discussion of the film in chapter 1.

10. Freud, *Civilization and Its Discontents*, 129.

11. Freud, *Civilization and Its Discontents*, 97.

12. Freud, *Civilization and Its Discontents*, 79–80.

13. Jacques Lacan, *Ethique de la psychanalyse*, Le Séminaire Livre VII (Paris : Seuil, 1986).

14. Dylan Evans, *An Introductory Dictionary of Lacanian Psychoanalysis* (New York: Routledge, 1996), 198–99.

15. Freud, *Civilization and Its Discontents*, 103–4.

16. Freud, *Civilization and Its Discontents*, 106, n. 3.

17. *L'Apport Freudien*, ed. Philippe Kaufmann (Paris: Bordas, 1993), 399–405.

18. Attempts to discredit Freud on the grounds of a failure on his part to understand women's demands, for example, fail totally to take this simple fact into account.

19. Herbert Marcuse, *Eros and Civilization* (London: Sphere Books, 1969), 23.

20. Russell Jacoby, *Social Amnesia* (Mahwah, N.J.: Transaction, 1997), xxviii. The first edition of *Social Amnesia* was published in 1975.

21. Jacoby, *Social Amnesia*, ix.

22. Freud, *Civilization and Its Discontents*, 143.

23. Socialist parties have always preferred "ethical commands" (i.e., right-thinking moralizing) to a genuinely materialist criticism of "possessions." We are now paying the price for this intellectual rejection of Marx.

24. Freud, *Civilization and Its Discontents*, 99.

25. Freud, *Civilization and Its Discontents*, 80.

26. Marcuse, *Eros and Civilization*, 170.

27. Marcuse, *Eros and Civilization*, 170.

28. Quoted in Marcuse, *Eros and Civilization*, 171.

29. Marcuse, *Eros and Civilization*, 44.

30. Marcuse, *Eros and Civilization*, 82.

31. Marcuse, *Eros and Civilization*, 47. The Freud quote is from *Civilization and Its Discontents*.

32. Marcuse, *Eros and Civilization*, 42.

33. Marcuse, *Eros and Civilization*, 41.

34. John Brenkman, *Culture and Domination* (Ithaca, N.Y.: Cornell University Press, 1987), 170–71.

35. T. W. Adorno, *Minima Moralia* (London: Verso, 1999), 22.

36. Marcuse, *Eros and Civilization*, 87.

37. The characters played by David Manners in *Dracula*, *The Mummy*, and *The Black Cat* and the character of Neil in *White Zombie* are instances of this. Present in only a small number of films, it resonates and insists in ways that indicate the repression of a notion that cannot become conscious.

38. Because the Margaret Herrick Library does not possess the PCA file on the film, I am unable to verify to what extent self-censorship functioned, the better to subvert the conservative ideologues at work in Hollywood. Censorship is, however,

by no means certain: the film dates from the pre-Breen era. The representation of Ivy—manifestly naked in bed when Jekyll examines her—is remarkably erotic. On the other hand, the words *prostitute* and *customer* are never pronounced. But that is a minor matter compared with what actually appears on the screen. Apparently it was Hyde's violence that worried the censors at the time.

39. He was, perhaps, jealous of his fame and notoriety, too. This jealousy possibly extends to his attitude to Muriel, as we shall argue later.

40. I use the word *captivating* as the film shows the two men to be captivated. The spectators are involved by the use of close-ups, POV shots, and Miriam Hopkins's extraordinary sensuality.

41. Freud, *Civilization and Its Discontents*, 84. It would also seem to show that sublimation is not permanent: I refer the reader back to the discussion in the previous section. Lanyon, who is a bachelor, has put professional obligations, his career and contacts with the aristocracy in the place of sexuality, but even he is forced to reinforce repression under certain circumstances, such as the visit to Ivy and its aftermath.

42. We raised this topic briefly in chapter 2 when discussing the heroine as the object of economic and social exchange between Vollin and the fiancé in *The Raven*.

43. In *Group Psychology and the Analysis of the Ego*, Freud states that the army and the church are two "artificial groups." *SE* XVIII, chapter 5.

44. Marcuse, *Eros and Civilization*, 43; italics in the original.

45. Marcuse, *Eros and Civilization*, 72.

46. A parallel can be made between Lanyon and Garth (*Dracula's Daughter*) as conservative defenders of the prerogatives of patriarchy and the social status quo.

47. As we have just pointed out, however, the feudal lord had obligations, so Hyde and Dracula strive to go "beyond" this form of power relations via the implacable nature of what drives them.

48. In our reflections on the signifier, we have not forgotten the *seme* "son." The notion of being the "son of a peer" clearly corresponds to the representation of Hyde in this scene. It also indicates the social position Jekyll could enjoy if he adopted the values of Lanyon who, as we have noted, gets invited to dinners at the homes of the aristocracy.

49. Jean-Jacques Lecercle, "Tissage et métissage," in *Dr. Jekyll and Mr. Hyde*, ed. Jean-Pierre Naugrette, Figures Mythiques (Paris: Autrement, 1997), 53–54.

50. The fact that the parson is later seen at a dinner party in the company of the "cream" of society and that he is played by Sir C. Aubrey Smith, notable for his portrayal of aristocrats and military men (Sir Charles + General Carew) is hardly coincidental.

51. Or, to formulate it in terms of Hollywood at that time, it was to defend Louis B. Mayer.

52. There is surely an striking and productive opposition, in an inverted form, set up between Hyde's behavior here and Carew's concern with "training" in the 1931 version.

53. A further case merits attention, that of the fascinating Terence Fisher-Wolf Mankowicz film of 1959, *The Two Faces of Dr. Jekyll*. Here a middle-aged Jekyll turns

into young and handsome Edward Hyde, a man given over to the realization of drives allowing for no obstacle of any kind. On discovering, in a club, Jekyll's wife in the arms of a friend of the doctor's (to whom Jekyll is accustomed to giving large sums of money to pay his gambling debts), Hyde hits on a scheme: he bails out the friend for a huge sum, then demands to have the favors of Mrs. Jekyll as payment. What is pertinent for our argument here is that, whereas the friend behaves in a like fashion but uses his love for the wife as a blind, Hyde calmly exhibits the nature of patriarchal capitalism: the woman as simple merchandise, circulating between men, an object to be exchanged for money in circumstances determined by the social and economic status of men alone.

54. I refer the reader to the discussion of the links among rationalism, superstition, and disavowal in chapter 1.

55. Jean Marigny refers to this remark by Van Helsing in his article "Un vampire renaît de ses cendres," in *Dracula*, ed. Jean Marigny, Figures Mythiques (Paris: Autrement, 1997), 72.

56. See the discussion of *Mark of the Vampire* in chapter 1.

57. Slavoj Zizek, *The Sublime Object of Ideology* (London: Verso, 1989), 25.

58. Anton and Gregor are the film's equivalent of Jekyll and Hyde, but here literally divided into two.

59. Quoted by Mandy Merck, "The Medium of Exchange," in *Ghosts: Deconstruction, Psychoanalysis, History*, ed. Peter Buse and Andrew Stott (London: Macmillan, 1999), 163. The quote is from *Capital*, unfortunately with no indication of either volume or chapter.

60. Slavoj Zizek, *The Plague of Fantasies* (London: Verso, 1997), 67.

61. Edward Lowry and Richard deCordova, "Enunciation and the Production of Horror in *White Zombie*," in *Planks of Reason: Essays on the Horror Film*, ed. Barry Keith Grant (Metuchen, N.J.: Scarecrow, 1984), 351.

62. See chapter 2 for a discussion of the various implications of the subject positions worked out in the film.

63. Sigmund Freud, *Group Psychology and the Analysis of the Ego*, in SE XVIII: 114.

64. Lowry and deCordova, "Enunciation," 354.

65. Lowry and deCordova, "Enunciation," 354.

66. We shall analyze these related themes in detail when discussing *The Mask of Fu Manchu* in chapter 4.

67. Yet, as Jean-Jacques Lecercle has pointed out, critics tend to interpret the burning windmill at the end of *Frankenstein* as a reference to the lynching activities of the Ku Klux Klan. *Frankenstein: mythe et philosophie* (Paris: Presses Universitaires de France, 1988), 113. This copresence of history and its denial in critical discourse will be addressed in the following chapter.

68. Chris Baldick, In *Frankenstein's Shadow: Myth, Monstrosity and Nineteenth-century Writing* (Oxford: Clarendon, 1987), 121–40.

69. Baldick, *In Frankenstein's Shadow*, 121.

70. Don G. Smith, "*Frankenstein*," in *Boris Karloff*, ed. Gary J. Svehla and Susan Svehla (Baltimore: Midnight Marquee, 1996), 10.

71. Bryan Senn, *Golden Horrors: An Illustrated Critical Filmography of Terror Cinema, 1931–1939* (Jefferson, N.C.: McFarland, 1996), 278, italics added.

72. Baldick, *In Frankenstein's Shadow*, 18, 19.

73. Fredric Jameson, "Marx's Purloined Letter," *New Left Review* 209 (January–February 1995), 83, 92.

74. Jean-Jacques Lecercle has also drawn attention to the fact that the monster can be interpreted as representing revolution. See *Frankenstein: mythe et philosophie*, 59.

75. Jameson, "Marx's Purloined Letter," 93–95.

76. See Slavoj Zizek, *The Plague of Fantasies* (London: Verso, 1997), 34, 68.

77. Zizek, *The Plague of Fantasies*, 21.

78. Baldick, *In Frankenstein's Shadow*, 131.

79. The scene assumes the creature has entered the Symbolic Order and is reacting negatively to the return of the repressed of the mirror stage. This in turn justifies the decision to allow the monster access to speech. In *Frankenstein*, the monster has clearly not entered the Symbolic Order, as his innocent playing with the little girl shows: he cannot distinguish between throwing flowers into the pond and throwing her in instead.

80. Slavoj Zizek, "Introduction," in *Mapping Ideology*, ed. Slavoj Zizek (London: Verso, 1994), 29.

81. Fredric Jameson, "Reification and Utopia in Mass Culture," *Social Text* (Winter 1979): 130.

82. Referring to Arno Mayer's *The Persistence of the Old Regime*, Fredric Jameson has pointed out that aspects of that regime survived in Europe until the end of World War II. *The Seeds of Time* (New York: Columbia, 1994), 13.

83. Fredric Jameson, *The Political Unconscious: Narrative as a Socially Symbolic Act* (London: Methuen, 1981), 105.

84. Jameson, *The Political Unconscious*, 148.

85. *SE* XXI: 68–69.

86. Marcuse, *Eros and Civilization*, 96.

87. Marcuse, *Eros and Civilization*, 51.

88. Baldick, *In Frankenstein's Shadow*, 51.

89. Baldick, *In Frankenstein's Shadow*, 138.

90. Jacques Lacan, *Les Psychoses*, Le Séminaire Livre III (Paris: Seuil, 1981), 150.

91. Baldick, *In Frankenstein's Shadow*, 128.

92. See the discussion of *The Crime of Dr. Crespi* in chapter 1. The Zizek quote comes from *The Sublime Object of Ideology*, 135.

93. Orloff's relation to the blind inmates of the Institute in *The Dark Eyes of London* bears a striking resemblance to that of Legendre to the zombies. Both films lend a precise political meaning to the concept of exploitation.

94. Clearly, *The Dark Eyes of London* is an exception, but it is not a Hollywood film. There is, however, another exception to the rule, as we shall see in chapter 4.

95. Baldick, *In Frankenstein's Shadow*, 130. I take the liberty of reminding the reader that this "thirst," like that of Jekyll in a different context, is a *drive*, not an instinct.

96. For a detailed discussion of this rare film, see the useful chapter in the collective volume *Bela Lugosi*, ed. Gary J. Svehla and Susan Svehla (Baltimore: Midnight Marquee Press, 1995), 137–44.

97. Jacques Derrida, *Spectres de Marx* (Paris: Galilée, 1993), 243–50.

98. Marcuse, *Eros and Civilization*, 170.

99. Marcuse, *Eros and Civilization*, 163.

100. Marcuse, *Eros and Civilization*, 151.

101. Georg Lukacs, "Reification and the Consciousness of the Proletariat," in *History and Class Consciousness* (London: Merlin, 1971), 149. A point that must be remembered, although its importance hardly needs to be insisted on in the context, is that Lukacs resorted to the eloquent expressions "phantom objectivity" and "ghostly objectivity" to describe the process in question. The "specter" haunts many texts.

102. Baldick, *In Frankenstein's Shadow*, 126.

103. I refer the reader to my discussion of this and related matters in chapter 1.

104. I refer the reader to my discussion of this publicity material in chapter 2.

105. The film was written by Paul Jarrico, who was to be blacklisted as a Communist in 1951 and to become the producer of *Salt of the Earth* in 1954.

106. Christina Britzolakis, "Phantasmagoria: Walter Benjamin and the Poetics of Urban Modernism," in *Ghosts: Deconstruction, Psychoanalysis, History*, ed. Peter Buse and Andrew Stott (London: Macmillan, 1999), 72, 73. The entire volume is of the greatest interest.

107. Adorno, *Minima Moralia*, 239.

108. Zizek, *Mapping Ideology*, 21.

109. Ruth Parkin-Gounelas, "Anachrony and Anatopia: Spectres of Marx, Derrida and Gothic Fiction," in *Ghosts*, 132.

110. Randy Loren Rasmussen, *Children of the Night: The Six Archetypal Characters of Classic Horror Films* (Jefferson, N.C.: McFarland, 1998), 182.

111. In his analysis of the film in *Boris Karloff*, 270.

112. The wind that buffets the characters is accompanied by the appearance on the screen of a shapeless, white form. I suggest we see this, like the fog vampires materialize from or fade into, as a further manifestation of the "fading" of the subject.

113. Steven Connor, "The Machine in the Ghost: Spiritualism, Technology and the 'Direct Voice,'" in *Ghosts*, 207.

114. In *Boris Karloff*, 268.

115. Dmytryk, of course, also returned later as a "specter" to haunt his former comrades and colleagues by naming names so as to be removed from the blacklist.

CHAPTER FOUR

~

History Is Made at Night

So much has been made of questions of history and temporality in books devoted to the horror film that it may seem wrong-headed, even perverse, to claim that the concept of history as it relates to the films of the period under discussion has been neglected. That, however, is precisely the claim I wish to make, by drawing attention to the fact that history tends all too often to be seen by critics in terms of linearity, of cause and effect, as if history were a full presence to be grasped in terms of dates and events. Rather, I wish to insist in this chapter on history as a "structuring absence" or, in the terms of Fredric Jameson, an "absent cause."[1]

Nor is it uncommon for specialists to put their finger on a key aspect of a film and then promptly nip in the bud any attempt to analyze it further. Thus, Randy Loren Rasmussen describes *Son of Frankenstein* in the following terms: "The village is a gloomy place full of depressed people obsessed with old hatreds. The surrounding landscape is desolate and lifeless, like a smoldering battlefield. Everything in the film has an unhealthy, post-apocalyptic appearance, perhaps echoing political tensions in late 1930s Europe."[2] This description is rather vague, but it at least opens the door to analyses concerning politics, negative representations of Otherness, and hidden secrets from the past that can arguably be interpreted in terms of class animosity and placed in a historical frame of reference rather than be put down simply to the experiments carried out by the son's notorious father. Suddenly, all this is dispelled: "Old antagonisms never die. Or, in terms related to then-current events, World War I inevitably leads to World War II."[3] To begin with, the "antagonisms" refer both to those within the film and to real-life situations in such a way that each reinforces the other without respecting the specificity of either. Rasmussen neglects in particular the fact that a historical event is transformed the moment it is constituted by and as a discourse, verbal or cinematic. Furthermore, "inevitably" begs far too many questions for us to accept its connotations of cause and effect. Even if we suppress it from the sentence, World War I is presented as a nonproblematic event or cause followed by just as nonproblematic an effect—namely, World War II. The problem, surely, is the unconscious effect of hindsight. By the time that Rasmussen came to write his book, it was known and generally accepted that precise links had to be made between the outcome of World War I and the conflagration of World War II. However, *Son of Frankenstein* was conceived and shot in the closing months of 1938, and it is surely its prescience that must be hailed, rather than some sort of inevitability. In other words, we would need to interrogate much more closely those textual elements highlighted by Rasmussen in order to understand in what way *something absent from the film* determines the articulation of the various themes and characters presented.

I suggest the same copresence of critical blindness and insight is at work in a remark by Andrew Tudor on the resurgence of ghosts in horror films of the mid- and late 1940s:

> Beyond their shared concern with ghosts, however, and therefore in several cases with haunted houses, these films have little in common. Viewed in context they do suggest a significant increase in interest in the life/death borderline, and accordingly in supernatural threats that seek to cross it—perhaps unsurprisingly in the wake of a world war.[4]

Just as Rasmussen unwittingly blocks his own analysis, so Tudor, by resorting to a sort of afterthought in the concluding nine words, puts the dominance of ghosts down to a single event construed as a sort of "present cause," even hedging his bets there ("perhaps unsurprisingly").

It is in such a context, and as a reaction against it, that I wish to insist, yet again, on the notion of the "absent cause," already very much present in the preceding pages. On two separate occasions David Skal unerringly highlights the "absent cause," albeit without going to the logical end of his own remarks. The following observation is most suggestive:

> Like *Dracula* earlier in the year, *Frankenstein* seemed to tap the public's need to confront images of dread during what turned out to be the most dreadful year of the Great Depression. A general anxiety about the prospects of resurrecting a dead economy was curiously refracted in the back-from-the-grave themes of both films.[5]

If the first sentence falls into the cause-effect trap again, the reference to "a dead economy," by linking the economic to that ghoulish and vampiric dimension of capitalism we discussed in chapter 3, implies quite rightly that the Depression was not an event in its own right, the simple cause of misery, but the *effect* of another cause: history itself. And when the author evokes nicely "the shuffling spectacle of the walking dead in films like *White Zombie*" as "a nightmare vision of a breadline," he is taking up an earlier comment of his: "Untold millions had been left with the feeling that modern life—and death—was nothing but an anonymous, crushing assembly line."[6] More pertinently, Skal has drawn a parallel over the years separating his two volumes between the "bread*line*" and the "assembly *line*." Whether queuing up to receive food day after day or being submitted to another form of alienating repetition inside the factory, the proletariat becomes the effect of an absent cause, the historical opposition between capital and labor. The three sections of this chapter will pursue these and related concepts.

From the Hysterical to the Historical

I shall open the discussion by referring again to *King Kong*. The film is exemplary because, by evoking the Depression as being at least partly responsible for the weakened condition of Ann Darrow (she faints because she is, quite simply, starving), it in fact masks the real reasons for such a parlous state of affairs. The film both suggests a cause without raising the conditions for its existence and disavows this via the Women's Home Mission in the opening sequences. Ann declares that there are "lots of girls like me," but we also see old women in the mission, which suggests general poverty that is not limited to young women who cannot find work. Class and social conditions are uppermost, a fact we shall see returning again and again. Such disavowal is also evident linguistically, via certain formulas and words. Ann's situation is put down to "bad luck," a classic example of the individual being brought into focus to blur the objective economic factors at work. Moreover, Denham stresses that his interest in her is "strictly business," and he assures her that there will be " no funny business." Thus, the film harnesses the economic and the sexual via a play on words that functions precisely to bracket the real nature of Denham's hiring Ann—a contract between an entrepreneur and a worker where equality of status and opportunity is purely imaginary—and to suggest again what has been denied via the presence of the mission: that Ann is a prostitute and hence a victim of economic madness.

Although *King Kong* makes it clear that Denham considers himself lucky to have found so talented an amateur as Ann, it insists more on Ann's good luck (as opposed to her aforementioned "bad luck") in finding an entrepreneur with the initiative of Denham.[7] It is hardly a coincidence that Denham behaves toward the natives on Skull Island in a way that, while not being identical to his treatment of Ann (after all, they're only savages; Ann is at least white), is nevertheless part and parcel of the same economic ideology. Ann is forced to take any money offered to stave off starvation, whereas the natives can simply be filmed *for nothing*. They are turned into so many unpaid actors, without even the benefit of being considered as filling anonymous "walk-on" roles.[8] The presence of Denham and the ship's crew on this remote island is taken for granted, another coincidence that enables them to misrecognize their status as intruders in favor of a belief that any and every person, object and event is there to be exploited in one or another sense of the term. From this standpoint, the natives fulfill the same symbolic and historical function as Frankenstein's monster and Legendre's army of zombies. Press-ganged into service, they are transformed into images to be sold as part of a documentary from which they will derive no benefit, social or pecuniary. Skull Island is so remote that not even the ship's captain has ever visited it before; it is as if it had suddenly appeared from nowhere, perhaps emerging from the ocean floor after some cataclysm, another version of Atlantis, the lost continent.

This is not just idle speculation on my part. What are we to make of the presence of dinosaurs, such as the pterodactyl and tyrannosaurus rex? The fact that such creatures became extinct tens of millions of years ago can only lead us to interpret Skull Island as the signifier of prehistory, the land that time has forgotten. We can, of course, interpret this along the usual racial lines of the superiority of white Western civilization, but we are also surely entitled to see at work the "invisible hand of the market," the naturalization of the economic in a society such as ours where profit is the only motive. This is nowhere more present than in the celebrated sequence where Kong is put on display to New Yorkers, but a number of factors come into play that create an excess of meaning that becomes as impossible to control as Kong when he escapes.[9]

That the ape is turned into a spectacle for well-heeled New Yorkers is patent, so we would be advised not to lose from sight, first, that they are from the monied classes at a time of economic crisis and, second, that the notion of spectacle is not innocent in the film. By getting Ann to look off-screen, see something, and scream, Denham is both shooting a spectacle and turning Ann into one (somewhat like the natives, inasmuch as she is being tried out to see if she will fit the role being written for her in the context of a documentary incorporating the natives). Whether it intends to or not, *King*

Kong is setting up parallels among Ann, Kong, and the natives: in one way or another they are alienated from their "labor."

I in no way wish to neglect the infamous fantasy of blacks and primates being linked in the racial Western unconscious. Thus, when the giant ape breaks loose and creates panic, we can present this both as the objective fear of the bourgeoisie faced with possible proletarian insurrection and a paraphrase of Marx: "blacks and women unite: you have nothing to lose but your chains!" The very size of Kong, like Frankenstein's monster, works in favor of a giant (= the proletariat) dominating and triumphing over a dwarf (= the capitalist).

There is clearly a fetishistic dimension to the spectacle of Kong on display, functioning on the mode of disavowal. Kong being worshipped by the natives and Ann being offered as a sacrifice to placate him will both be put down to superstition by the characters of the film and the audience of the film. The New Yorkers—who form an audience within the film and therefore can be said to represent us—would certainly reject the accusation that they are "worshipping" Kong in the same way, but they have been praying at another shrine for years: that of the stock exchange. We can perhaps use this to see the train crash caused by Kong as an unconscious displacement and inversion of the real historical situation obtaining. For it is ordinary working people (from working-class or lower middle-class backgrounds) who are the victims of the train crash that I propose to see as the text's literal representation of another "crash" of a figurative kind: the stock market crash of 1929 so present on the mode of absence from the very opening sequence of *King Kong*. If we return now to the famous shot of Ann screaming at the sight of something off-screen that we never see, it is undoubtedly true to argue that we finally do see the absent "something": when Kong suddenly appears and provokes Ann's next bout of screaming. Ann's patent *fear* when coached by Denham takes the form of *anguish* for us—fear without an object. To a certain extent, therefore, Kong is a form of hallucination, the result of something foreclosed in the Symbolic returning in the Real. Kong in the absent off-screen of Ann's look stands in for history itself, something real but invisible. Thus, making Kong massively present and sowing destruction is the way, the film both materializes what is a real threat to capitalism—the unleashed forces of proletarian fury—and represses the historical nature of the conditions that have wrought havoc on capitalism's victims. Denham's remark about "Beauty and the Beast" is yet another instance of ideology turning one victim against another, made necessary by the fact that we cannot but sympathize with Kong's plight. His being shot down by planes, symbols of bourgeois economic and political power, is a warning that no sacrifice is too great to be demanded by those in power of those whose own plight is uncannily akin to that of the giant ape.

The Son of Kong has the distinction of being a dispiriting cinematic experience and a truly fascinating text, almost a textbook working-out of capitalist ideology with its attendant contradictions and subterfuges. It is also, as we shall see, an openly political film and an attempt to defuse the criticisms of capitalism at once implied by the status of Ann Darrow and denied in the ways we have analyzed already. It is therefore interesting to note that this narrative strategy is first put to work by dividing the character of Ann into two characters: the journalist who comes to interview a besieged Carl Denham (ruined by Kong and pursued by avid creditors); and the young woman whom Denham takes back to Skull Island with the captain and himself and whom he agrees to marry at the end. A short B feature in which the son of Kong plays a subordinate role, the film nevertheless has a script that demands close attention.[10]

It is surely revealing that Denham is presented as ruined because of Kong, which eliminates all question of responsibility on his part, an aspect of the situation that is not shared by those prosecuting/persecuting him for the damage caused by the marauding ape. The film explicitly takes the side of the entrepreneur, thus validating the notion of initiative *whatever the cost*.[11] It is therefore just as revealing that the young woman journalist says she will lose her job if Denham refuses an interview, which he does: he shows complete indifference, and she is represented as barging in on him like just another writ server. Only Denham, it would seem, has the right to show initiative, not this woman who is at the mercy of the whims of her boss and potential interviewees, much as Ann was at the mercy of New York low life, until "saved" by Denham. Placed back to back, the two films give the impression that Denham comes out on top ethically, whatever happens.

This interpretation is perfectly logical, given *Son of Kong*'s deep commitment to the ideology of capital as opposed to the interests of labor. Thus, the boatswain hired by the captain is called a "troublemaker" (i.e., trade unionist), and the delegation of crew members who have come to protest about wages and conditions are referred to as "the workers' committee," complete with a sarcastic reference to the Soviet Union. However, the script gets itself embroiled in a non sequitur that reveals its political hand and the real economic relations at work. The crew members mutiny and cast adrift Denham, the captain, the young woman he has befriended after the death of her father,[12] and the man responsible for his death, Helstrom, a character straight out of Joseph Conrad's *The Nigger of the "Narcissus"*: like the mediocre Donkin, he is consumed by *resentment*. This feeling is due to the captain having his own ship, a sign of private property that is a symbol of intelligence, foresight and saving. But times are hard, and the captain doesn't know how he can pay the crew. Apparently he finds business along the route taken because the crew is paid, although the boatswain complains it's not a "living wage." *Son of Kong* therefore presents the captain as a man of initiative *because* he sets off without knowing what business he will find and without knowing whether he will be able to pay the crew; the money he has saved is needed to launch this new expedition and not to be used as wages. Lest audiences at a time of economic crisis find it abnormal not to pay workers for their labor, the entire crew is shown to be lazy and shifty (they squint and are unshaven!).

Here the script finds itself at an ideological impasse. The skipper can only set off on a new expedition because he has found a crew *and* put enough money aside. This premise in turn suggests thrift and foresight, but it conveniently represses the fact that *anyone* is supposed to be able to become his own boss and succeed within the American system of free enterprise. In that case, not only does the film hide the role of surplus value—a captain pays his crew and has something to show for it after (profit)—but also denies the right of each crew member to strive to become a captain himself. There was obviously a time when the captain was not his own boss but became one by a stint of hard work and saving. If crew members are deprived of wages so that their captain can use the money to equip his ship for a new voyage, then how will they be able to earn enough money to save and have the opportunity to buy their own ship in due course? The film cannot give a historical answer to the question of capital and labor, so it must perforce resort to visual and ideological stereotypes to present workers protesting about wages and working conditions as loafers incapable of understanding the problems an employer has to face.

Both the captain and Denham are single-minded and selfish, but the film tries to present them as the opposite. It does so by having Denham say he is "conscience-stricken" over what happened to Kong, although he has shown no remorse whatsoever in *King Kong* for the sailors killed on the island, sacrificed to his obsession with making a film.[13] Denham even says at one point in *Son of Kong*, "I owe his family something," referring to the ape. This way of anthropomorphizing the animal comes down to a form of reification, with animals taking the place of things. Denham's sense of initiative is made clear: learning from Helstrom that the island contains hidden treasure, he resolves to find and take it. That way he will be able to pay off his creditors—by stealing from someone else, in this case the islanders. Just as *Son of Kong* cashes in on *King Kong*, so Denham cashes in on the first expedition; he does not entertain the idea that he might owe the natives something. At one point Denham, reflecting ruefully on his fate since Kong escaped, says, "I'm sure paying for what I did to you," which is quite wrong. Everyone is paying ex-cept Denham. As we have seen, he and the captain are prepared not to pay the crew in order to get their business back on its feet. In other words, if something can be said to be "strictly business," then it is certainly "no funny business."

As the ship sails out of New York harbor on its way to prove the equation "trade = profit," we are shown the Statue of Liberty. Because we already know we are in New York, it would be unwise to see this as a piece of local color. The image returns to give a particular meaning to the ending where a gigantic earthquake destroys Skull Island, which gradually sinks beneath the waves until it has entirely disappeared. Denham and the young woman are saved by the son of Kong, who holds them aloft above the water until the Captain can get to them by boat. Then the ape, too, sinks beneath the waves, his arm raised so that he bears a striking resemblance to the Statue of Liberty. What is happening here? Bryan Senn points out that, after the storm and the earthquake begin we see "a violent hurricane buffeting a handful of natives." He then adds significantly, "Not only does the storm suddenly ap-pear as if by magic, the natives *disappear* just as abruptly, for this is the last time we see any of Skull Island's indigenous human inhabitants."[14] The na-tives, the sailors on the first expedition, and the crew members who mutiny all disappear without a trace, with Senn's most pertinent formula "as if by magic" summing up how capitalist ideology removes all traces of labor from the products of the world we inhabit so that it appears as natural as the ele-ments themselves. The son of Kong saves Denham as the latter represents free enterprise. Thus, the historical significance of the Statue of Liberty, which insisted on the existence of poverty and exploitation, has been hidden so as to result in the extolling of initiative as something existing outside time, a concept without a past and therefore without a history.

I would suggest that two other levels of meaning are created by the juxta-position of the ape as the Statue of Liberty and the disappearance of the na-tives. One meaning is that all the natives needed to survive was to believe in the benefits of American democratic capitalism and that those who do not are condemned to disappear into the abyss of prehistory—not for nothing do dinosaurs appear again in this film. However, as one of the latter resembles no dinosaur that really existed but is rather a hybrid product of the studios more in keeping with a fantasy world, we can say that the film is revealing its "fairytale" dimension at the very moment it is presenting a highly biased view of history. The second meaning is even closer to home: the natives stand in for the American Indian who had to "disappear" in order for expansionism to take place. This tragic aspect of the American past is foreclosed rather than repressed; it is as if it never took place. This view corresponds perfectly to Skull Island disappearing without a trace, permanently, as if it had never existed. I propose to interpret this example of the film's political unconscious as an indication, via denial, that Skull Island is the film's signifier of history.

At the end, the heroine renounces her share of the treasure to be with Denham, a form of sacrifice that has interesting implications. Since the woman is about to marry the man, she is expected to give up what is owed her, much as the workers in the film are expected to renounce their wages and trust the captain. Here the "rights" of capitalism and those of patriarchy merge into one, with the young woman accepting her condition without ever considering she is a willing victim, unlike Ann Darrow at the opening of *King Kong*. *Son of Kong* serves to eliminate any trace of social criticism the earlier film might have countenanced.

One film that most definitely does countenance forms of such criticism, via the presence/absence dialectic of money and labor, is *The Devil-Doll*.[15] A striking example of this dialectic occurs at one point. Former banker Lavond has been imprisoned for life on Devil's Island, victim of a plot by his three colleagues to have him found guilty for their own criminal financial activities. Lavond escapes, returns to France, and, with the help of the widow of the prisoner who escaped with him but dies of heart failure on his return home, exploits the latter's experiments, which consist of reducing people and animals to a fraction of their size—he sends tiny assassins to eliminate his former colleagues. (The implications of this experiment and the various themes it evokes will be discussed later.) As soon as the three men hear of the escape, they put up a reward for Lavond: a shot of the inside of a police station shows that the amount is one hundred thousand francs. Next to the poster advertising the reward is another informing the public/the spectator of a "child missing." Significantly, no reward is being offered for information concerning her whereabouts. However, if the role of money is explicit in the film, its real social function remains profoundly ambiguous.

Let us first see how the theme of money is highlighted. What I assume to be a private joke introduces the concept: One of the bankers is called Radin, which is a homophone of *radin*, French for "miserly." How appropriate a name! Joke or not, elsewhere the script is deadly serious when it comes to representing the effects of money and social position. Lavond's daughter (who blames her father for everything, a striking example of the subject repressing the collective in favor of a purely imaginary individual relationship) works in a laundry to survive.[16] The visibly unpleasant working conditions and the presence of steam (a useful "naturalistic" detail) form a neat metaphor for "sweated labor," where the literal introduces the figurative and, hence, the real social conditions.[17] What is also striking is that the female proprietor upbraids the young women if they use too much soap. In other words, she, too, is "miserly" like the bankers, and making her a woman shows it is a question of *class, not sex*. The daughter, who would have lived a life of luxury if her father had continued in the banking business, is now forced to sell her labor and is turned into a member of the proletariat. However, she is convinced that her father is to blame, despite her mother's determined support for her husband. Thus, the daughter listens to the ideological discourse of men representing the class of the bankers; one form of patriarchy replaces another, the perverse effects of which we shall return to presently. At the same time, the script gives another reason for this hatred and bitterness on her part: she has a second, part-time job as a sort of "hostess" in a bar where she earns one centime for every drink bought by men who come to leer at her. Such a form of prostitution is an integral part of the economy of a society under the sway of fetishism and reification.

The beautiful irony lying behind the offer of a large sum for Lavond's capture is that this money is really his, so his colleagues are having recourse to the surplus value that the four of them used to share out and that has increased for the three others since Lavond's imprisonment. This is further elaborated (the script is one of the most sophisticated of the period) in a scene where Lavond, disguised as doll maker Mrs. Mandelip to carry out his plan of revenge, visits one of his future victims to sell a doll (in reality a shrunken version of a real person who will obey Lavond's will and kill). The wife is about to buy one but the husband protests because the price is far too high. Lavond/Mandelip makes a reference to the cost of the wife's jewelry, and the banker gives in. The sequence neatly represents the effects of an absent cause (the jewelry purchased thanks to the surplus value created by the labor of workers, all invisible for the couple) and the fact that a small entrepreneur runs the risk of his or her prices being forced down by those in charge of the means of production: Mrs. Mandelip may be an independent artisan, but her control over her products, it is being subtly suggested, is not absolute.

The Devil-Doll insists that Lavond is interested only in revenge; he remains a capitalist at heart. For him the people reduced to the size of dolls are just so many guinea pigs to be exploited. Moreover, they have no minds of their own when so reduced, which sets up a link between them and Legendre's zombies who are at his beck and call in much the same way.

Legendre's look and his gesture with his hands find an echo in Lavond's mental concentration to set the dolls off on their missions. It is revealing that both Lavond and the late scientist's widow wish to use the results of his experiments for purely negative reasons: she is power crazy. They both come to Paris to work together and have a peasant girl as their servant; she is retarded and walks with a pronounced limp. A fascinating parallel is set up between her and Lavond's second victim who is paralyzed by poison rather than murdered outright. His new and permanent state is described thus by his intimates: "a brilliant mind imprisoned in a useless body." Nothing has shown him to be particularly brilliant, except as a wily crook (the film's subversive aspect lies in its equating bankers with organized theft on a grand scale), so this perversion of the truth by his friends can be interpreted as pure ideology and allows us to see another meaning a historically determined one, hiding behind the remark quoted earlier. The bodies of the proletariat, useful in producing surplus value, are deemed socially useless because they are not endowed with that "brilliant mind" that distinguishes the capitalist from those whose labor he transforms into surplus value.

We must not forget that Lavond was a banker who made a fortune and not allow ourselves to have the wool pulled over our eyes by the perfidy of his colleagues. It is here that the film retreats from its often radical criticism of capitalism to a position that ultimately shores it up. The daughter is engaged to a young man who is in the taxi business: he transports Lavond early in the film and announces proudly to him (as he does immediately after to his fiancée) that he has just bought his third taxi. It is his words that are of interest here: "We capitalists must take risks: nothing ventured, nothing gained." Lavond heartily concurs, which is hardly surprising: he remains a capitalist to his fingertips and is about to venture on an undertaking that involves not a few risks. From that standpoint, the remark of the young man is one of unconscious irony: how many risks, if any, did Lavond take in order to become rich? The fiancé is as much a victim of the discourse of individual success as the daughter. The film, however, ends up by justifying him in the name of the happy end, whose implications we must now analyze.

At one point in the film, the fiancé takes the daughter up to the top of the Eiffel Tower, and they gaze down on the people, tiny specks, hundreds of feet below. "Everything seems so small and unimportant from up here," says the young man. Through him the film is assimilating the Parisians to the characters reduced to the size of dolls by Lavond, which sets up an ideological parallel between the taxi driver and the ex-banker. His belief in taking risks indicates he has not only become part of the ideological world of the banking system but that he is implicitly ready to treat anyone who threatens his

"right" to succeed, just as his fiancée's employer does, just as the bankers do—
and just as Lavond does with the tiny humans at his disposal. At the end of
the film, Lavond ascends to the top of the Eiffel Tower with the fiancé in order to reveal who he is and how he has decided to "disappear," now that his
revenge is complete. He wishes him and his daughter good luck and, to all
extents and purposes, hands her over to the young man as a wedding gift,
thus renouncing his own phallic rights and granting them to the fiancé. The
unwritten laws of patriarchy and capitalism thus remain intact, indeed secret;
his daughter, Lavond insists, must never know. Since the daughter is the
film's signifier of the proletariat and the fiancé the signifier of democratic
capitalism, this secrecy parallels that of the way capitalism hides all traces of
labor in the fabrication of products to be exchanged on the market for money
and, crucially, in the creation of surplus value. The fact of his disappearance
can only underscore the profoundly ideological notion that making money is
a normal and natural state of affairs and that the origin of any form of wealth
is simply the person who works hard and is ready to take risks.

One aspect of the plot, however, remains to be brought to light because it
undercuts the ending. When discussing his experiments with Lavond, the
scientist admits to one failure: when a person is reduced in size, "all records
are wiped off, no memory left, no will of its own." This erasure of memory is
crucial, for memory is the only obstacle in the way of triumphant capitalism
that naturalizes the economy and turns it into an ahistorical phenomenon
with no origin. This in turn justifies class exploitation and the social phenomenon called "profit." If the "absent cause" of history insists, it is a "lost
cause" at the end where Lavond descends the Eiffel Tower in the elevator,
and a fade-out to black symbolizes his future annihilation and the disappearance of the past as an influence on the present and the future.

The theme of invisibility is taken literally in *The Invisible Man*. In
Whale's film, the drive for recognition lies in the fact of succeeding with
an experiment that makes the subject invisible. The hero's dilemma stems
from his inability to reverse the process, and he returns to physical normality only at the end when he is shot dead. Much of the film is marred by
Whale's dubious concept of humor. As in *Bride of Frankenstein*, the dreadful Una O'Connor character throws a spanner in the works every time she
opens her mouth (usually to scream to no effect whatsoever). I shall argue
that the film's interest lies not in the success or failure of its special effects
but in the way it gives symbolic meaning to the very concept of being invisible and to the research of a young and poor scientist. The hero's poverty
encourages a search for wealth, and the film implies he is from a proletarian background: he wants "wealth, fame, and honor." The film thus rightly

dismisses the ideological ploy that recognition from one's peers is sufficient reward for a scientist; that can be the case only if he is financed by the public sphere where his work will belong to the collectivity and resources made available for him to pursue further fundamental research. In the present-day context of research being funded increasingly by the private sphere, often to further its own interests, the film has something of interest and importance to say to us.

If *The Invisible Man* opts for the "mad scientist" approach, this can be justified in the light of Jack Griffin's going rapidly and inexorably mad. For what is his madness but a question of social *alienation* and, as such, the film's way of showing how even intellectual labor can be a victim of a system based on money and exploitation? It is here that Whale's weakness for humor gets in the way of a genuine critical discourse. I am thinking in particular of the representation of the village locals and Griffin's treatment of them: contemptuous and unnecessarily aggressive. Had Whale chosen to represent the villagers as people frightened by something they don't understand, rather than as moronic and suspicious yokels, then *The Invisible Man* would have been a thoughtful comment on alienation generally and how one sector of the community, misrecognizing its real social and historical status, turns another sector (here: a solitary intellectual) into a scapegoat. The parallel with the director's two Frankenstein movies would have been striking, and it is regrettable that Whale should have failed to understand the subversive ideological thrust of this aspect of his own work.

A political reading of this film made in 1933 is not difficult and needs to be mentioned. Griffin is anxious to "put the world right," but the context in which he makes the remark indicates not a progressive but a fascist program. This point only confirms what we have already heard: "An invisible man can rule the world; no one can see him come, no one can see him go . . . he can rob, wreck, and kill." Which he promptly proceeds to do: the derailing of a train suffices to show his contempt for human life. A revealing shot follows his speech: we see a Jewish jeweler putting diamonds away in order to protect his business from looters in a context of general confusion and the breakdown of order. What could be taken for anti-Semitism (the Jew as miser) is surely just the opposite: an uncanny anticipation of a nationwide phenomenon that was already under way in Hitler's Germany, the organized pogrom. I will argue now that this anti-Nazi dimension of the film has been introduced not to make a simple political point (surely deliberate) but to do something quite different: to reveal what forces were at work to ensure the victory of Nazism and the complicity with fascism shown by the international community during the decade.

In one scene, the Invisible Man commits the most heinous crime possible in a capitalist society: he robs a bank.[18] What is intriguing is that he does so not to finance his continued research but to create confusion. He throws handfuls of bills in the direction of passers-by who scramble frantically for the loot. Several things are happening here. We must not forget that Hitler was defended, within Germany and without, for supposedly increasing the living standards of the German people. The film seems to be suggesting how easily people can be hoodwinked when easy gain is at hand. The scene also stresses the true social nature of money by having *invisible hands* as the source of this unexpected wealth. These hands symbolize the proletariat whose labor produced the goods that are exchanged for money, while at the same time producing surplus value for the person who hires the laborer. One of the favorite gambits of capitalism is to tell the truth the better to deceive. Let us take the formula "Money doesn't grow on trees." Clearly the Invisible Man is trying to show the opposite, but his gesture nevertheless reveals the truth. When the capitalist quotes this saying, he is not telling us that it is labor power that produces wealth, but that people should accept working ever harder in order to earn the same amount of money. The subject who takes up this saying as if he or she were making an earth-shattering discovery and were the original subject of the enunciation, is in reality only revealing the unconscious truth of his or her social and psychic alienation. In Germany in the 1930s, Hitler and the economic forces underpinning his regime exploited this alienation in ways undreamed of before, except by Marx and Freud.

At one point in *The Most Dangerous Game*, Count Zaroff, sporting a hunting rifle, comes running down a flight of steps leading from the huge hall of his island castle down into the depths of the dungeons where he brings his future victims prior to sending them out to be hunted by himself. He is dressed all in black and is wearing breeches; the resemblance with Mussolini or a Gestapo officer is flagrant. That the film is an extended antifascist allegory surely no longer needs to be demonstrated. What does need to be highlighted, however, are the numerous links between Zaroff and his unwilling guest Rainsford, for it is in these links forged between them, notably by the dialogue, that the particular interest of this remarkable film lies.

A clear parallel is made between the opening scene onboard the yacht that is soon to founder (Rainsford alone will escape) and the sequence involving Zaroff and Rainsford in the hall/salon where they discuss hunting. This is the topic that occupies Rainsford's companions, all of whom are obviously from the monied classes, some of them with considerable independent means. This, too, assimilates them to Zaroff, whose castle is surely the equivalent of the yacht, a private world where each owner can do just what he likes. Rainsford's comments on the tiger he has just shot during a hunting expedition are revealing of the film's subtext on class, labor, and history, although the full implications will become clear only later. Rainsford talks of the animal as if it were a person, enjoying the hunt as much as he. He thus establishes a purely imaginary identity of purpose, a matching of minds, as if there were some sort of equality of opportunity at work, with the tiger as free to take part (or not) in the hunt as Rainsford. When asked whether he would change places with the tiger, Rainsford replies with a grin, "Not now," thus disavowing his own argument. I would claim that what is being presented here is the meeting (every bit as antagonistic as that between hunter and hunted) between the capitalist and the worker, always presented as freedom of choice, as if the worker had the possibility of refusing a job offer, in reality made him on a "take it or leave it" basis. The lack of balance is patent to anyone willing to think about it. The capitalist has a large reserve of workers to choose from (especially in times of high unemployment: the film dates from 1932 and was made during the shooting of *King Kong*), whereas the worker has the choice between a wage and starvation.[19] Therefore, when Rainsford claims that there are "two kinds of people: hunter and hunted," he is unwittingly admitting to the truth of the intersubjective relation between employer and employee, showing that the fact of talking about the tiger as a person was a slip of the tongue. This is what he meant all along but failed to recognize his true subject position as privileged hunter/capitalist.[20]

In case readers feel that I am claiming too much by my reference to the film's date, let us turn to a conversation between Zaroff, Rainsford, and the heroine's drunken brother. To start off with, Zaroff presents himself as a refugee from the Bolshevik Revolution, fleeing a country where his father had owned vast tracts of land and loved to hunt. Fortunately for him, Zaroff has managed to escape with the surplus value produced by the serfs, several of whom he has brought with him; they do the dirty work for him on the island, sometimes paying the supreme penalty so that their master can hunt. However, times are hard: Zaroff is bored and is looking for new sport. It is in this context that the brother says, "Conditions are bad everywhere these days," a clear reference to the economic situation and a remark that one would not expect from so stupid and selfish a character as the boorish brother. It is a hint to the audience, for neither Zaroff nor Rainsford (nor his companions on the yacht) are lacking for anything. Zaroff's admiration for Rainsford is partly narcissistic—he sees a kindred spirit. However, this narcissism must be taken on another level: Rainsford is Zaroff's mirror image. For both the count and Rainsford, certain people were born to hunt. This concept indicates a supposedly natural state of affairs that eliminates any class antagonism, not to mention history itself.

Zaroff has no respect for the brother, who cannot follow a particular state of affairs to its logical conclusion; he has resorted to alcohol to hide his alienation from the world around him. Even Rainsford disappoints him in his refusal to participate in the count's new sport: hunting humans, of which there are several ready and waiting on the island. Rainsford is appalled, and it is not difficult to see why. As we have already shown, his tendency to turn prey into humans via discourse betrays an unconscious system of values that is identical to that of Zaroff but on the mode of reversal: turning humans into prey by an act. Only Zaroff recognizes it openly and denounces Rainsford as "one who dare not follow his own convictions to their logical conclusion." Zaroff is the perfect example of Lacan's *plus-de-jouir* (surplus enjoyment), where the subject strives to go as far as possible, beyond the point where he or she needs to go to obtain satisfaction, producing an *excess* of enjoyment that the subject does not need in order to survive. This, of course, corresponds to surplus value, what Zaroff has brought with him to his island, something the capitalist enjoys but which he does not need to ensure his basic existence.[21] Hence the film's need to set up a rift between the two men who are so alike, with the count referring to them as "we barbarians," a call for solidarity to which Rainsford can respond only by a horrified rejection. The nature of the society he inhabits is suddenly revealed to him in all its nakedness, a fact he must refuse. When Zaroff offers the heroine as a prize, he is not only showing himself a true representative of the competitive spirit but a man deeply versed in the phallocentric values of patriarchy.

All this is too much for Rainsford. Unfortunately for the conscious logic of the film, certain details insist on the identity they share. Zaroff claims to believe in fair play but tries to shoot Rainsford when the latter returns from the hunt which he has therefore won according to the rules. The men fight, and Rainsford manages to stab the count fatally with one of his arrows. To be precise, he *stabs him in the back*, thus showing he has betrayed the logic of power and enjoyment at the basis of both Zaroff's code and Rainsford's supposedly civilized version of it. The fact that the count starts the hunt with a bow and arrow before resorting to a rifle suggests a certain feudalism, a notion underscored by the seeming opposition between the modern yacht and the medieval castle. These oppositions are surely the film's admitting the true state of affairs via the unconscious tactic of denial. The crew members are the first victims when the boat crashes into the reefs, which it does because nobody takes the captain seriously when he urges the owner to take another course. And, as I have already pointed out, Zaroff cares not a jot when his faithful henchman is killed. Such is the logic of the system, the survival of the fittest, one person's failure (i.e., death) leading to another's success (i.e., money and power).

Thanks to the accident, Rainsford has the impression that he is "living on borrowed time" because he alone has survived; perhaps the next time the hunter/hunted opposition might change. It is interesting to notice that he has learned something from his experience, although just how much cannot be ascertained. For the yacht ran into the reef just after Rainsford stated, with utter confidence, that nothing would change the "hunter/hunted" opposition. What has occurred here with this accident, if not the manifestation of the Real, showing that the best laid plans can come to naught? The Real, or history itself. It is as if the film wants us to take seriously the problems posed by the national and international situation, although Zaroff would have none of this: "You don't excuse what needs no excuse," he tells Rainsford, showing himself to be the perfect capitalist. Perhaps, then, we are entitled to see the animal-hunter confrontation as that between communism or Marxism and capitalism: just as the animal kills only to eat, so for Marx production was for consumption, not for profit. The hunter, however, kills for fun: it is Rainsford himself who claims the animal enjoys the hunt. This, then, indicates the hero's *plus-de-jouir*. The discussion on the yacht, which resembles nothing if not a meeting in a businessmen's board room, shows that no amount of equating Zaroff with the feudal or the medieval can change the film's thrust and its profound historical meaning.

A clash between two worlds is also central to *The Mask of Fu Manchu*, but in this case East and West are presented as totally alien to one another, the better to excuse the film's prejudices and hide the significance of the real meaning of history as opposed to the profoundly ideological one represented. The patent racism is sufficiently extreme and obnoxious to unite against it everyone from the Old Right to the New Left, a fact that should give us cause to pause: it is all too simple, too simply *moral*. To dismiss this fascinating, if repugnant, film out of hand because of its gross xenophobia would be to miss the point entirely. Asians in the film function much as the Jew in Slavoj Zizek's example:

> Society is not prevented from achieving its full identity because of Jews: it is prevented *by its own antagonistic nature*, by its own immanent blockage, and it "projects" this internal negativity into the figure of the "Jew." In other words, what is excluded from the Symbolic (from the frame of the corporate socio-symbolic order) returns in the Real as a paranoid construction of the "Jew."[22]

We must not be led astray by the fact that the first shot of Fu Manchu in the film shows his face reflected in a mirror, huge and massively distorted, as

if he were some monster. There is some truth in approaching the film thus—
the other as absolute Otherness, to be cast out like the Devil—but its meaning returns in the very last sequence of the film, at precisely the moment
when the Evil One has been conquered. Let us, however, begin at the beginning.

The tone is set by the question Nayland Smith of the Secret Service puts
to archaeologist Sir Lionel Barton, whom he has summoned to help him
combat Fu Manchu: "Do you love your country?" At once there is communicated to the audience the idea of a homogeneous entity "Britain," devoid
of any difference whatsoever, as natural a political entity as it is a geograph-
ical one. The antagonistic nature of that society, however, is also made abundantly clear by Sir Lionel's reply: "All through the war and the Depression.
And the high taxes and the low rents." In other words, the two men are the
representatives of the owners of the means of production, living off the (fat
of the) land and surplus value, the latter compromised in their eyes by "low
rents": they cannot exploit the locals (represented in the film by the coolies)
as much as they would like. Then Nayland Smith asks him whether he has
heard of Fu Manchu, and Sir Lionel asks whether he is an archaeologist. The
fact that this exchange enables Smith to launch into a tirade concerning the
danger represented by Fu Manchu should not prevent us from interpreting
the meaning of the reply. Since Sir Lionel is an archaeologist, he at once attributes that function to Fu Manchu, not to welcome him into the club, as
it were, but to deny that he, Sir Lionel, can be anything else, that he can
represent any interests other than those of disinterested science and the love
of art. Fu Manchu's interest in Genghis Khan's mask and scimitar, however,
has already been commented on unwittingly by a real-life nineteenth-
century Orientalist, William Muir: "the sword of Muhammad, and the Ko-
ran, are the most stubborn enemies of Civilization, Liberty, and the Truth
which the world has yet known."[23] The fact that Nayland Smith is in charge
is a perfect example of what Said has called that "appropriation by which Europe, or the European awareness of the Orient, transformed itself from being
textual and contemplative into being administrative, economic, and even
military."[24] All ulterior motives—apart from a "natural" wish to "save the
world"—have thus been foreclosed as quite simply not existing in order to
set Fu Manchu up as a sort of bogeyman.[25] From then on, from an ideological standpoint, everything is meant to be plain sailing, and it is not without
unconscious irony that the last scene takes place aboard an ocean liner on a
placid sea. Between the opening and closing scenes, however, the film's
racist and colonialist discourse comes to grief on the reefs of representation,
both visual and verbal.

Denial and inversion are frequent, which need hardly surprise us. Claims of neutrality and projecting one's desires onto the other are staple tactics in ideological warfare. Captured by Fu Manchu and offered one million pounds for the mask and scimitar of Genghis Khan that will make Fu Manchu all-powerful, Sir Lionel replies, "I am not for sale." And, of course, he is not, given his social and economic situation. He is not like the Chinese coolies who work with the British team to unearth the tomb; they have been bought because their labor power is needed, and they have accepted because they have no choice. Nayland Smith and Sir Lionel, Zaroff and Rainsford, Lavond and the bankers, Denham and the ship's captain are all part of a given economic and political system. Such a disclaimer concerning the importance of the monetary value of the objects sought after fits in badly with the remark made by von Berg, one of the team, the moment he sets his eyes on the objects: "Worth a king's ransom!" The repressed of the conversation between Nayland Smith and Sir Lionel returns to haunt the text: the implications of the link between "the interests of Britain" and "the interests of archaeology." The remark of von Berg is a condensation of unsaid motives impossible to admit. First, the exchange value of the mask and scimitar is of the utmost importance; second, violating the East for treasures belonging there poses no problem (after all, they are destined to end up in the British Museum). It is hardly surprising that *The Mummy* tries to pass off the British presence in Egypt as purely altruistic, from which all pecuniary interests must be excluded, nor that the British expedition of 1921 (the basis of the script of *The Mummy*) should be evoked in *The Mask of Fu Manchu*.[26]

This is an opportune point at which to return, from another angle, to the question of the role played by excrement that we raised in chapter 2 in the context of *The Mask of Fu Manchu*. Freud frequently made reference to the link between money and feces, and it is obvious that in our society money occupies a superior place—indeed, the only place, the excremental being repressed.[27] The film is thus patently, if unconsciously, suggesting that Fu Manchu is inferior to Sir Lionel because he is obsessed by excrement and wants to overcome this by boasting about how much money he has. Once again, however, we must not lose from sight that the representation of Fu Manchu is very much a subjective racist fantasy, and we could therefore argue that the film is anxious to set off the Oriental's abnormal concern with bodily functions against the West's more noble attitudes. However, as we have just seen from the example of von Berg, the film fetishizes money, and we would be justified in setting up an opposition between the natural (excrement) and the artificial (money). Or, to put it more concretely, the value of excrement and money will depend on the circumstances. If, like Robinson Crusoe, I find myself cast away on a desert island, then I shall prize my excrement far more highly than a gold ingot: the former will be very useful as a fertilizer to help me cultivate the soil. Continuing this comparison, I would point out that, if the capitalist desires his excrement to be turned into gold, I on my desert island would wish exactly the reverse. My excrement has *use value* for me, whereas my ingot has only *exchange value*, a question to which I shall return in the next section.

Another hallowed realm of Western fantasy is opened up when Fu Manchu offers Sir Lionel his daughter, not in marriage but as an object for his sexual pleasure: what Orientals (and blacks, much in evidence as Fu Manchu's servants[28]) do with their women. The role of the female body as commodity in the West does not need to be stressed further, but even a cursory glance at advertising material used to sell films in general and horror films in particular in the 1930s (to keep to that decade) show that those in charge of publicity left no (grave)stone unturned in their feverish search for cunning stunts. The way Sir Lionel's daughter is presented as she is about to be sacrificed at the end, with masses of Asians attempting to paw her helpless body, tells us more about Western fantasies than anything else, as we can ascertain from the sacrifice of the native girl and Ann Darrow in *King Kong*.[29]

The coolies, who represent Asia in general, have no rights whatsoever.[30] When the birthplace of Genghis Khan is finally discovered, the British team descend into the bowels of the earth[31] without so much as a "by your leave." It goes without saying that it all belongs to them, just as it goes without saying that, when the coolies descend to prostrate themselves before the grave, they are behaving as simple-minded fetishists. There is, of course, nothing fetishistic in calling the relics "priceless," a way of disavowing their real meaning, their ideological and imperialist "value" beyond what they can bring on the market: "surplus value" in a very special sense, in that case. However, it is precisely at this moment, the penetration into the tomb, that the film resorts to a device that is used systematically throughout the film and proves to be its ideological undoing: the coolies looking. A shot, taken from *inside* the tomb, shows them forming a circle around the rim of the opening and looking in. The spectator is therefore "with" the explorers, looking *out* at the coolies looking *in*. It would be difficult to find an image summing up more succinctly an unconscious ideology and its meaning. The West has a natural right to be in the East, while the Easterners are but *onlookers* in their own country, in their own history: "The Orient is watched . . . the European, whose sensibility tours the Orient, is a watcher."[32] Fredric Jameson has pressed matters further: "the fact of objectification is grasped as that to which the Other (or myself) must necessarily submit. To make other people over into things by way of the Look thus becomes the primal source of a domination and a subjection which can only be overcome by looking back or 're-turning the gaze.'"[33] We can take the question even further. The anxiety pro-duced in the subject by the understanding that the Other is indifferent to him and does not return his look is inscribed into the film in the form of a projection that condenses a paranoid fear of being watched and a desire to be watched, on the grounds that this desire returns to the subject as part of his being threatened by the indifference of the Other.[34]

In its use of the coolie looking, the film betrays a paranoid attitude that we can better understand by interpreting it less as a danger from *without* than one from *within*. What is so striking is that this paranoia becomes quite patent, with shot after shot of "sinister" coolies peering out from behind walls to watch the progress of the British. We can surely see this as an inversion of the disinterested look of the West, as supposedly neutral as that of the scien-tist gazing through his microscope. This helps us to understand what obtain-ing the mask and scimitar means to Nayland Smith and the British govern-ment in terms other than those of plunder and science. The paranoid dimension lies in the fear that the Oriental may turn out not only to be more educated than expected but also to be more educated than Westerners, which explains why Sir Lionel is so sarcastic when Fu Manchu informs him that he has three doctorates from famous Western universities. It is also, I would suggest, a case of anxiety faced with the impossibility of representing the Oriental: any attempt to pin him down to a stable signified produces an excess due to the fantasy situation inherent in the Western point of view. As we shall see, this information concerning Fu Manchu's knowledge—swept aside as irrelevant, indeed foreclosed—returns in no uncertain fashion in the last sequence of the film.

Before turning to that sequence, however, it is necessary to describe and analyze the first textual manifestation of a coolie looking.[35] It occurs in the British Museum near the beginning of the film and involves the kidnapping of Sir Lionel. We see a face, with prominent eyes, painted on a vertical sar-cophagus containing an Egyptian mummy. Then the lid opens slightly, to re-veal a coolie inside looking out. Two other coolies, dressed as mummies, emerge from their hiding places, and Sir Lionel is overpowered and spirited away. I would suggest that this shot annihilates the Orientalist discourse in-scribed into the film at the very moment it seeks to reinforce it. The fact that the coolie is inside looking out places him in the same position as the British and the spectators in the tomb looking out later in the film. Thus, the coolie suddenly occupies the place of knowledge and power, even if it does take three of them to overpower Sir Lionel.[36] This power of the coolie must be trans-formed into an act of treachery and inverted so as to render the Westerner a victim at the precise moment where he is shown *not* to be omnipotent. More-over, by concentrating on the eyes painted on the coffin, the film implicitly draws a comparison between them and the look of the coolie, thus assimilat-ing the Chinese to several thousand years of history, far more than the British can boast of. This scene, to which the others add their grain of subversion, also indicates that whatever the British do the Asians have the drop on them, a fact pointed out by reviewers at the time.[37] This must be disavowed, which is the function of the last sequence.

Fu Manchu is dead, and the mask and scimitar are safely in British hands. On the return journey to civilization onboard an ocean liner—that symbol of Western knowledge and the superiority of its class system[38]—Nayland Smith informs his companions that it is too dangerous to keep the sword; it must be consigned to the sea, lest another Fu Manchu come to claim it. Thus, the hypocrisy of pretending that people like Sir Lionel are interested only in the historical value of the sword is maintained to the end. As he makes this remark, a gong is heard and the Westerners turn around in hor-ror. But it is only a waiter announcing dinner. The scene shows the triumph of the power of the word—mention someone's name and the person will promptly appear—which is not only a question of the Uncanny, the return of a superstitious belief one thought to be part of the past, but also of a fear of the power of the signifier to mean something beyond what one can con-trol. Fu Manchu is dead, but another like him can return to stir up the same trouble. The menace, invisible, is everywhere, a notion perfectly captured by a comment by one newspaper at the time that the film evoked "a band of brave men struggling against the ever-present, yet unseen, evil of the Asiatic monster."[39] This unconscious caricature of institutionalized paranoia sums up not only the coolies looking, "ever-present, yet unseen," but also the Lacan-ian Real. Nayland Smith addresses the waiter to ask him whether he has doc-torates from universities. The bemused man assures him he does not, and Smith shakes his hand to thank him. The Oriental—the waiter, of course, is Chinese—is acceptable as long as he not only is ignorant but admits it and considers it normal. Unlike Dr. Fu Manchu.

We can now see what has been excluded from the Symbolic and has re-turned in the Real in the form of an auditory hallucination. The hordes evoked and shown in the film are nothing if not working men massed for (strike) action. By throwing the scimitar overboard, Nayland Smith is acting as if the object, and nothing else, could have ensured the power of Fu Manchu. In so doing, he is at the same time admitting that the power of Fu Manchu and the Asian hordes may be superior to Western might and dis-avowing what lies behind a striving for power and domination: economic strength and the omnipresent fear of class conflict. What is so horrifying for the characters on hearing the gong is the simple possibility of the return of the repressed of social agitation, a bourgeois obsession since 1848. The *outside looking in* is in the process of being transformed into the *inside looking out*. For the film, the "evil" is within British society from the very outset, in that most august of institutions, the British Museum, the signifier at once of history and of the past. The scene onboard the liner, that signifier of bourgeois order and economic power, is like a ghost from the past reappearing, yet another specter haunting the social order: the specter of Fu Manchu represented, as it were, by the waiter/coolie. *The Mask of Fu Manchu* is a displaced and racist representation of the fear inspired by *The Communist Manifesto*, a fear concerning the very bodies of the workers, the proletariat as "the body politic."

The juxtaposition of the modern and the medieval that we have seen at work in *The Most Dangerous Game* and in the clash of two worlds in *The Mask of Fu Manchu* are central to the project of *The Wolf Man*. Larry Talbot, who has been educated in the United States, returns to the family home when his elder brother is killed in a hunting accident. The film turns less on his being transformed into a werewolf after being bitten by Bela (the werewolf son of an old gypsy woman called Maleva) than on this tension between the two worlds represented by Larry and his father. Or, to be more precise: Larry's werewolfery is a symptom of the unconscious conflicts within him triggered by the impossible demands at the basis of this tension. That symptom is *hysteria*.

Larry's father is a curious condensation of modern science and feudal despotism, a fact that we would be advised not to put down simply to a need to construct a script. He is an amateur astronomer. At the same time, he reigns over the entire village: when he tells Larry forthrightly, "They're your people," he is designating all the villagers and not simply the workers on his estate. When Larry, realizing with horror what is happening to him, raises the question of the police coming for him, his father retorts in anger and astonishment: "You believe those men can come in here and take you out?" The father therefore substitutes himself for the law, precisely inasmuch as he sees himself as the Law, outside time because of a "natural" state of things that has always existed. Thus does the father foreclose history, which, expelled from the Symbolic, returns in the Real in the form of an hallucination. What this latter represents will be our concern here.

With his manifest contempt for democracy and through the economic power he wields, the father represents a particular brand of British aristocratic landowner and capitalist, that which gave support to fascist regimes in the 1930s as a bulwark against the changes heralded by Bolshevism and such dangerous offshoots as trade unionism and workers' rights. The estate's working-class members are suitably deferential, even toward Larry, and their superior is the gamekeeper, a faithful and conservative retainer. I write "even toward Larry" because of the anti-American prejudices of many Britons (not to mention the anti-British prejudices present in certain horror films of the period, discussed later). The film's latent content suggests that none of this would have happened if Larry had remained in the States, immune from European decadence, medieval prejudices, and supernatural powers existing only in the Old World. Such an opposition is due to far more complex factors than Gothic novels being English in origin. I would go so far as to suggest that what Hollywood is unconsciously exploiting—and reacting against—is precisely the historical tradition of an entire continent, not in an attempt to hide its own lack of history (which is a false argument) but as part of an unconscious strategy aimed at presenting history as something nefarious, belonging to a past that America must triumph over and eliminate in order to be modern (i.e., capitalist).

Larry is both British born and an American, thanks to the formative years he has spent in the States. As such, he has already been subjected to a form of cleavage on the level of his ego that, on his return, will find an outlet in an extreme and tragic form. He is shown to be a "normal" and "healthy" male from the outset. He uses his father's telescope (already a phallic symbol) to scrutinize the village, where his unerring heterosexual gaze falls on a comely wench whom he promptly courts in a rather boorish and arrogant manner. As this is very much part of his male heritage, particularly the American aspect of it, we are surely entitled to put it down to phallocentrism, not to a simply feudal belief in his hereditary male rights. Put in his place by the energetic young woman, he becomes confused and claims he really came into the shop to buy a cane. He chooses one with a wolf's head made out of silver, a symbolism going beyond an anticipation of the curse soon to be visited on him.

The cane is more than an object (Larry's father beats him to death with it on discovering the truth about his son) or a phallic symbol, however much the film may wish us to read things thus. It is a signifier of which both the film's characters and its spectators are the unconscious effect. It fascinates the gamekeeper who, crucially, fills a function that bears some resemblance to that which now falls to Larry after the death of his elder brother: Larry will inherit the estate on his father's death and will therefore be the man's employer. As both Larry and the gamekeeper are in love with the same woman (she is engaged to the latter), the script obligingly introduces the theme of rivalry, which we shall take in a wider sense than that of two men fighting over a woman. For this rivalry is intimately linked to the question of the real and imaginary relationships between Larry and his father, on the one hand, and the gamekeeper and the father, on the other. Larry is doubly an intruder: because it has always been to the elder brother that the gamekeeper swore allegiance in the event of the father's death; and because sex now rears its head—like that of the cane—to complicate matters.

We are therefore dealing with an unconscious textual manifestation of a form of sibling rivalry akin to Cain and Abel in the Bible (the unconscious play on words is obvious, especially as the gamekeeper is shown to be competent, or *able*).[40] Indeed, the gamekeeper wishes to appropriate the cane because of its patent phallic symbolism. Not, I might add, because it is long and terminates in a big knob, but for far more serious reasons that we must now try to elucidate. The rivalry between the two men stems partly from the fact that, unconsciously, the gamekeeper would have liked to replace the dead brother, hence his devotion to the father. There is nothing obsequious about this: other factors are at stake. I would argue that Larry's real past identification with his brother finds an equivalent in the gamekeeper's imaginary identification with him. In other words, Larry and the gamekeeper are each the double of the other: "Actually, and considered externally, the double is the rival of his prototype in anything and everything, but primarily in the love for women—a trait which he may partly owe to the identification with the brother."[41] Because the gamekeeper was there first as far as the love for a woman is concerned, Larry is an interloper, a fact he experiences as the prodigal son returning in tragic circumstances beyond anyone's control; things had not been planned this way.

The father is a perfect representative of the stern paternal superego, praising or punishing, making decisions for everyone on everything. Significantly, this symbolic structure is to be found everywhere in the village: Gwen, the young woman courted by Larry and the gamekeeper, is subjected to her father's wishes, her friend Jenny (killed by werewolf Bela) to her mother's. Just as significantly, Larry's mother is absent, presumably long dead, but in fact never mentioned. In her place we find Maleva, the gypsy woman and mother of Bela, another double inasmuch as, once bitten, Larry becomes literally like him. However, the main point of contact is the mother (figure) Maleva. If Larry's cane is a phallic symbol, then it is as a sign of his excessive identification with the mother at the expense of the father: Larry wants to be the phallus that the mother does not have and to accede to her desire, a desire that questions in an impossible and unacceptable manner the phallic and patriarchal rights of Larry's father. At the same time, the gamekeeper's fascination with the cane stands in for his desire to submit to precisely those rights in order to please the father. Thus he, rather than Larry, has submitted to the Name-of-the-Father, a fact that poses a major problem of sexual identity for Larry. Which brings us back to his hysteria and its function in determining the film's meaning.

Dylan Evans has written on the subject as follows:

> Hysteria concerns the question of the subject's sexual position. This question may be phrased "Am I a man or a woman?" or, more precisely, "What is a woman?" This is true for both male and female hysterics. Lacan thus reaffirms the ancient view that there is an intimate connection between hysteria and femininity. Indeed, most hysterics are women. . . .
>
> The structure of desire, as desire of the Other, is shown more clearly in hysteria than in any other clinical structure: the hysteric is precisely someone who appropriates another's desire by identifying with them.[42]

Larry is a hysteric because of his doubts about his sexual identity due to his identification with Maleva, the substitute mother, at the expense of that with the father. Nor should we forget the important parallel between the werewolf and a woman. Both function according to the lunar cycle: the human turns into a beast; the woman has her menstrual cycle. This problem in no way concerns the gamekeeper, a "normal" male. The gamekeeper's unconscious knowledge of the father's desire is accurate—rather a son like the gamekeeper, faithful to tradition, than one like Larry who has inherited the values of the New World and questions the place his father has assigned him. It is important to remember that the villagers are suspicious of him to the point of rejecting him when he comes to church but cannot sum up the courage to sit down at his father's side. We find here a fascinating reworking of the situation in eighteenth-century Britain: the elder son looked after the estate, while the younger one became a parson. Even this latter function is being symbolically refused Larry, who can only run away. At one point his father makes the remark, "You can't run away." Maleva says exactly the same thing but means something quite different. For her his fate was "predestined," whereas the father is imposing a social obligation on his son.[43] Both the father and Maleva are obscurantist reactionaries, transforming the "absent cause" of history into a continuum untouched by change and time.

I have kept to the end of this section a discussion of perhaps the most unusual and unexpected representation of history in the corpus of films chosen, a situation due not to the nature of the textual element in question but to the film in which it figures: *Dracula's Daughter*. The most useful angle of approach is to return to the mask—not the mask as signifier of desires and drives that cannot speak their name (see chapter 1), but the mask as a "simple" element of decor. Both spatially and structurally, it echoes another piece of decor, observed but not insisted on in any way by the camera, presented to the spectator's gaze early in the film. I say "spatially" because both items are hanging on a wall; "structurally" because they refer to one another within the film's strategies of narrative and representation. This earlier element is a photograph of Lord Kitchener, who has gone down in history because he figured in propaganda material during World War I to encourage young Britons to join the army and fight the Germans. This material included not only a photo of Kitchener pointing his finger out at the public—the photo's "spectators"—but also the written message "Your Country Needs You!" This written element is absent from *Dracula's Daughter*, and it is precisely this absence that lends meaning to the film's discourse at this point.

Von Helsing has just placed himself under arrest for killing Dracula. Cut to the office of Scotland Yard Commissioner Sir Basil Humphrey, then to a close-up of Von Helsing wiping his glasses. The camera tracks back and pans to the left to reveal Sir Basil behind his desk. When it comes to a stop, we are able to see on the wall in the background, between the two men, the photo of Kitchener. What is happening here? I hardly need to insist on the fact that such an item of decor is no less innocent than the propaganda actually used during the war, although it functions in quite a different fashion. It must be pointed out at once that the photo is already present in the frame, as the camera moves to reveal Sir Basil but *before* the commissioner actually appears; it thus creates a privileged link between Von Helsing and Kitchener. This link is in turn overdetermined by the link between the two men, the representative of the law and the representative of scientific knowledge. This should be sufficient to make us pause. It is Von Helsing, here as in *Dracula*, who is responsible for drawing attention to the evil represented by vampirism, but this point raises certain ideological problems: he is a foreigner, yet it is he whom Britain needs to save it. Let us now attempt to unravel these enigmas.

If the action of *Dracula's Daughter* takes place in England, one must not forget it is an American film, with all the unconscious prejudices concerning things British; the subtext of gayness can, in part, be attributed to this. The police are shown as stupid and cowardly, Sir Basil as well-meaning but hardly up to fighting evil effectively. At one point, a policeman orders his subordinate to guard Von Helsing and then rummages about in a drawer and takes out—a revolver, despite the fact that the British police are not armed. This is a perfect example of viewing the other from the standpoint of one's own social values. However, there is a sort of switch in midstream, a displacement at work on the level of character and narration, one that is naturalized by the theme of love but that cannot be imposed without a certain violence being committed against the story's logic: Von Helsing is ousted from his position of knowledge in favor of Dr. Garth. The latter is a sort of "compromise formation," destined to enable the film to concentrate on the love of the countess for Garth and, by so doing, to have her eliminated by Sandor, who is in turn eliminated by the police under the control of the commissioner.

Garth stands halfway between Von Helsing and the commissioner: he has been the former's pupil and owes him what he knows from a scientific point of view; and he represents the law inasmuch as he is called on as an expert by the commissioner. However, Garth stands for much more than that. He represents the same class as the commissioner and the Law in the Lacanian sense: the transmission to the next generation of certain values and constraints, one of which is capitalist patriarchy. When I say Garth "stands" between the two other men, I mean that both literally and metaphorically: he is also a condensation of their social and ideological functions. As such, he takes the place literally, both spatially and structurally, of the photo of Kitchener, which can only mean one thing: it is Garth and people like him that Britain needs.

In other words, an unconscious ideological discourse on the place of the male in preserving the law and a country's identity is set in motion from the outset. I would argue therefore that the displacement of the center of interest from Von Helsing to Garth is necessary for the unconscious meaning of the film and is both overdetermined and undermined simultaneously by the cut to the mask, an example of displacement in the strictly Freudian sense. For the film systematically shows that the countess is much stronger than Garth and thus possesses that which is the male prerogative: the phallus. This scandalous contradiction must be repressed at all costs, hence the manifestations of disavowal that occur throughout the film: Garth's failure to save Lili and to vanquish the countess and his inferior position in relation to his secretary whom he just happens to "save" at the end of the film have that very function. None of this is convincing, yet it works as disavowal always works: to leave the spectator in a state of imaginary fullness, along with the profoundly repressive and phallocentric discourse around which the entire film is built, however shakily.

In the film, Kitchener, of course, is looking out at the spectators, thus implicitly telling us, "Your country needs you." The film attempts to reassure at the same time as it represents a complete breakdown of the codes needed for that reassurance to function: the drawing up of clear boundaries based on anatomical sexual difference and its concomitant unconscious social values. This state of affairs can be seen as evidence that, once censorship both institutional and psychic is in place, such appeals to identity are nothing other than the disavowal of the Other whose discourse leaves its traces everywhere. One such trace is in the change in the name of the great vampire hunter: *Van Helsing* is transformed into *Von Helsing*, or, a Dutchman becomes a German. This does not mean that we are to distrust the man; the change of name functions to displace the center of interest onto the character of Garth, as we have just seen. Representing Garth as a modern Kitchener is a way of defusing his representation as being insufficiently virile and, more crucially, of suggesting that the class and economic system of which he is a part must be upheld as the only feasible one. Grouse shooting in Scotland may make him as feudal as Larry Talbot's father, but it also implies a long tradition that can be appealed to as a means to combat that medieval phenomenon, vampirism. *Dracula's Daughter* presents us with yet another unbroken continuum destined to stand in for history and foreclose any other version of it.

I have had occasion to insist in certain of the analyses above on the significance of the notion of "disappearance," far less innocent and neutral than it appears at first sight. I shall now return to it for the last time in the context of *Murders in the Rue Morgue*. As we shall see, the film is exemplary from other standpoints that, however, can best be approached via the character of the young prostitute who serves as guinea pig for Mirakle's experiments: the mingling of the blood of an ape and a woman to show our "kinship with the ape." Mirakle picks the prostitute up, escorts her to his secret laboratory, and ties her to a sort of cross (the Christian symbolism need not bother us here) in order to take a sample of her blood prior to pushing the experiment in the desired direction. However, her blood is diseased, which provokes this outburst from our mad scientist: "You cheated me; your beauty was a lie." How beautifully the torturer becomes the victim and the victim the exploiter! Could we find a better instance of ideology turning things upside down? In fact, Mirakle is a good capitalist bemoaning his fate at not being able to draw instant profit from the body at his disposal, a body that he simply has "disappear" in a sleight of hand that makes one think of a conjurer's trick: it falls through a trap door into the river below. Randy Loren Rasmussen has perfectly summed up the implications of this encounter:

> She is nothing more to him than raw material, to be unceremoniously dumped into the river below, like so much garbage, when she proves useless. The additional fact that the prostitute's venereal-disease ridden blood renders her inappropriate for Mirakle's experiment, while the heroine's uncontaminated blood makes her an ideal subject, emphasizes the moral distinction between heroine and shadow heroine. . . . That she is nameless makes her all the more pitiable.[44]

Rasmussen is referring to the fact that the film's heroine is abducted by Eric the ape so that Mirakle, knowing she is as pure as the driven snow, can at last find a victim worthy of his madness. As it turns out, the mingling of blood is a euphemism for something as scandalous as the experiment of Dr. Moreau in *Island of Lost Souls* where he hopes to mate the hero and Lota the panther woman (see chapter 2; we shall return to Dr. Moreau in the next section). One shot shows in close-up the ape bending over the supine and unconscious body of the heroine and moving backward and forward in a way that quite clearly implies sexual intercourse. Both female victims, then, are the victims of forms of rape, which allows us to compare the two young women, rather than see them as being radically different.

This point takes up what we have already had the occasion to argue in chapter 2. This parallel between women as victims finds its counterpart in the vocabulary used by the hero's friend Paul who calls him a "vampire" and a "body snatcher" because of the way he recuperates from the morgue the nameless bodies transported there. As the morgue attendant is gratified with the epithet "ghoul," *Murders in the Rue Morgue* is patently presenting both the mad scientist Mirakle and the up-and-coming doctor Dupin as capitalist profiteers exploiting the bodies of the living and the dead for personal advancement, the ideological problem lying in the fact that Dupin is part and parcel of a social system that is seen to be normal, whereas Mirakle is an outcast.

However pertinent this may be for our argument about the exploited being made to disappear so as not to tarnish a biased view of history as neutral continuum, something more complex and subtle is at work in *Murders in the Rue Morgue* that will help us to extend our argument into other realms. Eric the ape is on show in a sort of fairground where we first see belly dancers plying their trade. One bourgeois gentleman says to his companion, "Do they bite?" to which the other replies, "You have to pay more for that." This obviously transforms the Arabian women into prostitutes, the typical fate of "exotic" females in Hollywood and everyday life. Customers from the same bourgeois background have already drawn a comparison between the Apache Indians we see pretending to scalp a white victim and "waterfront rats." This is more than just another example of the inversion "exploiter/victim." We are dealing here with an interesting linguistic phenomenon that needs pursuing. Whether we are dealing with Indians, foreign women, prostitutes, or the homeless makes no difference for the locals. All the lower orders are to be classified as "rats," and the fact that the homeless watch the prostitute's body being fished out of the Seine from the vantage point of the *waterfront* can only strengthen the link between the literal and the figurative when evoking those whose sole existence is reduced to that of "raw material" endowed with a certain value. *Murders in the Rue Morgue* thus foregrounds the notion of exploitation inasmuch as it involves both Nature and the human body. This will be the basis of our reflections in the next section.

Today the Laboratory, Tomorrow the Universe!

Murders in the Rue Morgue, like *King Kong* (and other films that will be discussed later in this section), shows the exploitation of both animals and humans for power and profit. It soon becomes clear, however, that what is at stake is not a particular animal but *nature itself*, the overarching theme that will concern us here. At the same time, I would argue that we must see both Mirakle's experiment and Denham's movie camera as part of the concept of *technology*. This can take the form of Jekyll's creation of a potion and Moreau's scalpels or the quite explicit paraphernalia on show in *Frankenstein* and the two sequels, in *The Invisible Ray*, *The Devil-Doll*, *Dr. Cyclops*, and *Man Made Monster*.[45] Similarly, it is through this technology that the mad scientist acts as God, assuming a right that is not his. We shall not let ourselves be sidetracked by the concept of blasphemy, a purely ideological ploy in the service of the socioeconomic status quo where the mad scientist is in reality a stand-in for the capitalist, acting as the return of the repressed of the latter's real historical function: assuming "rights" that are not his. Instead, we shall focus on the different ways the films of the period show how people and animals both tend to become part of nature in the eyes of the mad scientist, to be exploited like so much raw material, like the prostitute by Dr. Mirakle, and hence to become so many instances of *objectification*.

This concept is perhaps to be seen at its clearest in *Frankenstein* where the eponymous character digs up dead bodies—humans who have literally returned to a natural state—in order to galvanize the reconstructed result. Frankenstein, however, is no Dr. Mirakle, no Dr. Moreau, no Dr. Thorkel, no Dr. Rigas (*Man Made Monster*); he is neither ruthless nor hungry for power. What he does is nevertheless significant of social attitudes concerning the exploitation of nature and humanity. We can perhaps best glean some idea of the complexity of the various situations on display in these films, some idea of how they give us a particular vision of history at work invisibly, by turning to a film Karloff made in England during this period: *The Man Who Changed His Mind*. The Karloff character, a recluse called Dr. Laurience, is convinced that he can prevent knowledge from dying with the individual by transplanting the thoughts of a person shortly before he or she dies into the mind of a much younger recipient who will keep that knowledge alive for decades until he or she can pass it on to another, and so on. Hired by a wealthy newspaper magnate who hopes that the success of Laurience's experiments will bring him (the magnate) increased fame and fortune, Laurience fails to convince other scientists and makes the magnate a laughing stock. Furious, he fires the scientist who gets his revenge by transmitting the mind of his crippled assistant into the body of the magnate, but destroying the magnate's mind along with the cripple's body. Rendered insane by notions of power and wealth, Laurience now kills the assistant/magnate. Knowing that he will be arrested for murder, Laurience arranges yet another switch: his mind into the body of the magnate's son. That way the son will be executed for murder, while Laurience will inherit the magnate's fortune. Needless to say, things go wrong and Laurience dies, asking that his experiments be destroyed, as "the mind is sacred."

The film opens with two surgeons emerging from an operating theater and going to wash their hands while their surgical masks are being removed by nurses. The two characters stand side by side, each in front of a mirror. Until we see that one is a man and the other a woman, the film gives the impression that each could stand—literally or metaphorically speaking—in the place of the other. I would argue that this introduces the film's unconscious central theme: exchange value. Discussing Marx's theory of the function of exchange under capitalism, Thomas Keenan writes:

> When things are exchanged as commodities, they are related to each other not as use values but as exchange values, in terms of something else. This shared third term, the axis of similarity, enables a comparison, makes the different uses or things commensurable, relatable as quantities of the same thing rather than different uses or qualities. . . .
> Exchange is a matter of *substitution*, of one thing's standing in for another, on the basis of something similar or equal.[46]

In the context of *The Man Who Changed His Mind*, knowledge—in the widest sense—is the third element that enables the film's plot to function and to take on, beyond the question of money and power, an economic dimension. The problem lies in the kind of knowledge represented. If we grant that the knowledge of the male surgeon can be exchanged for that of the female surgeon on the basis of equality, this can hardly be upheld in the case of the knowledge of Laurience's assistant in the place of that of the magnate, or Laurience's in the place of that of the latter's son. Knowledge as an abstract concept is thus a blind to hide radical difference and a factor that we shall approach through a certain number of reflections on exchange.

Now we all know that famous expression "fair exchange is no robbery," a perfect summing-up, through denial, of capitalist exploitation, a naturalization through language of the relations of production. Once again, we need to advance with some precaution. If X produces with his own labor an object he exchanges for one produced by Y with his own labor, a transaction from which profit is absent, then the object does not assume the form of a commodity and we remain in the realm of use values. Should money play a role in exchange, then the objects take on the function of commodities. In which case, the object has both a use value and a value form. Commenting on this analysis by Marx in the first chapter of *Capital*, Abdul JanMohamed writes of commodities, "As depositaries of value, they are also the bearers of whatever power relations have been invested in their production and exchange. . . . Value, like power, constitutes itself only through the processes of production and exchange."[47] If we now return to my remark about the knowledge of the two surgeons, it must become clear that the notion of equality, of "fair exchange," is possible only if we go on the assumption that each of them is a self-sufficient individual. The film is taking a protofeminist stance in showing that a young woman can participate in an operation on the same terms as an older man, but it hedges its bets: ultimately she is as much his collaborator as she will become Laurience's collaborator for the rest of the film. The whole question of what knowledge is, who possesses it, and under what circumstances is thus elided, however well-meaning the film's conscious discourse may be.

The basic situation has been summed up by two theorists: "Bourgeois economic theory . . . has derived equal exchange from its assumption of the individual with a set of given attributes. If trade is understood as taking place between agents naturally constituted as individuals, then this trade appears, and is immediately explained, as an exchange of equivalents."[48] By effacing any difference due to class, upbringing, access to knowledge, or the prejudice encountered by a young woman (especially in the 1930s), the film quite simply endorses the notion that the mind—or brain, or the knowledge the subject has at his or her disposal—is a *commodity*. It is therefore only "natural" that the capitalist magnate should consider that he is *buying* Laurience's knowledge when he offers him ideal working conditions for his experiments. Laurience, a typical idealist, goes on the assumption that the man is being philanthropic, a perfect indication of his own fetishization of knowledge and of his position within reified social relations, one that he clearly shares with the other characters and the film's own discourse. Laurience naively believes that he will have the right to use the results of his experiments for the common good, whereas the magnate has the firm intention of exploiting them for profit and power. In other words, Laurience suddenly becomes aware that he is nothing but a *laborer*—an intellectual one, for sure, but nevertheless a social subject forced to sell his knowledge to produce more knowledge that, transformed into a social commodity, will benefit solely the person holding the purse strings. In a typically idealist way, Laurience is determined to keep his knowledge for himself (i.e., as use value), as though the fact of having produced this extra knowledge under precise working conditions had not inscribed him, along with the magnate, into an equally precise power relation based on production and exchange. A classic case of misrecognition.

What is fascinating about the theme of knowledge in the film is Laurience's concern with its transmission from generation to generation. Knowledge is what must not be allowed to die as it is part of the heritage of humanity. We can interpret this in Marxist terms: the knowledge produced by one generation of manual and intellectual workers belongs to that generation *and to every future generation*. There is no need to produce it again and again, and its very existence enriches every human being affected by it. This collective notion enters into direct and permanent conflict with the capitalist notion of individualism and the right to private property, a right that perforce encompasses knowledge that is part of our common heritage. The capitalist wants to enrich only himself.

Interesting linguistic parallels can be found at work here. I have used the word *transplant* to refer to the thoughts contained in the brain of one person being placed in that of another. I could have used the word *graft*. If we turn to *Collins English Dictionary*, we find two meanings of *graft*, the first taken from horticulture, the second from surgery: "a small piece of plant tissue (the scion) that is made to unite with an established plant (the stock), which supports and nourishes it"; "a piece of tissue or an organ transplanted from a donor or from the patient's own body to an area of the body in need of the tissue." The surgical definition corresponds to the situation to be found in certain films under discussion. In *The Monster and the Girl*, mad scientist Dr. Parry (George Zucco) transplants the brain of a man wrongly executed for murder into a gorilla which promptly goes looking for the gangsters responsible. In *Black Friday*, the Boris Karloff character, grief-stricken at the accidental death of a mild-mannered university colleague, transplants into him the brain of a gangster killed at the same time in another road accident that left his body mutilated, only to find that his former colleague's body is now housing the mind of a psychopath. In both cases, we can see knowledge living on after death in another form, which takes up what we have just analyzed as a result of our reflections on *The Man Who Changed His Mind*.

It is hardly a coincidence that both *The Monster and the Girl* and *Black Friday* are also gangster movies involving a third, familiar, meaning of *graft*: "the acquisition of money, power, etc. by dishonest or unfair means, esp. by taking advantage of a position of trust." This concept corresponds closely to the plot of *The Walking Dead* where gangsters, posing socially as businessmen (as is the case with Paul Lukas and his associates in *The Monster and the Girl*), use money and threats to control the city's elected officials. It is precisely because they cannot bribe or frighten a judge that they murder him and succeed in framing John Elman (Karloff) who is executed. Brought back to life by the film's scientist, played by Edmund Gwenn, he has experienced death and seems to remember nothing of what happened. Yet he is driven by something to seek out the gangsters, one by one, who contrive to die in accidents, although his presence—not surprisingly—triggers their panic and the carelessness that leads to their deaths.

Elman can be seen as a particularly naive member of the working class. He is used for a job and then paid off in no uncertain fashion by being executed by the state, which thus stands in for the capitalist gangsters. We could even go so far as to say that state and gangsters can be *exchanged* for each other as far as Elman's fate is concerned. He then returns from the dead, like a zombie, to exact his revenge, and much of the film's power derives from the fact that Elman is a genuinely tragic victim. We can also note an interesting parallel with *White Zombie*, where the Bela Lugosi character is killed by those he enslaved. The unconscious meaning of *The Walking Dead*, however, is made more explicit by the publicity material used for the film (see chapter 3). As I have pointed out, if Elman is portrayed as a vampire in the publicity material, this is precisely what the capitalist gangsters are in the film according to the rhetoric resorted to systematically by Marx: they suck out Elman's life blood by using his labor and then discard him. The gangster-capitalist latches onto Elman's physical body which unwittingly nourishes him and is destroyed in the process. Elman is therefore very much like a plant onto which something artificial and destructive is grafted. His fate is an eloquent instance of the negative effects on nature of capitalism's insatiable drive for profit.

Thus, both language itself—the ultimate product and manifestation of history—and the very themes and concerns of the films discussed allow us to articulate humanity and nature and their exploitation, often via technology, for power and profit. It is instructive at this point, and prior to resuming the discussion of certain films in our corpus, to turn to a film of the period that would seem to be light years from the horror genre but that deals with similar topics: *Zoo in Budapest* (Rowland V. Lee, 1933). The entire action takes place within the zoo and turns on a love affair between a young orphan, who stays at the zoo rather than return to the institution, which is meant to look after the interests of girls like her, and a young man, also orphaned since his father was killed by a tiger in the zoo, who looks after the animals. However, his love for the creatures leads him to steal fur stoles, which leads to the police coming to arrest him. Simultaneously, a little boy decides to spend the night at the zoo and opens one of the cages, allowing a tiger to escape. The animal attacks at elephant and chaos reigns. What can such a film possibly have to say to us? Quite a few things.

Early in the film the zoo's director, a humanist of enlightened and progressive views, states that a zoo is where animals are "protected from their natural enemies." Because all creatures are either predators or victims of predators, it is clear he is talking of human beings, a specimen of which is on show in the film: a bourgeois lady with a penchant for precisely those fur stoles the young hero Zani steals because he is opposed to animals being killed for their fur. The woman goes so far as to ask her husband, who gives donations to the zoo, to buy one of its foxes so she may have a matching stole. Here the economic element, rather than the purely ecological one, rears its head: the husband can exert pressure on her behalf because he contributes to the upkeep of the institution. Thus, private interests, albeit on a small scale, are represented as ever ready to exploit nature, on the one hand, and their economic power, on the other, for self-interest, as if this went without saying, as if it were some timeless social right. We are therefore at the heart of the matter.

The true interest of the script, however, lies elsewhere: in the treatment of the orphan girls and the rebellion of the heroine.[49] Her only idea is to escape from the orphanage where the girls are kept behind bars (the parallel is quite explicit). Now that she has reached the age of eighteen, the woman in charge can send her out to work in a tannery for five years or, as this woman herself obligingly puts it when she discovers the girl has disappeared: they could have "bonded her out to a tannery for five years." In other words, she will be forced to work in a tannery without payment, and the tannery will pay a sum of money to the orphanage. The girl will get nothing; she will be a literal example of "slave labor," which enables both the tannery to make a profit (no wages to pay—shades of Legendre and the zombies in *White Zombie*!) and the orphanage to pay for the upkeep of the girls. The parallel set up between the fur stoles and the girls—humans and animals both reduced to "raw materials" ripe for exploitation—is striking, and the closing minutes of the film introduce a delightful ambiguity that maintains its subversive discourse at the expense of the apparently conventional happy ending.

Zani is responsible for saving the life of the little boy whose love for animals leads him to want to spend a night in the zoo where he can see the animals in a more natural state. The father is a wealthy landowner who offers Zani employment on his estate where he will look after the animals. He also accepts to look after the girl for five years to compensate for the orphanage's loss of revenue, but in fact she will marry Zani. Although we would be justified in interpreting this as a form of "tenant farming," it is the heroine's remark closing the film that is of interest here: "We're just like other people." Clearly this comment is meant to indicate that orphans are humans, too, but in fact she and Zani are now members of the proletariat working for a wealthy capitalist. They have no choice: for her it is that or the orphanage; for Zani, imprisonment for theft.[50] The repressive aspect of society can be seen in the way the police search for Zani and the girl with the aid of torches. Dressed in black, they resemble Count Zaroff and his henchmen, a visual parallel overdetermined by a shot at night of Zani carrying the girl through the zoo's ponds and undergrowth. They could be Rainsford and the heroine of *The Most Dangerous Game* trying to escape through the swamp.

Further parallels can be seen between *Zoo in Budapest* and the horror film made the same year that we have already had cause to analyze from a quite different perspective: *Murders in the Zoo* (see chapter 1). Businessman Eric Gorman, a paranoid sadist played with relish and gusto by the excellent Lionel Atwill, makes this remark: "Leave an animal alone and it'll leave you alone, which is more than you can say of most humans." Made in another context by a different person, this would seem to partake of the same discourse as that of Zani and the director of the zoo in *Zoo in Budapest*. Gorman, however, is simply revealing the truth about himself. In fact, he admires the primitive emotions of animals: "They love, they hate, they kill." Given the lengths to which he is ready to go to eliminate rivals and his wife, he is in fact talking more of himself as a man given over totally to his drives and the *jouissance* they bring him. His staring eyes refer back to those of Count Zaroff during the hunt, and Gorman's fate (crushed to death by a python) echoes that of Zaroff (fatally wounded, he falls into the pit where his dogs devour him) and, crucially, highlights via the notion of nature "getting its own back," the relationship between nature and the worst predator, man. Which brings us back to our point of departure.

We are fortunate at having at our disposal one of the most dramatic theoretical statements of recent years, Teresa Brennan's *History after Lacan*. Aside from its exceptional intellectual rigor, this study is invaluable in any number of ways, in particular the author's concern to articulate a psychoanalytic and political reading of the Freudian ego the better to explain humankind's aggressivity toward his or her peers in general and the environment in particular. Although *History after Lacan* is in no way whatsoever concerned with the cinema, certain remarks resonate uncannily in the context of the films under discussion and will hopefully enable us to clarify the complex issue of how history itself is the "absent cause" that can help to explain aspects too often neglected or relegated to the categories of "War" and "the Depression," as we saw at the beginning of this chapter. It is not therefore a question of direct influence but of approaches to themes that must be approached historically when being applied to a particular field of research.

At one point, Brennan evokes certain texts of Jacques Derrida in which he "linked logic and truth to the narcissism of the 'self-identified subject' whose narcissism requires that he take possession of, and lay claim to truth, while excluding others from the right to any such claim."[51] I propose we apply this "logic and truth" to the question of nature and precise geographic areas of the globe, duly taken possession of in historic reality by imperialists and in the horror film of the 1930s by the mad doctor/scientist, much as the latter also takes possession of the bodies of animals and humans, alive in the former case, dead or alive in the latter, according to the nature of the experiment. This narcissism is that of the Westerner with his prejudices concerning the Oriental as morally and intellectually inferior, the better to foreclose history as having anything to do with the West's presence in the East. Elsewhere Brennan quotes Homi Bhabba writing on Franz Fanon, notably, "the exchange of looks between native and settler that structures this psychic relation in the paranoid fantasy of boundless possession and the familiar language of reversal: 'They want to take our place.'"[52]

We have already analyzed just such a phenomenon in the previous section: the coolies looking in *The Mask of Fu Manchu*. What we have not done is to address the question of rivalry: "The problem starts when the rival is perceived as like the self. Because of this, it becomes a threat to one's separate identity, and a threat to one's 'space,' a potential invader of one's territory."[53] I would argue this point enables us to bring together the real dimension of imperialism, where the imperial subject imposes itself on the representative of Otherness the better to avoid the same fate being visited on itself because it cannot conceive the other might not act thus, and its figurative expression in a fictional text. Thus, the presence of the Chinese in the British Museum where Sir Lionel is abducted indicates a paranoid fear of being "taken over" which is simply the projection onto the other of one's own aggressive fantasies.[54] *The Mask of Fu Manchu* is remarkable for the ways in which it narrates history as a series of reversals and paranoid projections destined to bolster the Western subject's delusions and illusions, how the subject is led to misrecognize the truth about itself as a supposedly self-centered ego: "The ego has more in common with the unconscious characteristics of narcissism;

it does not want to know about what Lacan terms 'truth.' It is a 'carapace': a rigid construction harboring the resistances to self-understanding, the defenses against what the subject wants to conceal from itself."[55]

Can we not read this passage as a peculiarly apposite definition of the mad doctor/scientist? If so, it is not because the mad scientist is opposed to the truth, after which he is supposed to strive, however insanely or simply wrongheadedly. It is because the mad scientist—and the filmic text along with him—refuses to see the search for truth in other than individual and narcissistic terms, completely cut off, as both he and it are, from any social and historical context other than society's blindness and refusal to recognize "genius."[56] More is at stake, however, such as the unconscious motivations underpinning such films. For the freedom the mad scientist claims for himself is one that other members of society have lost in the name of "progress," where they have to toil and sell their labor power to the owner of the means of production. In this context the mad scientist is the object of *unconscious longing*, duly transformed into its opposite: a *conscious rejection*. Moreover, on a more collective level, what the mad scientist represents is that which society also strives after—mastery and control, recognition and success—in aggressive and destructive ways that are shown in the films in ways that can come uncomfortably close to the truth and hence precipitate that rejection I have just mentioned.

Early in her study, Brennan brings together the strands of Lacan's theory concerning the aggressivity of the ego and draws a certain number of conclusions:

> The aggressive imperative involved in making the other into a slave, or object, will lead to spatial expansion (territorial imperialism). This is because the objectification of the other depends on establishing a spatial boundary by which the other and the self are fixed. But this fixing of the other leads to the fear that the other will retaliate, which in turn leads to a feeling of spatial constriction. Moreover, the feeling of spatial constriction is related to the physical environment. These changes have physical effects on the psyche, which in turn alter the psychical perception of the environment, and of one's own boundaries. With spatial constriction, one's boundaries are threatened, and the resultant fear increases the need to control the object.[57]

Toward the end of her study, the author evokes certain tendencies of postmodernism, such as "a distrust of history," and stresses the collusion "with the ego's tendency to deny its own totalizing history, and its fantasy that it is the source of life."[58] I propose to indicate briefly how aspects of certain films can be explained by the remarks in this long quote before passing on to the notion of "the source of life" as it is represented in the experiments of various mad doctors and scientists, along with the themes of natural resources and technology.

I make no claim here to an overall explanation of a particular film. Rather, I want to highlight certain parallels that show the filmic subject and the spectator as unconscious effects of the signifier as a historical phenomenon. In *Murders in the Zoo*, Eric Gorman travels to the four corners of the globe to capture animals for a zoo, living out a fantasy of complete freedom that stems from imposing himself as a sort of colonial. Already suspicious of his wife, he not only literally turns her into an object (so much meat to be thrown to the alligators) but feels increasingly hemmed in by the confines of the zoo and the economic limits imposed on his activities. He is forced back on subsidies to keep the zoo going and thus loses a precious, if illusory, commodity: freedom. In light of the use of the word *constriction* in the earlier quote, we can savor the coincidence that has him die in the "embrace" of a python, or a boa *constrictor*. I have already drawn the reader's attention to the irrational and illogical reaction of Dr. Thorkel in *Dr. Cyclops*: he accuses the scientists he has reduced to the size of dolls of spying on him, as if they constituted a threat. In fact, their presence in Peru where his laboratory is situated can only remind him of his own expropriation of land that does not belong to him; the fear of not controlling everyone and everything leads to anxiety and paranoia. If we move to a character who is apparently as far removed as possible from that of the mad doctor/scientist, Carl Denham of *King Kong*, we find a similar pathology at work. In fact, his arrogance and incipient megalomania lead him to interpret his real social situation as one that compels him to go ever further and to seek out Skull Island, so remote that it does not even figure on maritime charts. That way he can take possession of the island and the natives via the image (and the gun, if necessary), all in the name of art and knowledge.

As our corpus is both thematically and ideologically heterogeneous, I have no wish to give the impression that all the films involved can be forced into a mold that would explain them and, by implication, mask their differences in the name of an overarching theory. We must not lose sight of the fact that the intimately related notions of exploitation, possession and the "territorial imperative" apply to nature in general and human beings in particular, and not exclusively to areas of the globe. Take, for instance, the cases of Dr. Crespi and Dr. Gogol. A perfect case of unconscious reversal on the part of *The Crime of Dr. Crespi* is the eponymous character's burying alive his sexual rival, a form of rivalry that is a possible displacement for a real-life economic rivalry. Certainly no space is more constricted and terror evoking than a coffin underground.[59] Gogol's drive to possess the ideal female body in the form of the heroine of *Mad Love*, although clearly Oedipal, finds an interesting parallel in Dr. Mirakle's experiment on the prostitute in *Murders in the Rue Morgue*. Gogol experiences *jouissance* via the torture of the heroine-as-actress in the play with which *Mad Love* opens and thus behaves like Mirakle: the heroine is punished for her sexual "crime," just as the prostitute is to blame for the failure of yet another experiment on Mirakle's part. Another more complex form of reversal can be seen at work through the behavior of Frankenstein. I would argue that he seeks to free himself from the imperative of imposing the patriarchal order on both himself and his fiancée in the form of a marriage that is yet another form of domination and control. The case of Jekyll is more complex still. Somewhere within him, inaccessible to his ego's conscious analysis, is the desire to possess his beloved, despite the seemingly egalitarian thrust of his opposition to the repressive father figure. In such a case, Hyde does indeed represent a part of himself Jekyll rejects, while simultaneously desiring to give in to it.

Brennan is rightly anxious to extend Lacanian theory "in a dialectical discussion of the relation between the ego's need for fixity and technological domination."[60] One of her theses she expounds as follows:

> The subject is founded by a hallucinatory fantasy in which it conceives itself as the locus of active agency and the environment as passive; its subjectivity is secured by a projection onto the environment, apparently beginning with the mother, which makes her into an object which the subject in fantasy controls."[61]

Calling attention to the theories of Melanie Klein concerning the mother's body, Brennan argues that "in drawing out the relation between the psychical fantasy and technology, Klein's 'mother's body' has to be correlated with living nature."[62] She goes on:

> Instead of the length of an individual's lifetime, or the years of their madness, 'the ego's era' spans a few centuries. Instead of megalomanic fantasies that are dreamed, technologies that make them come true, increasing their coverage of the earth's surface and corruption of its temporal parameters in the process.
>
> Developing technologies permit the subject to construct a world of objects which fulfill its fantasies. When the world is actually turned into a world of objects, when living nature is consumed in this process, the power of the fantasy, the extent to which it takes hold psychically is reinforced.[63]

We shall have occasion to take up the most felicitous (from the standpoint of our concerns here) expression "corruption of its temporal parameters" in the following section. For the time being, let us turn, in the light of the various remarks quoted above, to certain films that will enable us to carry our argument forward to complete this section: *Island of Lost Souls, Dr. Cyclops, The Devil-Doll, Man Made Monster,* and *The Invisible Ray.*

The "lost souls" of the film's title are the "manimals" created by Dr. Moreau, whose scalpel transforms animals into creatures with certain human characteristics: M'ling was a dog, Lota a panther, and so forth. Much is always made of Moreau's insane notion that he is God, speeding up the normal cycle of evolution, but we need to turn to another and more materialist meaning of his vision of society. Moreau gets his creations to work for him, feeds and houses them: they live in a sort of compound in the jungle looking suspiciously like the sort of village natives inhabit in Hollywood movies set in Africa. Moreover, the island is Moreau's, which implies that he has reappropriated the soil (referred to as "fertile") that he can now exploit for his own profit. He does not have to share this natural "treasure" with anyone. Similarly, Denham simply steals from the natives the real treasure he finds on Skull Island in *Son of Kong.* The relations set up by Moreau are those of master and slave. He behaves like a feudal baron, wields a whip, and punishes the recalcitrant by threats concerning the "House of Pain," his own version of the dungeon or the torture chamber. This, however, is only part of the story, for a form of hierarchy exists between the "manimals," whom Moreau considers as semihuman, and the products of what he calls his "less successful experiments," the creatures who "provide power to create others." Moreau is thus a capitalist: there can be no production without labor. Moreau, true to capitalist ideology, keeps in watertight compartments the notion of intellectual labor (with its occasional failures) and manual labor, which allows him to carry on his experiments by having his "workers" produce food for the daily sustenance of all.

Moreau's obsession with speeding up evolution both condenses the historical shift from feudalism to capitalism into a few years and stands in for the capitalist wanting to get ever more surplus value from those forced to work for him. What is fascinating about the film is that it both presents Moreau as akin to God (for which he must be punished) and introduces elements showing he has succeeded in ways we need to scrutinize. Thus, Lota's sexuality is human, not animal, and the manimals know how to use knives. *Both phenomena are therefore cultural in nature.* The latter is a clear manifestation of knowledge produced by and throughout history itself. Knowing what a knife is used for is a form of knowledge transmitted both consciously and unconsciously over the generations and centuries. It is transmitted consciously when a worker communicates to an apprentice, destined also to become a worker, *how* to make a knife. The use value of the object is also learned consciously, but the fact the knife is a tool with a variety of functions is also part of an unconscious heritage. The capitalist steps in when the knife is ex-changed, not for another tool that the producer needs, but for food, clothing, and shelter, where the producer must use the knife to produce something for the capitalist, in return for which he is given the wherewithal to live. The knife's use value for the producer has thus been taken from him, much as Moreau has reappropriated nature (the island) for himself.

Capitalist ideology has naturalized this situation so as to justify exploitation. Significantly, Moreau harps on this particular angle by presenting himself as im-mortal, the source of the Law that he imposes. In such ways is history foreclosed and a given situation is passed off as having always existed as a law of nature. Moreau's immortality is another instance of "the opium of the people," but Moreau falls victim to our old friend "contradiction": he breaks the Law himself by condoning murder, a fact that the "manimals" do not fail to grasp, a nice ex-ample of "false consciousness" being transformed into a real knowledge of the truth. Seen from this standpoint, the moment where the "manimals" see them-selves as "Things!" has a certain ironic ring to it: in a reified society this is what they are, how Moreau really sees them. Despite the film's affirmations to the contrary, the proper significance of Moreau in no way lies with his wish to be God. He has simply taken at its face value the ideology which fools the capital-ist into believing that he has created all by himself the enterprise he owns and the wealth he has accumulated. Moreau's denial of history catches up with him in a revolt of the exploited who give the scalpels—which they call "little knives"—a use value in their own terms.

With *Dr. Cyclops*, we find ourselves in the domain of raw material and technology, the body and sexuality, power, domination, and control. Dr. Thorkel and an associate have discovered a rich radium deposit in Peru, and the latter has developed a plan to use it to heal. Thorkel has other plans: "We can shape life, mold it like putty," he cries and promptly murders his associ-ate when he protests. Thorkel is the "perfect" capitalist. He transforms a nat-ural resource into a source of power and profit and eliminates his colleague—whom he has transformed discursively into an economic rival, the better to justify eliminating him literally, as competing firms do one another—so as to enjoy a monopoly he hopes to wield internationally to obtain power. How-ever, I have deliberately overlooked an important detail of the script: the original idea on discovering the deposit was to use it to found an institute and cure illness, whereas Thorkel reappropriates it for himself. But this appar-ently altruistic plan involves a form of *exploitation by appropriation:* the West-erner has the right to intervene in nature. Walter Benjamin expressed this in terms which apply to Thorkel's descending into the bowels of the earth to lo-cate the deposit: "Everywhere sacrificial shafts were dug in Mother Earth."[64]

This fetishization of technology finds a parallel in the film where the scientists simply reify science: doing research is cut off from any consideration other than knowledge, such as the fact of plundering another country. It comes as no surprise that their local guide, Pedro, is a sympathetic but intellectually limited peasant and that the mule owner who accompanies them to Thorkel's laboratory shows no interest in money. How can one possible entrust scientific discoveries to such people?[65] The scientists' status as historical subjects has been repressed and, significantly, they immediately denounce Thorkel as insane. Which he is, but he at least has the honesty within his paranoid delirium to recognize the *power* of science, according to the use to which one puts it. If you change the "subject" of science, then the object itself shifts from being a way to heal the sick to a way to control the world.

We can see the death of Thorkel at the end (falling down his own shaft) as a return of the repressed of an *ecological* relation to nature and raw materials: he who would rape and exploit nature literally returns to it. It is a relation none of the scientists in the film entertains. It would, however, be wrong to dismiss the importance for humanity of a selfless and neutral use of science, where its use value in no way becomes an exchange value enabling the Americans who are the film's heroes to impose their presence on the country on the grounds that they have made an important discovery. The ending puts an end to any idea that the film is unequivocally in favor of such altruism. The sudden and unconvincing announcement that hero and heroine are to marry must be seen, not as a simple "happy ending" tacked on, but as an ideological ploy that undercuts the "science is neutral" discourse. As we have shown in chapter 2, the young female scientist takes charge when the group, reduced to a fraction of their size and fighting for their lives, faces various dangers; she shows herself both more intelligent and courageous than her male colleagues. By indicating that she is a woman first and a scientist second, the film creates for her and her sex a barrier, a boundary that is not to be crossed, suggesting that science (like war, politics and economics) is a male preserve. This attempt to foreclose difference as a social and therefore historical phenomenon founders by the very clumsiness with which it is put across.

The Devil-Doll also turns on the theme of people reduced to a fraction of their size, but the film is more clearly political. As in *Dr. Cyclops*, we are dealing with a person with a noble scientific project in mind (albeit a crazy one) and another obsessed with power alone. Moreover, the plundering of a country is absent. The prisoner with whom Lavond escapes from Devil's Island has invented a process by which he can reduce humans and animals to the size of dolls, his intention being to create a new race that will not consume so fast and thereby avoid using up the earth's resources. His aim is diametrically opposed to that of the capitalist: "To make a profit, capital has to produce commodities at a faster rate than the time taken by living nature to reproduce itself. As the only substances out of which commodities can be produced are those supplied by living nature, this means that the profit factor tends to exhaust natural resources."[66] This ecological dimension given to technology, however, is masked in the film by making the scientist's wife the instigator of a scheme that will help Lavond wreak his vengeance on the bankers who framed him, while enabling her to use her husband's invention for pure personal profit in the form of control. For the scientist dies without solving a major problem: those reduced in size lose their memories and act like so many automata. As the deranged wife says to Lavond when showing him how to proceed with a young woman so reduced, "She'll respond to your will." All Lavond—or anyone else—needs to do is to concentrate and make the "doll" act according to his wishes. The crucial difference between *Dr. Cyclops* and *The Devil-Doll* lies here. Apart from Thorkel, none of the scientists is impaired mentally in Schoedsack's film. The Nazi undertones of the wife's ravings are surely patent, but more pertinent for our argument is the notion of memory and forgetting. If the control of another's mind helps, say, a dictator to hide the real reasons behind a coup d'état, then memory is an obstacle to this. Despite its ambiguities, *The Devil-Doll* constitutes an implicit defense of working-class memory in the face of capitalism's reorganization of past society along lines of profit and private property.

Man Made Monster (aka *The Electric Man*) is a shoddy B feature endowed with a truly fascinating script. As such, like *Son of Kong*, it merits our close attention. Dan (Lon Chaney) survives an accident where the bus in which he is traveling collides with a pylon, and everyone else aboard is electrocuted. Doctors cannot explain what happened to him, but a scientist, Dr. Rigas, realizes he can use Dan for his experiments on electricity. Pretending he merely wishes to study the effects of electricity on him, Rigas transforms Dan into a guinea pig, submitting him to increasing doses of electricity until Dan becomes immune to electrocution but also becomes the helpless tool of Rigas for whom "electricity is life; men can be motivated and controlled by the electrical impulse." The mad scientist gets Dan to murder his colleague Dr. Laurience, who considers that the theories of Rigas are destructive when there are so many constructive experiments to be carried out. Clad in a rubber suit designed to prevent the electricity escaping from his body, the now-indestructible Dan goes on the rampage but dies when barbed wire tears the suit and the electricity, his sole source of life and power, escapes.

This summary hardly justifies my claims concerning the script, readers will say. In fact, the script both comments on the contemporary period and looks ahead to more recent horror movies. It also looks back to *White Zombie* and elaborates a theory of value, energy and labor that coincides with aspects of our argument in this section. Rigas wishes to create "a superior race of men whose only wants will be electricity." They will have no desires, only drives to be satisfied. If he succeeds, one half of humanity will serve the other half. That a film made in 1941 should reproduce—deliberately, surely, given the use of the formula "a superior race"—the ideology of Nazism via a mad scientist is not surprising. What is less to be expected is the economic and historical dimension of Rigas's theory, for it becomes clear later that Rigas wants to create an army of men like Dan, ready to do battle and serve as the workers of the future. There must therefore be another race, superior to Dan and his future coworkers/soldiers, who will control them, bend them to their will and exploit their labor and energy. It is the masters and the slaves, yet again, with Rigas and others in the role of a new capitalist/politician class wielding unlimited power without having to submit to such nonsense as wages and democratic elections. The surplus value produced will thus be beyond a capitalist's wildest dreams, and society's values a thing of the past, banished as part of the film's intriguing anticipation (in another historical context) of current notions of "prehistory."[67]

To refer to slaves evokes, of course, the fate of blacks in the United States, and *Man Made Monster* reveals unconsciously an element of Nazism rarely commented on: blacks in concentration camps.[68] The notion of racial superiority had already been sketched in via the character of a surgeon in *The Return of Dr. X* who exclaims, "The time's coming when man will be able to control blood; and when that time comes he'll be able to control his destiny." Because the surgeon sports a small beard and a monocle, he can be "read" as a German, and therefore a Nazi, given the film's date.[69] Much earlier in the decade, however, an anti-Negro discourse that had little to envy Nazi ideology held sway. Thus, in *The Monster Walks* the black chauffeur played by Willie Best is not only stupid and cowardly but is placed at the center of a remark on Darwin (of whom the poor ignoramus has never heard), which evokes evolution. Informed that apes are our ancestors, the Best character evokes the ape who plays a key role in the film's plot and asks, "Do you mean he's related to me?" That the other character (a lawyer) makes no attempt to correct him by saying "us" instead of "me" can only reinforce white prejudices by implying that the Best character accepts his assimilation to primates as a trait particular to blacks only.[70]

Returning to *Man Made Monster*, we find that much of the film's dialogue reads like an economic/political treatise where fascism and capitalism meet and shake hands over the corpse of the rights of humanity in general and workers in particular. For Rigas, most people are born to be mediocre and un-educated, but they have to be "fed by a superior intelligence." I suggest we read "fed" both literally and metaphorically, as *Man Made Monster* creates here a link with *The Devil-Doll*. Rigas turns the lower orders into slaves who need no food or money, whereas Lavond's scientist coprisoner dreamed of a scheme to feed everyone without depleting the world's resources. In the dis-course of Rigas, however, these resources become a source of personal wealth and power as they will be privatized by those whose knowledge and breeding will bring them permanent control. Thus, "fed" in no way implies the intel-lectual nourishment one person with knowledge shares on a democratic ba-sis with others but rather the imposition of a certain order destined to repro-duce itself indefinitely.

In the scheme of Rigas, an army of men like Dan is a throwback to Legendre's zombies.[71] Various visual elements in *Man Made Monster* create links with Frankenstein's monster: Dan is strapped to a huge table to be elec-trocuted and, in the film's final sequence, lumbers across the fields, the hero-ine helpless in his arms. A further parallel, equally eloquent, is created with Fritz Lang's *Metropolis*. At one point, the heroine states that Dan has "slowed down"; he walks with difficulty and his body is no longer his own, thus echo-ing the mechanical and repetitive movements carried out by the workers in the underground city. In fact, Rigas starts his experiments by giving Dan five times the normal maximum dose of electricity (beyond which a human would expire) before he faints, then proceeds in stages until Dan no longer faints. Dan is thus being forced to adapt to an ever-changing situation until he reaches the point where he can be ordered to carry out any task: the per-fect worker in capitalist eyes. It is in this context that Rigas states that Dan is "doing the work of the world," implying that the self-styled elite live off him and those destined to resemble him.

Rigas is the film's incarnation of a literal "triumph of the will." Focusing intently on his victim, he obliges him to repeat "I killed him," a reference to the murder of Dr. Laurience. Here, however, Rigas is almost betrayed by "the political unconscious." A psychiatrist attempts to get Dan to admit he killed Laurience and makes use of the Oedipus complex to prove that Dan killed Laurience to get even unconsciously with the man who mistreated him when he was in an orphanage. Unfortunately for the psychiatrist and for Rigas, this (ab)use of Freud rebounds on them by provoking an outburst from Dan, quickly suppressed by Rigas. What is happening here? Dan has kept alive an unconscious recognition of the fact that it was Laurience who befriended him and helped him when he most needed it. Laurience's views on science have a vaguely socialist tinge to them: knowledge for the common good and, more crucially, knowledge as a common heritage transmitted from one generation to the next. Laurience was therefore Dan's ego ideal, the benign and positive father figure. Rigas stands in as the perfect manifestation of the bad father, the father of endless enjoyment, an early example of that indispensable modern figure Freddy Krueger: both seek to exploit the body of the other for their own gain, but *Man Made Monster* makes this *jouissance* more explicitly economic and political.[72]

Certain little details in the film merit our continued attention. After a period under observation, Dan leaves hospital, as he puts it himself, "under my own power," insisting on the fact that his body is his own. This recalls the character of Ruth Rogen in *Supernatural* who refused to trade her body in after execution as it is the only thing she possesses that is really her own (see chapter 3). By transforming Dan's body into a receptacle for electricity that he controls, Rigas expropriates Dan's labor power totally to his own advantage. Indeed, Dan's body is the locus of *accumulation* (of energy), which Rigas draws on for his own benefit, replenishing Dan periodically to "maintain," as it were, the machine in perfect working order and to reinforce his own power and social status. It is clear that, just as the workers in *Metropolis* are so many adjuncts of the machines, so Dan becomes a new form of machine for Rigas. Similarly, when the electricity drains away at the film's climax, it is as if not only the energy but also memory and knowledge have drained away too, inasmuch as this loss of energy results in Dan's death. The ending thus becomes a sort of parable of worker-capitalist relations, with Dan in death corresponding to the living dead in *White Zombie* or the assorted body parts that go to make up Frankenstein's monster. The script of *Man Made Monster* is a little history lesson in its own right.

We can easily imagine Rigas crying out triumphantly, "Today the laboratory, tomorrow the world!" suitably paraphrasing the Nazi call for worldwide domination by the Third Reich. If I have substituted the word *universe* in the title of this section, it is to take account of *The Invisible Ray*, a noteworthy and neglected film. Brennan has pointed out that for Lacan, "the ego would act as if there were no limits, pushing off into outer space on the strength of its imperative to expand."[73] If history has proved Lacan right, *The Invisible Ray* provides us with earlier proof of this, albeit in an inverted form that we shall analyze presently.

First, it is necessary to furnish information provided by the script. Dr. Rukh (Karloff) has invited scientists to witness the result of an experiment proving his "belief that a great meteor, bearing an element even more powerful than radium, struck an uncharted spot somewhere in the continent of Africa." Using special equipment, he has discovered that this event has been recorded by a ray from Andromeda. "Everything that has ever happened has left its record on nature's film," he informs his skeptical guests, who soon learn that he has been telling the truth. They and the film's spectators—who are led to identify with the guests by the way the latter are invited by Rukh to sit down and watch the spectacle—are "transported" out into space until they encounter the ray from Andromeda, at which moment the point of view changes and we are located in outer space, watching the meteor in question colliding with Africa.

I would argue that, by according its spectators two privileged points of view, *The Invisible Ray* is in fact representing a split subject position that, if the two positions are copresent in the subject's unconscious, resembles the condition of paranoia: looking *out* at X is transformed into X looking *in* at the subject. The parallel with *The Mask of Fu Manchu* is striking. This is crucial to understanding the character of Rukh who, anxious to obtain recognition from the scientific community that has hitherto rejected him, soon suspects a plot mounted by Dr. Benet (Lugosi) to deprive him of fame. In fact, Benet sees the medical possibilities involved in the substance, whereas Rukh gradually but inexorably comes to see it as belonging exclusively to him. The parallels with *The Devil-Doll*, *Dr. Cyclops*, and *Mad Made Monster* are clear. I would also argue that the ray from Andromeda plays a very particular role in Rukh's psychic constitution, especially in light of the function of religion and fetishism in the film and his insane belief in his quasi-divine status. Rukh is horror cinema's version of Dr. Schreber: "Schreber believes that he is the special beneficiary of the 'rays of God,' just as a psychotic suffering from a different delusion believes he is the persecuted (but therefore privileged) object of, say, Communist plots."[74] If we replace "Communist" by the group of scientists and explorers suspected by Rukh of wanting to steal his discoveries, we have the situation represented in the film.

These considerations interest us in the present context only inasmuch as they help us to understand the way the film deals with the continent of Africa and the concomitant representation of religion and fetishism. The fact that Rukh refers to the meteor striking "an uncharted spot" should surely make us sit up and take notice, with its implications of a wilderness open to the first comers who can do with it what they will. This is the equivalent in *The Invisible Ray* of Moreau's island in *Island of Lost Souls* and of Skull Island in *King Kong*: a colonialist's paradise or dream world.[75] The fact that we are dealing with an event that happened countless millions of years before at once forecloses all discussion of time and history: they simply do not exist within such a conceptual framework. Once he has discovered the substance, Rukh uses it to melt a rock in the presence of his native bearers, thus simultaneously confirming his theory of its power and impressing the natives who are seen "cowering in awe and fear."[76] This brief scene is surely a perfect manifestation of the use of technology by the West to dominate the third world, whether physically or by means assimilated by the "superstitious" natives to a divine substitute which they treat as a fetish.

The only problem, from an ideological standpoint, is that Westerns behave in exactly the same fashion when Rukh melts statues adorning a Paris church,[77] and it is in this context that we can question the film's unconscious relation to history. Just as films as different as *The Most Dangerous Game* and *The Wolfman* incorporate elements of the feudal and the modern, so *The Invisible Ray* incorporates the medieval and a vision of today that looks ahead to tomorrow. This is done, however, not via the attitudes of characters (Zaroff; Larry Talbot's father) but through certain visuals. Thus, Rukh's home is a castle, the form of whose gigantic rooms resembles nothing if not the vaults of a cathedral. At this point, we would be advised to pay attention to the representation of his mother, whose hair and clothes make her bear a strange resemblance to a *bishop*. This religious attribute makes her *masculine* and can only reinforce the parallel between Rukh and Schreber who adopted a *feminine* position toward God. More germane to our argument here is the way religion functions to eliminate from time and history any properly materialist elements of class and social agitation.[78]

The film also brings us back to the theme of energy, waiting throughout countless centuries to be released for a variety of purposes, none of which is innocent: medicine is used as an ideological marker to justify the penetration of the so-called Dark Continent. Brennan quotes a reference to energy in Lacan's Seminar IV: "energy begins to be of interest to us in this instance [the current of a river] only beginning with the moment in which it is accumulated, and it is accumulated only beginning with the moment when machines are put to work in a certain way."[79] This view implies, as with the use of electricity in *Frankenstein* and *Man Made Monster* (to take just two examples), that we are dealing with an intervention on man's part at a precise moment of history, an intervention inseparable from the notion of exploitation of nature and the economic benefits that can accrue. Just as Frankenstein uses electricity as a natural force (a lightning storm), so *The Invisible Ray* uses the "universal" phenomenon of the meteor to displace the centre of interest and focus it on the experiments of an individual (mad) scientist. The harnessing of electricity is no more due to mere chance than Freud's discovery of the unconscious in turn-of-the-century Vienna. As that other great theoretician Karl Marx pointed out, it is people who make history, but they are not aware that they are doing so.

The reader will have noticed that I have referred on more than one occasion to the juxtaposition of incompatible elements in certain films discussed in this chapter, most notably in the realm of different periods of history. It is to a systematic appraisal of this question that we shall now turn in our concluding section.

Far from the Madding Crowd

I have had occasion to quote Teresa Brennan on technologies that enable "megalomanic fantasies" to "come true, increasing their coverage of the earth's surface and corruption of its temporal parameters in the process."[80] This juxtaposition of time and space (but not "outer space," which will not concern us beyond our comments on *The Invisible Ray*) is crucial for our argument here, most notably in the context of the preceding section's concluding paragraph concerning "incompatible elements" that, as we shall see, always turn on time and space in one manifestation or the other of these notions. Brennan quotes Heidegger, who "situates metaphysics as a privileging of space over temporality, and argues that this privileging results in a repression of the historical process."[81] This argument of Heidegger's is most suggestive and productive when applied to the horror film of the 1930s, but I wish to adopt a second line of approach at the same time, one that seeks to demonstrate how time itself also poses problems that can be shown to exist in their own right in a number of films. Let us commence, however, by considering the matter of space.

"Remote places" are the setting of many a horror film. Drawing attention to "a period setting in what looked like a kind of stylized nineteenth century," Andrew Tudor has written that "castles, old manor houses, country inns and elaborate laboratories repeat themselves from film to film, forming a highly distinctive setting and, no doubt, serving to divorce the fictions from their audience's immediate context of experience."[82]

I propose here a division into three major categories, with a certain amount of overlap in certain films:

- Castles and mansions: *Dracula*, *White Zombie*, *Dr. X*, *The Old Dark House*, *The Black Cat*, *The Raven*, *The Invisible Ray*, and *The Devil Commands*
- Uncharted islands: *The Most Dangerous Game*, *Island of Lost Souls*, *King Kong*, and *Son of Kong*. A variant within this category would be Africa in *The Invisible Ray* and the Peruvian jungle in *Dr. Cyclops*.

- (Secret) laboratories: *Frankenstein, Dr. Jekyll and Mr. Hyde, Murders in the Rue Morgue, Dr. X, Mystery of the Wax Museum, The Vampire Bat, Bride of Frankenstein, Werewolf of London, The Devil-Doll, The Man Who Changed His Mind, Son of Frankenstein, The Dark Eyes of London, Dr. Cyclops, The Devil Bat,* and *The Devil Commands.* A variant within this category is to be found in those films where the laboratory has been transformed into a torture chamber (*The Mask of Fu Manchu, The Raven*) or a secret room (*The Black Room*).

If we turn to the question of temporality, we can note a small number of factors returning in a limited corpus. The role of peasants tends to place a film outside time (*Dracula, Frankenstein, Bride of Frankenstein*), a factor also present, but less obvious, when villagers act as substitutes for peasants: *Son of Frankenstein, The Wolf Man.* To put it more concretely, Renfield seems to belong to another "time zone" in the opening sequences of *Dracula,* which could also be attributed to the fact that he is traveling in a "backward" country, a Hollywood stereotype we find at work in the representation of the indigenous population in *The Mummy, The Mask of Fu Manchu, The Invisible Ray,* and *Dr. Cyclops. Bride of Frankenstein* is most instructive here. On the one hand, it introduces Mary Shelley and the poets Byron and Shelley as belonging explicitly to the early years of the nineteenth century, whereas the rest of the film seems to be taking place in a more recent period. On the other hand, the film makes of Pretorius a specialist in alchemy, which shifts the focus back to the Middle Ages and complicates the entire question of temporality.

Before even attempting to draw any conclusions, we need to consider a further parameter: the actors who dominated the genre. I propose the following list, along with the films in which they appeared:

- Lionel Atwill: *Dr. X, Mystery of the Wax Museum, The Vampire Bat, Murders in the Zoo, Son of Frankenstein,* and *Man Made Monster*
- Boris Karloff: *Frankenstein, The Old Dark House, The Mummy, The Mask of Fu Manchu, The Ghoul, The Black Cat, The Raven, The Invisible Ray, The Walking Dead, The Man Who Changed His Mind, Son of Frankenstein, Black Friday, The Devil Commands,* and the trilogy directed by Nick Grindé
- Bela Lugosi: *Dracula, Murders in the Rue Morgue, White Zombie, Island of Lost Souls, The Black Cat, The Raven, Mark of the Vampire, The Invisible Ray, Son of Frankenstein, Black Friday, The Devil Bat, The Wolf Man,* and the film he made in England, *The Dark Eyes of London*

Other major contributions were made by the following actors:

- Leslie Banks: *The Most Dangerous Game*
- Colin Clive: *Frankenstein, Bride of Frankenstein*, and *Mad Love*
- Charles Laughton: *The Old Dark House* and *Island of Lost Souls*
- Peter Lorre: *Mad Love* and *The Face behind the Mask*
- Claude Raines: *The Invisible Man* and *The Wolf Man*
- Edward Van Sloan: *Dracula, Frankenstein, The Mummy*, and *Dracula's Daughter*

Every single one of these actors was European in origin, and few actors in the films of the period were American: Fredric March (*Dr. Jekyll and Mr. Hyde*), Lionel Barrymore (*Mark of the Vampire, The Devil-Doll*), Albert Dekker (*Dr. Cyclops*), and Lon Chaney Jr. (*The Wolf Man*). A few comments are in order.

One line of reasoning that needs to be firmly rejected is introduced by David Skal:

> March's casting is notable in that he is so obviously an American. A recurrent feature in thirties horror films is the injection of American characters and performers into nightmarish "European" situations. As Frank McConnell has noted, "the 'England' of *Dracula* is transparently New England, even to the accents of most of the major characters."[83]

Just as the first sentence is accurate and highlights the point under discussion, so the rest is both inaccurate and wrong-headed: the two main characters in *Dracula* are played by Lugosi and Van Sloan; and what is paramount in these films is not "the injection of American characters" but the massive presence of Europeans and a certain number of elements that refuse to "gel." As I have just pointed out, Skal is quite right to insist on actor Fredric March's American origins, but he fails to draw the correct conclusion. His remark neglects the fact that European actors sometimes played American characters, or else characters of European origin, in films set in America. I have already insisted on the anachronisms present in *Dr. X*, where the Atwill character, Dr. Xavier, wears spats and the journalist (played by American Lee Tracy) drives up to his house in a horse-drawn carriage, although the film is set in the America of the period (1932). No, something else is happening here. Not all horror films were European in origin, far from it, but this frequent recourse to "remote places" does have a significance.

As we have seen, "remote places" can be diverse indeed: Dracula's castle, the cliff-top dwellings of Murder Legendre and Dr. Blair (*The Devil Commands*), the laboratories of Frankenstein and Dr. Thorkel, sundry islands, and so forth.[84] To this parameter we can add the question of temporality (time has indeed "forgotten" Skull Island, with its assorted dinosaurs), nature, and technology. And even when the setting is seemingly banal—Dr. Crespi's hospital, Dr. Vollin's mansion (*The Raven*), the home of Dr. Laurience (*Man Made Monster*)—nameless horrors are at work that highlight the theme of good and evil that traverses the genre from beginning to end, whether the mad doctor/scientist is evil incarnate from the outset or has allowed ambition to corrupt him. Discussing binary oppositions in general and that of good and evil in particular, Jameson has made the following incisive comment:

> Yet surely, in the shrinking world of the present day, with its gradual leveling of class and national and racial differences, and its imminent abolition of Nature (as some ultimate term of Otherness or difference), it ought to be less difficult to understand to what degree the concept of good and evil is a positional one that coincides with categories of Otherness. Evil thus, as Nietzsche taught us, continues to characterize whatever is radically different from me, whatever by virtue of precisely that difference seems to constitute a real and urgent threat to my own existence.[85]

Jameson goes on to list some of "the archetypal figures of the Other, about whom the essential point to be made is not so much that he is feared because he is evil; rather he is evil *because* he is Other, alien, different, strange, unclean, and unfamiliar."

Otherness can thus be represented by one or another foreign actor ("foreign," that is, to American audiences) playing a character who may or may not be completely evil or mad or who takes the form of truly monstrous evil, such as Dr. Fu Manchu. Incidentally, cannot we attribute his status as doctor (of medicine, literature, and philosophy) to a further ploy, perhaps unconscious, of alienating him from spectators, of designating him as always already evil incarnate? This ploy, of course, is not simply textual but an integral part of the "social landscape" that is at once represented within the films under discussion and constructed through the context in which the films were conceived in the first place. Binary oppositions are obviously part of what Brennan, following Lacan, insists on: the need of the ego to expel from itself those elements it cannot accept precisely because they seem to question its status as self-centered source of knowledge. The mad doctor/scientist is "evil" precisely because what he strives to attain is too close for comfort, too akin to the ideology of wealth and individual success. In that case, we must also see the "remote places" as something specific to the psyche of the mad scientist: a place where he can find peace of mind, where he can exercise a freedom of action and spirit that pushes to its logical and ultimate conclusion the basis of capitalist ideology where the success of one person perforce passes via the failure and, if necessary, the destruction of the other.

One of Jameson's "magical narratives" is romance literature (he is not concerned with film), which he contrasts with the realist novel. We are entitled to see a similar contrast between Hollywood realism and the horror film, at least on a formal level. I am arguing here, as I have done from the outset, that the horror film of the 1930s came closer to historical realism than most of the studio productions of the time. Thus, a comment by Jameson on romance is pertinent:

> As for romance, it would seem that its ultimate condition of figuration . . . is to be found in a transitional moment in which two distinct modes of production, or moments of socioeconomic development, coexist. Their antagonism is not yet articulated in terms of the struggle of social classes, so that its resolution can be projected in the form of a nostalgic (or less often, a Utopian) harmony.[86]

Referring to Eichendorff, he remarks that the author's "opposition between good and evil threatens so closely to approximate the incompatibility between the older aristocratic traditions and the new middle-class life situation that the narrative must not be allowed to press on to any decisive conclusion."[87] These comments go a long way to helping us understand, say, the blatant opposition between Frankenstein's father and the peasants on the one hand, and Frankenstein's attempt to bring science into the modern world on the other; the reference to alchemy in *Bride of Frankenstein*; the copresence of the feudal and the modern in *The Most Dangerous Game* and *The Wolf Man*; Hyde's drives as the extreme untrammeled expression of the semifeudal mentality of General Carew; the fairytale atmosphere and decor of *Son of Frankenstein*; the son of Kong as symbol of the Statue of Liberty on an uncharted island whose population comprises natives and dinosaurs; love crossing the centuries to conquer history itself in *The Mummy*; and so on.

Yet some of the examples I have just given—Frankenstein, the mummy Imhotep—are also surely attempts to represent the positive aspects of the characters' drives, what Jameson refers to as "Utopian harmony." It is the notion of "Utopia" that concerns us here.[88] In an attempt to clarify its meaning, I shall turn to another text by Jameson where he evokes it in the context of a discussion on reification, which he sees "as a fragmentation of the psyche and of its world that opens up the semiautonomous and henceforth compartmentalized spaces of lived time over against clock time, bodily or perceptual experience over against rational and instrumental conscious-ness."[89] He goes on:

> Ultimately of course, this fragmentation generates a psychic division of labor which reorders all the others into a fundamental opposition between the sub-ject and the object, between the private or the psychological and a henceforth inert scientifically and technologically manipulable external "reality." But if this is the case, then it becomes clear that modernism not only reflects and re-inforces such fragmentation and commodification of the psyche as its basic precondition, but that the various modernisms all seek to overcome that reifi-cation as well, by the exploration of a new Utopian and libidinal experience of the various sealed realms or psychic compartments to which they are con-demned, but which they also reinvent.[90]

Perhaps some readers will also have experienced, as I did on reading this passage, a feeling of the Uncanny, for what is Jameson describing here if not the characters of the various mad doctors and scientists, their conditions of work in their laboratories, and the lives they live on their islands? It is not only high modernism that reflects reification and commodification at work and the Utopian striving to overcome them at the very moment of repre-senting their effects. Should we not also ask ourselves why the mad doctor/scientist is considered to be irrational when he claims to be aiming for a new form of reason, whether it is intended to benefit humanity (Frankenstein, Jekyll, Laurience) or serve the interests of a tiny elite (Moreau, Thorkel, Rigas)? For he is surely the locus of contradiction, at once striving for some impossible Utopia while succumbing to an extreme form of rationalization:

> The rationalization process is first and foremost to be described as the analyti-cal dismantling of the various traditional or "natural" unities (social groups, in-stitutions, human relationships, forms of authority, activities of a cultural and ideological as well as of a productive nature) into their component parts with a view to their "Taylorization," that is, their reorganization into more efficient systems which function according to an instrumental, or binary, means/ends logic.[91]

The mad doctor/scientist sees the world in terms of himself and the object of his experiment, be it human or animal, while simultaneously refusing to consider the result in terms of an efficiency that takes no account of his ge-nius, which he does not see in purely economic terms. Frankenstein is looked on with suspicion, on the one hand because he is a threat to an archaic so-cial system and, on the other because he refuses modern bourgeois marriage. The same could be said of Jekyll. More generally, the mad doctor/scientist is revolting against a system that reduces all genuine intellectual and cultural effort to its lowest common denominator, whereas the films strive to make out that any attempt to kick against the traces, to return to a less regimented form of social order, is an act of transgression that cannot go unpunished. The "remote place" can also be seen as the spatial manifestation of a form of nostalgia, more common—and also more reactionary—than the push toward Utopia, a retreat to a past where those who wielded power could do so without hindrance, but in circumstances where there was more collective activity. The peasants and villagers or the mobs are instances of the latter, either on a fanciful mode (the peasants) or a negative mode (the mobs). I am thinking, among others, of the Frankenstein films, *Dracula*, *The Vampire Bat*, *The Invisible Man*, and *The Devil Commands*. A more genuinely radical version is surely *Island of Lost Souls*, the moment of the rebellion where the "manimals," filmed in extreme close-up, denounce their status as "Things!" and appear as so many "grimaces of the Real" in the oft-used formula of Slavoj Zizek, where something that cannot be represented finds a particular form of expression—in this case, the "absent cause" that enables us to grasp the meaning of their suffering: history itself.

In the extended quote cited earlier from Jameson's *Fables of Aggression* figures the expression "the various sealed realms or psychic compartments to which they are condemned." We can see this notion at work in the assorted laboratories and islands where the main characters cut themselves off from those who would at once curtail their freedom to experiment as they see fit and remind them that their behavior is unacceptable, while simultaneously defining "behavior" in economic and social terms totally hostile to any form of cultural and intellectual endeavor. More literally, it is the coffin in *The Crime of Dr. Crespi*, the secret room in *The Black Room*, and the secret corridors in *Son of Frankenstein*. In *The Mask of Fu Manchu*, the scene where the coolies emerge from sarcophagi to kidnap Sir Lionel is the representation by reversal of the West's sealing itself off from the East to avoid "contamination" by and all knowledge of the Other, while using this "difference" as a threat to justify aggression.

The theme, taken literally and figuratively, finds a most complex formal expression in *The Raven*: Dr. Vollin's mansion itself. In few films does the old adage "A man's home is his castle" resonate with such determination. His home is not only the place where Vollin has retreated to cut himself off from those surgeons who have refused to recognize his exceptional talent, it is organized to resemble spatially the cultural and psychic forms his condition assumes. At the touch of a switch, steel shutters descend over the windows, thus transforming the house into a literal "sealed realm." At the touch of another switch, rooms descend into the basement like so many lifts from which there can be no escape. The basement itself is a dungeon—so we have the copresence of the medieval and the modern in as pure a form as one could hope for—designed to resemble the pit in Poe's "The Pit and the Pendulum." Thus the spatial, the temporal and the aesthetic coexist. That Vollin should die hideously, crushed to death in a room whose walls close in on their victim, is peculiarly appropriate. Once the walls, floor, and ceiling meet, the room ceases to exist as if it had never been there, which is also the fate of Vollin. Both he and this "sealed realm" are as if foreclosed, much like history itself.

The film that gives us the most elaborate representation of the topics under discussion here is *The Black Cat*. Death, time, and war are the film's dominant themes; they are inextricably linked and rendered explicit by the script. Vitus Werdegast returns to Marmorus in his native Hungary to seek revenge on architect Hjalmar Poelzig, who sold out his troops to the Russians at the end of World War I and has built a splendid house on what Werdegast calls "the greatest graveyard in the world": thousands died as a result of Poelzig's treachery. Werdegast has rotted in prison for fifteen years and now wants to know what became of his wife and daughter whom Poelzig stole from him. In due course, he learns that Poelzig married the former, embalmed her after her death, and then married the daughter, Karen. Werdegast is accompanied by a newly married American couple, Peter and Joan Alison, whom he helped following a train crash to reach Poelzig's dwelling.

These are the bare bones of the plot of one of the most complex and remarkable horror films of the period. Poelzig reifies time by embalming his first wife's body and transforming it into a cult, an object of fascination that he comes to stare at adoringly in the dungeon on which he has erected his house. Thus for him time stands still, a denial of history overdetermined unconsciously by his marriage to the daughter (whom his wife had from her marriage to Werdegast), surely a way of going *back* in time to begin the first marriage all over again. Everything in the film, from Poelzig's now-notorious remark "Even the phone is dead" to shots of him rising up suddenly and all erect from his bed like some corpse galvanized by electricity in Dr. Frankenstein's laboratory, turns on his obsession with death. As we have already pointed out, Poelzig is an obsessional neurotic, multiplying acts able to convince him that he can keep death at bay and continue to live as if time were standing still. It is hardly surprising, therefore, that Poelzig refers to Werdegast and himself as "the living dead." The chess game, where he and Werdegast play for the lives of the young couple, must surely be seen as play serving as an imaginary mastery of time and also looks ahead to the cinema's best-known chess game: that between the Knight and Death in Ingmar

Bergman's *The Seventh Seal* (1956). Shots of the heroine moving around as if sleepwalking only add to the overall unsettling atmosphere of a world cut off from all spatial and temporal parameters.

The thrust of my argument here is that this "unsettling atmosphere"—the hero says the house has an "atmosphere hard to describe"—is the manifestation of the Real, that which cannot be described but only felt and that, following in the footsteps of Fredric Jameson, I interpret as none other than history, the absent cause that structures the text. The fact that Werdegast returns makes of him a ghost from the past as far as Poelzig is concerned, none other in fact than the return of the repressed history. Survival for Poelzig has meant the extermination of thousands of his troops in exchange for wealth, which turns him into a particularly grisly signifier of capitalism. What is so truly fascinating about *The Black Cat* is that it foregrounds history and politics in terms of class and economic survival and, in a very special way that we shall discuss in a moment, disavows this by its very narrative structure.

The chess game can be interpreted in different ways, however, the most obvious—and explicit—being that of a game to possess the other. Let us strip this scene of its metaphysical and moral implications and see it for what it is: a naked exercise of power (in Poelzig's case at least; Werdegast is fighting for three lives, his and the couple's, against a mass murderer who will stop at nothing). We can surely see a parallel with *The Most Dangerous Game* where Rainsford is offered the heroine as a prize, as if people were objects within a system based on exchange. The central role played by money and class— Poelzig the officer who exchanges (the lives of) his soldiers/workers for hard cash—is also implicit in the earlier film. I have already compared the discussions on board the yacht to decisions made in a boardroom concerning the future of a firm. As millions of people know today to their cost, that entails unemployment as a means to increase dividends and weaken even further employees and their unions. That the dynamite Werdegast uses to blow up the house at the end sounds like cannons firing only serves to underline the role of history, in the form of World War I, returning implacably. Moreover, the theme of possession has a precise sexual connotation, itself explicit in *The Black Cat*. On the train prior to the accident, the hero catches Werdegast in the act of stroking his wife's hair, which the unhappy man explains as being due to his memories of his lost wife. Karen lying motionless in bed beside Poelzig, and the theme of embalming both raise the morbid theme of necrophilia, a symbolic way of submitting to mortality via a particularly gruesome form of disavowal. This is an intimate part of Poelzig's fetishism and is also the structure of misrecognition that is at the basis of ideology as opposed to true knowledge.

It is, however, in its use of spatial parameters that *The Black Cat* provides us with the most unusual representation of history, one that simultaneously highlights and denies it. Much has been made of the strikingly modern decor and layout of Poelzig's home, but the fact that he has built it on the ruins of Fort Marmorus, which exists as a sort of autonomous space directly beneath it, has not been commented on sufficiently.[92] For here, even more than in *The Raven*, we find ourselves in the presence of those "sealed realms" that concern us in this section. These twin manifestations of Poelzig's existence—an ultramodern home and vestiges that look like a medieval dungeon—enable him to seal himself off physically and psychically from the past or, to put it more accurately, to create an imaginary continuum through the presence of his former wife's embalmed corpse that inhabits the former fort. The latter is thus transformed into a sort of church by which Poelzig can escape the meaning and consequences of his past actions and thus the historical context determining them. I am reminded here of a remark made by Freud on his most famous patient, the Wolfman, whose unconscious memories he compared to religion in ancient Egypt: throughout its evolution it kept alive the earliest divinities and allowed them to exist alongside the more recent ones.[93] In this context, Poelzig's function as head of a coven of Satanists must surely be seen as yet another instance of his neurotic encounter with death and his foreclosure of history, rather than as some facile symbol of evil, that all-purpose signified that critics love to brandish and dissect outside questions of history.

The Black Cat's atmosphere, discussed earlier, is one that could be described as "dreamlike," and it is precisely this that has enabled us to evoke the Real as history itself. However, the film's overall narrative structure can also be said to resemble a nightmare from which one awakens, distraught and then relieved, and it is this structure that disavows—indeed, represses—the significance of everything that occurs between the arrival at Poelzig's home and its destruction by dynamite. As I have already mentioned, it is a train crash that precipitates the encounter with Poelzig, and it is with a train journey that the film ends, the couple taking up their honeymoon trip to its destination, *much as if nothing had happened*. Something important has occurred, however: the hero is a novelist and learns in the closing moments that his new novel has just been published. A happy ending thus elevates a work of *fiction* to the point where it takes precedence over history, seen as an unpleasant interruption within a journey that symbolizes everyday life, one far removed from such collective dramas as World War I and ultimately devoted to the couple as the symbol of the future.

I would suggest that it is Hollywood's need to impose such endings that can help to explain certain odd and unconvincing aspects of the film. To begin with, why is Werdegast shot by the hero? Edgar Ulmer certainly presents the scene as if the man were threatening the hero's wife, but we are surely entitled to consider the husband's interpretation as a classic instance of misinterpretation due to his inability to comprehend what is going on around him. Werdegast's behavior places him within the sphere of the mad doctor: he starts to flay Poelzig alive and seems to have lost all self-control. His death is necessary within another logic, one where Werdegast's function as a sort of "emissary" of history must be replaced by the "laws" of the genre. To put it another way: the film represses history for a second time, just as Poelzig has always done. We are faced with an example of history repeating itself, first as tragedy and then as farce: the ending is rather silly and unconvincing, due not to a lack of talent but to a lack of logic, the Symbolic yielding to the Imaginary.

A rather painful moment is the scene where two gendarmes argue over the respective beauty of the towns in which they were born. A supposedly comic moment of the kind that disfigures certain films by James Whale, it also comes over as a reworking of scenes where peasants frolic in a bucolic setting. Things, not surprisingly in this film, are not that simple. One of the gendarmes says in a most superior tone that his colleague's village "used to be all right ten to fifteen years ago." As Werdegast has just returned from the supposed oblivion of the past after fifteen years, this remark is hinting not so much that World War I is responsible for such a deterioration, but that countries have not learned the history lessons laid out before them.

These two instances return us to the notion of "romance" referred to earlier, most notably in light of the fact that the husband is a novelist. I quote Jameson again:

> A first specification of romance would then be achieved if we could account for the way in which, in contrast to realism, its inner-worldly objects such as landscape or village, forest or mansion—mere temporary stopping places on the lumbering coach or express-train itinerary of realistic representation—are somehow transformed into folds in space, into discontinuous pockets of homogeneous time and of heightened symbolic closure.[94]

This uncannily accurate summary of 1930s horror in general and of *The Black Cat* in particular will enable us to conclude our analyses. There is a shot in *Son of Frankenstein*, taken from within the train transporting the eponymous central character and wife and child to his family home, where we are suddenly confronted with a desolate countryside, as dead as that in the opening sequence of Roger Corman's *House of Usher* (1960) and resembling perhaps a landscape devastated by war. However, it is so devoid of life, as if definitively dead, that it looks more like a residue from the past that refuses to go away. A similar shot occurs in *The Black Cat* but in a more extreme form; Werdegast looks out of the train window and all we see is a sort of void, with streaks of smoke from the engine. Then we see a vague reflection of his face in the glass. Both shots, I would argue, represent history, the first as something repressed that refuses to go away, the second as yet another "grimace of the Real." The ending of *The Black Cat*, with Werdegast safely dead, shows that this extraordinary film, despite its exceptional insights, has ultimately missed the true significance of its encounter with history.

Notes

1. I am thinking in particular of *The Political Unconscious*.

2. Randy Loren Rasmussen, *Children of the Night: The Six Archetypal Characters of Classic Horror Films* (Jefferson, N.C.: McFarland, 1998), 246.

3. Rasmussen, *Children of the Night*, 247.

4. Andrew Tudor, *Monsters and Mad Scientists: A Cultural History of the Horror Movie* (Oxford: Blackwell, 1989), 37.

5. David Skal, *Screams of Reason: Mad Science and Modern Culture* (New York: Norton, 1998), 130.

6. David Skal, *The Monster Show: A Cultural History of Horror* (London: Plexus, 1993), 168–69, 135.

7. We shall return to this presently when analyzing *Son of Kong*. Judith Mayne has called Denham "a typical petty-bourgeois entrepreneur." In "*King Kong* and the Ideology of Spectacle," *Quarterly Review of Film Studies* 1, no. 4 (November 1976): 378.

8. Or, without the benefit of a union. See my later comments on *Son of Kong*.

9. I have not forgotten that I have argued in chapter 2 against considering Kong as male and am using the masculine here for reasons of simplicity. Resorting to "he or she" when discussing a primate whose symbolism is polyvalent does not strike me as pertinent.

10. It comes as no surprise that the film's title insists on Kong's virility, but the script makes no attempt to explain how Kong could sire a son without female help. It is as if the gay subtext of *Frankenstein* and *Bride of Frankenstein*—men creating life without the benefit of procreation (see chapter 2)—were returning here to haunt both the film and its critics. I have already mentioned in chapter 1 the reference to the young ape as "something of a pansy," which in no way corresponds to what we see: he defends "manfully" Denham and the young woman from attacks by the island's assorted animals and is clearly presented as a chip off the old block.

11. To shift genre and periods, this is surely the "message" of Martin Scorsese's *The Aviator* (2005). It is history repeating itself.

12. She and her father had been touring the islands putting on a musical show.

13. Not to mention the natives, of course, but for Denham they're not worth mentioning anyway.

14. Bryan Senn, *Golden Horrors: An Illustrated Critical Filmography of Terror Cinema, 1931–1939* (Jefferson, N.C.: McFarland, 1996), 229; emphasis in the original.

15. Erich von Stroheim collaborated on the script, as did a leading Hollywood Marxist theoretician of the 1930s (and future blacklistee in the 1950s), Guy Endore.

16. This is the other exception to the absence of any representation of proletarian toil that I mentioned when discussing *White Zombie* and *The Dark Eyes of London* in chapter 3.

17. Senn calls the laundry a "sweatshop." *Golden Horrors*, 369.

18. British readers old enough to remember the Great Train Robbery of the early 1960s will also recall the hysterical denunciation of its organizer Ronald Briggs by the right-wing press (notably the populist *Daily Express*). The money stolen was on its way to be pulped and therefore no longer had any use value, except ideologically as signifier of the sacrosanct banking system.

19. An interesting parallel can be drawn between reality and fiction, and actresses Fay Wray (heroine of both films) and Ann Darrow. Because of the unusually long shooting schedule of *King Kong*, Wray was used in other films "between takes" so that the money invested in her would not be "wasted" due to her being "idle." And Ann is starving at the opening of the story.

20. Zaroff collects trophies from his hunts: the heads of his victims. As such, he is a "head hunter," a formula used figuratively today in the field of hiring executives. Rainsford is clearly in the executive category and is also a head hunter (those of tigers, for example).

21. On this, see Slavoj Zizek, *The Sublime Object of Ideology* (London: Verso, 1989), 50–53.

22. Zizek, *The Sublime Object of Ideology*, 127; emphasis added.

23. Quoted by Edward W. Said, *Orientalism* (London: Penguin Books, 1985), 151.

24. Said, *Orientalism*, 210.

25. The "specter" of communism was also set up as a bogey in order to take people's minds off the real nature of the social relations determining their lives. See Chris Baldick, *In Frankenstein's Shadow: Myth, Monstrosity and Nineteenth-century Writing* (Oxford: Clarendon, 1987), 121.

26. *The Mask of Fu Manchu* was released in November 1932, *The Mummy* in December.

27. It is therefore surely interesting to reflect briefly on the expression "filthy lucre." It denounces the importance of money, which seems to contradict what I have just said. Not a bit of it. The word *lucre* comes from the Latin word for "gain," so "filthy lucre" is a denunciation of the profit motive. On another level, the expression can be seen as a manifestation of denial by reversal: we as social subjects are encouraged to believe that money is not the driving force in life—or, rather, *were* encouraged, whereas in these glorious days of neoliberalism nothing is more important.

28. Is this not in itself a denial of History via an inversion: the West made slaves of blacks, whereas here it is a power-crazy Asiatic who does so? Note, too, the shift from the nation to the individual, a perfect way of repressing politics in the best Hollywood tradition.

29. Needless to say, I use the verb *paw* deliberately in the context of a reference to *King Kong*.

30. Any more than they had the right to oppose the Treaty of Tien-Tsin (1858), which "opened" China to Western investors and to the "pleasures" of opium.

31. The formula "bowels of the earth" is not used lightly on my part: the anal connotations of the expression are de rigueur in a context where money is the ultimate prize.

32. Said, *Orientalism*, 103.

33. Fredric Jameson, *The Cultural Turn* (London: Verso, 1998), 105.

34. See Joan Copjec, *Read My Desire* (Cambridge, Mass.: MIT Press, 1995), 36.

35. I have not forgotten other meanings of the look that I approached in chapter 2. My concerns are different here.

36. It is hardly coincidental that Fu Manchu has *three* degrees, suggesting that a combination of force and knowledge is sufficient to seize power. This is exactly what happened historically, but in an inverted form. It is interesting to note that, thirty years later, a shabby film such as *55 Days at Peking* stresses the need for the "Great Powers" to pull together in order to conquer the barbaric Chinese hordes.

37. A review in the *Boston Transcript* (12 November 1932) not only calls attention to Fu Manchu's degree from Harvard but points out that the British are not very bright as they fall into every trap he sets for them. See Jean Hersholt Collection, vol. 10 (1930–1932), Special Collections, MHL. Hersholt played von Berg in the film.

38. "The ego-ideal of society" as Zizek succinctly puts it in a discussion of the Titanic in *The Sublime Object of Ideology*, 70.

39. *New York American*, 3 December 1932, Jean Hersholt Collection, MHL.

40. The fact that in *The Wolf Man* it is rather Abel who would slay Cain is perfectly in keeping with denial that represents a desire via its opposite.

41. Otto Rank, *The Double* (London: Maresfield Library, 1989), 75.

42. Dylan Evans, *An Introductory Dictionary of Lacanian Psychoanalysis* (New York: Routledge, 1996), 78–79.

43. It is customary, in both films and critical writing, to use the word *curse* to designate the fate that befalls the werewolf. Examples are to be found in the very titles of certain films: *Curse of the Werewolf* (Terence Fisher, 1961) and the recent Wes Craven–Kevin Williamson fiasco, *Cursed* (2004). I remind readers that "the curse" is a familiar expression designating a woman's period.

44. Rasmussen, *Children of the Night*, 42–43.

45. In *The Raven*, this paraphernalia takes the form of Vollin's torture chamber, indeed of his entire house, as we shall see later in this chapter.

46. Thomas Keenan, "The Point Is to (Ex)change It: Reading *Capital*, Rhetorically," in *Fetishism as Cultural Discourse*, ed. Emily Apter and William Pietz (Ithaca, N.Y.: Cornell University Press, 1993), 162–63.

47. Abdul JanMohamed, "Refiguring Values, Power, Knowledge," in *Whither Marxism?* ed. Bernd Magnus and Stephen Cullenberg (New York: Routledge, 1995), 41.

48. Jack Amariglio and Antonio Callari, "Marxian Value Theory and the Problem of the Subject: The Role of Commodity Fetishism," in *Fetishism as Cultural Discourse*, ed. Emily Apter and William Pietz (Ithaca, N.Y.: Cornell University Press, 1993), 203.

49. Interestingly, the French title of the film is *Révolte au Zoo*, which makes explicit the notion of rebellion, as the zoo is the place the girl chooses to rebel against the orphanage. We are not entitled to talk of animals in the same manner, unless we wish to anthropomorphize them.

50. The manifest level of the script becomes thus the unconscious effect of language. Just as Zani is accused of theft, so the girl's labor will be stolen. If both are real victims of the laws of bourgeois society, the ideology underpinning *Zoo in Budapest* becomes a victim of another sort. That the matching fur the wife demands is called a "stole," which happens to be the past tense of *steal*, is a nice instance of the signifier insisting and giving the last word, as it were, to the class victims.

51. Teresa Brennan, *History After Lacan* (New York: Routledge, 1993), 88.

52. Brennan, *History After Lacan*, 59.

53. Brennan, *History After Lacan*, 53.

54. Think of sci-fi movies of the 1950s where the "takeover" by aliens concerns both the Red scare and the anxiety produced by an economic "takeover" (or "merger") where social alienation prevents the subject from recognizing the way capitalism functions within Western society itself. I have written on this subject elsewhere, notably in the context of *Invasion of the Body Snatchers* (Don Siegel, 1955). See Reynold Humphries, *The American Horror Film: An Introduction* (Edinburgh: Edinburgh University Press, 2002), 60–62.

55. Brennan, *History After Lacan*, 30.

56. The symbolic and historical significance of being literally "cut off" from one's surroundings will be analyzed later in this chapter.

57. Brennan, *History After Lacan*, 8–9.

58. Brennan, *History After Lacan*, 195.

59. The fact that Tod Browning earned his living before going to Hollywood in a fairground sideshow where he was "buried alive" is perhaps to be interpreted less in terms of an individual pathology than as a case of economic necessity in which the notion of "choice" of career is a classic instance of social alienation. See Skal, *The Monster Show*, 26.

60. Brennan, *History After Lacan*, 9.

61. Brennan, *History After Lacan*, 11.

62. Brennan, *History After Lacan*, 13–14. One is reminded irresistibly of the expression "mother earth" and of Freud's "dark continent," where it is impossible to separate the literal from the figurative. Unconsciously the subject shifts endlessly from one level of meaning to the other, ever interchangeable.

63. Brennan, *History After Lacan*, 14.

64. Quoted by Brennan, *History After Lacan*, 79. Benjamin was writing in 1925. The reader will have noticed that I have had recourse again to the formula "the bowels of the earth." See n. 31.

65. After the scientists and their local guide, Pedro, have been reduced in size by Thorkel, their clothes no longer fit them, so Thorkel (or rather, the wardrobe department) creates new habits for them: togas for the scientists, a loincloth for Pedro! In such mysterious ways does class insist in Hollywood's (unconscious) fantasies.

66. Brennan, *History After Lacan*, 18.

67. As I write this in the run-up to the French referendum on the European Constitution, neoliberal guru Alain Minc has denounced as "antidemocratic" the call to vote no. In other words, exercising one's democratic rights is an affront to "democracy" as conceived of by the neoliberal consensus and thus to be suppressed.

68. The subject of a documentary (1995) and a book by Serge Bilé, both entitled *Noirs dans les camps nazis*.

69. *The Return of Dr. X* was a Warner Brothers production, like the controversial *Confessions of a Nazi Spy* the same year (1939). It can perhaps be considered as much a piece of anti-Nazi propaganda as a follow-up to *Dr. X*. Like *The Walking Dead*, *Dr. X* brings different genres together, notably the gangster film and the horror film. See also *The Monster and the Girl* and *Black Friday*. *The Face Behind the Mask* is the most striking instance of this.

70. The fact that Best's nickname was "Sleep 'n Eat" only serves to reinforce his assimilation to animals.

71. *Man Made Monster* also looks ahead to the recent and underrated *Dog Soldiers*, in which the British army's attempt to use werewolves as soldiers because they cannot be killed backfires disastrously. *Dog Soldiers* is more complex politically than *Man Made Monster*, however, as the state and power politics are involved, and not an individual "mad scientist."

72. On this Lacanian aspect of Freddy, see Reynold Humphries, *The American Horror Film*, 158–62. Once again, I remind the reader of my debt to the work of Slavoj Zizek.

73. Brennan, *History After Lacan*, 3.

74. Brennan, *History After Lacan*, 115.

75. Or China in *The Mask of Fu Manchu*, given that Orientals are supposedly inferior specimens.

76. Senn, *Golden Horrors*, 339.

77. See my reference to this aspect of the plot in chapter 1.

78. However, as Andrew Tudor rightly points out, *The Invisible Ray* anticipates by twenty years, through its reference to a substance more powerful than radium, the nuclear anxieties of science-fiction films of the 1950s. Hollywood was making history in its own way, but without realizing it. See Tudor, *Monsters and Mad Scientists*, 140.

79. Brennan, *History After Lacan*, 48.

80. Brennan, *History After Lacan*, 14.

81. Brennan, *History After Lacan*, 15.

82. Tudor, *Monsters and Mad Scientists*, 123.

83. Skal, *The Monster Show*, 142.

84. To a certain extent, "remote places" can be interpreted as a metaphor for "the Old World" as opposed to "the New World," but there are too many exceptions to this for it to be operative. Similarly, it would be unwise to consider "remote places" as being simply another manifestation (unconscious this time) of Hollywood's rejection of east coast intellectuals. Both interpretations contain an element of truth but fail to grasp the complexity of the issue.

85. Fredric Jameson, "Magical Narratives: On the Dialectical Use of Genre Criticism," *The Political Unconscious: Narrative as a Socially Symbolic Act* (London: Methuen, 1981), 114–15.

86. Jameson, "Magical Narratives," 148.

87. Jameson, "Magical Narratives," 149.

88. For an application of this notion to the contemporary horror film, see Reynold Humphries, "David Cronenberg and the Utopian Imperative: A Political Reading of *Shivers* (1974)," in *Memory, Imagination and Desire in Contemporary Anglo-American Literature and Film*, ed. Constanza des Rio-Alvaro and Luis Miguel Garcia-Mainar (Heidelberg: Universitätsverlag Winter, 2004), 197–210.

89. Fredric Jameson, *Fables of Aggression: Wyndham Lewis, the Modernist as Fascist* (Berkeley: University of California Press, 1979), 14.

90. Jameson, *Fables of Aggression*, 14.

91. Jameson, *The Political Unconscious*, 227.

92. The Bauhaus has been cited as an influence, but one does not have to go to Europe to find a possible real-life example: Frank Lloyd Wright's Hollyhock House in Barnsdall Park, Los Angeles. The fact that you have to look up a hill to see it when driving down North Vermont from Los Feliz reproduces the way the house is shot in the film. I suggest this point not to fix a source but to question the ease with which other critics have seen fit to "identify" Poelzig's construction. Clearly many influences are possible.

93. Sigmund Freud, "From the History of an Infantile Neurosis," in SE XVII: 119.

94. Jameson, *The Political Unconscious*, 112.

CHAPTER FIVE

~

Conclusion

Fifty-three films figure in our corpus.[1] Of these, thirty-eight were made between 1931 and 1936, and fifteen between 1939 and 1941. Seventeen films were made in the two-year period 1932–1933. And seventeen (a third of the total) were produced by Universal, from *Dracula* and *Frankenstein* in 1931 to *Man Made Monster* and *The Wolf Man* in 1941. Taken out of context, these figures seem to indicate the considerable importance of the horror genre, yet these films represent less than 1 percent of Hollywood's output in that period. Before we draw any conclusions from these various facts, some remarks are clearly in order.

I would be the first to recognize that the concentration of so many films (in proportion to the number of horror films actually produced) in so short a period doubtless has something to tell us. Those who have no time for the theories I have mustered in the preceding pages will doubtless put the phenomenon down to Hollywood's notorious desire to make money, which would be nothing but a vulgar appropriation of the Marxist notion that, in the last instance, economic factors take precedence. "In the last instance," perhaps, but certainly not as the sole criterion, especially if one sees unconscious factors at work, not to mention the notion of an "absent cause" that we have made ours here. Moreover, to lend credence, at the expense of all other factors, to the drive for profit is to distort Marx and to interpret the formula as applying "in the *first* instance."[2]

If we take up the argument that precise historical events—World War I, the Depression, European fascism—were instrumental in the existence and success of the genre, then certain problems arise. Why did so many years elapse before the production of *Freaks* if the theme of mutilation is to be traced to those who returned diminished from the battlefields of World War I? It is not a question of denying the link but rather of stressing that it would be unwise to locate some smooth transition from cause to effect. Similarly, to use the explicit presence of World War I as the basis of the very narrative of *The Black Cat* would be to reduce the film to a question of vengeance, shutting off the far more interesting and productive aspects of this dense and polysemic text. On the other hand, given the role of the desolate landscape in *Son of Frankenstein*, the clear references to the Nazi ideology of the superior race in *Man Made Monster* and the articulation, on a bitterly ironic mode, of the themes of the idealistic immigrant, freedom, and crime in *The Face Behind the Mask*, one could more easily make a case for seeing these films as a direct result of Nazi aggression in Europe and of the outbreak of World War II.

Let us look at the matter in another way by returning to that impressive body of films made in those two great "years of horror," 1932 and 1933. To begin with, it would be counterproductive and perverse to deny the influence of current events: European fascism in *The Most Dangerous Game* and *The Invisible Man*, and the Depression in *King Kong*. Yet it is not a question of an event being represented directly or in some displaced or disguised form, but rather of history finding a "textual form" and of becoming accessible to us "through its prior textualization, its narrativization in the political unconscious."[3] Hence the emphasis I have put on the notion of *isolation*, clearly present in the films in question as a theme that can be separated from the storyline and shown to exist via characters, incidents, and settings. For what is this theme if not the representation of certain values that coexist uneasily—indeed, contradict one another: unbridled individualism and selfishness; the importance of research as an activity that is not dependent on financing by private capital or to be applied along utilitarian lines; the negation of the collective?

The fact that the mad doctor or scientist is a signifier of extreme individualism, often undertaking research for reasons of power, need not necessarily be interpreted either as an attack on science or as some vaguely noble statement in favor of teamwork as essential to scientific endeavor. Rather, it can be interpreted politically as an unconscious manifestation of something else, what Fredric Jameson has strikingly called that "sense of the ineradicable drive towards collectivity that can be detected, no matter how faintly and feebly, in the most degraded works of mass culture just as surely as in the classics of modernism."[4] In which case, I would "rewrite" the character of Dr. Frankenstein as he appears in the film of 1931 as follows: He exists not simply as a mad, albeit well-meaning, scientist cutting himself off from society, but one who has unconsciously understood that the results of research are always put at the disposal of the "collective" in the very special sense of the selfish, rapacious and conservative class to which he, along with his father, Victor and Dr. Waldman, belongs. Hence, Frankenstein's isolation becomes the equally unconscious manifestation of its *opposite*, a political act aimed at transforming research into part of the collective in a radically different sense: humanity itself. Never mind that Henry is not aware of this; what concerns us is precisely the presence of this theme as an "absent cause" within the body of the film.

The fact that Henry, unlike his peers, lives to continue his experiments can be seen as the site of the film's—and the genre's—contradictions and incoherencies. Frankenstein the man becomes Frankenstein the monster, which, in its role as a hapless and witless victim, is an ideal scapegoat for such contradictions in the society that produced the film and the textual incoherencies thus produced. That Henry be allowed to live can be attributed to the fact that a scapegoat has been found but also to an unconscious factor representing a form of recognition that Henry is a victim of negative, repressive and reactionary forces.[5]

These concerns are also apparent if we go to the other extreme: the case of Dr. Moreau in *Island of Lost Souls*. What is so disturbing for audiences here is the unacceptable blurring of boundaries between the animal and the human, triggering an anxiety stemming from a certain dreadful apprehension that a supposedly natural difference may not be absolute. This return of the repressed (as Freud pointed out, young children do not make the same distinction between the animal and the human that adults do) explains why Moreau must be punished. However, as we have seen, it is also a case of the exploited animals standing in for exploited workers—exploited and ill treated on the most material level possible: their bodies, their sole possession—and of taking things into their own hands to rid themselves of their tormentor/capitalist exploiter.

We return, then, to the notion of Utopia that figured so prominently in chapter 4, a political notion that strikes me as particularly adapted to a genre so firmly anchored in the unconscious. What I am saying, ultimately, is that we can interpret the surge in horror films at a precise moment as indicating, inter alia, the attraction of the public for a cinema whose Utopian dimension, as part of the Real in both the Marxist and Lacanian senses, had no ready and immediate access to symbolization. One critic has put it in a different context:

In claiming that psychoanalysis is *essential* for understanding the attraction of horror, I mean that horror as a genre, and most cases of being attracted by horror, cannot be understood without it. This does *not* mean that psychoanalysis might not need to be supplemented by other theories and explanations in some cases—or even that psychoanalysis might not be immediately necessary in *all* cases.[6]

As far as my own reading of the horror films of the 1930s is concerned, it is rather a case, not of politics supplementing psychoanalysis—or vice versa—but of the need to articulate the theories of Marxism and psychoanalysis in ways that highlight their dependence on one another.

To conclude—very tentatively—I refer the reader to my comments on anxiety in the introduction: it is not necessarily a state conducive to conservatism. Since classic Hollywood's main thrust was to preserve the status quo, it is not helpful to see such conservatism as inherent to horror cinema alone. The very themes and concerns of horror, touching as they do on forbidden and repressed desires, produce excesses of meaning which can never be reduced to a simple signified, such as "progressive" or "reactionary." The way class persists in making its presence felt is a factor that I have stressed again and again. Contradictions are rife and insist in the conflict between the individual and the collective, between ideology as the way subjects live out in the Imaginary their real social relations and conditions and some more human alternative, long repressed but capable of finding textual form in ways it is the critic's task to pinpoint, explain, and analyze. It is this task that we set ourselves to pursue in the present study.

Notes

1. For full details on titles and dates, see the filmography.

2. It also eliminates, of course, such seemingly irrelevant questions as aesthetics and the relative autonomy of the text, which helps to explain why such criticism is steeped in the ideology of "context" where one discusses everything *except* the film.

3. Fredric Jameson, *The Political Unconscious: Narrative as a Socially Symbolic Act* (London: Methuen, 1981), 35.

4. Fredric Jameson, "Reification and Utopia in Mass Culture," *Social Text* 1 (Winter 1979): 148.

5. We reject as both irrelevant and a dismal manifestation of the "cause-effect" syndrome the notion that some cunning executive had a remake up his sleeve. See also n. 2.

6. Michael Levine, "A Fun Night Out: Horror and Other Pleasures of the Cinema," in *Horror Film and Psychoanalysis*, ed. Steven Jay Schneider (Cambridge: Cambridge University Press, 2004), 48, emphasis in the original.

~

Filmography

A few films were shot in England. As they were vehicles for Boris Karloff (*The Ghoul* and *The Man Who Changed His Mind*) and Bela Lugosi (*The Dark Eyes of London*), I have chosen to consider them as part of my corpus.

Chronological List, 1931–1941

1931

Dracula (Tod Browning)
Frankenstein (James Whale)
Svengali (Archie Mayo)
The Mad Genius (Michael Curtiz)
Dr. Jekyll and Mr. Hyde (Rouben Mamoulian)
Murders in the Rue Morgue (Robert Florey)

1932

Dr. X (Michael Curtiz)
Freaks (Tod Browning)
White Zombie (Victor Halperin)
The Most Dangerous Game (Ernest B. Schoedsack and Irving Pichel)
The Mask of Fu Manchu (Charles Brabin)
Island of Lost Souls (Erle C. Kenton)
The Old Dark House (James Whale)
The Mummy (Karl Freund)
The Monster Walks (Frank Strayer)

1933

Mystery of the Wax Museum (Michael Curtiz)
King Kong (Ernest B. Schoedsack)
The Invisible Man (James Whale)
The Ghoul (T. Hayes Hunter)
The Vampire Bat (Frank Strayer)
Murders in the Zoo (Edward Sutherland)
Supernatural (Victor Halperin)
Son of Kong (Ernest B. Schoedsack)

1934

Death Takes a Holiday (Mitchell Leisen)
The Black Cat (Edgar G. Ulmer)
Maniac (Dwain Esper)

1935

The Raven (Louis Friedlander)
Mad Love (Karl Freund)
Werewolf of London (Stuart Walker)
Bride of Frankenstein (James Whale)
The Black Room (Roy William Neill)
Mark of the Vampire (Tod Browning)
The Crime of Dr. Crespi (John H. Auer)

1936

The Invisible Ray (Lambert Hillyer)
Dracula's Daughter (Lambert Hillyer)
The Devil-Doll (Tod Browning)
The Walking Dead (Michael Curtiz)
The Man Who Changed His Mind (Robert Stevenson)

1939

Son of Frankenstein (Rowland V. Lee)
The Return of Dr. X (Vincent Sherman)
The Man They Could Not Hang (Nick Grindé)
The Dark Eyes of London (Walter Summers)

1940

Dr. Cyclops (Ernest B. Schoedsack)
The Man with Nine Lives (Nick Grindé)

Before I Hang (Nick Grindé)
The Devil Bat (Jean Yarbrough)
The Monster and the Girl (Stuart Heisler)
Black Friday (Arthur Lubin)

1941

Man Made Monster (George Waggner)
The Wolf Man (George Waggner)
The Face behind the Mask (Robert Florey)
Dr. Jekyll and Mr. Hyde (Victor Fleming)
The Devil Commands (Edward Dmytryk)

Breakdown by Studio

Universal

Dracula (1931)
Frankenstein (1931)
Murders in the Rue Morgue (1931)
The Old Dark House (1932)
The Mummy (1932)
The Vampire Bat (1933)
The Invisible Man (1933)
The Black Cat (1934)
The Raven (1935)
Bride of Frankenstein (1935)
Werewolf of London (1935)
The Invisible Ray (1936)
Dracula's Daughter (1936)
Son of Frankenstein (1939)
Black Friday (1940)
Man Made Monster (1941)
The Wolf Man (1941)

Paramount

Dr. Jekyll and Mr. Hyde (1931)
Island of Lost Souls (1932)
Murders in the Zoo (1933)
Supernatural (1933)
Death Takes a Holiday (1934)

Dr. Cyclops (1940)
The Monster and the Girl (1940)

MGM
Freaks (1932)
The Mask of Fu Manchu (1932)
Mark of the Vampire (1935)
Mad Love (1935)
The Devil Doll (1936)
Dr. Jekyll and Mr. Hyde (1941)

Warner Brothers
Svengali (1931)
The Mad Genius (1931)
Dr. X (1932)
Mystery of the Wax Museum (1933)
The Walking Dead (1936)
Return of Dr. X (1939)

Columbia
The Black Room (1935)
The Man They Could Not Hang (1939)
The Man with Nine Lives (1940)
Before I Hang (1940)
The Devil Commands (1941)
The Face behind the Mask (1941)

RKO
The Most Dangerous Game (1932)
King Kong (1933)
Son of Kong (1933)

United Artists
White Zombie (1932)

Biograph Studios
The Crime of Dr. Crespi (1935)

Commonwealth Pictures
The Monster Walks (1932)

Roadshow Attractions
Maniac (1934)

PRC
The Devil Bat (1940)

Argyle Productions
The Dark Eyes of London (1939)

British Gaumont
The Ghoul (1933)
The Man Who Changed His Mind (1936)

~

Bibliography

Adorno, T. W. *Minima Moralia*. London: Verso, 1999.

Aguerre, Jean-Claude. "Si la chair n'était pas faible." Pages 141–51 in *Dracula*, ed. Jean Marigny. Figures Mythiques. Paris: Autrement, 1997.

Ameriglio, Jack, and Antonio Callari. "Marxian Value Theory and the Problem of the Subject." Pages 186–206 in *Fetishism as Cultural Discourse*, ed. Emily Apter and William Pietz. Ithaca, N.Y.: Cornell University Press, 1993.

Apter, Emily, and William Pietz, ed. *Fetishism as Cultural Discourse*. Ithaca, N.Y.: Cornell University Press, 1993.

Baldick, Chris. *In Frankenstein's Shadow: Myth, Monstrosity and Nineteenth-century Writing*. Oxford: Clarendon, 1987.

Bellour, Raymond. "Symboliques." Pages 184–92 in *Le Cinéma américain: Analyses de films*, Vol. 1, ed. Raymond Bellour. Paris: Flammarion, 1980.

Benshoff, Harry M. *Monsters in the Closet: Homosexuality and the Horror Film*. Manchester: Manchester University Press, 1997.

Berenstein, Rhona J. *Attack of the Leading Ladies: Gender, Sexuality, and Spectatorship in Classic Horror Cinema*. New York: Columbia University Press, 1996.

Bernard, Kenneth. "*King Kong*: A Meditation." Pages 122–30 in *The Girl in the Hairy Paw*, ed. Ronald Gottesmann and Harry Geduld. New York: Avon, 1976.

Brenkman, John. *Culture and Domination*. Ithaca, N.Y.: Cornell University Press, 1987.

Brennan, Teresa. *History After Lacan*. New York: Routledge, 1993.

Britzolakis, Christina. "Phantasmagoria: Walter Benjamin and the Poetics of Urban Modernism." Pages 72–91 in *Ghosts: Deconstruction, Psychoanalysis, History*, ed. Peter Buse and Andrew Stott. London: Macmillan, 1999.

Buse, Peter, and Andrew Stott, eds. *Ghosts: Deconstruction, Psychoanalysis, History*. London: Macmillan, 1999.

Clover, Carol J. *Men, Women and Chain Saws: Gender in the Modern Horror Film*. London: BFI Publishing, 1992.

Connor, Steven. "The Machine in the Ghost: Spiritualism, Technology and the 'Direct Voice.'" Pages 203–25 in *Ghosts: Deconstruction, Psychoanalysis, History*, ed. Peter Buse and Andrew Stott. London: Macmillan, 1999.

Copjec, Joan. *Read My Desire*. Cambridge, Mass.: MIT Press, 1995.

Craft, Christopher. "'Kiss Me with Those Red Lips'. Gender and Inversion in Bram Stoker's *Dracula*." Pages 444–59 in *Dracula*, ed. Nina Auerbach and David J. Skal. New York: Norton, 1997.

Crane, Jonathan Lake. *Terror and Everyday Life: Singular Moments in the History of the Horror Film*. Thousand Oaks, Calif.: Sage, 1994.

Creed, Barbara. *The Monstrous-Feminine: Film, Feminism, Psychoanalysis*. New York: Routledge, 1993.

Dadoun, Roger. "Fetishism in the Horror Film." Pages 39–61 in *Fantasy and the Cinema*, ed. James Donald. London: BFI Publishing, 1989.

Dale, R. C. "Narrative Fable and Dream in *King Kong*." Pages 117–21 in *The Girl in the Hairy Paw*, ed. Ronald Gottesmann and Harry Geduld. New York: Avon, 1976.

Derrida, Jacques. *Spectres de Marx*. Paris: Galilée, 1993.

Donald, James. "The Fantastic, the Sublime and the Popular, Or, What's at Stake in Vampire Films?" Pages 232–51 in *Fantasy and the Cinema*, ed. James Donald. London: BFI Publishing, 1989.

———, ed. *Fantasy and the Cinema*. London: BFI Publishing, 1989.

Evans, Dylan. *An Introductory Dictionary of Lacanian Psychoanalysis*. New York: Routledge, 1996.

Freud, Sigmund. *Civilization and Its Discontents*. Vol. XXI: 64–145 of *The Complete Standard Edition of the Psychological Works of Sigmund Freud*, ed. James Strachey, 24 vols. London: Hogarth and the Institute for Psycho-Analysis, 1966–1974.

———. *The Complete Standard Edition of the Psychological Works of Sigmund Freud*. ed. James Strachey, 24 vols. London: Hogarth and the Institute for Psycho-Analysis, 1966–1974. (Hereafter abbreviated *SE*.)

———. "Family Romances." In *SE* IX: 235–41.

———. "Fetishism." In *SE* XXI: 152–57.

———. "From the History of an Infantile Neurosis." In *SE* XVII:7–122.

———. *Group Psychology and the Analysis of the Ego*. In *SE* XVIII: 69–143.

———. "Hysterical Fantasies and Their Relation to Bisexuality." In *SE* IX: 159–66.

———. *Inhibitions, Symptoms and Anxiety*. In *SE* XX: 87–174.

———. *The Interpretation of Dreams*. In *SE* IV.

———. "On Narcissism: An Introduction." In *SE* XIV: 73–102.

———. "A Seventeenth-Century Demonological Neurosis." In *SE* XIX: 72–109.

———. "The Theme of the Three Caskets." In *SE* XII: 291–301.

———. "The Uncanny." In *SE* XVII: 217–52.

Gottesmann, Ronald, and Harry Geduld, eds. *The Girl in the Hairy Paw*. New York: Avon, 1976.

Grant, Barry Keith, ed. *The Dread of Difference: Gender and the Horror Film*. Austin: University of Texas Press, 1996.

———, ed. *Planks of Reason: Essays on the Horror Film*. Metuchen, N.J.: Scarecrow, 1984.

Hardy, Phil, ed. *The Aurum Film Encyclopedia of Horror*. London: Aurum, 1996.

Hawkins, Joan. *Cutting Edge: Art-Horror and the Horrific Avant-Garde*. Minneapolis: University of Minnesota Press, 2000.

Hogan, David. *Dark Romance: Sexuality in the Horror Film*. Jefferson, N.C.: McFarland, 1997.

———. "The Old Dark House." Pages 72–89 in *Boris Karloff*, ed. Gary J. Svehla and Susan Svehla. Baltimore: Midnight Marquee, 1996.

Humphries, Reynold. *The American Horror Film: An Introduction*. Edinburgh: Edinburgh University Press, 2002.

———. "David Cronenberg and the Utopian Imperative: A Political Reading of *Shivers* (1974)." Pages 197–210 in *Memory, Imagination and Desire in Contemporary Anglo-American Literature and Film*, ed. Constanza des Rio-Alvaro and Luis Miguel Garcia-Mainar. Heidelberg: Universitätsverlag Winter, 2004.

———. "On the Road Again: Rehearsing the Death Drive in Modern Realist Horror Cinema." *Post Script*. Realist Horror Cinema, Part II: Serial Killers, ed. Steven Jay Schneider, 22, no. 2 (Winter/Spring 2003): 64–80.

———. "The Semiotics of Horror: The Case of *Dracula's Daughter*." *Interdisciplinary Journal for German Linguistics and Semiotic Analysis* 51, no. 2 (Fall 2000): 273–89.

Jacoby, Russell. *Social Amnesia*. Mahwah, N.J.: Transaction, 1997.

Jameson, Fredric. *The Cultural Turn*. London: Verso, 1998.

———. *Fables of Aggression: Wyndham Lewis, the Modernist as Fascist*. Berkeley: California University Press, 1979.

———. *Marxism and Form*. Princeton, N.J.: Princeton University Press, 1971.

———. "Marx's Purloined Letter." *New Left Review* 209 (January–February 1995): 75–109.

———. *The Political Unconscious: Narrative as a Socially Symbolic Act*. London: Methuen, 1981.

———. "Reification and Utopia in Mass Culture." *Social Text* 1 (Winter 1979): 130–48. Reprinted in Fredric Jameson, *Signatures of the Visible*. New York: Routledge, 1992.

———. *The Seeds of Time*. New York: Columbia University Press, 1994.

JanMohamed, Abdul. "Refiguring Values, Power, Knowledge." Pages 31–64 in *Whither Marxism?* ed. Bernd Magnus and Stephen Cullenberg. New York: Routledge, 1995.

Jensen, Paul M. "The Mummy." Pages 54–71 in *Boris Karloff*, ed. Gary J. Svehla and Susan Svehla. Baltimore: Midnight Marquee, 1996.

Kaufmann, Pierre, ed. *L'Apport freudien*. Paris: Bordas, 1993.

Keenan, Thomas. "The Point Is to (Ex)change It: Reading *Capital*, Rhetorically." Pages 152–85 in *Fetishism as Cultural Discourse*, ed. Emily Apter and William Pietz. Ithaca, N.Y.: Cornell University Press, 1993.

Krutnik, Frank. *In a Lonely Street: Film Noir, Genre, Masculinity*. London: Routledge, 1991.

Krzywinska, Tanya. *A Skin for Dancing In: Possession, Witchcraft and Voodoo in Film*. Wiltshire, England: Flicks Books, 2000.

Lacan, Jacques. *L'Ethique de la psychanalyse*. Le Séminaire Livre VII. Paris: Seuil, 1986.

———. "The Mirror-Phase as Formative of the Function of the I." Pages 93–99 in *Mapping Ideology*, ed. Slavoj Zizek. London: Verso, 1994.

———. *Les Psychoses*. Le Séminaire Livre III. Paris: Seuil, 1981.

———. *La Relation d'objet*. Le Séminaire Livre IV. Paris: Seuil, 1991.

Lant, Antonia. "The Curse of the Pharaoh, or How Cinema Contracted Egyptomania." *October* 59 (1992): 87–112.

Lecercle, Jean-Jacques. *Frankenstein: mythe et philosophie*. Paris: Presses Universitaires de France, 1988.

———. "Tissage et métissage." Pages 41–58 in *Dr. Jekyll and Mr. Hyde*, ed. Jean-Pierre Naugrette. Paris: Autrement, 1997.

Lenne, Gérard. *Le Cinéma fantastique et ses mythologies*. Paris: Cerf, 1970.

Levine, Michael. "A Fun Night Out: Horror and Other Pleasures of the Cinema." Pages 35–54 in *Horror Film and Psychoanalysis: Freud's Worst Nightmare*, ed. Steven Jay Schneider. Cambridge: Cambridge University Press, 2004.

Lowry, Edward, and Richard deCordova. "Enunciation and the Production of Horror in *White Zombie*." Pages 346–89 in *Planks of Reason: Essays on the Horror Film*, ed. Barry Keith Grant. Metuchen, N.J.: Scarecrow, 1984.

Luhr, William, and Peter Lehman. *Authorship and Narrative in the Cinema*. New York: Putnam, 1971.

Lukacs, Georg. "Reification and the Consciousness of the Proletariat." Pages 83–222 in Georg Lukacs, *History and Class Consciousness*. London: Merlin, 1971.

Magnus, Bernd, and Stephen Cullenberg. *Whither Marxism?* New York: Routledge, 1995.

Mank, Gregory William. "*The Mummy* Revisited." *Films in Review* (August–September 1984).

———. *Women in Horror Films, 1930s*. Jefferson, N.C.: McFarland, 1999.

Marcuse, Herbert. *Eros and Civilization*. London: Sphere Books, 1969.

Marigny, Jean, ed. *Dracula*. Paris: Autrement, 1997.

———."Un Vampire renaît de ses cendres." Pages 7–79 in *Dracula*, ed. Jean Marigny. Paris: Autrement, 1997.

Mayne, Judith. "*King Kong* and the Ideology of Spectacle." *Quarterly Review of Film Studies* 1, no. 4 (November 1976): 373–87.

Menegaldo, Gilles, ed. *Frankenstein*. Paris: Autrement, 1998.

Merck, Mandy. "The Medium of Exchange." Pages 163–78 in *Ghosts: Deconstruction, Psychoanalysis, History*, ed. Peter Buse and Andrew Stott. London: Macmillan, 1999.

Naugrette, Jean-Pierre, ed. *Dr. Jekyll & Mr. Hyde*. Paris: Autrement, 1997.

Newman, Kim, ed. *The BFI Companion to Horror*. London: Cassell and the British Film Institute, 1996.

Parkin-Gounelas, Ruth. "Anachrony and Anatopia: Spectres of Marx, Derrida and Gothic Fiction." Pages 127–43 in *Ghosts: Deconstruction, Psychoanalysis, History*, ed. Peter Buse and Andrew Stott. London: Macmillan, 1999.

Prawer, S. S. *Caligari's Children: The Film as Tale of Terror*. New York: Da Capo, 1980.

Punter, David. *The Literature of Terror: A History of Gothic Fiction 1765 to the Present Day*. Essex, England: Addison Wesley Longman, 1996.

Rank, Otto. *The Double*. London: Maresfield Library, 1989.

Rasmussen, Randy Loren. *Children of the Night: The Six Archetypal Characters of Classic Horror Films*. Jefferson, N.C.: McFarland, 1998.

Rhodes, Gary D. White Zombie: *Anatomy of a Horror Film*. Jefferson, N.C.: McFarland, 2001.

Rhodes, Gary D., and John Parris Springer. "They Give Us the 'Weird Feeling': Vampiric Women in Films of the Thirties." Pages 24–49 in *Bitches, Bimbos, and Virgins*, ed. Gary J. Svehla and Susan Svehla. Baltimore: Midnight Marquee, 1996.

Russo, Vito. *The Celluloid Closet: Homosexuality in the Movies*. New York: Harper & Row, 1987.

Said, Edward W. *Orientalism*. London: Penguin, 1985.

Schneider, Steven Jay, ed. *Horror Film and Psychoanalysis: Freud's Worst Nightmare*. Cambridge: Cambridge University Press, 2004.

Senn, Bryan. *Golden Horrors: An Illustrated Critical Filmography of Terror Cinema, 1931–1939*. Jefferson, N.C.: McFarland, 1996.

Silver, Alain, and James Ursini. *The Vampire Film*. New York: Limelight Editions, 1993.

Skal, David. *The Monster Show: A Cultural History of Horror*. London: Plexus, 1993.

———. *Screams of Reason: Mad Science and Modern Culture*. New York: Norton, 1998.

Smith, David H. "*The Devil Commands*." Pages 258–71 in *Boris Karloff*, ed. Gary J. Svehla and Susan Svehla. Baltimore: Midnight Marquee, 1996.

Smith, Don G. "*The Black Cat*." Pages 90–113 in *Boris Karloff*, ed. Gary J. Svehla and Susan Svehla. Baltimore: Midnight Marquee, 1996.

———. "*Frankenstein*." Pages 8–19 in *Boris Karloff*, ed. Gary J. Svehla and Susan Svehla. Baltimore: Midnight Marquee, 1996.

Svehla, Gary J. "*The Devil Bat*." Pages 137–44 in *Bela Lugosi*, ed. Gary J. Svehla and Susan Svehla. Baltimore: Midnight Marquee, 1995.

Svehla, Gary J., and Susan Svehla, eds. *Bela Lugosi*. Baltimore: Midnight Marquee, 1995.

———, eds. *Bitches, Bimbos, and Virgins*. Baltimore: Midnight Marquee, 1996.

———, eds. *Boris Karloff*. Baltimore: Midnight Marquee, 1996.

Tudor, Andrew. *Monsters and Mad Scientists: A Cultural History of the Horror Movie.* Oxford: Blackwell, 1989.

Turner, George E., ed. *The Cinema of Adventure, Romance and Terror.* Hollywood: ASC, 1989.

Twitchell, James. *Dreadful Pleasures: An Anatomy of Modern Horror.* New York: Oxford University Press, 1985.

Williams, Tony. *Hearths of Darkness: The Family in the American Horror Film.* Madison, Wisc., and London: Fairleigh Dickinson University Press and Associated University Presses, 1996.

Wood, Robin. "Foreword." Pages xiii–xviii in *Horror Film and Psychoanalysis: Freud's Worst Nightmare*, ed. Steven Jay Schneider. Cambridge: Cambridge University Press, 2004.

Zizek, Slavoj. *Enjoy Your Symptom! Jacques Lacan in Hollywood and Out.* New York: Routledge, 1992.

———. *Looking Awry: An Introduction to Jacques Lacan through Popular Culture.* Cambridge, Mass.: MIT Press, 1991.

———. *The Plague of Fantasies.* London: Verso, 1997.

———. *The Sublime Object of Ideology.* London: Verso, 1989.

———, ed. *Mapping Ideology.* London: Verso, 1994.

Index

~

About the Author

Reynold Humphries is professor of film studies at the University of Lille 3 in northern France. He has written three previous books: *Fritz Lang cinéaste américain* (1982), *Fritz Lang: Genre and Representation in His American Films* (1989), and *The American Horror Film: An Introduction* (2002). Collective volumes to which he has contributed chapters include *Film Noir Reader 4*, *Docufictions*, and the forthcoming *The Gangster Film*, *Monstrous Adaptations*, and volumes devoted to Stanley Kubrick and Tod Browning, as well as French-language volumes devoted to the contemporary American horror film and George A. Romero. He has also contributed to the special issues of *Post Script* and *Paradoxa* devoted to the horror film. Directors he has published on include Bunuel, Cronenberg, Losey, Mizoguchi, Peckinpah, Powell, and Tourneur. Numerous articles on Joseph Conrad's fiction have appeared in specialized journals in the United States, Britain, and France. His latest book, *Hollywood's Blacklists: Politics and Culture in Context*, will be published in 2008.